STARTING STRENGTH *2ⁿᵈ Edition*

BASIC BARBELL TRAINING

Mark Rippetoe
& Lon Kilgore

2nd Edition (revised)

Editor – Stef Bradford, Ph.D.

ISBN 0-9768054-2-1

Printed in the United States of America 10 9 8 7

The Aasgaard Company
3118 Buchanan, Wichita Falls, TX 76308, USA

Contents

Strength: Why and How 2

The Squat 8

The Bench Press 66

The Deadlift 104

The Press 148

The Power Clean 168

Useful Assistance Exercises 208

Programming 284

Credits 314

Index 316

A human being should be able to change a diaper, plan an invasion, butcher a hog, conn a ship, design a building, write a sonnet, balance accounts, build a wall, set a bone, comfort the dying, take orders, give orders, cooperate, act alone, solve equations, analyze a new problem, pitch manure, program a computer, cook a tasty meal, fight efficiently, and die gallantly. Specialization is for insects.

Robert Heinlein

Foreword

Many things have happened since I started the writing of Starting Strength: A Simple and Practical Guide for Coaching Beginners in 2004. As a result of its publication I have had the opportunity to meet and learn from many new people. It is my sincerest hope that the additions to this book that are the direct result of their input make a difference in its usefulness. Greg Glassman, Tony Budding, Carrie Klumpar, Michael Street, Kyle Gulledge, Becky Kudrna, Dr. Kelly Starrett, and Mike Burgener have all contributed to this work.

As always, I am indebted to Glenn Pendlay and Lon Kilgore for many years of lab time, as we trained, worked, and learned together. Stef Bradford has, quite literally, made all this possible through her many kinds of support. She provided the finish edit for the manuscript, and thereby immeasurably increased its quality. Bill Starr started me down this path many years ago, and my continued association with him has been productive, interesting, and at times very weird. He is the Hunter. S Thompson of strength and conditioning, a very important part of our industry and our profession. We have had a lot of fun.

Also in this interim, my teacher Philip S. Colee passed away after a long – and let me assure you, a very hard-fought – battle with cancer. You have not witnessed determination until you have seen a man wearing an oxygen bottle do deep squats for sets of five across. In the process of telling metastatic cancer to Go To Hell – that it was not going to prevent him from living his remaining days as he saw fit – he taught many of us here at the gym what was possibly the most valuable lesson of his long career in education: no matter what your personal circumstances might be (the universe is unconcerned with such details), you get out of life exactly what you have contributed to the effort. It is my honor to have been his student. He will be missed. This book is dedicated to him.

Rip

"When one teaches, two learn."

Robert Heinlein

Strength: Why and How

Physical strength is the most important thing in life. This is true whether we want it to be or not. As humanity has developed throughout history, physical strength has become less critical to our daily existence, but no less important to our lives. Our strength, more than any other thing we possess, still determines the quality and the quantity of our time here in these bodies. Whereas previously our physical strength determined how much food we ate and how warm and dry we stayed, it now merely determines how well we function in these new surroundings we have crafted for ourselves as our culture has accumulated. But we are still animals – our physical existence is, in the final analysis, the only one that actually matters. A weak man is not as happy as that same man would be if he were strong. This reality is offensive to some people who would like the intellectual or spiritual to take precedence. It is instructive to see what happens to these very people as their squat strength goes up.

As the nature of our culture has changed, our relationship with physical activity has changed along with it. We previously were physically strong as a function of our continued existence in a simple physical world. We were adapted to this existence well, since we had no other choice. Those whose strength was adequate to the task of staying alive continued doing so. This shaped our basic physiology, and that of all our vertebrate associates on the bushy little tree of life. It remains with us today. The relatively recent innovation known as the Division of Labor is not so remote that our genetic composition has had time to adapt again. Since most of us now have been freed from the necessity of personally obtaining our subsistence, physical activity is regarded as optional. Indeed it is, from the standpoint of immediate necessity, but the reality of millions of years of adaptation to a ruggedly physical existence will not just go away because desks were invented.

Like it or not, we remain the possessors of potentially strong muscle, bone, sinew, and nerve, and these hard-won commodities demand our attention. They were too long in the making to just be ignored, and we do so at our peril. They are the very components of our existence, the quality of which now depends on our conscious, directed effort at giving them the stimulus they need to stay in the condition that is normal to them. Exercise is that stimulus.

Over and above any considerations of performance for sports, exercise is the stimulus that returns our bodies to the conditions for which they were designed. Humans are not physically normal in the absence of hard physical effort. Exercise is not a thing we do to fix a problem – it is a thing we must do anyway, a thing without which there will always *be* problems. Exercise is the thing we must do to replicate the conditions under which our physiology was – and still is – adapted, the conditions under which we are physically normal. In other words, exercise is substitute cave-man activity, the thing we need to make our bodies, and in fact our minds, normal in the 21st century. And merely normal, for most worthwhile humans, is not good enough.

An athlete's decision to begin a strength training program may be motivated by a desire to join a team sport that requires it, or it might be for more personal reasons. Many individuals feel that their strength is inadequate, or could be improved beyond what it is, without the carrot of team membership. It is for those people that find themselves in this position that this book is intended.

Why barbells?

Training for strength is as old as civilization itself. The Greek tale of Milo serves to date the antiquity of an interest in physical development, and an understanding of the processes by which it is acquired. Milo is said to have lifted a calf every day, and grew stronger as the calf grew larger. The progressive nature of strength development was known thousands of years ago, but only recently (in terms of the scope of history) has the problem of how best to facilitate progressive resistance training been tackled by technology.

Among the first tools developed to practice resistance exercise was the barbell, a long metal shaft with some type of weight on each end. The earliest barbells used globes or spheres for weight, which could be adjusted for balance and load by filling them with sand or shot. David Willoughby's superb book, The Super Athletes (A.S. Barnes and Co., 1970) details the history of weightlifting and the equipment that made it possible.

But in a development unforeseen by Mr. Willoughby, things changed rapidly in the mid-1970s. A gentleman named Arthur Jones invented a type of exercise equipment that revolutionized resistance exercise. Unfortunately, not all revolutions are universally productive. Nautilus utilized the "principle of variable resistance", which claimed to take advantage of the fact that different parts of the range of motion of each limb were stronger than others. A machine was designed for each limb or body part, and a cam was incorporated into the chain attached to the weight stack that varied the resistance against the joint during the movement. The machines were designed to be used in a specific order, one after another without a pause between sets, since different bodyparts were being worked consecutively. And the central idea (from a commercial standpoint) was that if enough machines – each working a separate bodypart – were added together in a circuit, the entire body was being trained. The machines were exceptionally well made and handsome, and soon most gyms had the obligatory, very expensive, 12-station Nautilus circuit.

Exercise machines were nothing new. Most high schools had a Universal Gladiator multi-station unit, and leg extensions and lat pulldowns were familiar to everybody that trained with weights. The difference was the marketing behind the new equipment. Nautilus touted the total-body effect of the complete circuit, something that had never before been emphasized. We were treated to a series of before-and-after ads featuring one Casey Viator, an individual who had apparently gained a considerable amount of weight using only Nautilus equipment. Missing from the ads was the information that Mr. Viator was regaining size he previously had acquired through more conventional methods as an experienced bodybuilder.

Jones even went so far as to claim that strength could be gained on Nautilus and transferred to complicated movement patterns like the Olympic lifts without having to do the lifts with heavy weights, a thing which flies in the face of exercise theory and practical experience. But the momentum had been established and Nautilus became a huge commercial success. Equipment like it remains the modern standard in commercial exercise facilities all over the world.

The primary reason for this was that Nautilus equipment allowed the health club (at the time known as the "health spa") industry to offer to the general public a thing which had been previously unavailable. Prior to the invention of Nautilus, if a member wanted to train hard, in a more elaborate way than Universal equipment permitted, he had to learn how to use barbells. Someone had to teach him this. Moreover, someone had to teach the heath spa staff *how* to teach him this. Such professional education was, and still is, time consuming and not widely available.

But with Nautilus equipment, a minimum-wage employee could be taught very quickly how to use the whole circuit, ostensibly providing a total-body workout with little invested in employee education. Furthermore, the entire circuit could be performed in about 30 minutes, thus decreasing member time on the exercise floor, increasing traffic capacity in the club, and maximizing sales exposure to more traffic. Nautilus equipment quite literally made the existence of the modern health club possible.

The problem, of course, is that machine-based training did not work as it was advertised. It was almost impossible to gain muscular bodyweight doing a circuit. People who were trying to do so would train faithfully for months without gaining any significant muscular weight at all. When they went to barbell training, a miraculous thing would happen: they would immediately gain – within a week – more weight than they had gained in the entire time they had fought with the 12-station circuit.

The reason that isolated body-part training on machines doesn't work is the same reason that barbells work so well, better than any other tools we can use to gain strength. The human body functions as a complete system – it works that way, and it likes to be trained that way. It doesn't like to be separated into its constituent components and then have those components exercised separately, since the strength obtained from training will not be utilized in this way. The general pattern of strength acquisition must be the same as that in which the strength will be used. The nervous system controls the muscles, and the relationship between them is referred to as "neuromuscular." When strength is acquired in ways that do not correspond to the patterns in which it is intended to actually be used, the neuromuscular aspects of training have not been considered. Neuromuscular specificity is an unfortunate reality, and exercise programs must respect this principle the same way they respect the Law of Gravity.

Barbells, and the primary exercises we use them to do, are far superior to any other training tools that have ever been devised. **Properly performed, full range-of-motion barbell exercises are essentially the functional expression of human skeletal and muscular anatomy under a load.** The exercise is controlled by and the result of each trainee's particular movement patterns, minutely fine-tuned by each individual limb length, muscular attachment position, strength level, flexibility, and neuromuscular efficiency. Balance between all the muscles involved in a movement is inherent in the exercise, since all the muscles involved contribute their anatomically-determined share of the work. Muscles move the joints between the bones which transfer force to the load, and the way this is done is a function of the design of the system – when that system is used in the manner of its design, it functions optimally, and training should follow this design. Barbells allow weight to be moved in exactly the way the body is designed to move it, since every aspect of the movement is determined by the body.

Machines, on the other hand, force the body to move the weight according to the design of the machine. This places some rather serious limitations on the ability of the exercise to meet the specific needs of the athlete. For instance, there is no way for a human being to utilize the quadriceps muscles in isolation from the hamstrings in any movement pattern that exists independent of a machine *designed* for this purpose. No natural movement can be performed that does this. Quadriceps and hamstrings *always* function together, at the same time, to balance the forces on either side of the knee. Since they *always* work together, why should they be *exercised* separately? Because somebody invented a machine that lets us?

Even machines that allow multiple joints to be worked at the same time are less than optimal, since the pattern of the movement through space is determined by the machine, not the individual biomechanics of the human using it. Barbells permit the minute adjustments during the movement that allow individual anthropometry to be expressed.

Furthermore, barbells *require* the individual to make these adjustments, and any other ones that might be necessary to retain control over the movement of the weight. This aspect of exercise cannot be overstated – the control of the bar, and the balance and coordination demanded of the trainee, are unique to barbell exercise and completely absent in machine-based training. Since every aspect of the movement of the load is controlled by the trainee, every aspect of that movement is being trained.

There are other benefits as well. All of the exercises described in this book involve varying degrees of skeletal loading. After all, the bones are what ultimately support the weight on the bar. Bone is living, stress-responsive tissue, just like muscle, ligament, tendon, skin, nerve, and brain. It adapts to stress just like any other tissue, and becomes denser and harder in response to heavier weight. This aspect of barbell training is very important to older trainees and women, whose bone density is a major factor in continued health.

And barbells are very economical to use. In practical terms, five or six very functional weight rooms – in which can be done literally hundreds of different exercises - can be built for the cost of one circuit of any brand of modern exercise machine. Even if cost is not a factor, utility should be. In an institutional situation, the number of people training at a given time per dollar spent equipping them might be an important consideration in deciding which type of equipment to buy. The correct decision about this may directly affect the quality of your training experience.

The only problem with barbell training is the fact that the vast, overwhelming majority of people don't know how to do it correctly. This is sufficiently serious and legitimate a concern as to justifiably discourage many people from training with barbells in the absence of a way to learn how. This book is my humble attempt to address this problem. This method of teaching the barbell exercises has been developed over 25 years in the commercial fitness industry, the tiny little part of it that remains in the hands of individuals committed to results, honesty about what works, and the time-honored principles of exercise science. I hope it works as well for you as it has for me.

This York Barbell model 38 Olympic Barbell set
was obtained from the Wichita Falls Downtown YMCA.
It was used for nearly 50 years by thousands of men and
women. Among them was Bill Starr, famous strength coach,
Olympic weightlifter, and one of the first competitors in the
new sport of Powerlifting. Bill was the editor of Hoffman's
"Strength and Health" magazine and Joe Weider's "Muscle" magazine.
He was the coach of numerous national, international, and Olympic
teams, as well as one of the very first full-time strength coaches
at the collegiate and professional level. He is one of the most
prolific writers in the Iron Game, with books and articles published
over 5 decades. His influence is still felt today through the
accomplishments of his many athletes and training partners.
His first weightlifting was done on this set.

The Squat

The squat has been the most important yet most poorly understood exercise in the training arsenal for a very long time. The full range of motion exercise known as the squat is the single most useful exercise in the weight room, and our most valuable tool for building strength, power, and size (fig. 2-1).

The squat is so effective an exercise because of the way it uses the muscles around the core of the body. Much is made of core strength, and fortunes have been made selling new ways to train the core muscles. A correct squat perfectly balances all the forces around the knees and the hips, using these muscles in exactly the way the skeletal biomechanics are designed for them to be used, over their anatomically full range of motion. The postural muscles of the lower back, the upper back, the abdominals and lateral trunk muscles, the costal (ribcage) muscles, and even the shoulders and arms are used isometrically. Their static contraction supports the trunk and transfers kinetic power from the prime movers to the bar. The trunk muscles function as the transmission while the hips and legs are the engine. Notice that the core of the body is at the center of the squat, that the muscles get smaller the farther away from the core they are, and that the squat works them in exactly this priority (fig. 2-2). Balance is provided by the interaction of the postural muscles with the hips and legs, starting on the ground at the feet and proceeding up to the bar, and controlled by a massive amount of central nervous system activity under the conscious direction of the athlete's mind. In addition, the systemic nature of the movement when done with heavy weights produces hormonal responses that affect the entire body. Not only is the core strengthened, it is strengthened in the context of a total physical and mental experience.

The squat is poorly understood because it involves the use of many muscles – more than most people realize – and most of the people that don't understand it have never done it correctly themselves. This means that they can't appreciate the true nature of the movement and the interactions of all the muscles working in a coordinated manner, since to truly understand a thing it must be experienced personally. The more people who learn to squat correctly, the more people who will understand the squat and, like ripples in a pond, knowledge and strength will spread through the masses. This process starts here, with you.

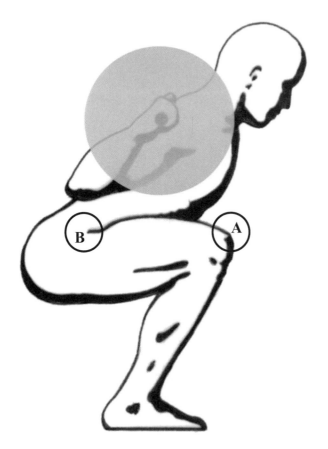

Figure 2-1. Depth landmarks for the full squat. The top of the patella (A) and the hip joint as identified by the apex of the crease in the shorts (B). The B-side of the plane formed by these two points must drop below parallel with the ground.

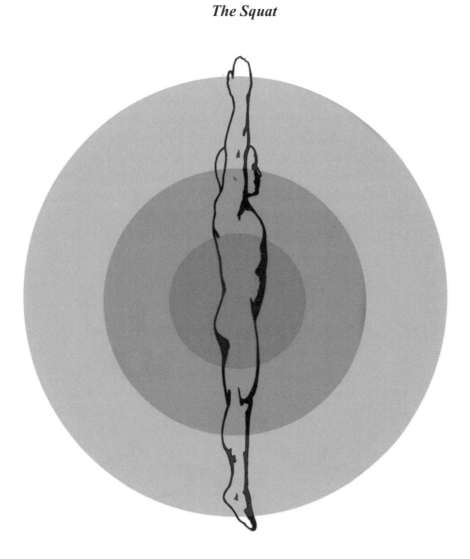

Figure 2-2. Total-body power development originates in the hips, and the ability to generate power diminishes with distance from the hips. Note also that the further from the center of the body, the greater the angular velocity with which the bodypart can move, enabling the application of power through acceleration. From a concept by David Webster, versions of which have been used by Tommy Kono and Bill Starr. This concept has recently gained new traction under the names "core strength," "core stability," and "functional training". It seems rather obvious to the authors that an athlete with a 500 lb. squat has a more stable core that that same athlete would with a 200 lb. squat.

Squat depth – safety and importance

The full squat is the preferred lower body exercise for safety as well as athletic strength. The squat, when performed correctly, is not only the safest leg exercise for the knees, it produces a more stable knee than any other leg exercise. The important part of the last statement is the "when performed correctly" qualifier. Correctly is deep, with hips dropping below level with the top of the patella. Correctly is full range of motion.

Any squat that is not deep is a partial squat, and partial squats stress the knee and the quadriceps without stressing the glutes, the adductors, and the hamstrings. The hamstrings, groin muscles, and glutes perform their function in the squat when the hips are stretched to the point of full flexion, where they get tight – the deep squat position (fig. 2-3). The hamstring muscles, attached to the tibia and to the ischial tuberosity of the pelvis, and the adductors, attached between the medial femur and various points on the medial pelvis, reach a full stretch at the very bottom of the squat, where the pelvis tilts forward with the torso, stretching the ends of the muscles apart. At this stretched position they provide a slight rebound out of the bottom, which will look like a "bounce," and which you will learn more about later. The tension of the stretch pulls the tibia backwards, the posterior direction, balancing the forward-pulling force produced by the quadriceps, which pull from the front. The hamstrings finish their work, with help from the adductors and glutes, by straightening out, or "extending," the hip.

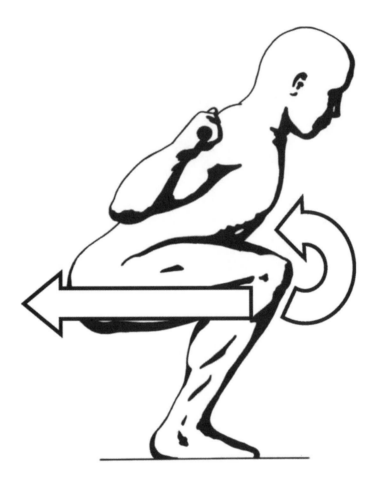

Figure 2-3. Muscular actions on the knee. The anterior force provided by the quadriceps is balanced by the posterior force provided by the hamstrings in the deep squat position. The depth is the key: partial (high) squats are predominately quadriceps/anterior, and lack balance.

In a partial squat, which fails to provide a full stretch for the hamstrings, most of the force against the tibia is upward and forward, from the quadriceps and their attachment to the front of the tibia below the knee. This produces an anterior shear, a forward-directed sliding force, on the knee, with the tibia being pulled forward from the patellar tendon and without a balancing pull from the opposing hamstrings. This shearing force – and the resulting unbalanced strain on the prepatellar area – may be the biggest problem with partial squats. Many spectacular doses of tendinitis have been produced this way, with "squats" getting the blame.

Figure 2-4. The variation in squat depths commonly seen in the gym. A. Quarter-squat. B. Half-squat. C. A position often confused with parallel, where the undersurface of the thigh is parallel with the ground. D. A parallel squat according to the criteria established in fig. 2-1.

The hamstrings benefit from their involvement in the full squat by getting strong in direct proportion to their anatomically proper share of the work in the movement, as determined by the mechanics of the movement itself. This fact is often overlooked when considering anterior cruciate tears and their relationship to the conditioning program. The ACL stabilizes the knee: it prevents the tibia from sliding forward relative to the femur. As we have already seen, so does the hamstring group of muscles. Underdeveloped, weak hamstrings thus play a role in ACL injuries, and full squats work the hamstrings while partial squats do not. In the same way the hamstrings protect the knee during a full squat, hamstrings that are stronger due to full squats can protect the ACL during the activities that we are squatting to condition for. In fact, athletes who are missing an ACL can safely squat heavy weights, because the ACL is under no stress in a correctly performed full squat (fig. 2-5).

Another problem with partial squats is the fact that very heavy loads may be moved, due to the short range of motion and the greater mechanical efficiency of the quarter squat position. This predisposes the trainee to back injuries as a result of the extreme spinal loading that results from putting a weight on his back that is possibly in excess of three times the weight that can be safely handled in a correct deep squat. A lot of football coaches are fond of partial squats, since it allows them to claim that their 17 year-old linemen are all squatting 600 lbs. Your interest is in getting strong (at least it should be), not in playing meaningless games with numbers. If it's too heavy to squat below parallel, it's too heavy to have on your back.

Olympic weightlifters provide a perfect illustration of the safety and benefits of the full squat. As of the 2004 Olympics 167 of the 192 countries in the world compete in Olympic Weightlifting. More than 10,000 individuals compete annually in IWF (International Weightlifting Federation) events alone, and the number of participants in total from the 167 countries would be staggering, likely on the order of 2 to 5 million (China alone boasts over 1 million lifters). All over the world, weightlifters squat way below parallel safely, most often using some form of the exercise, either back squats or front squats, every day. That is correct: they squat way below parallel every training day, and most programs call for six days per week. Isn't it fascinating that they are both strong and not under the care of an orthopedic surgeon?

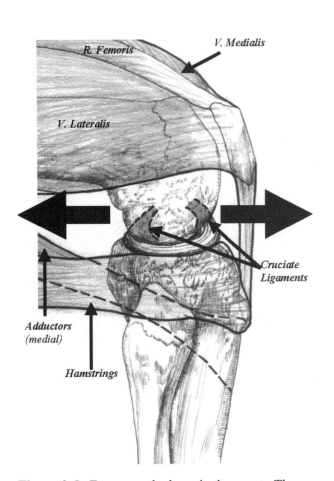

Figure 2-5. Forces on the knee in the squat. The hamstrings and adductors exert a posterior tension on the tibia, and the net effect of the anterior quadriceps tendon insertion is an anterior force against the tibial plateau. With sufficient depth, anterior and posterior forces on the knee are balanced. The anterior and posterior cruciate ligaments stabilize anterior and posterior movement of the distal femur relative to the tibial plateau. In the correct squat, these ligaments have very little to do.

There is simply no other exercise, and certainly no machine, that produces the level of central nervous system activity, improved balance and coordination, skeletal loading and bone density enhancement, muscular stimulation and growth, connective tissue stress and strength, psychological demand and toughness, and overall systemic conditioning than the correctly performed full squat. In the absence of an injury that prevents their being performed at all, everyone that lifts weights should learn to squat, correctly.

Learning to squat

The squat begins at the rack, or the squat stands, whichever is available. Set the rack height so that the bar in the rack is at about the level of your mid-sternum. Many will perceive this as too low, but it's better to be a little low taking the bar out of the rack than to have to tiptoe back into the rack with a heavy weight. Often the empty rack at this position will look low, because the diameter of the bar sitting in the hooks tells the eye a different story about its true height in the rack. When the bar is placed in the rack, the eye will be more comfortable with the setting.

We will use a fairly neutral foot placement, with the heels about shoulder width apart, the toes pointed out at about 30 degrees (fig. 2-6). Excessive width tightens the hips at the bottom, and excessive narrowness prevents adductor stretch and causes the quads to jam against the belly in heavier trainees, both of which prevent proper depth. Many people will use too narrow a stance, so make sure you're wide enough to permit a good position at the bottom. Look down at your feet and make a mental picture of what you see.

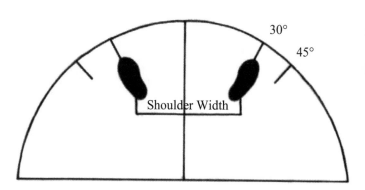

Figure 2-6. Map of foot placement in the squat, as seen from above.

Figure 2-7. Your point of view of your stance.

Now comes the crucial part of learning the movement. You are going to assume the position you will be in at the bottom of a correct squat, without the bar. This is far superior to doing it first with the bar, because any errors in position can be easily corrected without the bar adding to the complexity of the system. And if you've already been there without the bar, getting to that position again with the bar is much easier. Assume the correct stance, and squat down, all the way. Don't even think about stopping high, just go on down to the bottom. Make sure that your correct foot position has been maintained, because sometimes a lack of flexibility will alter your stance on the way down. If it has changed when you get to the bottom, correct it now. Next, put your elbows against your knees, palms of your hands together, and shove your knees out. This will usually be a decent bottom position, and if your flexibility is not great, the position acts as a stretch if you maintain it for a few seconds. Remember, proper depth is essential in the squat, and this low bottom position lays the groundwork for your attaining good depth from now on.

Stay in the bottom position for a few seconds, to allow for some stretching. If you get fatigued by holding the position, it might indicate that your flexibility is not quite what it should be. Stand up and rest a few seconds and go back down to get some more stretching done and to reinforce your familiarity with the bottom position. This is the most important part of learning to squat correctly, since good depth is the difference between a squat and a partial squat.

Figure 2-8. Use your elbows to stretch into the correct position at the bottom. The femurs are parallel to the feet, feet are flat on the ground at the correct angle, hips are back, knees are just a little forward of the toes, and the back is at an angle that will place the bar over the middle of the foot, about 45 degrees.

Now is the time to notice some important details about the bottom position. Your feet should be flat on the floor, your knees are shoved out to where they are in a parallel line with your feet, and your knees are just a little in front of your toes. Your back should be as flat as you can get it, but if it's not perfect we'll fix it later. Also notice that it is inclined at about a forty five degree angle, not at all vertical. You may think it's vertical, but it won't be and it's not supposed to be.

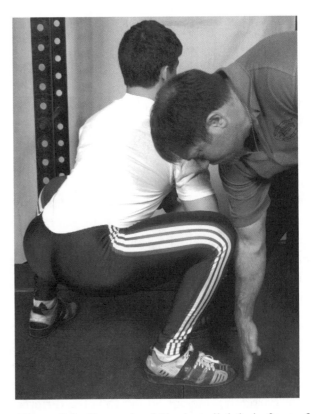

Figure 2-9. Knees should be just slightly in front of the toes.

A word now about knee position and adductor, or "groin" muscle function. This method utilizes a stance that requires a knees-out position, both at the bottom and on the way down. Knees-out does two important things for the squat: it allows for easier depth, and it adds the adductors to the movement. As for depth, the aforementioned jamming effect of the thighs against the belly affects most people, regardless of the degree of chubbiness. The tendency to stop the descent of the hips when the belly contacts the thighs is almost universal, as is the tendency to round the lower back when this happens. This, in combination with the fact that if the toes point forward, as is usual with a narrow stance, the knees will go forward too, makes good depth hard to reach. The knees can travel forward until they literally touch the floor, and the hip will not drop below the patella (fig. 2-10). Your knees should go to a point just in front of your toes, and this position will vary with your anthropometry (a fancy way of saying individual physical dimensions). If your knees stop too far back behind your toes, you have to lean too far forward to stay in balance. Knees too far forward produces too acute a knee angle, throwing your weight on your toes and making hip drive out of the bottom inefficient by loosening the hamstrings.

Figure 2-10. Knee position does not determine depth. Same depth, different knees. Depth is a function of hip position only.

The role of the adductors in the squat is a bit more difficult to understand. One sure indication of weak adductors is the inability to keep your knees out during the squat, a symptom that sometimes gets interpreted as weak *ab*-ductors, the muscles on the outside of the hip. So a good understanding of the anatomy here is important. Note that all these muscles essentially originate in the groin area and insert on the medial femur area. As such, their function will be to shorten the distance between these two points. When you squat, or simply squat down, notice what happens to the distance between these two points – it increases, as can be easily demonstrated by placing one finger on the origin in the groin area (do this in the private, please) and another finger placed on the inside of the knee (fig. 2-13). As you come back up, the points get closer together, illustrating the fact that these muscles contract during the squat. The adductors can function in the squat only when the knees are out. If the knees are together, as when they point forward and the thighs get parallel to each other, the groin muscles are in a position where they are already shortened without having lifted any of the weight. This forces the quads to do all of the work, while the adductors have contributed nothing to the movement. Since we are trying to strengthen more muscles and lift more weight, it makes sense to use the adductors during the squat. If the groin is injured, this information is useful as well: you can squat with a closer stance until it heals.

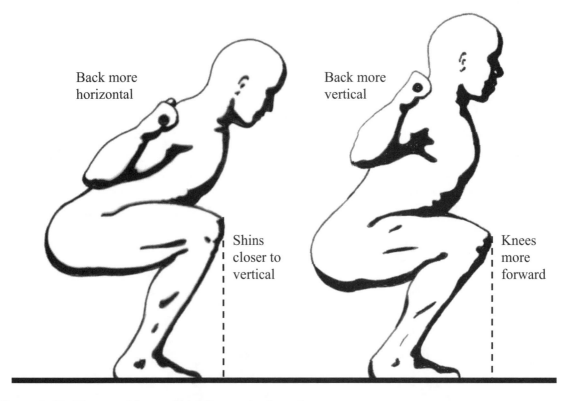

Figure 2-11. Knee position and its effect on back angle.

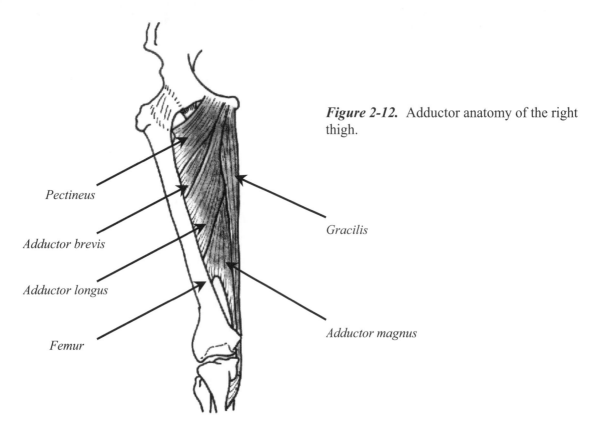

Figure 2-12. Adductor anatomy of the right thigh.

Pectineus

Adductor brevis

Adductor longus

Femur

Gracilis

Adductor magnus

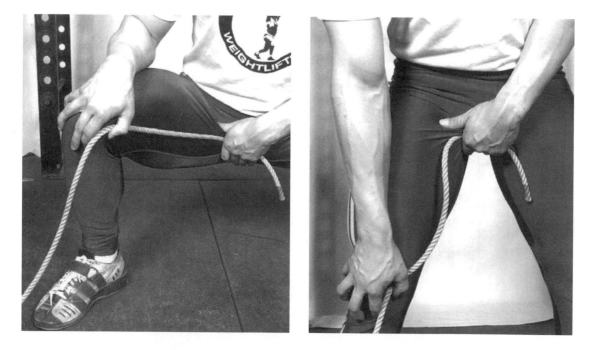

Figure 2-13. A demonstration of adductor function. Note the differences in the length of the rope laid alongside the inner thigh, illustrating the change in length of the adductor between the top and bottom of the squat. Adductors extend on the way down and contract on the way up, contributing to hip extension. Adductors are an important part of the "posterior chain".

Electromyography studies have shown that the glutes and hamstrings are the prime movers out of the bottom of the full squat, (adductors contribute as well, although this has not occurred to many researchers) and it is best thought of as a "hips" movement. After the bottom position has been established, come up out of the bottom by driving your butt straight up in the air. Up, not forward. This keeps your weight solidly over the whole foot instead of shifting to the toes. Think about a chain hooked to your hips, pulling you straight up out of the bottom (fig. 2-14). Don't think about your knees straightening out, don't think about your feet pushing against the floor, don't even think about your legs. Just drive your hips up out of the bottom and the rest will take care of itself. Keep the chest up while you are driving the hips, so that your back maintains a constant angle with the floor as you move out of the deep position.

This important point should not be missed. Our previous discussion about the use of the hamstrings in the squat is applied here. The squat is not a leg press, and pushing the floor with the feet provides an inadequate cue for the hamstrings, adductors, and glutes to provide their power out of the bottom. Hip extension is the first part of the upward drive out of the bottom. When you think about raising your butt up out of the bottom, the nervous system has a simple, efficient way to fire the correct motor units to initiate hip extension. If you are having trouble with this movement, it will help to have a coach or training partner push down on your sacrum from above while you are in the bottom position, and then drive up against the pressure. If you can do this in balance you are driving up correctly.

17

Figure 2-14. An interesting way to visualize hip drive in the squat.

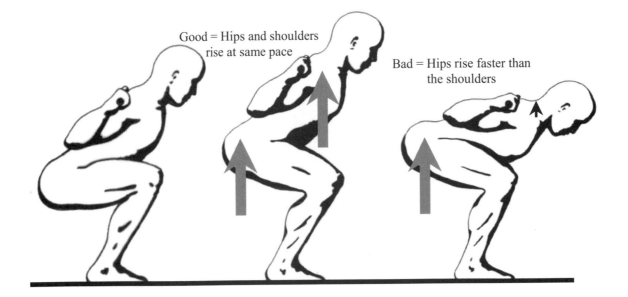

Good = Hips and shoulders rise at same pace

Bad = Hips rise faster than the shoulders

Figure 2-15. The back angle during the drive up from the bottom is critical to the correct use of the hips. The correct angle is produced when the bar is just below the spine of the scapula and directly vertical to the middle of the foot, the back is held tight in lumbar and thoracic extension, the knees are parallel to the correctly-placed feet, and the correct depth is reached, as discussed later.

Now you're ready to squat. You have already been in the position you will go to at the bottom – now you're just going back down there with the bar. First, chalk your hands. Chalk is always a good idea, because it dries out the skin, and dry skin is less prone to folding and abrasion than moist skin, and therefore is less prone to problem callus formation. If the weight room is not equipped with chalk, bring your own. If the gym complains, change gyms.

Face the bar. ALWAYS an empty bar at first. Always. There will plenty of time very soon to add weight. The rack should be set so that the bar hits you at about the middle of the sternum, a position that will be neither too high nor too low on the back when the bar is placed there. The preferred bar placement is NOT high on the traps, just below the neck, although that is the placement preferred by Olympic weightlifters. Use the lower position, where the bar is carried just below the spine of the scapula, on top of the posterior deltoids. This lower position shortens the lever arm formed by the weight of the bar transmitted down the back to the hips, producing less torque at the low back and consequently a safer exercise (fig. 2-18). If your shoulders are not flexible enough to assume this position at first, they will stretch out over a couple of weeks. The high-bar position can be used until then if necessary, but continue to shove the bar down as low as possible.

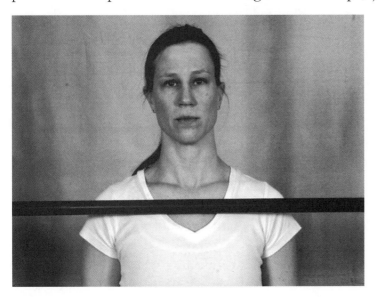

Figure 2-16. The position of the bar in the rack should be at about the middle of the sternum.

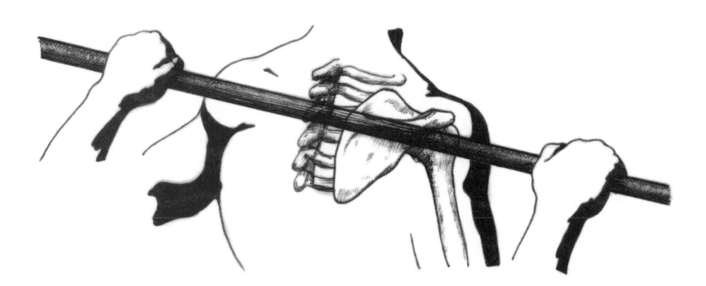

Figure 2-17. Position of the bar relative to the skeletal anatomy of the back.

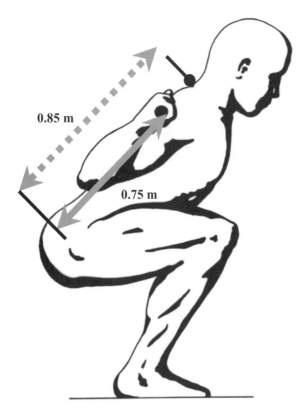

0.85 m

0.75 m

Figure 2-18. Torque against the lower back increases with the distance between the bar and the hips. The rigid trunk segment acts as a lever arm acting on the point of rotation at the hips. The longer the distance between the force of the weighted bar and the hips, the greater the torque against the lower back.

Take an even grip on the bar, measured from the markings placed on the bar for this purpose. A standard power bar has 16 ½ - 17 inches between the ends of the outside knurl, and 32 inches between the finger marks, those 1/8 inch gaps in the knurl indicating a legal bench press grip. Grip width for the squat will obviously vary with shoulder width and flexibility, but in general the hands will be between these two markings on this type bar. A narrower grip allows a flexible person to support the bar better with the muscles of the posterior shoulder when the elbows are lifted, and a wider grip allows an inflexible person to get more comfortable under the bar. In either case, a narrower grip tightens your shoulder muscles so that the bar is supported by muscle and doesn't dig into your back.

The thumb should be placed on top of the bar, so that the wrist can be held in a straight line with the forearm. If a lack of flexibility (usually in the chest and shoulders, not the wrists) prevents your achieving this position, use the high-bar position until proper stretching can establish enough flexibility to get it down to a better position.

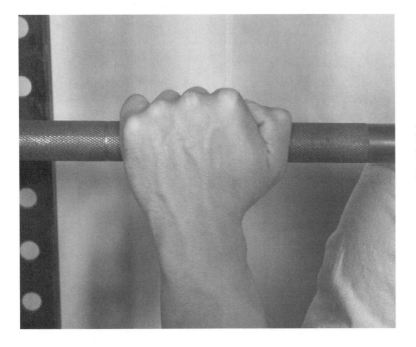

Figure 2-19. Hand placement on the bar. Note that the thumb is on top of the bar and the hand is between the outer ring and the inner edge of the knurling.

Figure 2-20. A comparison of wide and narrow grips. Note the difference in tightness of the upper back muscles, and the resulting difference in bar support potential.

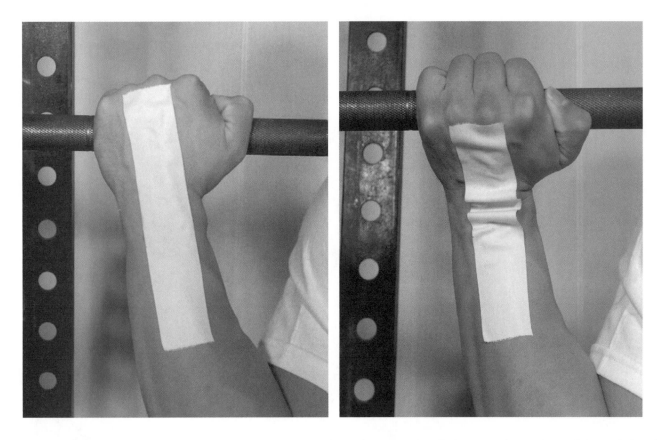

Figure 2-21. Wrist alignment on the bar. The correct grip keeps the hand above the bar and all of the weight of the bar on the back. An incorrect grip intercepts some of the weight, loading the wrists and elbows. The wrinkles in the tape illustrate the difference.

With your grip in place, dip your head under the bar, and come up into position with the bar on your back. The bar should be placed in the correct position – just immediately under the "bone" you feel at the top of the shoulder blades, with the hands and thumb on top of the bar – and then secured in place by lifting the elbows and the chest at the same time (fig. 2-22). This action tightens the muscles of your back, and lifts your chest, placing the thoracic spine in an extended, "straight" position, and fixes many of the problems often encountered earlier with a round-back position. Enormous weights can be safely handled this way later.

First and foremost, ALWAYS STEP BACK OUT OF THE RACK. ALWAYS. NEVER PUT THE BAR BACK IN THE RACK BY STEPPING BACKWARDS. NEVER. This cannot be done safely. You should never be in a position to have to step backwards and rack a weight at the end of a set. You cannot see the hooks, and even if you have spotters there will eventually be a wreck. The bar should be taken out of the rack in the same position in which it is to be squatted, with the torso and shoulders tightened, the chest and elbows lifted, and the head position "down". Everything should be the same as it is for the full squat, and the bar should be taken off of the hooks by extending the knees and hips, just like the top of a squat. In this way, any weight can be taken safely out of the rack. Many problems are caused by doing this improperly. It is very common to take the bar out of the rack on a loose back and chest, and then attempt to tighten everything just before squatting. It is obviously much easier to tighten the muscles and THEN take the weight onto tight muscles, than it is to take the weight, let it mash down into the back through loose muscles until it stops on some crucial skeletal component, and then try to tighten everything up underneath it. Unrack the bar exactly like it is a squat, and you'll have no problems.

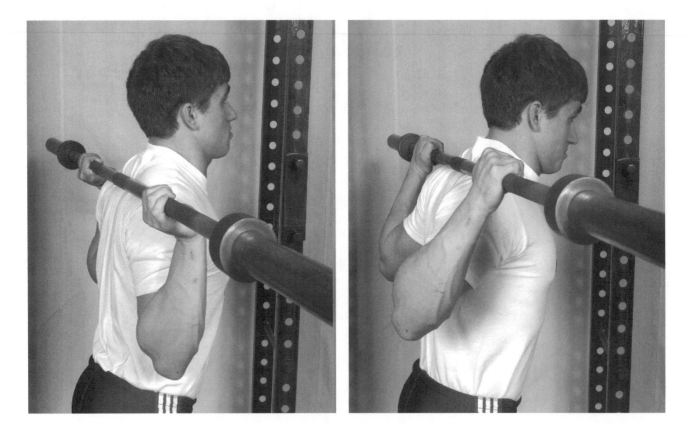

Figure 2-22. Simultaneous lifting of the elbows and the chest "trap" the bar between the hands and the back, creating a stable back and chest position and a tight bar placement on top of the posterior delts.

Figure 2-23. The proper position to receive the bar from the racks.

Once the bar leaves the rack, don't take a hike with it, backing up three or four steps before setting up to squat. This is unnecessary, and could become a problem if the set is heavy, spotters are unreliable, and the trip back to the rack is just too far on this particular day. One step back out of the rack with good form is enough to clear the rack and allow for any spotters to do their job while minimizing the trouble getting back home.

The stance should be the same as the one used during the stretch. Again, heels should be about shoulder-width apart, toes pointed out about 30 degrees. You might need to point the toes out more than you want to, to get them in a good position.

At this point, you are ready to squat with the empty bar. THE EMPTY BAR. All of the groundwork has been laid, the correct bottom position is fresh in your mind, and you are now in the correct starting position. Everything you are about to do is the same as you did during the stretch. Only two things are different: one, you don't have your elbows available to help push your knees out, so you need to do this with your brain. And two, don't stop at the bottom. Just go down and immediately come back up, driving your butt straight up, not forward, out of the bottom. Now, take a big breath and hold it, look down at a spot on the floor about 6 feet in front of your position, and squat.

Looking up at the ceiling when squatting has so many detrimental effects on proper technique that some law against it will eventually have to be adopted. It is the enemy of correct bottom position, hip drive out of the bottom, and correct chest position, the three most important factors in a safe, correct squat. This bizarre neck position is inherently unsafe anyway. To place the cervical spine in extreme hyperextension and then to place a heavy weight on the trapezius muscles directly underneath it is, at best, imprudent.

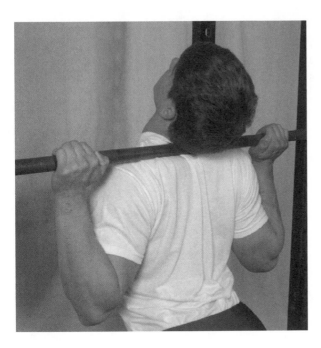

Figure 2-24. Don't do this, you fool.

Figure 2-25 (below). Notice the difference in trunk position between looking down and looking up. An upward-directed eye gaze quite effectively diminishes the ability to use the posterior chain during the drive up from the bottom.

Try this: assume a good deep bottom position as described earlier, with knees out, toes out, and heels down. Put the chin slightly down and look at a point on the floor five or six feet in front of you. Now drive your hips up out of the bottom, and make note of how this feels. Now do the same thing while attempting to look at the ceiling (fig. 2-25). You will discover an amazing thing – that chin-down (looking down keeps the chin down) with the neck in a normal anatomical position enables your hip drive. And it helps you keep your chest up, so that your upper back is in the normal anatomical position for the thoracic spine under load. Correct chest position is an important factor in placing the lumbar spine in the correctly extended, slightly arched position. Correct lumbar position is essential for full utilization of the hamstrings and glutes out of the bottom, because when they are stretched more completely they can contract more completely and generate more power over a longer range. So bad neck position sets up a series of bad positions that greatly diminishes the safety and effectiveness of the squat.

"Lifting the chest" is an important thing to learn how to do. It is something you will need to do often in the weight room, with every exercise you do. It is the way you get your upper back into "normal anatomical position", the position in which your spine is safe while bearing a load. It may be confusing for some, who may interpret this as making the torso angle more vertical. Imagine someone touching you on the sternum and telling you to "Lift this up." And then realize that this "chest" movement can be done no matter where the back is relative to the floor. (It will be important to learn how to arch the lower back also.)

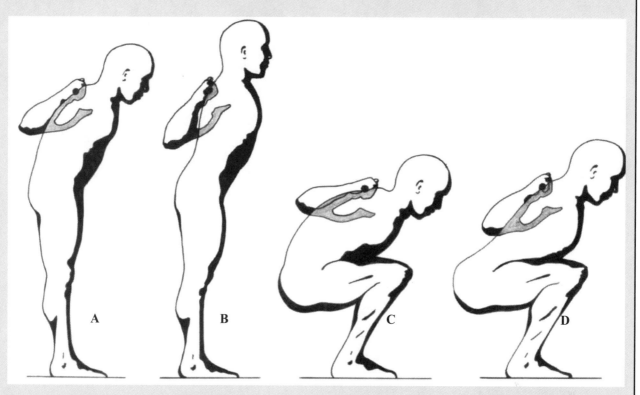

The difference in the position of the back relative to the ground and the position of the back relative to the chest and hips. A. Upright back in flexion. B. Upright back in extension. C. Inclined back in flexion. D. Inclined back in extension.

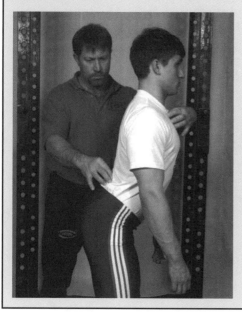

The "chest up" cue for learning to place the back in extension.

Figure 2-26. The effect of looking up on standing position. A. Justin has taken the bar out of the racks and is preparing to squat. B. Looking up has moved the bar into a position behind the mid-foot. C. An attempt to compensate has returned the bar to a position over the mid-foot, but at the expense of correct chest position.

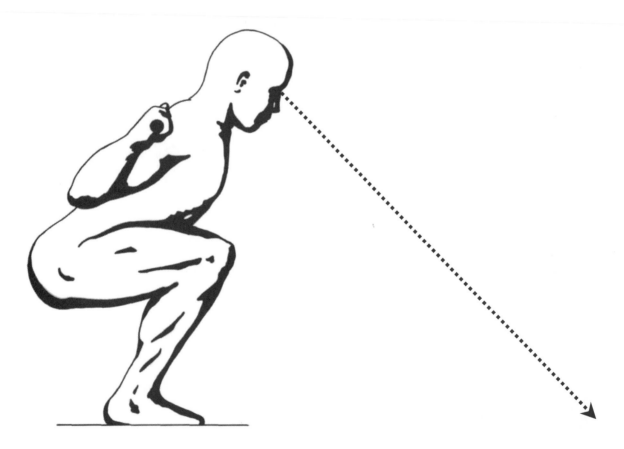

Figure 2-27. The point of focus should be 5-6 feet in front of you on the floor.

Looking at the floor also provides the eye with a fixed position reference. Any deviation from the correct movement pattern can be identified easily against this reference and can be adjusted as it happens. The ceiling also provides a reference, but at the expense of an unsafe neck position. And, generally speaking, the floor is closer to the eyes than the ceiling, and is therefore more useful as a reference – smaller movements can be detected against a closer point. To correct looking up, fix the eyes on a position on the floor five or six feet in front of you, or if training close to a wall, on a place low on the wall that results in the same neck position. Stare at this point, and get used to looking at it so that it requires no conscious effort. Most people will not raise their heads to the point where neck position is affected if they are looking down. Inventive coaches have used tennis balls for the purpose of illustrating a chin-down chest-up position (fig. 2-28).

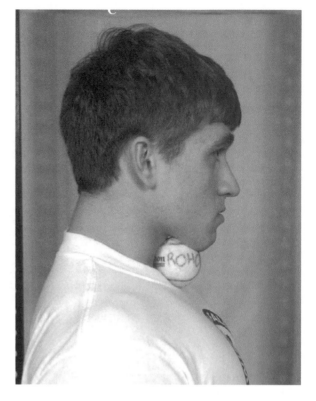

Figure 2-28. A tennis ball can teach the correct chin/neck relationship.

You should be in good balance at the bottom of the squat having been there already when you stretched. Your weight should stay evenly on your feet. The reference point your eyes have on the floor should help you maintain good position all the way down and all the way up. Get someone to verify that your depth is good, and DO NOT accept anything less than full depth, ever, from this point on. If your impartial critic tells you that you're high, check your stance to make sure you're wide enough but not too wide, and work toward good depth until you stretch out enough to get there. If you're sure the form is fairly good, do a set of five and rack the bar. If it is crazy bad, rack it and repeat the pre-squat procedure.

To rack the bar safely and easily, walk forward until the bar touches the vertical part of the rack. Find the uprights, not the hooks. You can't miss the uprights, and if you touch there, you'll be over the hook, but if you try to set the bar directly down on the hooks, you can and will eventually miss it on one side. Big wreck.

The general plan is to do a couple more sets of five reps with the empty bar to nail down the form, and then add weight, do another set of five, and keep increasing in even increments until form is compromised by the weight. Sets of five are a good number to learn with, not so many that fatigue affects form during the last reps, and enough to establish and practice the technique while handling enough weight to get strong. Increments will vary with the trainee. Lightweight, unconditioned kids need to go up in 10 lb. or 5 kg. jumps. Older, stronger trainees can use 20 or possibly 30 lb., or 10-15 kg. increments. Decide which jumps best fit your situation, being conservative since it is your first day. Go on up in weight, practicing good form and making sure to keep good depth, until the next jump up would alter your form, and do two more sets there, for a total of three sets across with the heaviest weight. And that is the first squat workout.

Figure 2-29. The squat.

Common Problems Everyone Should Know How to Solve

A correct squat will always have certain identifiable characteristics controlled by skeletal anatomy and muscle function. For any squat – low bar, high bar, or front squat (these two variations are discussed at length in chapter 7) – these conditions will be satisfied, making it relatively easy to determine whether form and position are correct. At the top, all the skeletal components that support the bar – the knees, hips, and spine – will be locked in extension so that the muscular components only have to exert enough force to maintain this resting position. The bar will be over the middle of the foot. The heavier the weight, the more true this will be.

When the squat begins its eccentric phase, all the muscles that will ultimately extend these joints, or in the case of the spinal erector muscles serve to maintain extension under increasing mechanical stress, come under active load as they resist extension on the way to the bottom position. During this ride to the bottom, the bar will maintain its position over the mid-foot. The correct bottom position is identified by definite anatomical position markers:

- The spine will be held rigid in lumbar and thoracic extension
- The bar will be directly vertical to the middle of the foot
- The feet will be flat on the ground at the correct angle for the stance width
- The thighs will be perfectly parallel to the feet
- The acetabulum will be in a position lower than the top of the patella

Any deviation from this position will constitute bad technique, as will any movement on the way down or back up that causes a deviation from this position. And actually, if the bar stays in the correct vertical position over the mid-foot on the way down and up you will have done it right. Your skeleton will have solved the problem of how most efficiently to use your muscles to get the job of squatting done. It will have done so within the constraints imposed upon it by the physics of the barbell/body/gravity system we all lift within.

The position of the bar on the torso will control the angle of the back, and the angle of the back and the stance will control the forward/back position of the knees. When the bar is in the front squat position the back will be quite vertical, since this angle is necessary to keep the bar over the mid-foot, and to keep it from falling forward off the shoulders. When the back is this vertical the hips are nearly directly under the bar, which forces the knees forward well in front of the toes, a position which the ankles must accommodate by allowing the tibias to incline. When the bar is in the low bar squat position advocated here, just below the spine of the scapula (closely approximating the same skeletal relationships that will be seen later in the

Squatting in front of a mirror is a really bad idea. Many weight rooms have mirrors on all the walls, making it impossible to squat without a mirror there, within eyesight, giving you its bad feedback. A mirror is a bad tool because it provides information about only one plane, the frontal, and depth cannot be judged by looking in the mirror from the front. Some obliqueness of angle is required to see the relationship between patella and hip crease, but a mirror set at an oblique angle would produce a twisting of the neck. Cervical rotation under a heavy bar is just as bad an idea as cervical hyperextension under a heavy bar. But the best reason not to use a mirror in front of any multijoint exercise is that you should be developing kinesthetic sense of movement by paying attention to all the sensory input provided by proprioception, rather than focusing merely on visual input from a mirror. "Learn to feel it, not just see it," is excellent advice.

deadlift), the back will be at a much less vertical angle, approximately forty five degrees for people of average proportions, and the knees will be back to a point just in front of the toes. The high bar squat places the back and the knees in a position intermediate to the two extremes.

The wider the stance, the wider the foot angle, and the wider the knees will have to be apart to keep the thighs parallel to the feet. At closer stances with more forward-pointing toes, the knees will travel further forward than they do at wider knee angles. This is because the narrower the stance, the longer the distance back to front from the knee to the hip, and the longer the distance the more forward the knees must travel to accommodate it. A close stance with toes pointed out like a wider stance will display the same knees-forward position that a moderate stance at the same foot angle will. At very wide stances like those favored by powerlifters using squat suits, there is very little forward travel of the knee at all, and their shins tend to stay nearly vertical. But a wide stance will not work if the toes are pointed forward, because of the twist it places in the knee; this is about the only squat stance that is really anatomically wrong.

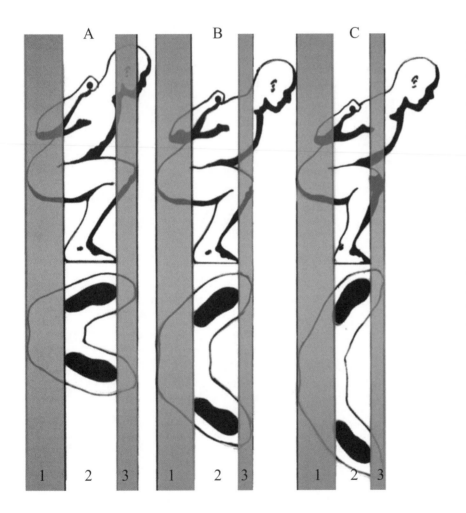

Figure 2-30. The variation in knee position, stance width, foot angle, and bar position. A. Narrow stance high-bar, with knees well forward of toes. B. The recommended stance for strength training purposes, with the bar just under the scapular spine. C. Modern powerlifting wide-stance, with the bar as low as the rules allow. Note that the distance between the front of the knees and the back of the hips appears to decrease with stance width, but that toe angle actually has more effect on this. Dimension 1 = butt to heel. Dimension 2 = Heel to toe. Dimension 3 = Toe to knee

Every barbell exercise that involves the feet on the floor and a barbell supported by the body will be in its best balance, both during the movement and at lockout, when the bar is vertically plumb to the middle of the foot. An assistance exercise like the barbell curl intentionally moves the bar out of line as a part of creating the resistance for the exercise, but any exercise that moves the bar through the frontal plane of the body conforms to this rule. All other considerations are secondary to this simple piece of physics, and correct form in these exercises is dictated by it.

For instance, knees too far forward would shift the bar to a position vertically forward of mid-foot; too horizontal a back would do the same thing. Too vertical a back would shift the bar behind mid-foot, as would insufficiently forward knees. These relationships are based on the position of the bar and the angle of the knees. If the high bar position is used, the angles change, as they will for the front squat. But for any given position of the bar and any acceptable knee angle, the angles formed by the body during the correct squat will be determined by the vertical relationship between the bar and the mid-foot, and the mechanics of the movement serve to maintain this relationship.

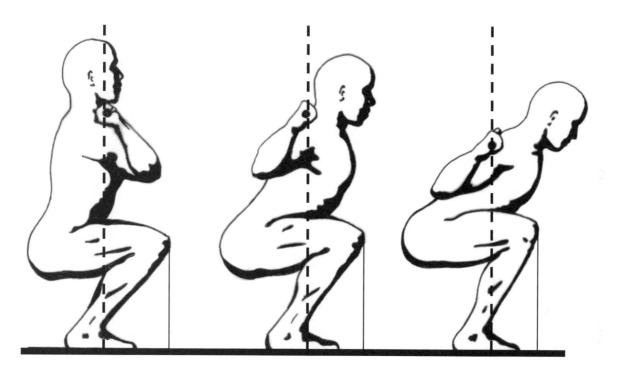

Figure 2-31. Bar position ultimately determines back angle, as seen in this comparison of the front squat, the high-bar squat, and the low-bar squat. Note that the bar remains balanced over the mid-foot in each case, and this requires that the back angle accommodate the bar position. This is the primary factor in the differences in technique between the three styles of squatting.

Grip and arms

Grip errors are common even among experienced lifters. The grip on the bar is the first part of your temporary relationship with the barbell that is referred to as a "set." If that grip is wrong, none of the reps in that set will be optimal, because the relationship of the body to the bar is determined first by hand position on the bar. For instance, an uncentered placement of the bar on your back results in an asymmetrical loading of all the components under the bar: more weight on one leg, hip, and knee than the other, as well as a spinal shear. A careless approach to grip placement could result in problems with heavy weights. Most people, as discussed earlier, will need to take an even grip somewhere between the score mark and the end of the knurl.

There is, however, an important exception to this rule: for a trainee with markedly different flexibility between the two shoulders – as might result from an injury – a symmetrical grip on the bar will result in an asymmetric bar position on the back. When the athlete goes under the bar, the tight shoulder keeps the upper arm from assuming the same angle as that on the good side. The tight shoulder thus drags the bar out toward that side, resulting in the bar being off-center and out-of-level on the back, and centered loading of the back should be your primary concern. If this is your situation – and it might require a third party or a mirror to identify this – you will need to experiment with your grip until you find the right position for each hand.

Figure 2-32. Asymmetrical (A) vs. symmetrical (B) bar placement. Uneven spinal loading affects the mechanics of the entire movement and predisposes for injury. Shoulder flexibility may be the cause of the uneven placement, and this should be analyzed and compensated for.

The vast majority of people will prefer to grip the bar with a thumbs-around grip. At lighter weights, this is fine since the load presents no problem to keep in place. But when heavier weights are being used – and, theoretically, they eventually should be – the thumbs can create problems.

The thumb should be placed on top of the bar, so that the wrist can be held in a straight line with the forearm. Most people have a mental picture of the hands holding up the weight, and this usually ends up being what happens. The bar sits in the grip with the thumbs around the bar, the elbows end up directly below the weight, and nothing really prevents the bar from sliding down the back from this position. People that do this will have sore elbows, a horrible, headache-like soreness in the inside of the elbow that makes them think the injury occurred doing curls. If the elbows are underneath the weight, and force of the weight is straight down (the nature of gravity is sometimes inconvenient), then the wrists and elbows will intercept some of the weight (fig. 2-33). With heavy weights, the loading is quite high, and these structures are not nearly as capable of supporting 500 lbs. as the back is. If the thumb is on top of the bar, the hand can assume a position that is straight in line with the forearm when the elbows are raised up. In this position, none of the weight is over any part of the arm, wrist, or hand, and all of the weight is on the back. A correct grip can prevent these problems before they start. If you learn to carry all of the weight of the bar on the back before your strength improves to the point where the weight becomes a problem, you'll have no problem at all.

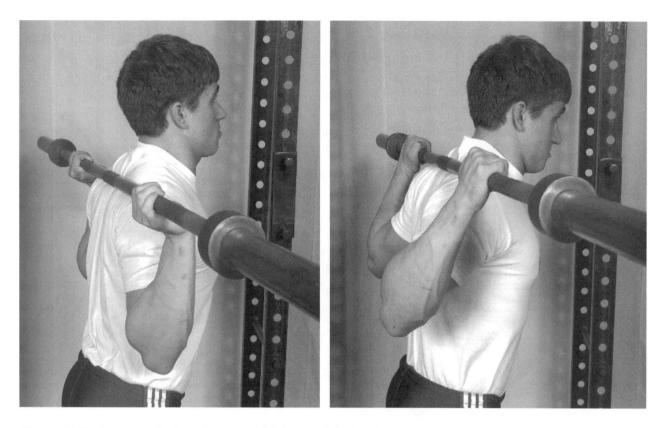

Figure 2-33. Incorrect (left) and correct (right) use of the hands and arms. Elbows should be elevated to the rear with the hands on top, not placed directly under the bar where they intercept part of the weight.

Occasionally a person gets misled into thinking that it is okay to put the hands out so wide on the bar that the fingers or even the palms of the hands are in contact with the plates. As bizarre as this sounds, you will eventually see this in the gym. As grip width increases, upper-back muscle tightness decreases, and muscular support for the bar is diminished, as previously discussed. If the posterior deltoids, rotator cuff muscles, traps, and rhomboids relax due to a widened grip, the skeleton becomes the default support structure. This is less than desirable. To add to the problem by placing the hands on the plates – a ROTATING pair of objects at the far end of the bar – is just silly. You must be in control of the bar, the bar must be secure on your back, and you must not be silly when you train.

As is often the case in athletics, one problem is intimately associated with another, and the solving of one fixes the other. A lack of shoulder tightness and failure to keep the chest up are almost the same problem, and may be fixed from either direction. If your elbows drop, your shoulders have relaxed; if you lift the elbows, your shoulders tighten. Most people will raise their chests when they raise their elbows, because not to do so would cause a forward shift in balance. Lifting the chest requires a contraction of the upper back muscles, especially the superior portion of the longissimus dorsi complex. So lifting the chest is thoracic spinal extension, a back movement. Tightening the shoulders and lifting the elbows aids the thoracic extension muscles by contributing to bar support at the point where it is mashing down into the back.

Many people seem to be making a flat, level spot for the bar to sit on by keeping the chest parallel to the floor. It is as if bending over into a position of spinal flexion makes the bar less likely to roll off the back. The bar will not roll off the back if you properly grip the bar and raise the elbows with the hands in the right position. When the elbows come up and the chest comes up, the hands are pushed forward and the bar is actually forced forward into the back, and cannot go anywhere at all (fig. 2-22). This "jamming" effect creates a tight, secure bar position that can tolerate changes of angle, acceleration, and deceleration.

Back

Although the squat has an undeserved, baseless reputation for knee injury, its greatest danger is to the spine. Lower back injuries – usually due to form problems – are more common by far than knee injuries, and care must be taken to prevent them. Most lower back errors fall into two broad categories: 1.) inadequate flexibility, and 2.) a lack of kinesthetic sense. Understanding the role of flexibility as it relates to squat form requires an understanding of the anatomy of the hip and leg musculature.

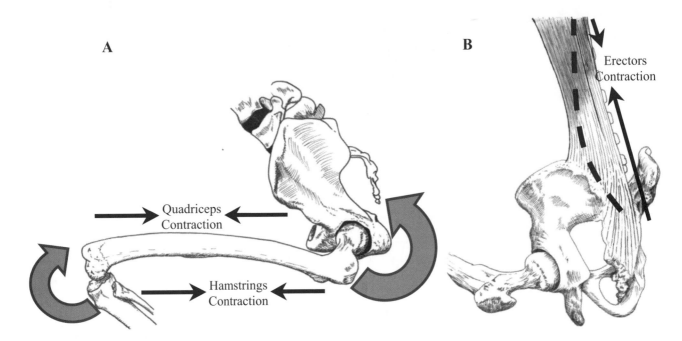

Figure 2-34. **A.** The relationship of the bones of the lumbar spine, pelvis, femur, and upper tibia, and the actions of the muscles that move them, in profile. The squat has the reputation of being a quadriceps exercise, but the hamstrings are also strongly developed during the full squat. **B.** The spinal erectors attach to the pelvis, ribs, and vertebrae, and extend the spine when in contraction. This "arching" action is accomplished in conjunction with the underlying multifidis, rotators, interspinales, and intertransversarii muscles. When contracted these muscles move the spine into the position shown by the dashed line.

The hamstrings are the key to good low back position. The hamstring group consists of the biceps femoris, the semimembranosus, and the semitendinosus, all three of which attach to the ischial tuberosity of the pelvis. They all insert at various points on the tibia, behind the knee on the lower leg. This configuration means that the hamstring group crosses two joints, the hip and the knee, and therefore has two functions: the proximal function, for hip extension, and the distal function, for knee flexion. When you squat, hip extension – straightening-out the hip joint – is what you do with the hamstrings, along with the glutes and adductors. The drive out of the bottom is hip extension, and the more efficiently you use hamstrings, adductors, and glutes, the more hip drive you have. This is another reason why good depth is important: the deeper you can squat with good form, the more the hamstrings are stretched, and the longer they are when they begin to contract the longer they can produce force during the contraction.

Squatting power is generated by the hips and legs and is transmitted up the rigid trunk segment to the load resting on the shoulders. The spinal column is held rigid in its normal anatomical position by the muscles of the back, sides, ribs and abs, so that the force may be safely transmitted to the load through the trunk. These muscles contract isometrically – that is, they stay in contraction but cause no movement to occur, and in doing so they permit no movement to occur. The pelvis articulates with the spine in the L5/S1 area of the lower back, the area above the tailbone. The muscles of the lower back – the erector spinae group – insert on the pelvis and at numerous points along the spinal column, so that when these muscles are in contraction the pelvis remains in a constant position relative to the lumbar vertebrae. The erector spinae serve to lock the pelvis and the lower back together, to fuse the pelvis and spine into a rigid structure, to protect the vertebral column from movement under load and to hold all these joints in normal anatomical position when lifting heavy loads so that the intervertebral discs are not damaged. These muscles, along with several ligaments and other connective tissue, act to keep the lower back in extension under a load. This area needs to stay "arched" to stay safe when lifting. And this is why the pelvis tilts forward at the same angle as the lower back as we lean forward with the back locked in a safe extended position.

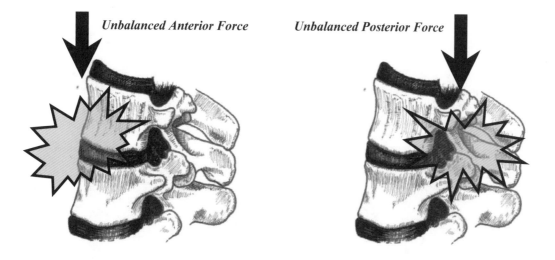

Figure 2-35. Proper spinal alignment ensures the anatomically correct distribution of forces across the intervertebral discs during loading. Improper vertebral position under load can result in either anterior or posterior squeezing of the discs and the injuries that accompany this bad position.

However, as the squat approaches the bottom position, the necessary forward lean of the trunk has a tendency to make the lower back assume a flexed, "rounded" position (fig. 2-36). This is due to the hamstring anatomy. As the squat depth increases and the torso assumes a more forward tilt, the bottom of the pelvis (the origin point of the hamstrings), locked into the rigid spine, tilts away from the back of the knee (the insertion point of the hamstrings). As these muscles reach the limit of their ability to stretch, they become tighter and begin to exert more pull on both the knee and their pelvic attachment. Here is the source of the lower back problem: your back muscles attach at the top of your pelvis, and your hamstrings attach to the bottom. If your hamstrings lack sufficient extensibility, they will exert enough tension on the bottom of your pelvis to pull it out of its locked position in the lower back, breaking muscular tension in the erector spinae, and permitting your entire lower back to come out of extension into a "round" position. The back muscles and the hamstrings are competing for control of your pelvis, and the back muscles must win if your spine is to stay safe.

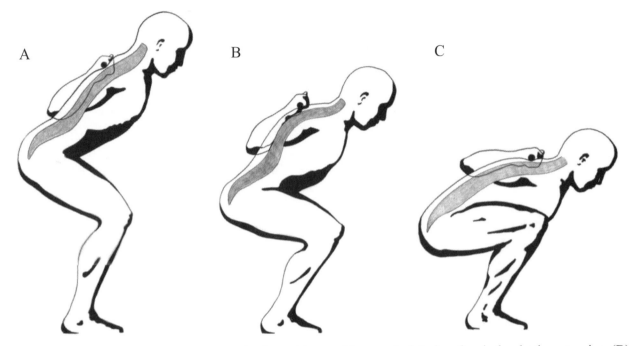

Figure 2-36. Tight hamstrings cause most back position problems. A deterioration in kyphotic extension (B) precedes the deterioration in lordotic extension (C), culminating in a round back at the bottom. This is due to the lack of extensibility in the hamstrings and the resultant ability to maintain a good pelvic tilt at depth, and the false perception of depth created by lowering just the bar.

Figure 2-37. The "Cat box position," a result of tight hamstrings. Knee and hip extension are limited by hamstring extensibility and the bar is then lowered by spinal flexion. This is an excellent way to produce a back injury.

Once the cause of this problem is understood, it can be corrected through diligent stretching. The squat itself acts as a stretch, and with careful attention to good lower back position it can correct itself in a short time – just a few workouts. Often, unfortunately, the lack of extensibility is paired with another problem: the inability to identify which position the lower back is in.

A lack of kinesthetic sense – the ability to identify the position of the body or a body part in spatial relation to the ground or the rest of the body – is very common. Some people have absolutely no idea that their lower back is round at the bottom of the squat, or that it is arched correctly at the top of the squat, or any idea what position it is in at all. It is as though all proprioceptive activity has ceased in this particular area of the body. Many inflexible trainees exhibit this problem, but many perfectly flexible people cannot assume a position of lumbar extension and hold it through a squat.

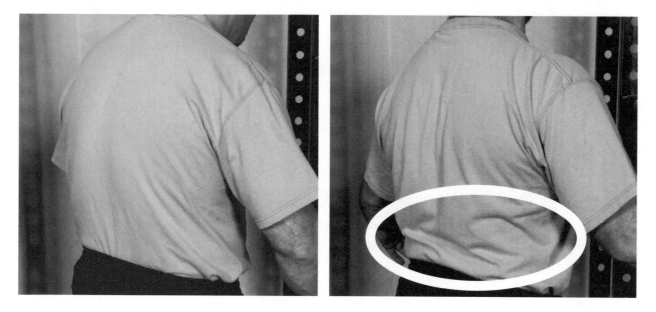

Figure 2-38. The easiest way to identify spinal extension – "arching the back" – is to look for wrinkles that appear in the cloth of the shirt as the top and bottom of the back get closer.

The key to learning the correct position for the lower back is to assume a position that is correct, and then memorizing the way it feels so that it can be reproduced every time. The best way to do it is to lie down on your belly on the floor, put your hands behind your head and raise your chest up off of the floor. Lift your elbows when you do this. Most of your back will now be in extension. Then lift your knees up off of the floor too. Don't push your toes down to lift the knees up, or you'll be using your quads instead of your back muscles. When you do this correctly, you'll be bending your knees slightly and using your glutes, hamstrings, and most importantly your low back to make this movement. When you get it right, the only thing touching the floor will be your belly. This is what it feels like to have your lower back in contraction. Feel this arch. Relax and do it again. By placing your back in a position where you have to contract your spinal erectors repeatedly without trying to do anything else at the same time, you can embed this new motor pathway quickly and easily, without having to try to distinguish it from other elements of an unfamiliar movement.

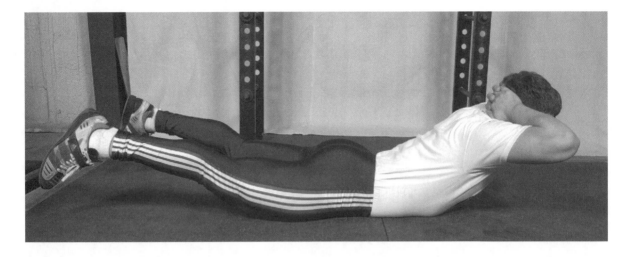

Figure 2-39. A good position for learning to identify the "feel" of spinal extension.

Now stand up and do this movement again immediately. Then put the bar on your back and repeat it several times. Just to be sure, unlock your knees and hips to about a half-squat position and see if you can still perform this lumbar extension. Since you can now identify the correct back position you should be able to keep your back arched through the whole squat, if you are sufficiently flexible.

Hips

The hips are the guts of the squat. Hips provide the power out of bottom, with the transition to the quads above parallel taking care of itself. Knees and hips are tied together, conceptually, as well as by the femur. If your hips are too forward, your knees are too. And if your hips are too far forward, and your knees are too far forward, you can't drive up out of the bottom. Hip drive is the basis for squatting power, and hip drive can be learned easily and quickly.

Look carefully at figure 2-40. As you assume the bottom position, imagine a hand placed on your sacrum, right at the base of the spine, and imagine pushing this hand straight up in the air with your butt. This is as clear a picture of the process of driving the hips up as can be drawn. If you have a training partner, get him to place his hand as in the picture and provide some resistance to your hip drive so that the effect can be felt. (This is also a good time to refresh your head/eye position lesson. Look both down and up at the ceiling while driving against the hand and see which you prefer. Twenty bucks says it's down.) There is only a subtle difference in appearance between good strong hip drive and a squat that lacks this, but you will be able to feel the power of this technique the first time you do it correctly.

A common error is the tendency for some lifters to drive the hips forward instead of upward, especially right before the transition point between hip drive and quads, a little above parallel (fig. 2-41). If your hips go forward, your knees will too, causing the weight to shift forward to the toes. This is bad for power, because anytime the knee angle closes, the hamstrings have shortened from the distal end, and if they have shortened without causing movement, they have been removed as a source of power. If the rebound out of the bottom is dependent on hamstring and adductor tightness, any relaxation of tension in these muscles represents a loss in stored elastic energy, not to mention the ability to contract and generate force. As we will see often, form errors in many exercises represent the loss of the ability to generate force due to a loss in the position required for productive contraction. Your best power is achieved when your hips continue straight up out of the bottom, your tibias serving as anchors for your hamstrings, your hamstrings and adductors contracting against the pelvis to produce hip extension, your quads then producing knee extension and then your knees and hips locking out simultaneously at the top.

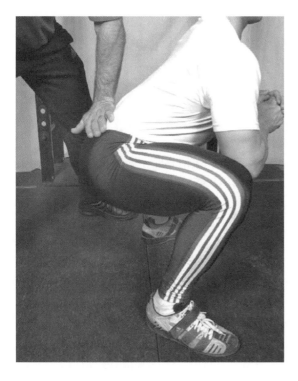

Figure 2-40. Learning hip drive with the aid of a coach.

Figure 2-41 (below). Driving chest up instead of hips up kills hamstring power in the middle of the squat. Raising the chest pulls the knees forward, and when the knee angle closes the hamstring shortens. Any muscle that assumes a position of contraction without moving a load during that contraction has not actively contributed to that movement. This phenomenon will be observed often throughout this examination of barbell training.

Rebound out of the bottom, the concept of "bounce," is very important. Once again, the bounce DOES NOT INVOLVE THE KNEE. **You bounce off of the hamstrings and adductors, not the quads.** It happens when the hamstrings, glutes, and adductors reach the limit of their normal range of motion due to the slight forward and outward motion of the knee and the more pronounced backward motion of the hips. Remember: the pelvis is locked in position – in line with the spine – by the low back muscles, the hamstrings attach to the ischial tuberosity at the bottom of the pelvis, and the pelvis tilts forward with the torso as squat depth increases, thus stretching out the hamstrings and glutes. At the same time, the adductors are tightening as the distance between their attachments on the inside of the femur and on the pubis area of the anterior pelvis are stretched apart. The bounce at the bottom of the squat is merely the correct use of the stretch reflex – a muscle contraction enhanced by the proprioceptive detection of muscle elongation immediately prior to the contraction – inherent in any dynamic muscle contraction, added to the rebound provided by the viscoelastic energy stored in the stretched muscles and tendons. Essentially, you are bouncing off your hamstrings, not your knees. It is safe, it is correct, and it is necessary if heavy weights are to be lifted. The only way it can hurt your knees is if your hamstrings relax at the bottom, which would result in your knees traveling forward, and which you should not do. If the hips are shoved back at the bottom while your knees are shoved out, your hamstrings and adductors will tighten, your knee will be protected, and power out of the bottom will increase.

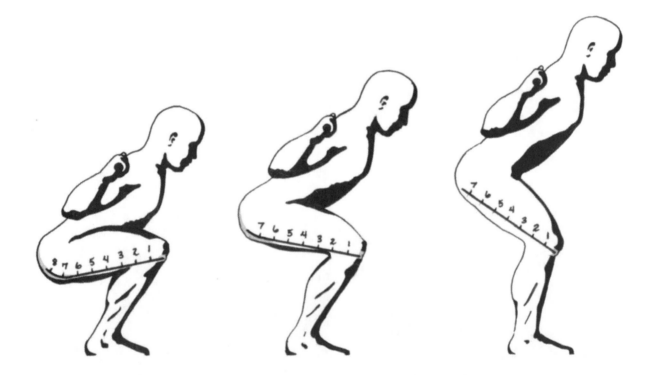

Figure 2-42. The correct bottom position of the squat stretches the hamstrings and adductors, and the drive up utilizes that stretch. The contraction is evident as the muscles shorten during the ascent. The "bounce" is the stretch-shortening cycle applied to the elastic rebound that tight, stretched muscles and tendons provide at the bottom of the squat.

Your timing here is important. If the bounce is used correctly, it will be immediately followed by a hard drive up of the hips. It is important that the bounce is not followed by a pause and then a drive up. The bounce must be incorporated into the drive – it must be anticipated as the first part of the drive. Think about the "up" drive all the way down during the descent. Don't think about going down while you're going down – think about coming up the whole time. This will reduce the tendency to separate the drive from the bounce, since it's being anticipated even before the bounce occurs.

The timing of your descent and rebound is critical to the performance of good squats. Bounce occurs optimally at the correct speed of descent. If your descent is too fast, the bounce will be less effective, and much less safe, because the only way to drop too fast is to relax something. Muscles tightened in the squat descent store elastic energy, as illustrated by our specific example of the hamstring rebound. Tight muscles also keep your back, hips, and knees in the correct, safe position. If you are loose enough to drop into the bottom of the squat much faster than you can come up, you need to tighten up more on the way down. And a loose descent can allow joints to be jammed into positions they should not occupy. This is how most people get hurt squatting – getting out of good position by going down so fast that proper technique cannot be maintained. This is how squats got an undeserved bad reputation. Don't contribute to the problem by dive-bombing into the bottom.

The term *posterior chain* often gets applied to matters regarding the spinal erectors, hamstrings, glutes, and adductors. This obviously refers to the anatomical position of these muscular components. It also indicates the nature of the problems most people experience under the bar, trying to improve their efficiency while squatting.

Humans are bipedal creatures with prehensile hands and opposable thumbs, a configuration that has profoundly affected our perception as well as our posture. We are used to doing things with our hands in a position where our eyes can see them, and we are therefore set up to think about things done with our hands. We are not used to thinking about our nether regions, at least those unrelated to toilet functions. The backside of your head, torso, and legs are seldom the focus of your attention unless they hurt, and they remain visually unobservable even with a mirror. The parts you can see in the mirror – the arms, chest, and abs, and the quads and calves if you're wearing shorts – always end up being the favorite things for most people to train. They are also the easiest parts to learn how to train, maybe because they are accessible visually while you learn them, and because they involve or facilitate the use of our hands.

The hard parts to train correctly are the ones you can't see. The posterior chain is the most important component of the musculature that directly contributes to gross movement of the body, as well as the source of whole-body power. It is also the hardest part to learn how to use correctly. And it would be easier if you didn't have any hands: how would you pick up a table without the ability to grab the edge of the thing and lift? You'd get under it and raise it with your upper back, or squat down and drive it up with your hips against the undersurface of it, or lay down on your back and drive it up with your feet, because without hands those would be the only options open to you. But your hands shift your focus away from these options and enable you to avoid thinking about them at all. So posterior chain matters remain largely unexplored by most people, and this makes their correct use a rather groundbreaking experience.

You will find that the posterior aspects of squatting and pulling present the most persistent problems, require the greatest amount of outside input from coaches and training partners, and will be the first aspects of form to deteriorate in the absence of outside reinforcement. For coaches, the posterior chain is the hardest part of the musculature to understand, to explain, and to influence. But it is also the most critical aspect of human movement from the perspective of athletic performance, and the mastery of its lore can determine the difference between an effective coach and a slightly-more-than-passive observer.

Knees

In a correct back squat of the style advocated here, there is one correct place for the knees: slightly out in front of the toes, the exact distance being determined by the anthropometry of the individual, and directly in line with the foot so that the femur and the foot are parallel. This basically means that the femur and the foot should be in a straight line as seen from directly above, so there is no twisting of the knee. Depending on your femur/tibia/trunk dimensions, your knee could be anywhere from directly above your toes to three or four inches in front of them. Since your knees will be directly in line with your toes, the angle of your feet in your stance will determine the angle of the knees as well. As shown in figure 2-6, about 30 degrees out from the perpendicular works for most people, although this varies as well. This angle allows the torso to clear the legs at the bottom so that good depth can be attained.

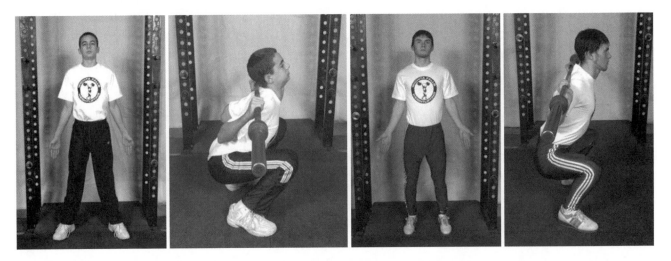

Figure 2-43. A dramatic example of the differences that anthropometry can produce in the appearance of the bottom position of the squat. Both are correct, but both are different due to variations in leg and trunk length.

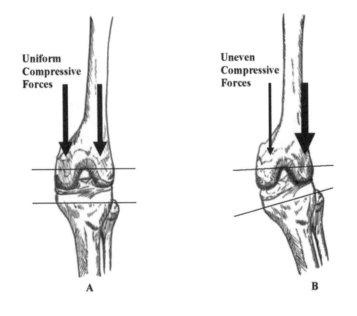

Figure 2-44. Distribution of compressive forces during a correct (left) and incorrect, knees-in (right) squat.

By far, the two most common knees errors are 1.) knees in too much and 2.) knees too far forward, either early in the descent or at the bottom. It is actually unusual to see a novice not make one or both of these errors the first time they squat. Both are related to flexibility and positional awareness, two things that are specifically developed and corrected by squatting.

If you allow your knees to come together during the squat at any time, you place your knees in a position that is not friendly to your knee anatomy. But this problem cannot be corrected if it is not identified. Look down when you squat even more than usual, to a point on the floor right between your toes where you can clearly see your knees, and check your position. If they move toward each other at any point during the squat, shove them out. You will probably have to exaggerate this shoving-out in order for it to put your knees in the correct position, since you thought they were in the right position anyway. When you get them back out to parallel with your feet and keep them there for a couple of sets, you will notice later that your adductors, or "groin" muscles, get sore. As previously discussed, adductors play an important role in squatting.

Figure 2-45. A. The knees-in position. B. The only way to fix the knees-in position: shoving the knees out and keeping them there until the adductors strengthen.

Knees too far forward presents a different challenge, as its cause can be either flexibility or perception. The problem with knees too far forward is not that it destroys the knees, but that it has a detrimental effect on hip extension out of the bottom. A knees-forward position produces a more acute knee angle, and the resultant shortened hamstrings have less room to contract from the other end. This makes the already-contracted hamstring's contribution to hip extension much less efficient than a longer, stretched-out hamstring's would be.

Tight hamstrings can throw the knees forward. But if you have a concept of the low-bar back squat that involves a mental image of your doing the movement with your back in a vertical position, your perception of what you're supposed to be doing is wrong, and will cause your knees to be forward. If your torso is too vertical, your knees will be forced forward, to maintain your balance. The advice to "lift with your legs – not your back" may be part of the problem, since most people interpret this to involve a vertical torso and legs pushing the floor. The saying should be, "lift with your hips, not your back." "Lifting with your back" is what happens when you bend over to lift and round your spine into flexion. It's a normal part of the movement to lean over (fig. 2-46). The correct mental picture usually fixes this problem.

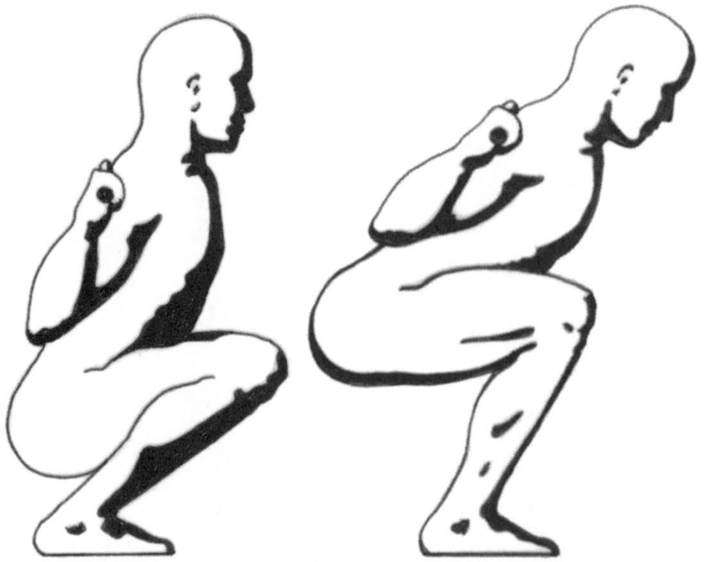

Figure 2-46. Quite often, the mental image of the squat involves a vertical torso (left), a position that kills posterior-chain involvement. The correct amount of trunk inclination is necessary (right) in order that correct mechanics can be expressed, and this will involve the appropriate mental picture of what your torso does during the squat. Don't be afraid to lean over, stick your butt back, and shove your knees out.

If it doesn't, there are other things that can get the knees back. If the weight is on the heels during the squat, the knees can't be too far forward. Think about the heels, and how it feels to have your weight balanced on them. Assume your squat stance and pick up your toes. You obviously can't pick up your toes without going on the heels. Once your weight is on your heels, squat. When you squat from the heels, your knees will stay back. Now, you will not be able to continue to squat on your heels, because this is also an unbalanced position, but after three or four reps this trick will have done its job and you will have settled into the middle of your foot with your knees in the correct position, not too far out over the toes. This position will feel balanced and strong, and done correctly a few times it will be the one you favor from then on.

Fig. 2-47. Picking up the toes is an excellent way to learn the feel of heels-down.

Figure 2-48. Letting the knees travel forward at the bottom of the squat is both inefficient for posterior chain involvement and detrimental to the health of the hip flexor tendons. Caused by a relaxation of the hamstrings at the bottom, the forward travel of the knee pulls the insertions of the hip flexors on the ASIS (see fig. 2-50 below).

A different problem often encountered in more advanced trainees is the tendency to let the knees slide forward at the bottom. It is usually a problem developed over time, and is a rather embedded movement pattern that can be hard to fix if you let it go uncorrected too long. If your knees move forward at the bottom of the squat, you have relaxed your hamstrings, because hamstrings pull the knee back. They insert on the tibia and provide posterior tension, which should increase with the depth of the squat as the other attachment point on the pelvis tilts away. If this tension is insufficient to keep the knees from sliding forward as the bottom of the squat is approached, something is wrong. And when knees move forward at the bottom, tension is put on the hip flexors as they insert on the ASIS, the anterior superior iliac spine, or point of the hip. The muscles in question – the rectus femoris, the sartorius, and the tensor fascia latae – cross both the hip and the knee joints, and therefore produce movement around both joints (fig. 2-49). In the squat, their knee extensor function (the distal function) is our concern, since active hip flexion does not occur. At the bottom of the squat, these muscles act with the other knee extensors in the quadriceps group to straighten the knee. All the muscles in the group are under tension, but only the three hip flexors cross the hip to attach at the ASIS. Now, if at the bottom of the squat the knee should be allowed to move forward, tension is increased on these muscles and their attachment at the hip as the knee angle becomes more acute (fig. 2-50). The ASIS is pulled on very hard by these muscles at their attachment, and a marvelous dose of the weirdest tendinitis you have ever seen can be the result. This condition is thankfully rare, and some people squat this way for years without trouble, but if it develops it takes many weeks to heal.

The fact is that most people don't like to keep tension on the posterior chain as they approach the bottom of the squat. For some reason most people would rather let the knees slide forward and settle into the quadriceps than maintain tension on the hamstrings, adductors, and glutes. Tempting as it may be to relax forward, it is inefficient and increases the risk of injury, since low-back relaxation often comes along for the ride.

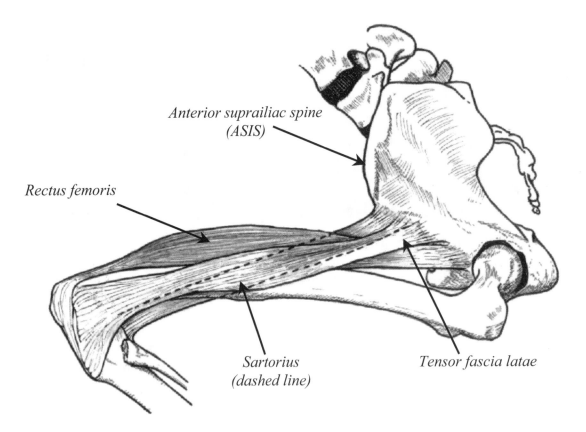

Anterior suprailiac spine
(ASIS)

Rectus femoris

Sartorius
(dashed line)

Tensor fascia latae

Figure 2-49. The relationship of the hip flexor muscles to the bones of the hip and knee. The hip flexors have two functions: knee extension is the distal function, and hip flexion – not used during the squat – is the proximal function.

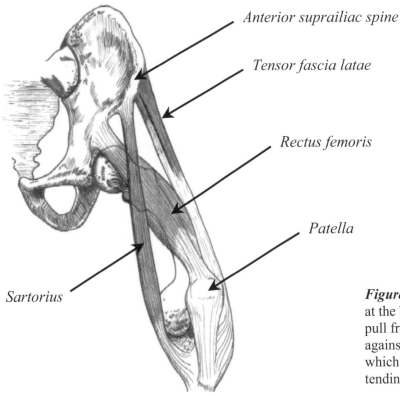

Anterior suprailiac spine

Tensor fascia latae

Rectus femoris

Patella

Sartorius

Figure 2-50. If the knee slides forward at the bottom of the squat, the increased pull from the knee develops high tension against the attachments on the pelvis, which can cause an interesting type of tendinitis.

The answer is to learn to squat with the knees in the proper place, and to move them correctly during the descent. One approach is to make all of the forward knee travel occur in the first third or half of the descent. From the top, shove the knees forward and out to the place they will end up, just in front of the toes, and then the rest of the movement will consist of the hips moving back and down. Make two movements out of this for a couple of reps, and then reduce this to a smooth single motion (fig. 2-51). A useful way to learn this is with the use of a block of wood, as illustrated in figure 2-52.

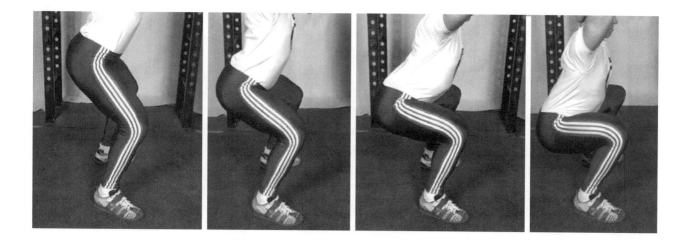

Figure 2-51. Note that the knees, once they move forward to their position over the toes, do not move during the remainder of the squat until the ascent carries them back up to this point.

Figure 2-52. A terribly useful block of wood. Touch the block, but don't knock it over.

As noted previously, a technique that can be used to correct all of these knee position problems is to actually look down at your knees. In your squat stance, at the top with the bar in position on your back, look straight down at a point on the floor between your toes. You will see a picture of your knees relative to your feet, and the movement of your knees relative to your toes will be apparent as you go down. Look at your knees all the way down and back up a couple of times with the empty bar. You will need to practice this because it will seem awkward at first. But as you watch your knees change position through the movement and as the sets get heavier, you will see exactly what the problems are and have immediate feedback on what you need to do to correct them. If your concept of the squat is correct, this is the best way to fix your knee problems.

Feet and stance

The recommended stance is heels at about shoulder width apart, toes pointed out at about 30 degrees. Stance is a highly individual thing, and will vary with hip width, hip ligament tightness, femur and tibia length and proportion, adductor and hamstring flexibility, knee joint alignment, and ankle flexibility. Everybody's stance will be slightly different. And as noted earlier, stance width will have an influence on knee position.

For example, if you are tall with very long femurs and relatively narrow shoulders, you need a wider stance than usually recommended, since your shoulders are not of typical width. If you have a long torso and short legs (not that uncommon a bodytype), you will need a bit narrower stance than our model would predict. Sometimes the foot angle needs to be adjusted for individual situations: if you are pigeon-toed, your foot angle will need to be slightly more forward-pointing than the model, or more commonly in the case of out-toeing the foot will need to be pointed out more. These corrections are necessary to keep the correct neutral relationship between the femur and the tibia, so that no twisting occurs in the capsular and medial/lateral ligaments of the knee. Expect a closer stance to drive the knees more forward, and a wider stance to place them further back (see fig. 2-30). But again, shoulder width heels produces the best effect for general strength training.

A trainee with very tight hips can benefit from a wider stance until flexibility is increased; in fact, if this adjustment allows you to squat to correct depth, it will cause the problem to correct itself, and very quickly allow you to assume a more useful narrower stance.

A narrow-stance squat, such as those frequently pictured in the muscle magazines, develops an aesthetically pleasing set of quads. But since you should plan on using the rest of the hip musculature too, it seems unwise to omit it from your training program. It is very difficult for people of normal flexibility to get deep enough with a narrow stance, and thus the hamstrings are never engaged as fully as with a more generalized wider stance. Also, the narrow stance does not involve the groin muscles, as discussed earlier. For this reason it can be useful in the event of a groin injury, and can be used for several weeks while the adductors are healing. If used all the time, narrow stance squatting predisposes you to a groin injury due to the lack of conditioning for these muscles.

What is wrong with a wide, modern powerlifting-type sumo-style squat stance? Especially if it allows you to squat more weight? The answer is nothing, if you are a powerlifter. But if you are training for general athletic strength and power, the thing that is wrong with it is the same thing that is wrong with half-squatting more weight above parallel. You are trying to get strong; you are not trying to see how much weight you can squat. The two things are NOT the same, especially if that squat style is not specific to your program or safe for you to use. A wide stance does allow more weight to be squatted, but no sport except powerlifting can use strength developed in this stance, because that stance does not occur in other sports. Strength is both general and specific: general in that it is always good to be stronger, specific in that the strength should be acquired in a way that allows it to be applied to movement patterns used in the sport for which we are conditioning. An extremely wide-stance squat omits much of the quadriceps function, and as such is not very specific to sports that use the quads. This includes pretty much all of them.

Powerlifters favor a wide stance for peak performance. Here Kevin McCloskey representing the Weight Room in Richmond, Virginia squats 277.5 kg. in the 90 kg. class at the 2006 USAPL Nationals.

One occasionally sees powerlifters squatting with their toes pointing almost forward. Some of the really strong ones do this to increase the joint tightness and resultant rebound obtained by placing additional torque on the knee ligaments. This is a practice best left to very experienced powerlifters. For you, it will be very important to have all the bones of the legs and hips in the best position to generate force without being injured. Here is a way to see this relationship: sit in a chair with your knees slightly bent and your feet out in front of you, without pushing hard on the floor. Put your legs together, and note that your toes are pointing straight forward. Spread them out wide and note that your toes are pointing out. In both positions your feet assume a position parallel to your femur, and your knee is in an anatomically neutral position, with no twisting (fig. 2-53). As your knees point out, your toes point out. The wider the knees, the more the toes point out. As the knees widen, the femur rotates externally, and the tibia must follow it to keep the knee ligaments in normal anatomical position, and the toe points out more because it is attached to the end of the tibia. This anatomical relationship must be understood and respected, so that unnecessary knee injuries don't happen.

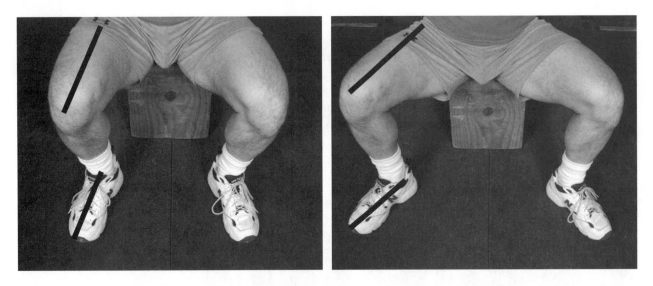

Figure 2-53. The relationship between stance width, stance angle, and knee angle. The wider the stance, the more the toes point out, due to the changing angle of the femur at the pelvis with increasing width. The feet keep the tibias rotated in line with the femur – and the stress off the knee – by changing their angle to accommodate the rotation.

The practice of placing a block or a 2x4 under the heels is common. Most gyms keep one lying around somewhere. The purpose of this is to make the full squat position easier to reach, and an understanding of the reason this works is necessary to the understanding of why it should not be done. A block under the heels tilts the shins forward by lifting the ankle up a little and allowing the knee to move forward without stretching the ankle joint. This shin angle causes the attachment point of the hamstrings on the back of the tibia to move back closer to their origin on the pelvis, unstretching the muscle a little and thus decreasing the amount of stretch necessary to get to full depth. If you are having flexibility problems severe enough to need a block under your heels to squat deep, you will not benefit by being prevented from stretching those muscles that are too tight. The squat, being a full range of motion exercise, provides an even better stretch than most stretches do. It is far better to approach full squat depth a little at a time each workout, with an exercise that will very quickly stretch you out, than to use an artificial aid that will prevent you from obtaining enough stretch to ever fix the problem.

Breathing

Much controversy exists about breathing patterns during exercise. It is thought by some that "inhaling on the way down and exhaling on the way up" is a good way to eliminate the possibility of cerebrovascular accidents during exercise, by lowering the peak blood pressure during the rep. Such advice reveals a misunderstanding of the mechanisms involved, overrates the likelihood of an exercise-related cerebrovascular injury, a breathtakingly uncommon event, and underrates the likelihood of an orthopedic injury, an all-too-common occurrence. It behooves us to understand the function of the Valsalva maneuver, the proper term for holding the breath against a closed glottis while pressure is applied by the abdominal and thoracic muscles, during the squat.

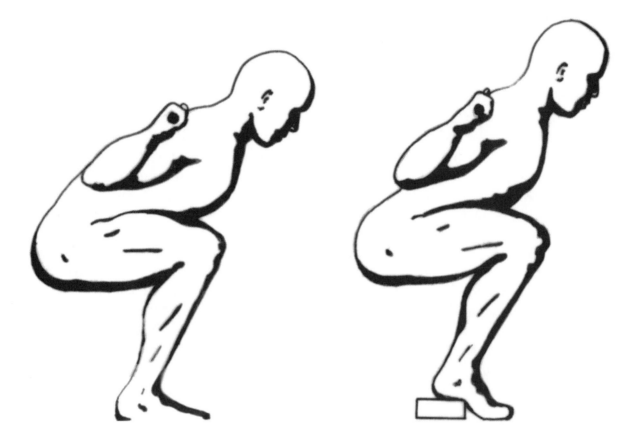

Figure 2-54. Placing a block under the heels allows the knees and hips to move forward, compensating for a lack of hamstring flexibility. This, of course, merely allows you to postpone solving the problem that makes the block helpful.

If your car runs out of gas in an intersection, and you have to push it out of the way or get killed, you will open your car door, put your shoulder on the doorframe, take a great big breath, and push the car. You will probably not exhale except to take another quick breath until the car and you are out of the way. Furthermore, you will not even think about this, since the many millions of years your ancestors have spent pushing on heavy things has taught your central nervous system the correct way to push. Or you might find yourself grunting aloud during the effort, a vocalization produced by a marked restriction in the airway at the glottis which produces an increase in pressure during the partial exhalation. This is perhaps the origin of the "kiyah" in martial arts, the vocalization that allows for an increased focus of power at the striking of a blow.

When you inhale, pressure increases in your thoracic cavity. When you hold your breath and tighten your trunk muscles, this pressure increases more. Since your thoracic and abdominal cavities are separated by only your diaphragm, abdominal pressure increases too. Thus, pressure in your abdominal and thoracic cavities is being applied to the anterior side of your spine, from the front to the back. The spinal vertebrae are being held in the correct anatomical position by your back musculature, and this correct position is reinforced by static pressure transmitted to the belly side of the spine across the hydrostatic column of the gut, the essentially non-compressible contents of the abdominal cavity (fig. 2-55). As pressure in the thoracic cavity increases with a big held breath, and this pressure is increased by the tightening of the abs and obliques, more anterior support develops for the spine. The back muscles position and support the spine from the back; the abs, with the aid of a big breath, support it from the front. A weightlifting belt adds to this effect, its main function being to add to anterior support rather than to apply pressure from the back.

The conventional wisdom is that this thoracic and abdominal pressure is also being applied to the cardiovascular system embedded in the trunk, and that the increase in pressure is being transmitted up the vascular column to the head, and that this increase in pressure has the potential to cause a cerebrovascular accident, such as a stroke or a blown aneurysm. This ignores the fact that the same pressure is being applied to the cerebrospinal fluid (CSF) in the spinal canal, which transmits pressure up through the subdural space in the skull and throughout the cranium, balancing cardiovascular pressure across the blood/brain interface (fig. 2-56). These opposing pressures remain in balance during the Valsalva maneuver, and the spinal support provided by the anterior thoraco-abdominal pressure is precisely why it is natural for us to do it when we lift or push. Fighter pilots perform the Valsalva when they are subjected to high G-forces in acrobatic maneuvers; the increased support maintains an open vascular column that supplies blood to the brain, so that consciousness can be salvaged under momentary high-G conditions that would otherwise cause a blackout.

Furthermore, no one gets under 405 lbs. and squats it without having trained enough to be able to do so. The cardiovascular system adapts to resistance training just like all of the other tissues and systems in the body, and this adaptation occurs as strength increases. Anyone who is capable of squatting extremely heavy weights is adapted for it in all the necessary ways. And no lifter has ever pulled 800 lbs. off the floor while exhaling. For the athlete using more than 5 lb. chrome dumbbells, it is far, far more likely that following the advice to "inhale on the way down and exhale on the way up" will actually cause an orthopedic injury than prevent a stroke.

In fact, it is a good practice to take and hold the biggest breath you can before each rep of your heaviest sets. Get in the habit of breathing correctly during your lighter sets, so that when the weight gets heavy the pattern will be established. The Valsalva maneuver will prevent far more problems that it has the potential to cause. It is a necessary and important technique for safety in the weight room.

The actual rates of cerebrovascular accidents (CVA) versus orthopedic injuries provide ample evidence that the greater risk is orthopedic. In Risser's 1990 study (*Am J Dis Child*, 144(9):1015-7, 1990) of junior high and high school athletes from all sports, 7.6% of all athletes incurred injuries that kept them out of training for 7 days. The rate of injury from all causes was 0.082 injuries per training year; 74% of all injuries were simple sprains and strains, and 59% of all injuries were classified as back injuries.

In contrast, the death rate from cerebrovascular accident in 2004 was about 0.000512 deaths per year (150,074 total) for the entire population of the US (293 million in 2004). The rate of survivable CVA in 2004 was 0.00305 incidents per year (895,000). So even if we compare the rates of orthopedic injury in a specialized small population engaging in exercise with the rate of CVA of the population of the entire United States, orthopedic injuries are still twenty-seven times more common than survivable strokes, and you are still ninety-four times as likely to hurt your back in sports as you are to die from a CVA if you don't even exercise. In reality, the difference is much greater, since athletes are far less likely than the general population to have cerebrovascular problems they have not inherited. There are no actual data for the rates of CVA in the weight room, because they occur so infrequently as to be statistically unmeasurable. More people drown in 5-gallon buckets each year than have had strokes in the weight room in the past decade.

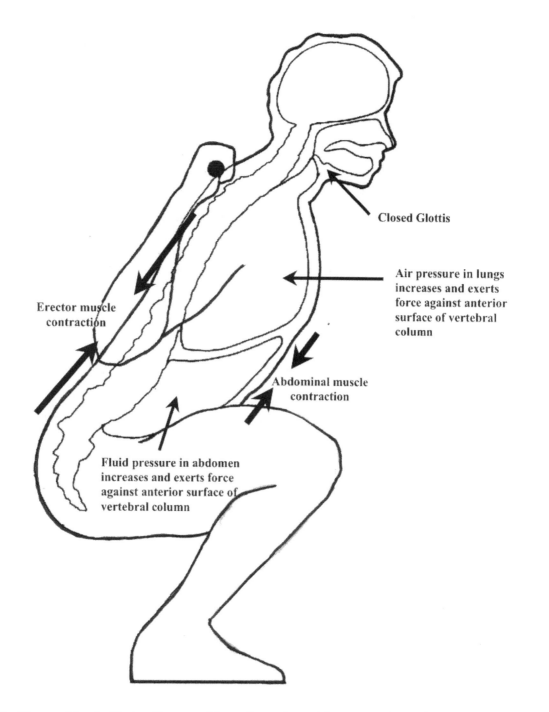

Closed Glottis

Air pressure in lungs increases and exerts force against anterior surface of vertebral column

Erector muscle contraction

Abdominal muscle contraction

Fluid pressure in abdomen increases and exerts force against anterior surface of vertebral column

Figure 2-55. The combined effects of increased lung (intra-thoracic) pressure, intra-abdominal pressure produced by abdominal muscle contraction, and spinal erector contraction on spinal stability during loading. The Valsalva maneuver increases the ability to produce this pressure and stability. Exhalation during heavy efforts prevents the development of sufficient pressure to stabilize the spine. At minimum, a vocalization should be performed during each rep, which ensures at least the partial closure of the glottis and the maintenance of some increased pressure during the effort. Best is a big, held breath during a heavy effort.

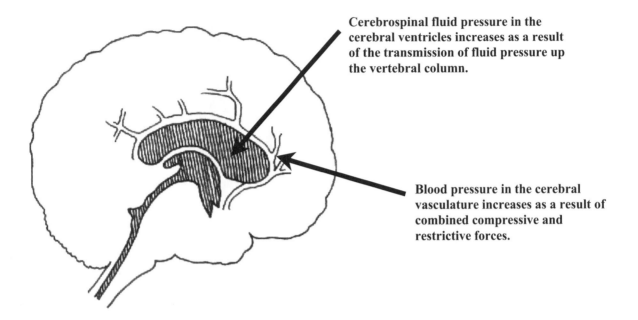

Cerebrospinal fluid pressure in the
cerebral ventricles increases as a result
of the transmission of fluid pressure up
the vertebral column.

Blood pressure in the cerebral
vasculature increases as a result of
combined compressive and
restrictive forces.

Figure 2-56. Cerebral vascular pressure does increase with strain and the Valsalva maneuver. However, the likelihood of vascular rupture is mitigated by a simultaneous increase in cerebral ventricular pressure transmitted up the cerebrospinal fluid column in the spinal canal – under the same pressure as the vascular column. The volume of the skull limits these two pressures and stabilizes vessel structures rather than predisposing them to rupture.

Spotting the squat

Weights used in the squat can be sufficiently heavy and are in such a position that it is not safe for one spotter to work alone. Any squat attempt or set of squats you are uncertain you can do or even a little worried about should be spotted by two people. The squat requires two spotters. They have to learn to watch each other and work carefully together to minimize the effects inherent in two people applying force to the same object. The differential loading caused by one spotter jerking the bar up while the other one doesn't is a potential wreck, and it has caused many back injuries. But this is a thing that can be managed by having spotters learn how to do it correctly. Spotters should apply force to the bar in a balanced way, coordinating their efforts to keep the bar as level as possible while minimizing the chance of hurting themselves in the process (fig. 2-57).

A one-person spot for a squat cannot be safely accomplished. One spotter standing behind the lifter, leaning over with arms wrapped around and under the lifter's chest, is not only an embarrassing position but also a terribly ineffective and unsafe one. After all, if you are so ungracious as to drop the bar off of your back, what will your single spotter do? Catch it? Coupled with the fact that any help he gives you from this position will be applied to your chest, thus altering your position at precisely the worst time it could be altered, a single squat spotter is usually a bad idea (fig. 2-58).

Figure 2-57. Spotting the squat requires attention, teamwork, and some finesse. Spotters should assume their positions prior to the start of the set. If the lifter misses the rep, the spotters use both hands and the crook of one elbow to catch each end of the bar. This effort must be balanced and coordinated, or the lifter gets uneven deloading of the bar and a possible torsion injury. Any lifter that bails out of the missed rep and leaves the spotters holding the bar needs to be beaten with a hammer.

In a dire emergency, a spotter might be able to help by standing directly behind and pushing up on the bar with as even a hand position as can be managed around your grip and bar placement (fig. 2-59). This may not work, and if so everybody needs to take care of himself by getting away from the bar as safely as is possible. (In fact, some coaches teach their athletes to dump the bar off the back when using rubber bumper plates and using no spotters, in the event of a miss. You can't hurt spotters this way, since there aren't any, and spotters can't hurt you either. This move requires practice. Don't try it without being shown how by a good coach.) But this is a completely avoidable situation, one that indicates that either the wrong weight is on the bar, or that there is not enough help in the weight room. Things should be changed so that it does not happen again.

"Squatting" in a Smith machine is an oxymoron. A squat cannot be performed on a Smith machine, as should be obvious from all previous discussion. Sorry. There is a gigantic difference between a machine that makes the bar path vertical and a squat that is executed correctly enough to have a vertical bar path. Muscle and skeleton should do the job of keeping the bar path vertical, not grease fittings and floor bolts. And a leg press machine – the "Hip Sled" – may be even less useful. This device restricts the movement of joints that normally adjust position during a squat, thus restricting the expression of your normal biomechanics. The leg press is particularly heinous in that it allows the use of huge weights, and therefore facilitates unwarranted bragging. A 1000 lb. leg press is as irrelevant as a 500 lb. quarter-squat.

Figure 2-58. The incorrect way to spot. Single-person spotting of the squat is tricky. The purpose of the spot is to take some of the weight of the rep so that it can be completed by the lifter. This cannot be safely accomplished by applying force to the lifter's body.

Figure 2-59. A better way to perform a one-person spot if necessary. Spot the bar, not the lifter.

Squatting inside a power rack is sometimes necessary. If the weight room is not set up correctly, i.e. the surface of the platform against the power rack is not flush with the inside floor of the rack so that you can walk the squat back across a level surface, or if your rack lacks a floor, it will be necessary to stay inside the rack to avoid stepping down or over things with the bar on your back. And if there are absolutely no spotters and it is squat day, it will have to be done inside the rack with the pins set at the correct height for the bar: low enough so that a below-parallel squat doesn't touch them, and high enough that a miss doesn't drive you into the floor. Power racks should be designed 1.) with a heavy floor inside that can be made flush with an adjacent platform, so that most of the time squats can be walked out, and 2.) with uprights built using the correct depth dimensions so that if necessary it can be used to squat inside. Squatting inside the rack as a matter of regular practice might be required because of a poorly designed rack and platform, but when squatting heavy it creates a potentially dangerous situation for the spotters and their hands. For the lifter, having the uprights visible peripherally may be distracting, their presence possibly altering the bar path in an attempt to stay away from contact with them. You can get accustomed to having them there, but squatting outside the rack is preferable, since available spotters remove the only reason to squat inside in a properly equipped weight room.

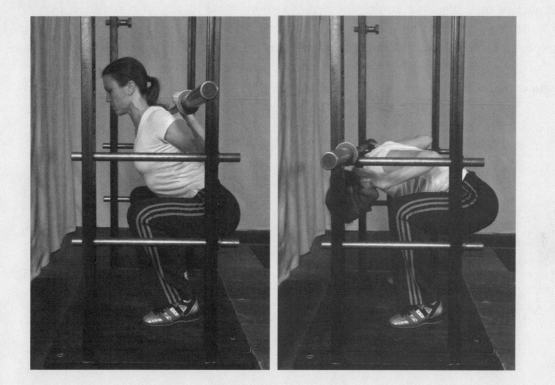

The proper use of the power rack if spotters are not available. The bar is dumped onto the pins, which have been carefully set at the correct height for this purpose.

Personal equipment

Supportive apparel, such as squat suits, squat briefs, power socks, bench press shirts, and such items are designed to help powerlifters lift more weight at a meet where such equipment is permitted. For purposes of strength training for athletics and fitness, it has no place in your program. Remember: lifting more weight is not always the same thing as getting stronger. This should be obvious in light of the principles already discussed regarding squatting and strength.

Less obvious is the role of belts and knee wraps. A properly designed and adjusted belt is useful as a safety device when squatting heavy weights. The role of the weightlifting belt in anterior support having just been discussed, it should be stated that a belt protects the spine while lifting heavy weights, but a suit actually makes it possible to lift weights that are heavier than you can squat. By storing some of the kinetic energy of the descending bar as elastic energy in the suit material and the compressed skin and muscle under the suit, and then making that energy available to the lifter as he rebounds up, the suit is in fact an artificial aid. It could be argued that the belt is too, but spinal support and safety are necessary, while a squat 30% heavier than that which could be done unaided is probably not.

A properly designed belt is four inches wide, all the way around. Many millions of cheap, junky belts have been produced with two-inch buckles and fronts, and either four or six inch backs. These were designed by someone that did not understand how a belt works. For it to function correctly it must act against the abs, not the back, and there is no reason for it to be wider in the back than in the front. Four inches is about the widest belt that most people can get between ribs and hips. If you're shorter, you may need to find a three-inch belt. Thickness is important in that a very thick, laminated suede belt feels very good under a big weight. Its almost complete lack of stretch makes for a comfortable ride. Such belts are expensive though, and any good single-ply 4 inch leather belt with a good buckle will work. Even a well-made Velcro belt will work.

Figure 2-60. Different types of weightlifting belts. They can be constructed in various ways, but useful belts are the same width along their entire length. Belts that widen in the back are designed by people who do not understand the function of a belt.

58

Using the belt correctly is a matter of practice. It must be worn in the right place at the right tightness to be effective, and if it's wrong it can actually screw up the lift it's designed to support. Put it on around your natural waist (higher than where you wear your pants) at a comfortable tightness, take your squat stance and squat down into the bottom position. The belt will adjust to the position it wants to settle in, the place where it functions most effectively, and it will have done so before the weight is a factor. Stand back up and tighten it to the point that it adds a little pressure to the gut. The right amount of tightness is a matter of individual preference, but as a general rule more experienced lifters can wear it tighter than novices. It is quite possible to have a belt on too tight; if you have to stretch "up" to get the belt in that last hole, you will be less able to exert pressure with your own abdominal musculature, thus negating the actual supportive function of the belt. Everyone has to do this once to see for themselves, and when you do you'll find that there is an optimum tension on the belt, and that too tight is worse than too loose.

Belt position varies a little for most people between the squat and the deadlift. The conventional deadlift starts from a different position than the bottom position of the squat, and the belt rides in a different position as well, a little lower in front and a little higher in back. Too tight a belt in the deadlift really makes it difficult to squeeze down into a good start position, since this position is assumed without the benefit of a bar on your bar on your back helping to squeeze you down into position with your lumbar arch loaded. The anterior pressure cannot reinforce a position that the lumbar muscles have not already established, and a really tight belt may in fact prevent the most important aspect of the deadlift starting position from being attained. This may require that the squat and the deadlift be done in competition with different belts; lots of powerlifters carry two belts, maybe even three since the belt also helps with the bench press if used correctly. Sumo deadlifters are not as concerned by these differences, since their technique is more squat-like than the conventional style recommended here.

Your belt should be used judiciously, possibly restricted to the last warm-up and work sets, if then. You may not need a belt at all for much of the early part of your training career, and if your abs are strong and your back is uninjured, you may prefer to never use one. This is a judgement call, but it is probably prudent to err on the side of safety if there is any question at all about it. A belt will not prevent your trunk from getting and staying strong. There is plenty of work for the trunk muscles even if a belt is worn on heavy sets; it's not as if your trunk muscles just go to sleep when you put on your belt. A belt does in fact help you lift more weight safely than you would without one, since a tight back feels better when squatting and that tightness allows you to develop more force against the bar.

Knee wraps are another matter. The vast majority of the time a lifter uses tight wraps, the one-meter or longer heavy kind with the various-colored stripes, he is doing so to lift more weight. The mechanism is the same with wraps as with squat suits. In the absence of an injury, knee wraps must be considered supportive gear, and should not be worn. But in the event of certain knee injuries, wraps can be helpful IF USED CORRECTLY. If you have an old ligament injury that has healed as well as it's going to, wraps are useful to add stability to the knee. A light wrap adds some pressure to the whole knee assembly, acting almost like an external capsule, as well as maintaining warmth and providing some proprioceptive input to the skin and superficial structures (a belt does the same thing if used correctly). The caveat is this: if your wraps are so tight that they must be loosened during the workout, then they are acting as aids and not as support. If the wraps can be kept on for the whole workout without cutting off circulation to the lower leg, they are loose enough to consider as only supportive. Some heavier powerlifting wraps are so heavy that they cannot actually be used as a loose support wrap. Lighter wraps are available at most sporting goods stores, and they work fine for our purposes, or rubber/cloth knee sleeves can be used if warmth is the primary objective.

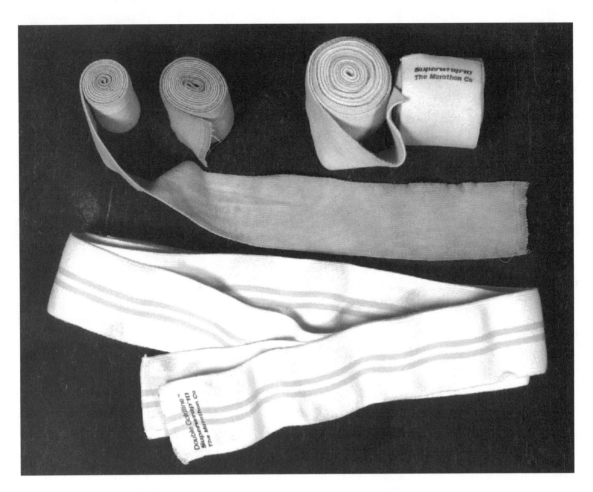

Figure 2-61. Wraps are used to assist in training with minor injuries, to provide for the maintenance of joint warmth, and to aid in the prevention of injuries by adding capsular support to the knee. For general strength training purposes they should NOT be used merely to lift bigger weights.

Shoes are the only piece of personal equipment that you really need to own. It only takes one set of five in a pair of squat shoes to demonstrate this convincingly to anybody who has done more than one squat workout. A good pair of squat shoes adds enough to the efficiency of the movement that the cost is easily justified. For anywhere from $50 for a used pair to $200 for the newest Adidas weightlifting shoes, a pair of proper shoes makes a big difference in the way a squat feels. Powerlifting squat shoes have relatively flat soles, and Olympic weightlifting shoes have a little lift in the heel that makes it easier to get the knees forward just in front of the toes. Your choice will depend on your squatting style and your flexibility. Most squat shoes have metatarsal straps to increase lateral stability and suck the foot back into the shoe to reduce intra-shoe movement.

But the main feature of a squat shoe is its lack of heel compressibility. The drive out of the bottom starts at the floor, where the feet start the kinetic chain. If the contact between the feet and the floor is the squishy gel or air cell of a running shoe, a percentage of the force of the drive will be absorbed by the compression of the cell. This compression is fine for running, but when

Fig. 2-62. Weightlifting shoes are the most important personal equipment a lifter can own. They provide solid contact with the floor and eliminate sole compressibility and the instability of squishy footing. Get a pair. It will be the best money you spend on your training gear.

squatting it reduces power transmission efficiency and prevents foot stability. Unstable footing interferes with the reproducibility of the movement pattern, rendering virtually every squat a whole new experience and preventing the development of good technique. Squatting in running shoes is like squatting on a bed. Many people get away with it for years, but serious lifters invest in squat shoes. They aren't that expensive, especially compared to brand new name-brand athletic shoes, and they make a huge difference in the way a squat feels.

Finally, a brief word about clothing is in order. It is best to squat in a t-shirt, as opposed to a tank top, because t-shirts cover more skin than tanks. Skin is slick when sweaty, and slick is not good for keeping the bar in place. The shirt should be cotton or 50/50, not nylon or all synthetic for the same reason. Shorts, sweats, or training pants should always be of stretch material. This is very important, because if your pants grab your legs, and they will because of the sweat, a non-stretch garment will restrict the movement of your legs and alter your form. Ditto with shorts that stop right below the knee, even if they are stretch. Mid-thigh stretchy shorts or simple gray sweats are the best pants for training. Clothing should not affect movement in any way, and should never, ever make it harder for you to do a thing that is hard already – squat correctly.

Figure 2-63. Training clothes should fit in a way that does not hinder the performance of the lifts or the ability of your technique to be observed. Baggy pants and shirts may be fashionable, but they are not terribly useful in the weight room. T-shirts are preferred over tank-tops, and shorts and sweats should be chosen for function, not appearance. But clever logos are always good.

Throughout this book the term "cue" will be used. A cue is a movement signal, and is an important concept in sports pedagogy. Cues are used both by coaches on the athletes they are handling and by athletes on themselves.

For a coach, a cue is a signal that reminds the athlete to change some part of the movement he is about to do, as previously discussed with the coach. It focuses the athlete's attention on the thing he should be thinking about at that time, instead of the thing he probably is thinking about. As such, a cue is not a long, expository explanation that introduces a brand new concept just before the lifter performs a PR attempt. It is a word or two, maybe three, seldom four, that reminds but does not explain. A cue should not have to be processed much by the mind that receives it; it should be heard by the ear and sent on down to the place that was waiting for it to trigger the action to which it refers.

An example of a cue would be "chest up." In contrast, "lift the chest so that your back gets flat" is not a cue. The former can be used after the lifter has assumed the starting position, right before he starts the pull. The latter must be used well before he assumes the starting position, when he can give some thought to what he is about to do.

Cues are worked out between the athlete and coach during training. They evolve naturally as the two people communicate with each other about the movement. A coach will develop his favorite ways of explaining key concepts to his athletes over his coaching career. He will tailor these explanations to fit the needs of the individuals he is working with and cues will develop. Some cues, like "chest up," are almost universal due to their usefulness, brevity, and sound. It almost barks the correct position at the athlete. Other cues, like "Now!" that appear to be so non-specific as to be useless, are in fact specific to a thing decided upon between coach and lifter, and are extremely individual to that particular situation. As such, cues must be given in the right circumstances and at exactly the right time, or they are useless and do not cue anything.

A cue can also be a reminder that you give yourself. It will not necessarily be spoken aloud, although this sometimes helps. It will be the same thing that a coach would say to you under the same circumstances, a reminder of a position problem that you have already worked out but that needs to be brought forward into a position of attention in your mind just before a movement occurs. As you learn the exercises covered in this book, you should develop your own set of cues that will serve to reinforce good form. As you become more experienced, you will find it necessary to build cues into your approach to each lift, to solve your own individual problems with each movement pattern. You will find that each lift responds to its own reminder, and if you train alone you'll have to remind yourself.

You will find that there are two basic types of cues: body cues and bar cues. Body cues are references to your body, like "chest up," "look forward," or "long, straight arms." They draw awareness to the thing doing the moving, the muscles or bodyparts that need correction.

In contrast, bar cues refer to the object being moved. Examples are "keep it close," "touch your shirt," or "rattle the plates," all referring to the barbell. A particularly helpful way to use a bar cue is to refer to the speed of the bar as it passes through a certain section of the lift. For instance, if your problem is jerking yourself out of position coming off the floor in a deadlift by getting in a hurry to get the bar moving fast, the cue might be "pull it slow" or "squeeze it up." Both cues refer to the bar, and if you do these things to the bar correctly your body will have solved the problem.

Some people process bar cues better than body cues, and what works for one exercise might not work for another. Deciding which to use is just one part of the skills that you will develop through experience.

The object of oratory is not truth,
but persuasion.

Unknown author - Fortune
cookie served at Ginza Sushi
Bar, San Diego, June 2007.

The Bench Press

There are few gyms left in the world that don't have a pressing bench. For good reason: the bench press, since the 1950's, has become the most widely-recognized resistance movement in the world, the one exercise most representative in the public mind of barbell training, the exercise the vast majority of trainees are most likely to want to do, and the exercise most often asked about by most people if they are interested in how strong you are.

Many incredibly strong men have benched big weights, long before the advent of modern supportive shirts, and even good benches. Men like Doug Hepburn, Pat Casey, Mel Hennessy, Don Reinhoudt, Jim Williams (who lifted in excess of 700 lbs. in a thin, cheap, white t-shirt), and Ronnie Ray were strong back in the early days of powerlifting, although the weights they lifted would, sad to say, scarcely turn a head at a 21st century national meet. Accomplished powerlifters of the 1980s, men like Larry Pacifico, the incredible Mike McDonald, George Hechter, John Kuc, Mike Bridges, Bill Kazmaier, Rickey Dale Crain, and the late, great Doug Young were masters of the bench press, using all the tricks at their disposal to establish national and world records in the lift (fig. 3-1).

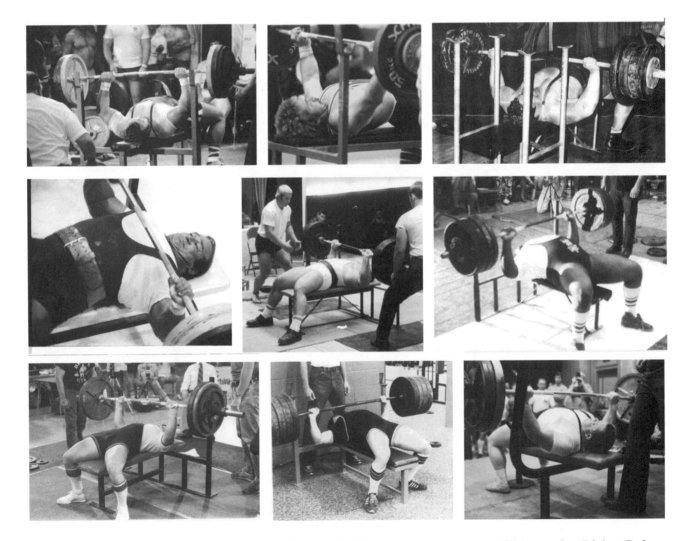

Figure 3-1. The bench press has a long, rich history. Left to right, top to bottom: Bill Kazmaier, Rickey Dale Crain, Pat Casey, Doug Young, Mel Hennessy, Jim Williams, Mike Bridges, Mike MacDonald, Ronny Ray.

The Bench Press

The modern version of the bench press, like the squat, depends on a piece of equipment other than the bar for its execution. Until the upright support bench came into widespread use in the 1950's, the bar had to be pulled into position while lying on the floor, or while lying on a flat bench pulled up from the floor over the head into position over the chest. Controversy abounded as technique was evolving, with questions about the legitimacy of assistance in getting the bar into position, the use of a heave from the belly, even the use of an arch in the lower back, causing debate among physical culturists all over the world. Nowadays, the bench-press bench is standard equipment, and only a few innovative thinkers in the powerlifting community bother with doing the exercise the old, harder, and probably better, way. After all, the more involved the exercise, the more the exercise involves, in terms of muscle, nerve, and control.

In fact, the dumbbell version of the exercise, which actually predates the barbell version due to its less specialized equipment requirements, is probably a better exercise for most purposes other than training for a powerlifting competition. This is especially true if the weights used are sufficiently heavy to challenge your ability to actually finish the set. Most trainees use them as a light assistance movement, and never appreciate how hard they are or how useful they can be. They are performed on a simple flat bench, and taking the dumbbells out of the rack or off the floor, getting into position on the flat bench, and getting up with them after the set is finished is a large part of the exercise. Dumbbells – being not tied together between the hands as with a barbell – require more active, conscious control, are harder to do, and are therefore less commonly done. There is a one-handed version, in which only one dumbbell is used, that requires a tremendous amount of core strength to just stay on the bench.

Nevertheless, you will be bench pressing with a barbell, as the weight of history and precedent demands. The bench press, or supine press (one occasionally sees old references to the "prone press" in badly edited sources), is a popular, useful exercise. It is arguably the best way to develop raw upper-body strength, and done correctly it is a valuable addition to your strength and conditioning program.

The bench press actively works the muscles of the anterior shoulder girdle and the triceps, as well as the forearm muscles isometrically. The primary movers are the pectoralis major and the anterior deltoid, which drive the bar up off the chest, and the triceps, which drive the elbow extension to lockout. The pectoralis minor and the posterior rotator cuff muscles act to stabilize and prevent the rotation of the humerus during the movement. The other posterior muscles - the trapezius, the rhomboidius, and other smaller muscles along the cervical and thoracic spine - act isometrically to adduct the shoulder blades and keep the back stable against the bench. The lats, or latissimus dorsi muscles, act to rotate the ribcage up, arched relative to the lower back, decreasing the distance the bar has to travel and adding to the stability of the position. They also act as a counter to the deltoids, preventing the elbows from adducting, or rising up toward the head, while the humerus is driving up out of the bottom, thus preventing the angle between the upper arm and torso from changing during the lift. The muscles of the lower back, hips, and legs act as a bridge between the upper body and the ground, anchoring and stabilizing the chest and arms as they do the work of handling the bar. And the neck muscles contract isometrically, stabilizing the head against the bench (fig. 3-2). Yes, bench pressing makes the neck grow too, making new dress shirts inevitable. Since the bench press is a free weight exercise, control of the bar is integral to the movement, and improvement in control is part of the benefit of doing it.

First, a small disclaimer: this is not a book about powerlifting, and it is not designed to be used as such. The bench press as a competitive lift will probably be approached differently than herein described. If aspiring powerlifters are able to obtain useful information from these comments, that is very cool. The author was never an accomplished bench presser, and this method was not derived from, nor is it intended to be used to develop, any special level of skill in the modern competitive powerlifting version of the bench press. This method is derived from the author's experience in teaching the movement to novices since 1978, and no claims are made otherwise.

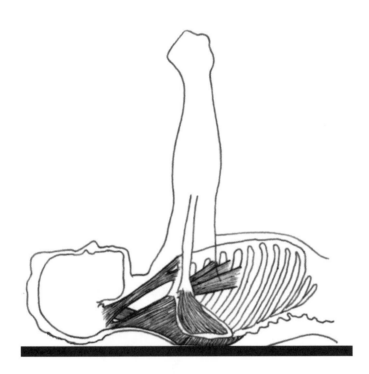

Figure 3-2. The muscles of the neck stabilize the head during the bench press, while the rotator cuff muscles and the pectoralis minor stabilize the shoulder joint. This makes the bench press a useful exercise for injury prevention in addition to its role in developing upper body strength.

You will be using standard power bars and benches for the bench press. Power standard bars are widely available, and this configuration has proven itself as the most useful over the years. It is probably the type that will be most available to you, at your gym or to buy. The specifications are simple: the bar diameter should be 28.5 to 29.5 mm., length is 7 feet, the knurling should be adequate but not too sharp, and will extend in from the sleeves so that a 17 inch gap is left in the middle, with center knurling of about 6 inches provided. The knurling will be scored with a ring at either end of the bar with a distance of 32 inches between the marks, denoting the maximum legal grip width for competition. If power standard bars are not available, use what you have until better equipment can be obtained. Bars are absolutely the wrong place to save money, either when you buy one or when your gym does (fig. 3-3).

The benches should also be to standard specs, although there is no standard configuration for constructing them. Standard specifications require the height of the bench surface to be 17 inches, and if this is too tall for short trainees, blocks for the lifter's feet (usually just barbell plates) will need to be provided. Uprights can either be fixed or adjustable, with a distance of about 45 inches between the uprights. Or you can use the power rack and a 17 inch flat bench for the bench press station (fig. 3-4). Most benches are provided with some type of vinyl upholstery, but auto seat fabric has proven itself over the years to last longer and provide better traction for the back during the lift.

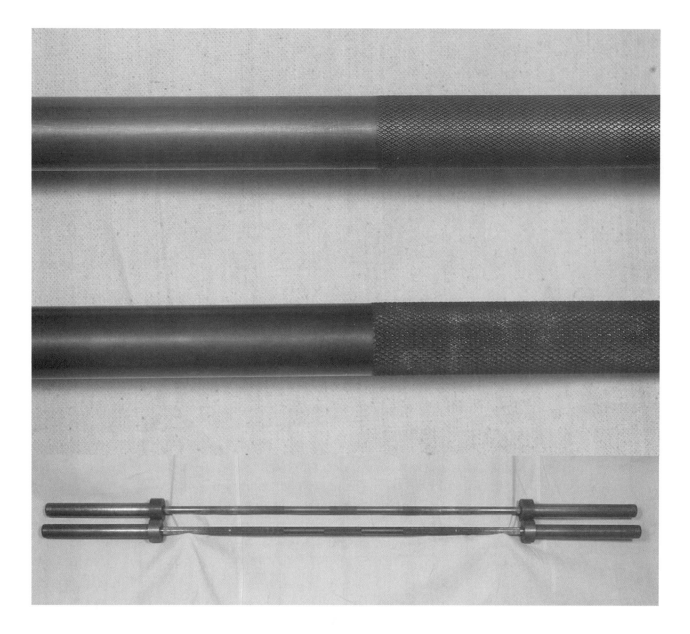

Figure 3-3. Bars for weight training can be obtained from several sources. "Power" bars are best for our purposes here, since they are marked in ways that are the most useful for the exercises that comprise the bulk of this program. Quality bars have uniform dimensions and similar mechanical characteristics, but there are differences that should be evaluated before you buy one. The close-up photo shows the differences in the knurling of the two bars. Subtle differences in diameter and tensile characteristics make some bars better for certain applications than others: whippier bars are better for cleans and presses, and stiffer bars are better for squats, benches, and deadlifts.

Figure 3-4. Two ways to use equipment for the bench press. The upright support bench is preferred by most lifters, but the power rack offers adjustability and a better use of space and limited resources.

Learning to Bench Press

When learning how to bench, it might be prudent to use a spotter if one is available. Spotting the bench press will be dealt with in detail later, but for our purposes in this early phase of learning, a spotter is there to keep the unracking/racking of the bar safe for the lifter. Although some would disagree, a spotter is not absolutely necessary, since you are using very light weights during the learning phase and should not have enough weight on the bar to give a spotter anything to do. A bad spotter that will not stay out of your way while you work is actually a detriment, and can quite often cause more problems for you than they can prevent. If you are worried about your ability to handle the bar, you have too much weight on it, and if a 45 lb. bar is too heavy – as it might be in your particular circumstances – use a lighter bar. If you are concerned, use a spotter, but make sure to use an experienced, competent, patient individual that will not insist on "helping" you just for the sake of participating in your exercise program.

As usual, start with an empty bar. ALWAYS start every lift with an empty bar, whether learning it for the first time or warming up for a personal record. Lie down on the bench with your eyes looking straight up. In this position, you should be far enough down (always meaning toward the foot-end of the bench) from the bar that when looking up your eyes are on the foot-side of the bar (fig. 3-5). Your feet should be flat on the ground in a comfortable spacing comparable to the squat stance, with your shins approximately vertical. Your upper back should be flat against the bench, with the lower back in an anatomically normal arched position.

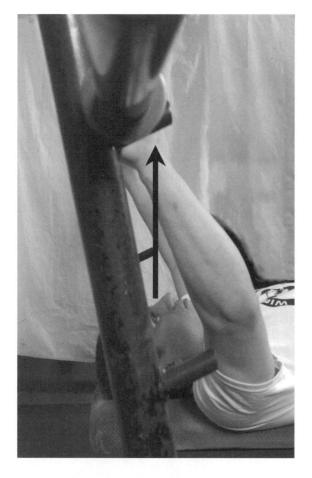

Figure 3-5. Eye position referenced to the bar before unracking.

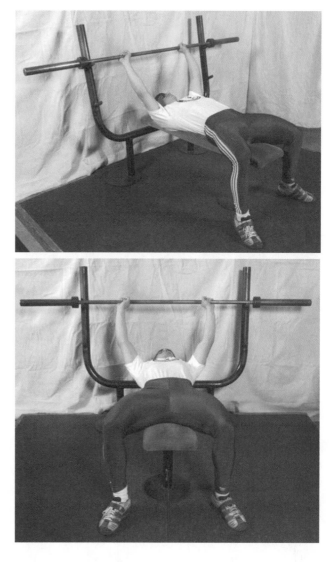

Figure 3-6. Foot and leg position on the bench

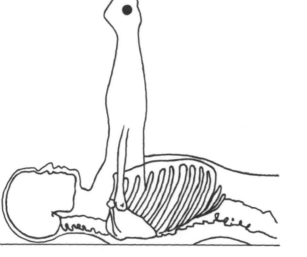

Figure 3-7. Spinal position on the bench, with normal kyphotic and lordotic curves.

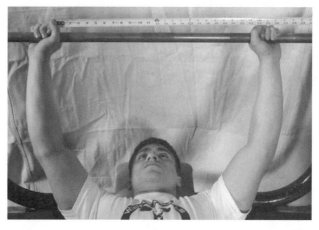

Figure 3-8. Grip width varies with the individual, but 22-28 inches works best for most people.

When this position has been established, take an overhand grip on the bar. Your grip should be somewhere between 22 and 28 inches, measured between the index fingers, the variation based on differences in shoulder width. An excessively wide or narrow grip should be avoided. The bar should rest on the heel of your palm, directly over the bones of the forearm, and not in the palm up near the fingers, so that power being transmitted to the bar up the arms goes directly to the bar without being channeled through the wrist. Your fingers should wrap around the bar AFTER the bar has been set correctly on the heel of your hand. This grip is best accomplished by turning your hands and elbows out, with a slight internal rotation of your arm. This will place the bar in a good position in your hand, and put your elbows in a useful position as well.

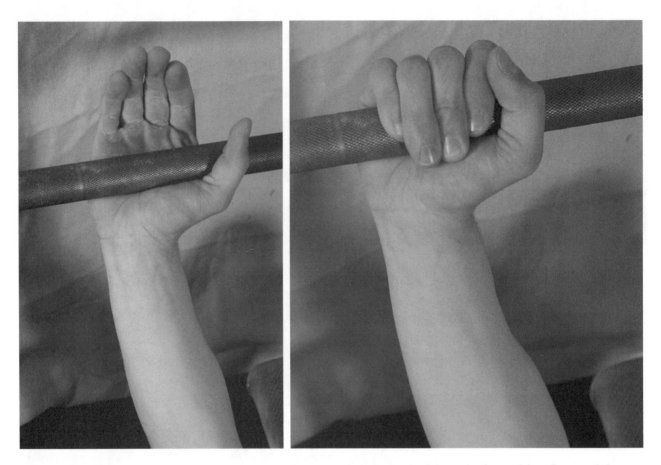

Figure 3-9. Grip the bar with the base of the palm by setting the heel of the palm in position first, and then wrapping the fingers around the bar.

You are now ready to take the bar out of the rack. Look directly up at the ceiling above your position on the bench and push up on the bar, locking out your elbows. With elbows locked, move the bar out to a position directly over the line of your nipples, your arms in a perfectly vertical position relative to the floor. Don't stop before you get it over your chest, since it will be over your chin or throat if you do. Make sure the bar gets out to the place it needs to be, right over the nipple line. This procedure should be accomplished quickly and positively, with your elbows locked out the entire time. Your spotter can help you do this the first few times, just making sure the bar clears your face and neck and gets all the way out over your chest.

As your bar becomes stable in the starting position, look at the very important picture directly overhead. You will be looking at the ceiling, and this picture is your reference for the path the bar will take as you move it down and up. You will see the bar against the ceiling in the lower half of your field of vision. Look at its position relative to the features you see on the surface of the ceiling. Don't look at the bar, look at the ceiling and just *see* the bar. Move the bar a tiny bit. Notice that if the bar moves even a little that you can tell by the change it makes against the ceiling. The bar moves and the ceiling does not, and the ceiling is therefore your position reference for the bar.

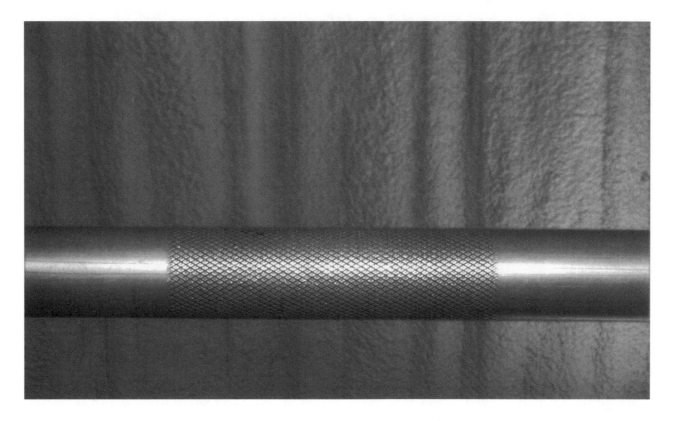

Figure 3-10. View from the trainee's position on the bench. The position of the bar is referenced against the ceiling; the eyes look at the ceiling, not the bar.

Note carefully the place the bar is in now. You are going to lower the bar to your chest, touch the chest, and then drive it right back to where it is now. Stare at the place on the ceiling where the bar is to go. DO NOT look at the bar as it moves; do NOT follow the bar with your eyes, but just stare at the ceiling. Make the bar go to that place every rep. Now, try it for a set of five reps. You'll notice immediately that if your eyes don't move from their fixed position, the bar will go to the same place every rep.

The key to the whole method is looking at the fixed position and not the moving bar. If you use a fixed reference for the bar position, you can make it go to the same place each rep, but if you follow the bar with your eyes you will have no way to direct the bar to that fixed, correct place since you are looking at the thing you are moving and not the place you want it to go. Oddly enough, this is the same principle as is used to hit a golf ball or a tennis ball: the implement moves to the target, and the target is the fixed object of the eye gaze. Granted, tennis balls move while golf balls don't, but the brain coordinates the hands to go to the target with the club, or racquet, or bar because the target is the reference for the eyes. When a tennis ball moves, the head and eyes move with it rendering it a stationary focal point. Fortunately, most ceilings don't move in most weight rooms, so our task is easier than McEnroe's, but it is similar in that we are driving an object in our hands toward a stationary thing we are actively looking at.

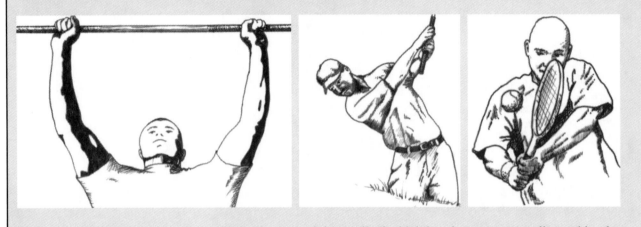

There are similarities between seemingly diverse activities, all of which involve movement directed by the eyes. Whether the object of the movement is stationary or in motion, the eyes focus on the point where the implement in the hands is going.

This little eyeball trick works 90% of the time the first time it is used to produce a correct bench press bar path. Even if you are "poorly coordinated," you should be able to do a fairly good bench press within a couple of sets using this technique. "Groove," as the bar path is often referred to by bench pressers, is the first and most frustrating problem that novice trainees will experience, and by focusing your eyes on the ceiling you can eliminate this problem the vast majority of the time. If the bar finds the groove automatically, as it does with this method, your attention can be directed to other aspects of the exercise that might be a problem.

Do another set of five with the bar, reinforcing your eye position, and then rack the bar. This is done with locked elbows after the last rep is finished, by moving the bar back to the uprights, touching them with the bar, and then setting it down in the hooks. Should you have a spotter, this movement back to the rack should be covered. Add weight a little at a time for the next sets of five reps, 10 pounds at a time for smaller kids and women, 20 or even 30 pounds for bigger trainees, until the bar speed begins to slow and form starts to change. Stay there for two more sets of five, and that is the first workout.

Figure 3-11. The bench press.

Common Problems Everyone Should Know How To Solve

Hands and grip

The bar, being in a position over the head, face, and neck during the bench press, presents some significant safety problems if certain common-sense precautions are not observed. The subject of spotters and spotting will be dealt with in detail later, so these comments will involve things that *you* must do.

Maybe the biggest, dumbest, most common problem involving the hands is the use of the thumbless grip. This is absolutely the worst habit you can develop with regard to safety, and is detrimental to performance as well. Many lifters start with a thumbless grip in an attempt to get the bar over the very end of the arm, off of the wrist, which is correct. But doing this with a thumbless grip is unnecessary, since the same position can be obtained with the thumb hooked around the bar with little change in the elbow position, and the risk of having an unsecured bar over the face and throat is just too great to be acceptable. The grip is thumbless in the squat because the bar is not moving – you are; for all movements where the bar moves, the full grip should be used. The thumb secures the bar in your grip, and without your thumb around the bar it is merely *balanced* over the end of your arm. The best spotter in the world cannot react quickly enough to save you from a dropped bar. The danger of this cannot truly be appreciated until one sees the effects of a dropped bar firsthand. If you insist on using a thumbless grip on the bench, you need to do it at home, so that when the ambulance comes (if anyone is there to call 911) it doesn't disrupt anyone else's training.

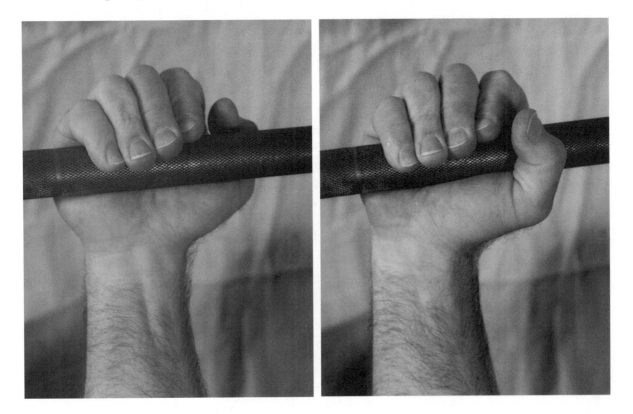

Figure 3-12. The thumbless vs. the thumbs-around grip. There are only a few ways to get badly hurt in the weight room, and using the thumbless grip is one of them. The same position over the end of the arm can be accomplished with the thumb around, without the potential risk of dropping the bar on your face, throat, or chest.

Another problem with the thumbless grip is that it diminishes lifting efficiency: what the hands cannot squeeze, the shoulders cannot drive. This phenomenon can be observed when using large diameter bars and fat-handled dumbbells: a 2 inch bar is about twice as hard to press as a standard 28.5 mm (1 1/8 inch) bar. This is due to the inability of a person with a normal-sized hand to effectively squeeze a bar that fat with a good tight grip. Squeezing involves closing the thumb and fingers around the bar until effective pressure can be applied with the forearm muscles in isometric contraction, increasing the tightness of the muscles on the forearm side of the elbow, making rebound out of the bottom more efficient, and increasing motor unit recruitment throughout the arms and upper body. Some lifters like to think about leaving their fingerprints in the bar, to increase their squeeze. The thumbless grip is an excellent way to voluntarily reduce the ability to squeeze the bar. Try it yourself for demonstration purposes, with a light weight, please.

Some people can effectively use a thumbless grip on the bench press, and many big benches have been done with a thumbless grip. The point is that since the standard grip is safer and more effective, it should be used by everybody that has thumbs.

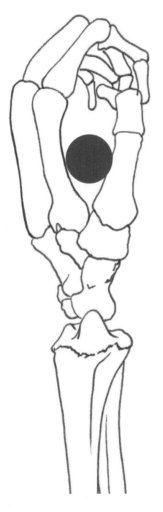

Figure 3-13. For maximum power transfer to the weight, the bones of the wrist and forearm should be lined up directly under the bar.

The thumbless grip is an attempt, as previously stated, to get the bar into a better position in the hand. The force generated by the shoulders and triceps is delivered to the bar through the bones of the forearm. The most efficient transmission of power to the bar would be directly from the heel of the palm to the bar through the forearm positioned vertically, perpendicular to the bar. Your grip should be positioned with this in mind, with the bar placed directly over the palm heel and then your hand rotated out so that the thumb can hook around the bar. Once your hand is in position, the palm should be tightened so that the bar is well supported and does not move during the rep. Squeeze your hand like you are trying to squeeze the bones of your forearm together. The thumb does not interfere with this position at all. Once your thumb position is secured, your fingers should wrap around the bar. Finger position is less important, as the bar is secured by the thumb, and you might have a tendency to hold the bar too far back in the hand if the fingers are thought to be the thing that grips and controls the bar.

It is common for the bar to shift back in your hand towards the fingers during the set, such that the bar ends up in a completely different position than where it started. This is the result of not maintaining a tight grip during the set. If the bar shifts much at all, it can change the lifting mechanics by altering the position of the load relative to the muscles driving it up, making a change in elbow or shoulder position during the lift likely. If the bar rolls back in the hand, it has also rolled back relative to the elbow and shoulder, and they have to adjust to maintain their drive. The bar should remain locked firmly in place during the set, for efficiency and safety.

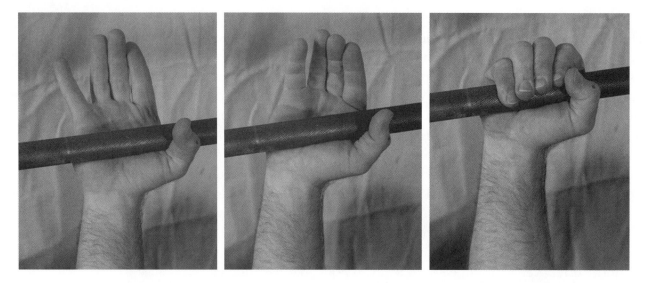

Figure 3-14. Most people will begin and end the grip process with the bar lying perpendicular to the line of the fingers (A). The best position is achieved by slightly rotating the hand in (B), and then setting the grip (C).

Grip width, within extremes, is largely a matter of individual preference. Since you are trying to develop strength, and not specifically a big contest bench press, your form should be generalized, without too much emphasis on any one muscle group and a lot of work for all of them. The greatest range of motion is obtained with a grip that places the forearms in a vertical position when the bar is on the chest. With a wider the grip, the bar doesn't move as far and locks out before the triceps have done much work, so the pecs and delts end up doing more of what gets done. But as long as the grip falls somewhere between 22 and 28 inches between index fingers, the purpose is served. This range allows enough leeway for people of all shoulder widths to find a grip they feel strongest with. Too much narrower will, for most people, take pounds off the work sets, and a wider grip shortens the range of motion excessively and takes out too much tricep. (Heavier weights can be benched with a wide grip since the bar doesn't have to move as far. The maximum legal width for powerlifting competition is 32 inches. But again, we are trying to make people strong using the bench press, which isn't necessarily the same thing as making people bench a heavier weight.) Most people will self-select a medium grip when they first do the exercise anyway. It feels more natural than a wide grip, which must be practiced extensively before it will be productive. A medium grip gives all the muscles of the shoulder girdle a share of the work, and produces the kind of overall shoulder and arm strength we want from the exercise.

Elbows

An understanding of elbow position is essential for lifting efficiency and, once again, safety. The elbow represents the distal end of the humerus, as it articulates with the radius and the ulna (*distal* is the end furthest from the center of the body, and *proximal* would be the closest to it). The pecs and delts attach to the anterior side of the humerus up by the shoulder, and the triceps attach to the olecranon process, the pointy part of the ulna that forms the outside of the elbow. Essentially, all the force being generated by the muscles involved in the bench press moves the elbow. The action around the shoulder joint contributes to the movement of the elbow, but the shoulder doesn't, or at least shouldn't, change its position against the bench while the humerus is moving (fig. 3-15).

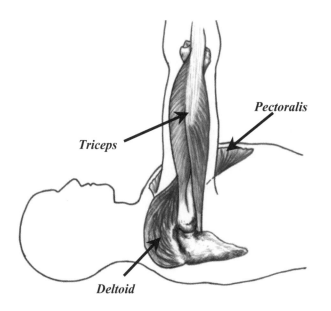

Figure 3-15. The major muscles involved in the bench press.

The position of the humerus while it moves the bar is crucial to the success of the movement. This position is determined by the angle the humerus makes with the torso, as seen from above. An angle of 90 degrees to the torso would have the arm at right angles to the bench, parallel to the bar, a rather extreme position. The other extreme would be allowing the elbows to come down to a position parallel with the torso, with the arms sliding against the ribcage at the bottom. The preferred position will be somewhere between these two extremes, but higher rather than lower. The forearm will always be vertical; since gravity operates in straight lines perpendicular to the floor, overcoming gravity must occur in exactly the opposite direction. The forearm must stay vertical or some of the load will begin to exert a rotational force, or torque, against the elbow (fig. 3-17).

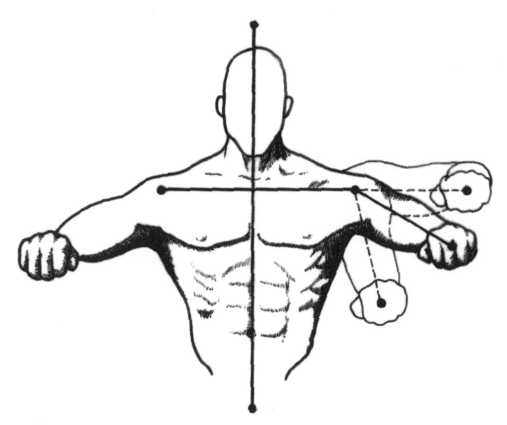

Figure 3-16. The best angle for the upper arm relative to the line of the body is somewhere between the extremes of 90 degrees to and parallel to the torso.

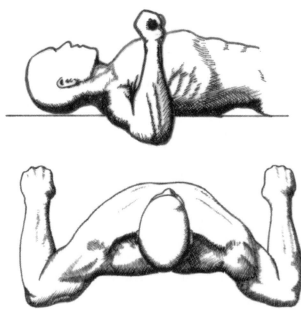

Figure 3-17. The forearm must be vertical from all angles to ensure optimum force transmission to the bar.

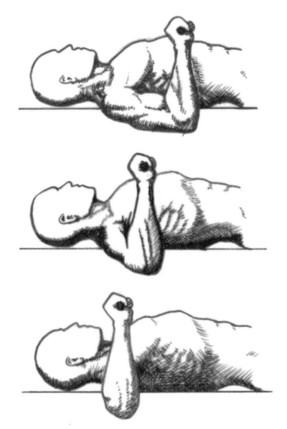

Figure 3-18. The upper arm angle determines the point where the bar will touch the chest. The lower the elbows, the lower the bar, and high elbows put the bar close to the throat.

Since your forearm must always be vertical at the bottom of the bench press, your elbow will always be directly under the bar. Because the forces driving the bar act at the elbow and on up through the forearm, this is a very good place for it to be. And since the forearm is vertical, the point on the chest the bar touches at the bottom is determined entirely by the angle of the humerus with the torso, and thus, the elbow. The bar follows the elbows: if the elbows rotate up away from the ribs, the bar goes up the chest toward the throat, and if the elbows slide down toward the ribcage, the bar moves down toward the belly.

Your elbow position is therefore related to the bar position, and to your individual anthropometry. For example, an experienced, proficient lifter with good upper back flexibility can arch his chest up high, thus allowing the bar a shorter trip down and up. This will have the bar touching lower on the chest towards the bottom of the sternum, as the ribcage rotates up. For a person with less flexibility in the upper spine, this bar position on the chest would require the elbows to be at an angle of perhaps 45 degrees to the torso, about halfway between touching the ribcage and in line with the shoulders. But since our experienced, flexible lifter has his chest up higher, his shoulders are closer vertically to the bottom of his sternum, when viewed from the side. This is due to the steeper angle his flexibility allows his upper back, and thus his chest, to attain. This steep chest angle allows his elbows to stay more in line with his shoulders than the less flexible trainee (fig. 3-19).

Elbows more in line with shoulders is important because the distance between the bar and the shoulder forms a lever arm against the shoulder. The greater the distance between the bar and the joint that is driving the bar, the more torque against the joint with the same weight. In figure 3-18, the top is the worst leverage, the bottom is the best, and the middle is the easiest on the shoulder.

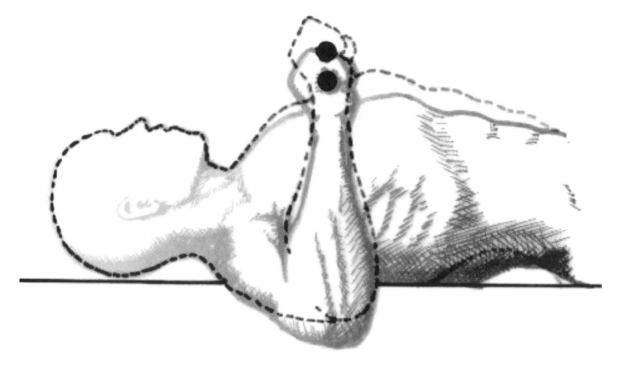

Figure 3-19. Chest angle, i.e. the steepness with which the chest can be inclined, affects the upper arm angle that can be used. More advanced flexible lifters can flatten out the kyphotic curve of the upper spine and make the chest taller (dashed line), allowing the bar to touch a place higher off the bench with a strong upper arm position, thus decreasing the distance the bar has to travel and improving leverage by lining up the bar closer to the shoulder.

The correct humeral angle can vary quite a bit among individual lifters, from 45 degrees, halfway between right angles and touching the ribs, to about 80 degrees. If the elbows are at a full ninety degrees, in line with the shoulders, the tendons of the biceps and the rotator cuff muscles are placed in an anatomically unfriendly position that can produce chronic shoulder pain. In contrast, the other extreme position, where the humerus is essentially parallel to the torso, is not particularly hazardous, but has the disadvantage of eliminating most of the pec function from the movement – reducing the efficiency of the lift as an exercise for the whole upper body – and radically increasing the length of the lever arm against the shoulder.

No matter what humeral angle is used, it is important that the angle not change during the rep. The eccentric phase of the movement should use the same elbow angle as the concentric. Stated another way, your elbows should be in the same vertical plane on the way down and on the way up. The humerus is kept in this constant position by the action of the lats and the deltoids, stabilizing the humerus by exerting equal opposing forces on the bone from top and bottom at the same time. Any variation in angle during the movement indicates that one of these two muscles is not countering the force of the other effectively (fig. 3-20). Shoulder problems are commonly associated with the bench press because of this elbow movement. The two tendons of the biceps, as they arise from and cross the shoulder joint on their way down to the elbow, are not very tolerant of the abrasion they are subjected to when the elbows flail around during an uncontrolled trip to the chest and back. One of these tendons lies in a groove in the humerus, and it likes to stay there as much as possible. When your elbows change position during the movement, the

81

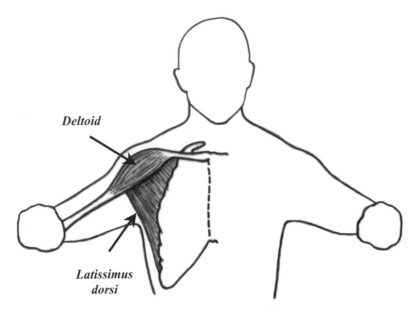

Figure 3-20. The latissimus dorsi and the and deltoids stabilize the humerus during the movement – the delts pulling from the top and the lats pulling from the bottom – holding it at the same angle all the way down and up.

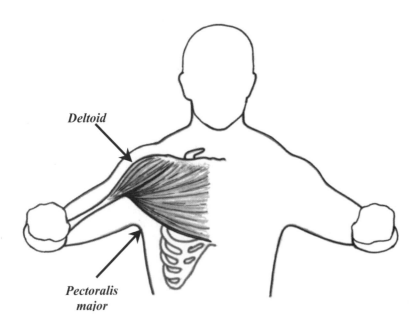

Figure 3-21. The primary musculature responsible for moving the upper arm.

bicep tendons get pulled against the limits of their normal position and become subject to abrasion from the edges of the groove and other positional abnormalities. Be careful about doing this.

Chest

The chest, for bench pressing purposes, is the anterior ribcage and the muscles attached to it. The main chest muscles – the pectoralis major, or pecs, and the anterior deltoids – attach to the humerus at a long insertion point along the upper third of the bone. They wrap across the ribcage to a long origin along a line from the bottom of the sternum, up to the clavicle, and along the clavicle back to its distal end at the shoulder, with the muscle fibers fanning out in a broad angle. This wide angle of origin allows the pec/delt muscle to apply force to the humerus over a range of angles of insertion, thus permitting a range of effective elbow positions.

It is also important to understand the relationship between the pec/delt muscle attachment to the humerus, and the angle of that attachment. Viewed from the horizontal, (a cross-section of your chest perpendicular to your spine) the pec/delt attachment occurs at an angle that varies with chest position. Refer to A. The higher the top of the chest – the highest point on the ribcage above the bench – the steeper the angle with which the pec/delt attaches to the humerus. The steeper the angle, the better, because of the increased mechanical efficiency of the contraction caused by the steeper angle of attack on the humerus. In a classic example of simple mechanics, a third class lever exhibits greater efficiency the more closely the force is perpendicular to the resistance, no matter what exercise. So the higher the chest position above the arms, the better the pull the pec/delt has on the arms. The short version: keep your chest up high when you bench.

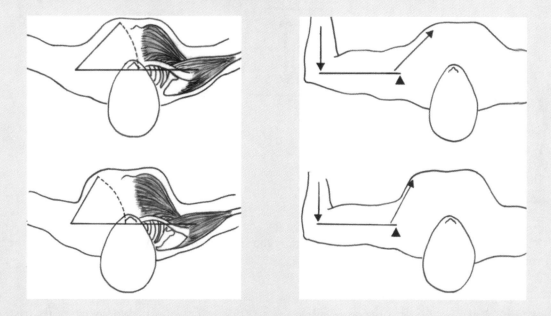

A. A bigger chest – whether from training or genetics – increases bench press efficiency. The increased steepness of the angle of attack of upper fibers of the pec/delt on the humerus increases the efficiency of the pull against the bone. This characteristic of third-class levers is the primary source of the advantages to be obtained by increased bodyweight, and is what is meant by the term "leverage." It applies throughout the barbell exercises.

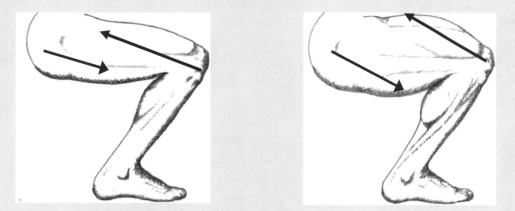

B. Leverage improvements in the squat. The angle of attack of the quad at the knee and of the hamstrings at the hips are all affected by an increase in size of the muscles

Let's address a common problem with the chest: not touching it with the bar every rep. Sometimes this is accidental, if you intend to touch but miss. If this is the case, you'll get it next rep, and this will only happen accidentally the first couple of times you bench. But don't play games with the weight on the bar by failing to do a complete rep. It is, after all, easier to move a load a shorter distance than a longer distance, and you are just trying to lift more at the expense of moving the bar through the whole rep. Work equals the force of gravity acting on the barbell multiplied by the distance the barbell moves. If, over the course of 3 month's training, the barbell doubles in weight but is only traveling half the distance it did on the first day of training, the work has stayed the same and you have wasted 3 months of training.

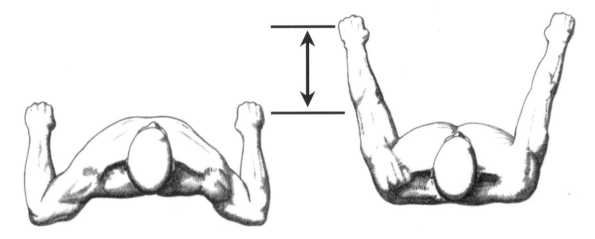

Figure 3-22. Work in the bench press is calculated using the simple work equation: force (weight of the bar) x distance (traveled by the bar up and down) = work.

Sometimes it may be on purpose. There is a school of thought that justifies the use of less than full range of motion by claiming that the pecs stop contributing to the movement when the humerus reaches a 90-degree angle with the forearm. (This same "analysis" requires an above parallel squat because the quads supposedly stop contributing when the femur gets to 90 degrees with the tibia.) The problem with this model is that full range of motion, multi-joint exercises are not *supposed* to isolate any one muscle. We use them precisely because they don't. We *want* them to work lots of muscles through a long range of motion. We like it when some muscles are called into function as other muscles drop out of function, and when muscles change function during the exercise. This is because we are training for strength. We are concerned with improving the functional motion around a joint. We are not just concerned about our "favorite muscles." We do not have favorite muscles.

The use of full range of motion is therefore important for two very good reasons. First, it allows you to quantify the amount of work you do: if you hold the range of motion of an exercise constant, you are holding constant the distance variable in your work equation. Then, if the force you can exert on the load increases (if you lift more weight) you know that your work has increased for a given number of reps. You know you're moving the weight the same distance, and the weight is heavier, so you know you're stronger. It allows you to compare performances, both between lifters and between your own performances over time. If you touch your chest with the bar every time you bench, progress – or lack thereof – can be assessed. This obviously applies to every exercise with a prescribed range of motion.

Second, full range of motion exercise ensures that strength is developed in every position that the joint can work. Strength development is extremely specific: muscles get strong in the positions they are made to get strong, and in precisely the way they are trained. For instance, a quadriceps muscle worked through 30 degrees of its range of motion on a leg extension machine will adapt to this work by improving its ability to work in that 30 degrees of motion. It will not get much stronger anywhere else in its range. If we want to prepare an athlete to use his legs for a sport where he might be called upon to use them in a variety of positions, then he must train through a full range of motion in a way that strengthens the whole range. Any joint about which movement can occur will benefit from having its entire function improved. So, all the muscles that move a joint should be exercised using a movement that calls into play as many of them as might be used in the sport for which we are training.

The bench press, like the squat, benefits from a certain amount of rebound out of the bottom, using the stretch reflex phenomenon that is a feature of skeletal muscle (fig. 3-23). It takes practice and good timing to tighten up the bottom of the movement enough that a correct rebound can be done every rep, without actually bouncing the bar off your sternum. A competition bench press (theoretically at least) has no rebound due to the technical rules, which specify that the bar must cease its motion at the bottom before being driven up off the chest. A touch-and-go bench press allows you to lift more weight than a paused bench press. It must be said that a cheated bench, where a heave of the chest, a hard bounce off the pecs, and a bridge with the hips allows more weight to be lifted than a strict touch-and-go. So why is a touch-and-go okay, but a bounce and bridge is not? It is not always our objective, as noted earlier, to lift more weight, but the touch-and-go is easier to learn than a paused bench, since the stretch reflex is such a natural movement; staying tight at the bottom during the pause is a skill difficult to master for competitive powerlifters. The bounced, heaved, bridged, butt-in-the-air version of the bench press uses ribcage resilience and hip extension to aid in driving the bar up, taking work away from the targeted muscles. So a strict touch-and-go is a good compromise, letting you lift more weight but still providing lots of work for the pressing muscles.

You should be able to recognize excessive bounce and know when a correction needs to be made. You bounce too much when the bar slams your chest hard enough to change your position with the impact, and then slows down markedly a couple of inches up from your chest, because the upward velocity of the bar was due more to the bounce than your active drive off the chest. If it's bad enough, the bar path will change right there as your elbows shift position from the lack of tightness in your lats and delts. The whole messy thing is a result of a lack of tightness on the way down, and can be remedied in a couple of ways.

One way to stay tight off the chest is to just barely touch the chest. You can't cheat it if you can't bounce it, and you can't bounce it if you just barely touch your chest. Think about touching just your shirt with the bar, not your chest. Or you might imagine a piece of glass on your chest that you have to touch but cannot break.

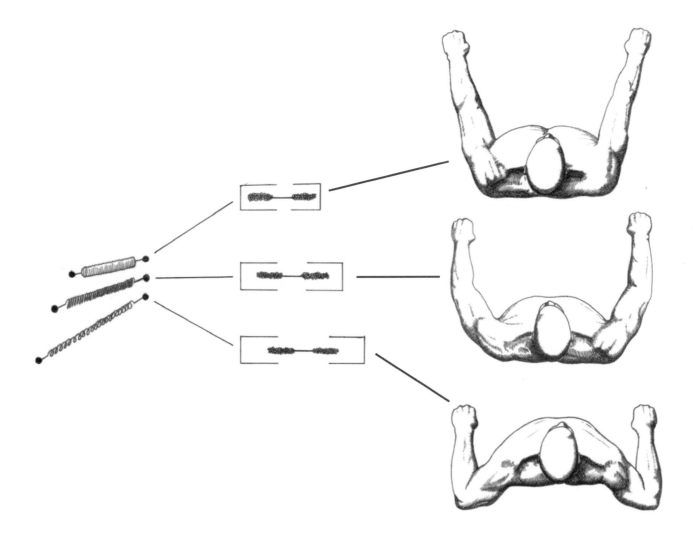

Figure 3-23. Several physiological and mechanical phenomena produce a rebound that makes for a stronger contraction. First, the viscoelastic nature of muscle makes it act like a spring – the longer you stretch it (up to a certain point), the more forceful the return. Second, there is an optimal sarcomeric length that results in the most force being generated by a contraction, and this optimal length is associated with a mild stretch. Lastly, the stretch reflex mediated by muscle spindles (intrafusal fibers) is activated by stretching and results in a more forceful contraction.

Visualizing a light touch usually works, but it deals with symptoms. The best way to fix a bouncing problem is to address the problem at its root, by learning to be tight during the movement, and in a way that can be applied to other lifts as well. It is a way to conceptualize the lift so that tightness is built in and elastic energy can be stored in the eccentric (negative) phase for use in the concentric drive-up. The bench press, like the squat, consists of two movements, lowering the bar and raising the bar. Don't think about lowering the bar, just think about driving it up. On the way down to the chest you should be thinking about driving up hard, not about down. Focus on **UP** only. In an attempt to get ready for the upward drive, you will slow down the descent and be tighter as you approach the chest, thus improving your rebound efficiency and minimizing bounce. By thinking about driving up while on the way down, you will have focused on the thing you are actually trying to do at the best point in the movement to start the process. Lowering the bar is awfully easy, and if you think past that to the drive, you will slow your descent as you prepare to actively drive the bar up. This excellent technique works for any exercise with an initial eccentric component.

Think about the drive up on the way down. This prepares the neuromuscular system for more efficient recruitment of motor units during the turnaround and drive up from the bottom.

Shoulders and Upper Back

"Shoulders" here refers to the lateral and posterior aspect of the shoulders, since the anterior deltoids were included in the discussion of the chest for functional reasons. This important group of muscles has two functions. First, the shoulders need to be planted firmly against the bench, and taken together with the muscles of the upper back (the ones between the shoulders), used as a platform to drive against while pushing the bar. When this is done correctly, the shoulder blades, or scapulae, will be adducted, or pulled together, to make a flat spot on the upper back to push against the bench itself. This stable platform is the anatomical surface on which the kinetic chain begins. Stated another way, when you bench press, you drive the bench and the bar apart – the bar moves and the bench doesn't, but you push against both (fig. 3-24). The upper back and shoulders push the bench and they need to be tight while doing so, just as the hands are tight against the bar. Second, the shoulders in their adducted position and the upper back muscles, as they contract and rotate or "tilt" the upper back into a chest-up position, push the ribcage up and hold the chest higher above the bench. This increases the mechanical efficiency of the pec/delt contraction by steepening the angle of attack on the humerus, as discussed earlier.

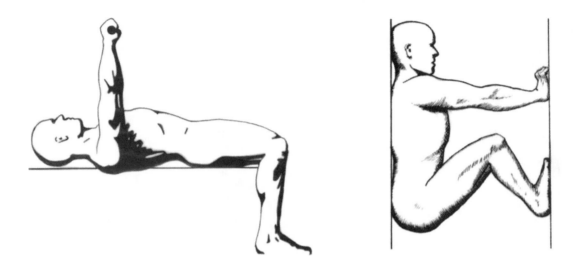

Figure 3-24. Just as we do when climbing a chimney (it still happens occasionally, really) when benching we are in between and pushing against two opposing things. When benching, the bar moves and the bench does not.

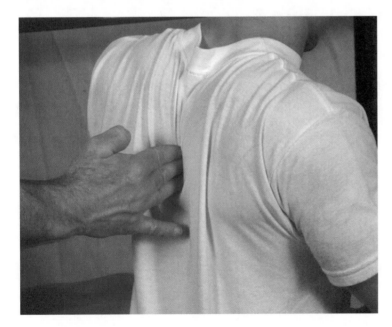

Figure 3-25. Retract the shoulder blades by thinking about pinching a hand between them. This effectively tightens the upper back for pushing against the bench.

Keeping your back tight is sometimes a difficult thing to do, since so many other things are going on at the same time. So it needs to be learned in a way such that it requires little active attention. Think about the "driving against the bench" model, and why you need your chest up. Then sit on the bench in the same position you assume before lying down to take the bar. Before you lie down, imagine a hand touching you right between the shoulder blades, as illustrated in figure 3-25 and pinching the hand between your shoulder blades. This will also cause you to raise your chest as your upper back tightens, further contributing to a good position. Now actively raise your chest, lifting it up as if to show it to someone. This is the position you will take against the bench, before you take the bar out of the rack. Now lie down and take the bar out and assume this position, making sure your shoulder blades are together and your chest is up high. Do a few reps, fixing your position before and after each one and focusing intently on the way it feels to do it correctly. This way, the position becomes embedded quickly and you can assume it without a lot of conscious thought or direction.

During the lift, minimal shoulder movement should occur. The thing that moves is the elbow. If the shoulder moves much, something in the upper back has loosened and the chest has lost some of its "up" position. Some minimal scapular movement is unavoidable, particularly in a set of more than a couple of reps, but if it is excessive it will compromise your efficiency by adding to the distance the bar has to travel to lockout. This can be illustrated by examining what happens during a shoulder shrug and the distance it adds to the bar movement.

Lie on the bench and pull your shoulders back into full adduction, with chest up in a good position and your back arched. Put your arms up with straight elbows in a position that simulates the start of the bench press. Note the position of your hands. Now shrug your shoulders up off the bench so that your shoulder blades come out of adduction, and note the difference in position. There will be a 4 to 6 inch difference in the distance from your hands to your chest from shrugged-back to shrugged-up. This is the extra distance you have to push the bar if you don't keep your shoulders back. You can illustrate this while standing as well, by shrugging one shoulder back and shrugging the other one forward and measuring the difference in distance from the chest between the two hands (fig. 3-27).

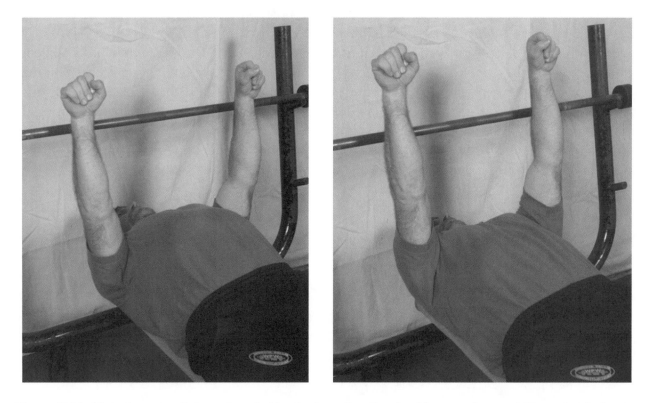

Figure 3-26. Note the extra distance traveled by the bar when the shoulders are shrugged forward at lockout.

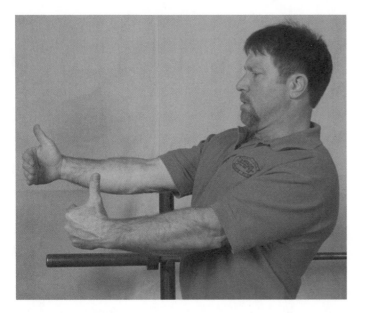

During a longer set (more than just a couple of reps) most inexperienced people will let their upper back deteriorate out of the shrugged position. If this happens, each rep is a little looser than the previous one and the bar must travel a little further each time. At the end of a set of five, reset your shoulder blades and chest-up position. If you are able to move them much at all, they have come out of position. Your goal is to be able to do all your reps without losing the set position.

Figure 3-27. A visual demonstration of the difference in distance between the shoulders kept back and shrugged forward.

Neck

The function of the neck muscles is to maintain head position, and to protect the cervical spine during the loading of the chest and upper back as the bar comes down on the chest. As such, the neck muscles work isometrically to maintain position, in a function similar to that of the lower back muscles during the deadlift. But unlike the back muscles, they should not transfer power along the neck to help with the lift. In other words, you do not use your head to bench press. *Do not push your head into the bench.* This is an excellent way to injure your neck. You need to learn how to tighten up your neck without pushing on the bench with the back of your head. As a practical matter, this involves holding your head about a half-inch off the bench during the rep. If your head is held off the bench your neck muscles are tight. It is tempting to use the neck to push the bench, as it adds contracted muscle and tightness to the upper back area, but it is too dangerous a habit to let become established.

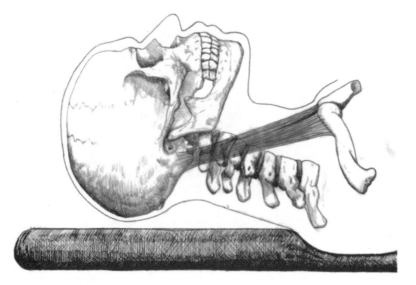

Figure 3-28. The preferred position of the neck and head during the bench press. Cervical injury often results from pressing the head into the bench under very heavy weights, and this position prevents the improper use of the neck muscles in this situation.

Lower back, hips, and legs

The bench press is an upper body exercise, but since the feet are on the floor, everything between the feet and the upper body has the potential to be somewhat involved in the exercise. The lower back and the hips and legs are thus the connection between the ground and the upper back. Strictly speaking, the kinetic chain begins at the bar and ends at the upper back/bench interface, but the correctly utilized back, hip, and leg position actually represents an extension of the kinetic chain down to the ground. The legs do more than stabilize the lower body as the bar is moved through its path, although that is a major part of their function. Used correctly, the legs drive against the floor, transferring force horizontally up the bench through the hips into the arched back to reinforce the arch and keep the chest in its high position, established when the shoulders were pulled back. The legs and hips thus function as a brace for the chest and shoulders, giving the upper body a connection to the floor, and allowing the lower body to contribute to the movement.

Figure 3-29. Force applied by the legs from the floor acts as a stabilizing force during the bench press and contributes to proper exercise posture.

Figure 3-30. Not the same thing as described in figure 3-29. This is bridging, and it is a bad habit to acquire.

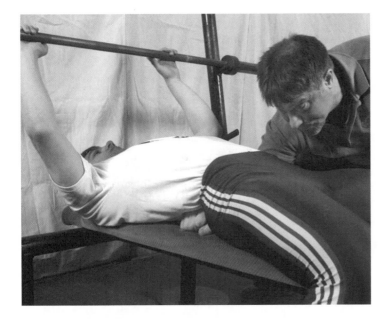

Figure 3-31. Learning to arch the lower back.

Before you have a chance to misinterpret, this is *not* the same thing as bridging or heaving the bar. That happens when the butt actually comes off the bench. Correct use of the legs and hips involves *only* the maintenance of chest and back position, with the force directed horizontally along the bench and not vertically up off of the bench. The descent of the bar unavoidably drives the elevated chest back down, by taking arch out of the back. The legs drive from the feet against the floor back up along the bench using a controlled isometric knee extension, with a slight hip extension produced by isometric contraction of the glutes and hamstrings. They actively counter the loss of arch in the back and chest height by reinforcing the arch from the floor.

But a common problem usually follows the realization that the legs are useful in the bench press. Bridging – the intentional heaving of the hips clear of contact with the bench – occurs as the lifter attempts to increase the chest height by using the lower body to steepen the angle of the upper back on the bench. Bridging takes work away from the target muscles by making the movement mechanically easier. (The popular gym exercise known as the decline bench press takes advantage of this position of increased mechanical efficiency. Most people can decline more than they bench, thus the popularity.) Some purists believe that we are cheating when we arch the back at all, but this program seeks to use all reasonable means to increase strength on the bench press. Bridging is a good place to draw the line. Lifting the butt has got to be learned as *verboten* in the same way that use of the hands is in soccer. The temptation is always there, but if the correct habits are learned early it will not usually be a problem.

The back arch is easy to learn. Assume your position on the bench, and imagine someone shoving a hand under your low back as you keep your butt in contact with it. Then imagine a clenched fist doing the same thing. Figure 3-31 provides a reference. It must be kept in mind that you cannot raise your butt up off of the bench, so it's much better to learn to arch without cheating from the beginning. Make yourself do it correctly, and resist the temptation to bridge your butt up.

Figure 3-32. The main parameters for foot placement in the bench are up/down (A) and in/out (B).

Figure 3-33. Feet too far up may lead to bridging.

Feet

Your feet are your connection to the ground. If your foot slips during a heavy bench, everything supported by the lower body – your upper body and all the muscles attached to it, everything you're using to push the bar – collapses. The feet must be in the correct position *on* the floor, and they must be positioned *against* the floor correctly.

Foot placement on the floor has two variables: up/down and in/out. The feet need to be wide enough apart to provide lateral stability for the hips and, through the tightness in the trunk muscles, the torso as it is planted on the bench. Excessive foot width is seldom a problem, as it is uncomfortable and hard to maintain. Narrow feet are much more commonly observed, many people having used the position without problems and never being corrected. Narrow feet do not guarantee disaster. They are merely a little less efficient, and you should learn to use an optimum stance from the beginning.

More a problem is placing the feet up too far, back under the hips with the knees at an acute angle. This position predisposes you to bridge your butt up in the air, and that is usually the reason people do it – if you have your feet too far up under your butt, and too close together with your heels up off the floor, you're going to bridge the heavy reps. If the feet are up too far, the knee extension, being done from a more acute knee angle, tends to raise the hips, while a more moderate knee angle generates force more parallel to the torso (fig. 3-34). Feet too far down, with the knees too straight, are commonly seen in novice lifters who have yet to learn how to use the hips and legs. This position makes it difficult to get enough "bite" against the floor to generate and maintain good tension in the upstream components (fig. 3-35). Your foot position should be set so that your shins are nearly vertical, give or take a few degrees either way, in both axes. This way, your knees are almost directly over your feet at any width without any adduction of the femurs. This position allows for efficient use of your legs in reinforcing the arch, but doesn't create a predisposition to bridge.

Figure 3-34. Correct positioning on the bench is important to learn. Ankle and knee placement happen first, and the hips are positioned as you lie down under the bar. In good position (left) the pelvis is flatter and the ankles and knees are positioned to drive against the floor and back up the bench to the shoulders. The bad position on the right is the perfect set-up for a bridge.

This is not to say that everybody with their feet up under the hips will bridge. But most lifters that bridge do so from this position. A little wider foot position, particularly with feet in full contact with the floor, will make it difficult to bridge because the slack has been taken out of the hips.

Proper foot position should be flat against the floor so that heels can be used as the base of the drive up the legs. As with most of the things in the weight room, your heels need to be nailed down to the floor. If you are up on your toes, you cannot use the force of knee extension nearly as efficiently as you can if your heels are planted. Flat feet are stickier feet, better connected to the ground through more surface area. A less than flat position represents a less than complete kinetic chain. Any rolling of the feet to either side during a rep implies that knees have moved, that the

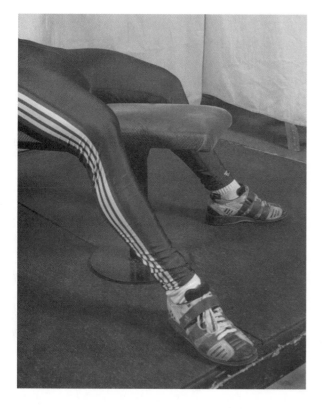

Figure 3-35. Too much "down" provides a poor brace against the floor.

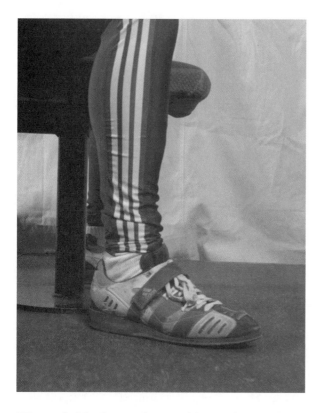

Figure 3-36. Proper foot position. The entire foot should be in contact with the floor.

chain has loosened, or that the floor connection has been interrupted. If you keep your heels down, driving off of them with flat feet, the problem goes away.

A bad problem when it occurs is an actual foot slip. It usually happens when the weight is very heavy and the floor connection is pressured up and therefore crucial. A foot slip results in a disruption and collapse of the kinetic chain, and most usually a missed rep or attempt, and any miss with a heavy bar can be dangerous. It is usually caused by conditions on the surface of the floor or the soles of the shoes, like the presence of baby powder (as is used in meets on the legs in the deadlift, or as an aid in putting on a tight squat suit), or just a dirty floor.

There are people – usually casual trainers, fitness enthusiasts, or retired powerlifters – who insist on benching with their feet up on the bench, or possibly held up in the air (fig. 3-37). The effect of this is to eliminate the use of the lower body during the movement and to make the bench press harder. This might be useful to an advanced trainee who, for various possible reasons, is not particularly concerned with benching heavy weights, but who wants to work hard during the exercise. It is also useful in the case of a trainee with a lower back injury that makes spinal extension painful, distracting, or otherwise contraindicated, but who still needs to bench. If you prefer to bench with your feet up, it might be due to lower back discomfort caused by a lack of lumbar flexibility; if the spinal ligaments are too tight to permit the degree of spinal extension that the normal bench position requires, stretching is in order. If your back is okay, you should be able to keep your feet down on the floor. Blocks or barbell plates can be used to add height to the floor for inflexible people until they stretch out, or to accommodate shorter-legged trainees. The net effect of the use of the lower body is to increase the weight that can be lifted, so putting feet up lowers the amount of weight lifted, but the exercise can still be done without it. The decision to do a feet-up bench should be made cognizant of the benefits of training around injuries and the limitations inherent in doing it this way.

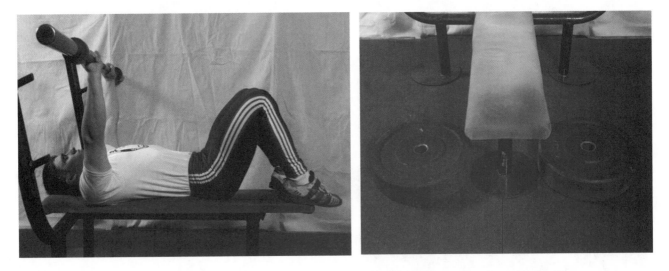

Figure 3-37. The knees-up position in the bench press is less stable than the conventional position, and should not be used by novice lifters.

Figure 3-38. Lifters with shorter legs can use any matched pair of stable objects to elevate the feet to a better position. Bumper plates or blocks built for this purpose work best.

Racking/un-racking errors

Taking the bar out of the rack and putting it back may seem like rather innocuous parts of the exercise and most people give it no thought. Please be aware of the fact that any time a loaded bar is located above your face and throat, you have a potential safety situation. The unrack/rack procedure needs to be done correctly from the beginning. At all times, when the bar is moving over your face and throat coming out of or going back into the rack, your elbows *must* be locked out straight.

When un-racking the bar, the elbows must lock out while the bar is still over the hooks of the rack. This means that the elbows drive the bar up along the uprights until they lock out, and only then does the bar move out over the chest to the start position. Many people get in the habit of taking the bar out on bent elbows and straightening them out as they move the bar down over the chest. This is a bad habit to acquire, one that may not cause an immediate problem but that has the potential to get you badly hurt. The triceps should lock the elbows over the rack hooks so that the bones of the arm are in a straight line and the weight is being supported by the skeletal components instead of the muscles when the bar moves over the head and neck.

The bar should move all the way out over the chest to the start position, without stopping above the chin or throat. It is common to see novices stop the bar short of the starting position at a point over the throat, lower the first rep to the chest at an angle, and come straight back up to the correct position to start the second rep. Only after the bar gets all the way to the start position and your eyes have found their place against the ceiling, should the bar start down.

Some people get in the habit of taking it down to the chest right out of the rack. It should never start down before it is in place – there will be bar path problems if it does, due to the lack of an initial ceiling reference for position, and the fact that the bar is going back to a different place than it started from. It makes your first rep different than the next ones. It prevents you from getting a good, tight start on the reps, since your shoulders and upper back cannot be correctly set until the bar is in position over your chest. And it might just indicate a lack of patience, an unwillingness to take the few extra seconds to prepare properly.

Even more important than un-racking properly, when your arms are not tired, is racking it correctly after the set has fatigued your muscles. This is normally where a wreck will occur. If you miss the rack hooks because a fatigued tricep has not locked out an elbow, and your spotter – if you have one – is not paying attention, at least one side of the bar is going to come down. **It is imperative that you get in the habit of finishing the last rep all the way to elbow lockout before you rack the bar.** It is common to see impatient people drive the last rep towards the rack right off the chest, producing a bar path that ends over the eyeballs instead of the chest. If

you're going to miss a bench press, and your spotter fails, it is preferable to have the bar come back down on your chest than on your face. The bench press *must* end in elbow lockout, directly above your chest, every time. The bench press is the source of the majority of training injuries involving free weights; your safety in the weight room may depend on this.

When racking the bar, make sure that you find the uprights with the bar. Don't try to set the bar down on the hooks. If you move the bar back with locked elbows until it touches the vertical part of the uprights, and then slide it down onto the hooks, you won't have to worry about whether it will stay in the rack. If the uprights are touched first, it will always be above the hooks. If straightening out your elbows got it clear of the hooks when taking it out, then locked elbows will ensure that it is high enough to get back over the hooks when putting it up. (If your arms are short, you need to use a bench with adjustable uprights.) But if you try to set the bar down on the *hooks first*, then you are not all the way back to the uprights as you try to set the bar down, and you will eventually miss the rack, usually one of the hooks on one side. This same advice applies to the squat, for exactly the same reasons.

Figure 3-39. On the final rep, it is common to push the bar back toward the rack before the rep is finished instead of driving into a proper lockout over the chest. If you miss the last rep (and if you miss a rep it will probably be the last one) where would you rather the bar come back down – on your chest or on your face? Get in the habit of finishing every rep correctly.

Breathing

The pattern of breathing during the bench is dependent on the length of the set and the abilities of the lifter. Novices should probably take a breath before each rep, hold it during the rep, and exhale at lockout, using the very brief break between reps to make sure everything is set correctly. More experienced lifters may prefer to use one breath for the whole set. Any exhalation involves a certain amount of loosening of the chest to exhale and re-inhale, and some may decide to stay tight and do the whole set on one breath if it is important, and if they can hold the breath that long. Most people can only manage five reps this way before the discomfort from the hypoxia becomes too distracting. For a longer set, some quick breaths will be required.

As it is for all barbell exercises, air is support for the bench press. In the squat and deadlift, the Valsalva maneuver (as described in the Squat chapter) provides increased back support. In the bench press, it provides support for the chest. This takes the form of increased tightness throughout the thoracic cavity due to the increase in pressure provided by the big, held breath. A tight ribcage allows for a more efficient transfer of power to the bar by the muscles attached to it when they contract. If the pec and delt origins on the external chest wall contract against a tight structure that does not move when they contract, then more of the force of that contraction can be transferred to the end of the kinetic chain that does move. When it's tight, less force gets absorbed, or dampened, by movement of the chest. This is analogous to trying to pick up a heavy weight while standing in a floating canoe as opposed to standing on a concrete driveway. This tightness, along with the support provided by the lower body connected to the ground, radically increases efficiency in the bench press. Also, in the extended spinal position that the arch requires on the bench, the abs cannot tighten. They cannot therefore effectively increase intra-abdominal pressure, and cannot contribute to the needed increase in intra-thoracic pressure, thus making the big breath the sole source of support for the chest.

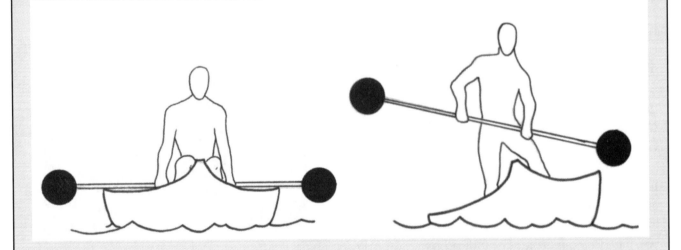

Getting into proper starting position against an unstable structure is not a huge problem. Applying force against an unstable structure can be. The boat moves erratically when the weight is lifted, thus reducing the height to which the weight can be lifted. An unstable spine against the bench reduces performance capacity for the same reason. Maximum strength cannot be developed by pushing against unstable structures since maximum force cannot be developed – and therefore cannot be trained – against an unstable structure.

The breath has to be taken *before* the rep. If the breath is taken *during* the rep, the lungs will incompletely fill due to the loading of the ribcage by the now-contracted pecs. If the breath is taken at the top with locked elbows, the pecs are not pulling on the ribcage and a more complete inhalation can take place. Moreover, when the bar actually starts down everything should be tight, from the floor to your fingernails, and this tightness will prevent a really big breath. If you can breathe during a rep, you're not tight enough.

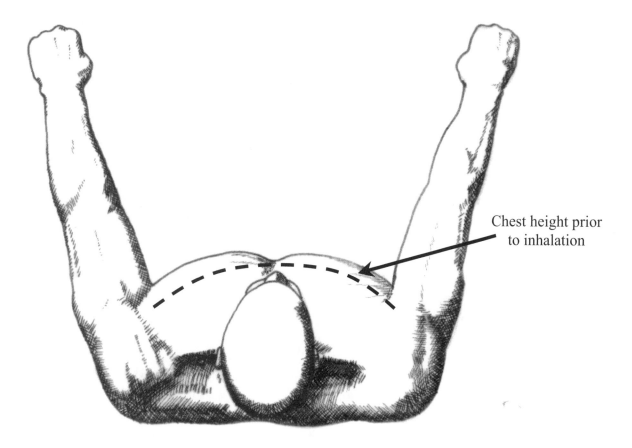

Chest height prior
to inhalation

Figure 3-40. Inhalation at the top with arms completely extended before the rep starts allows for a more complete filling of the lungs, a better chest angle, and better stability.

No breath taken during the set will involve the complete exhale/inhale of the full tidal volume of your lungs. This takes too long, requires too much relaxation, and is unnecessary. Breathing during the set consists only of topping off the huge breath taken before the first rep, after a quick exhalation that might consist of only 10% of tidal volume. This short refresher of air is just enough to allow the set to be finished more comfortably. The fact that it amounts to so little air is the reason you might decide to forego it in favor of maintaining tightness, after you practice it.

Spotters

In many gyms around the world, bench pressing is a team activity. The guy on the bench is "doing chest" while the guy standing over his head is working on his traps. It is truly amazing how much weight two guys working together like this can "bench press." It is not an exaggeration to say that most gym claims of big bench presses are exaggerations. If the spotter puts his hands on the bar during the first rep, and keeps them there for the rest of the set, then who lifted what, and why?

There is a perfectly legitimate place in the weight room for spotters, but it is not in the middle of someone else's work set. Spotters should be there for safety, when there is a question of safety. Spotters should *not* be there to help with a set. Make this your rule in the weight room: **No rep counts that is *touched* by anybody other than the lifter. No spotter touches any bar that is still moving up.** If this rule is followed by you and everyone you train with, all the personal records you set will be honest ones, and you won't have to slap anybody for interfering with a new personal record. Tell your spotters – and practice it yourself: *spotters stay away from any rep that the lifter might finish alone.*

This cannot be overstated: if the numbers written down in your training log are not honest, you have absolutely no way to evaluate the results of your program. This obviously applies to all lifts that customarily require spotters. The bench press has been particularly abused by bad spotters, with the result being inflated gym records and much unwarranted bragging (making a good case for a strength contest that replaces the bench press with the press). If you let your spotter help you on your work sets, you'll soon have absolutely no idea what you're really benching, and no idea if you're making progress.

Spotters should be there for safety, where a question of safety exists. For everybody except rank novices, the first warm-up sets are not a safety concern and do not require spotters, unless the spotter is also performing a coaching function. As the weight gets heavier, a spot becomes more necessary, some needing one on the last warm-up, until the work sets, where everybody should be spotted because the weight is supposed to be heavy. Excessive caution, and the insistence that every set be spotted, is inefficient, unnecessary, and bothersome to other people in the gym who are trying to train. But if your gym contains mostly people who can't be bothered to help you when it is legitimately necessary, you need to find a better gym. Get a spot when you need to, and know when this is.

For the bench press, a competent center spot will suffice for all but the very heaviest attempts. One of the actual functions of a spotter is the handoff. A good handoff is one of those rare commodities – there are more bad ones than good. A bad handoff interferes with the lifter's timing, balance, view of the ceiling, and concentration, by attempting to participate in the rep. A good handoff spotter is experienced and appropriate with the timing and amount of bar contact, respectful of the mental requirements of the lifter, and, above all, conservative about when and how much to help.

An entire chapter could be devoted to the art and science of spotting, and will be someday. But briefly, the bench press spotter stands behind the head of the lifter, in the center of the bar (fig. 3-41). This position can be adjusted a little if necessary. The primary requirement of the position is that it is close enough to grab the bar, but far enough back that after the handoff the lifter has an unobstructed view of the ceiling. From this position the spotter can do whatever might be necessary at the end of the set, from just watching the lifter finish the set, to securing the rack by shadowing the bar as it meets the uprights, to taking the bar out of a sticking point.

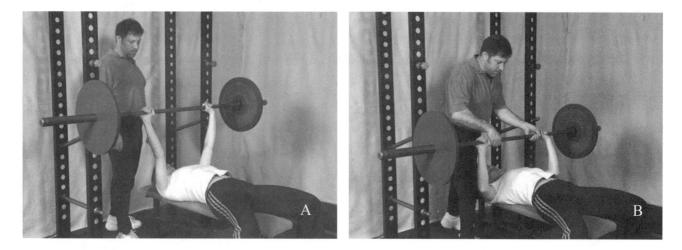

Figure 3-41. The standard spotting position (A) allows for a quick and safe response to problems. But the proper role of the spotter must be understood by the lifter. The spotter provides a measure of safety and confidence, and can help through a sticking point on the last rep and ensure that the bar is racked safely (B). IT IS NOT THE SPOTTER'S JOB TO ASSIST WITH ANY REP OTHER THAN THE LAST ONE, AND THEN ONLY IF NECESSARY.

If you actually get stuck during a rep, your spotter needs to be the one to decide that this has occurred, that he will take the bar, and how much of the weight to take when he does. The bar is stuck when it reaches a point of zero upward movement. This will shortly be followed by a deterioration in position as it begins to move down. Sometimes you may be able to tell the spotter to take the bar, and sometimes you won't. Your spotter has to accurately evaluate the bar velocity, being certain not to take a bar that is still moving up, yet not failing to take it before it sticks for too long or goes back down too much or too fast.

After the spotter decides to take the bar, the amount of help provided will depend on the situation and the correct assessment of it. When spotting an intermediate lifter with the last rep of the fifth set of five, the situation will warrant a different amount of help than in the case of an experienced lifter being spotted on a PR single, or the case of a novice trainee doing the first heavy work set of his third workout. Each instance requires a different response in terms of how fast to react, how closely the bar should be followed, the amount of weight to take off, whether or not to help maintain bar velocity, or whether to take the bar to the rack or the safety hooks.

Certain circumstances might require the use of two spotters, as at a power meet during the heavy attempts, but normal weight room conditions very seldom require more than one competent spotter. The problem with two spotters is the unalterable fact that two people cannot assist one lifter in a perfectly balanced way, especially in a situation where they must react quickly. The uneven loading that the lifter will inevitably experience is a potential source of injury. It is physically impossible for two people, even careful, experienced people, to pull upward with exactly the same amount of force on each side of a bar, thus subjecting the lifter to uneven loading at exactly the time when that stress is the most likely to cause an injury – during a rep that is too heavy to lift. This is true of both the squat and the bench press. The problem in the bench press is solved with the use of the single spotter, a perfectly reasonable way to spot for the vast majority of bench press workouts where the weight on the bar has been correctly selected.

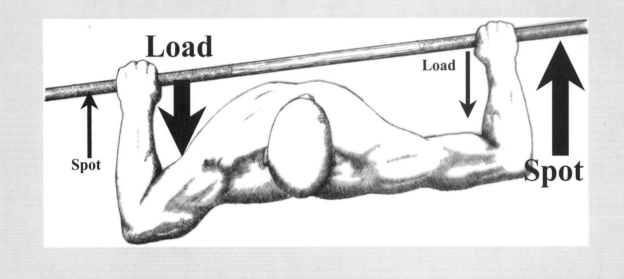

The danger inherent in the use of two spotters. No two people lifting on either end of a loaded bar that somebody else is pressing can possibly do so evenly. There will be an imbalance, and the only question is how much.

The Deadlift

Lower back strength is an important component of sports conditioning. The ability to maintain a rigid lumbar spine under a load is critical for both power transfer and safety. The deadlift builds back strength better than any other exercise, bar none. And back strength built with the deadlift is useful: while the bar is the most ergonomically friendly tool for lifting heavy weights, a 400 lb. barbell deadlift makes an awkward 85 lb. box more manageable.

The basic function of the lumbar muscles is to hold the low back in position so that power can be transferred through the trunk. They are aided in this task by all the muscles of the trunk: the abs, the obliques, the intercostals, and all of the many posterior muscles of the upper and lower back. These muscles function in isometric contraction – their main task is to prevent skeletal movement in the structures they are supporting. When the trunk is held rigid, it can function as a solid segment along which the force generated by the hips and legs can be transferred to the load – on the shoulders, as in the squat or the press, or across the shoulder blades and down the arms to the hands, as in the deadlift. There is no easy way to do a deadlift – no way to cheat, which explains their lack of popularity in most gyms around the world.

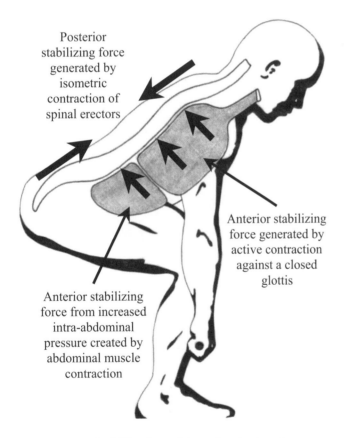

Posterior stabilizing force generated by isometric contraction of spinal erectors

Anterior stabilizing force generated by active contraction against a closed glottis

Anterior stabilizing force from increased intra-abdominal pressure created by abdominal muscle contraction

Figure 4-1. Stabilization of the spine during the deadlift is essential, and is accomplished the same way as in the squat. Intra-abdominal and intrathoracic pressures increase in response to the contraction of the trunk musculature coupled with the Valsalva maneuver.

The deadlift is a simple movement. The bar is pulled off the floor up the legs with straight arms until the knees, hips, and shoulders are locked out. Immense weights have been moved in this way by very strong men. In powerlifting, the deadlift is the last lift in the meet, and the expression, "The meet don't start till the bar gets on the floor!" is very telling. Many big subtotals have been overcome by strong deadlifts, especially in the days before squat suits and bench shirts. The meet was often won by a lifter with a bigger deadlift than his squat. It is hard to overstate the strength of a man with an 800 lb. + deadlift, a feat accomplished by only an elite few lifters. Nine hundred-pound contest deadlifts have occurred only a handful of times, although many more have accomplished this with straps (which eliminate the grip-strength aspect of the lift). As of this writing, a 1000 lb. deadlift had only been done by the UK lifter Andy Bolton.

But the deadlift is brutally hard, and can therefore complicate training if improperly used. It is very easy to do wrong, and a wrong deadlift is a potentially dangerous thing. There will be a few trainees that simply cannot perform this movement safely with heavy weights, due to previous injury or an inability to learn the movement correctly. The deadlift is also easy to overtrain; a heavy workout takes a long time to recover from, and this fact must be kept in mind when setting up your training schedule.

Figure 4-2. George Hechter (left) and John Kuc demonstrate the deadlift as done by brutally strong men.

For the majority that can benefit from this important exercise, the deadlift should be an essential part of training: an important assistance exercise for the squat, and especially the clean (for which it is an important introductory lesson in position and pulling mechanics), as well as a way to train the mind to do things that are hard.

There are two ways to perform the deadlift used in competition: the conventional, with the feet inside the grip, and the "sumo" style, with the feet outside the grip. Good sumo deadlifters typically have long torsos relative to the legs and are good squatters. This version of the lift allows for a more upright back angle so that leg strength may be used more efficiently (fig. 4-3). Since our purpose is the development of low back strength through the effective use of exercises that work these muscles, the sumo deadlift will not be used in this program.

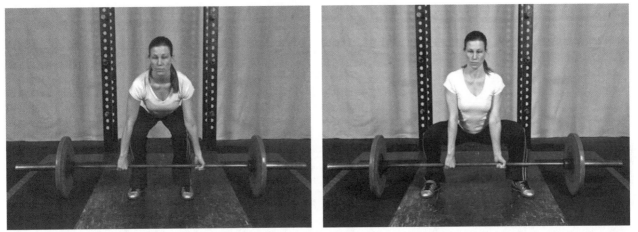

Figure 4-3. The conventional deadlift style (left), used in this program for strength training, and the Sumo style often used in powerlifting competition.

First, some general observations about the deadlift, in no particular order. It can be used as a leg exercise if injury prevents squatting. It is not nearly as effective as the squat for this purpose, due to the lack of hip depth used in the starting position (fig. 4-4). But this is the very reason it can be used if a knee or hip injury makes squats too difficult or painful, and at least some leg work can be done while healing takes place. A high rep deadlift workout can provide enough work to maintain some leg conditioning, even if the injury is of a nature that would prevent heavier, low-rep deadlifts, such as a groin pull or a not-too-severe quad tear.

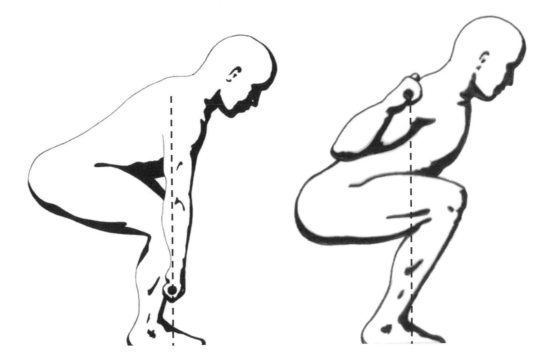

Figure 4-4. A comparison of the squat and the deadlift. Note that the bar in both exercises is centered over the mid-foot when balanced, and hangs below the same place in the deadlift that it sits in the squat. But the squat is carried to a much deeper hips position than the deadlift, which starts at the depth of a half-squat.

Tremendous leg power can be exerted in the deadlift starting position, essentially a half-squat depth, so the challenge is usually to keep your back tight to break the bar off the floor. Leg strength is seldom the limiting factor in the deadlift. If the bar comes off the floor, the legs can lock out what the back can support. If the bar stays on the floor, the problem is either the grip, an injury producing sufficient pain to distract from the pull, or a lack of experience with pulling a heavy weight that would rather stay where it is.

Grip strength is crucial to the deadlift, and the deadlift works grip strength better than any other major exercise. It is the limiting factor for many lifters with smaller hands or short fingers, or those that rely too much on their straps when training. The lift is famous for its alternate grip, but the use of the double-overhand grip as much as possible makes for stronger hands. The alternate grip keeps the bar from rolling in the hands, since it is always rolling up one hand as much as it's rolling down the other. So if all the warmups possible are done with a double-overhand grip and the alternate grip reserved for the really heavy sets, grip strength develops quickly. Novices are often able to pull their heaviest sets with a double-overhand grip; their hands are stronger than their backs. More advanced lifters find that it is necessary to flip a hand over to an alternate grip (most prefer the non-dexterous hand for the supine, or underhand, side) when the weight gets very heavy (fig. 4-5).

Figure 4-5. The alternate grip. Most people prefer to supinate the non-dexterous hand. This lifter is right-handed.

For those not intending to deadlift at a meet, straps may be a logical choice for the heavy sets, since one supine hand and one prone hand produces asymmetrical stress on the shoulders and can cause or aggravate bicep tendon problems on the supine side in some people. Your decision to strap the heavy sets will be based on personal preference, flexibility, and training goals. If the warm-ups are done without straps to as heavy as possible, the grip will still get most of the benefit of the exercise without the shoulder problems on the supine side that sometimes accompany the alternate grip.

Anybody who has trained the deadlift for a few months has had the experience of pulling on a weight that seemed too heavy even to break off the ground when tried with a double-overhand grip, only to find that it goes up surprisingly easily when the grip is alternated. The back will not pull off the floor what the hands cannot hold, due to proprioceptive feedback that tells the back the weight is too heavy. When the grip is flipped and the hands don't slip as the load increases off the floor, the back doesn't receive the signal that makes it stop the pull. A long, heavy deadlift can get dropped from higher up the legs with any style grip, but most lifters cannot even break a weight off the floor that is so heavy that it opens the hands at the start of the pull. Deadlift straps have a place in training, but judgement must be exercised here; they can cause as many problems as they solve. They can allow heavier back training if grip is the limiting factor, or they can cause grip to *be* a limiting factor, by keeping it from getting strong if used too often with too light a weight.

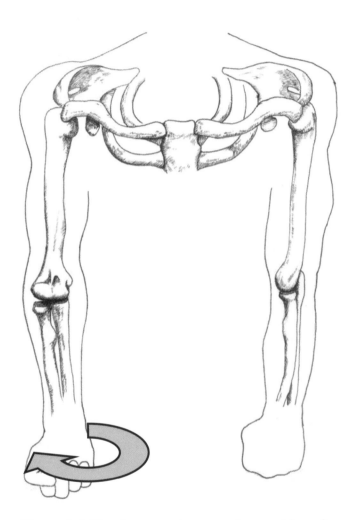

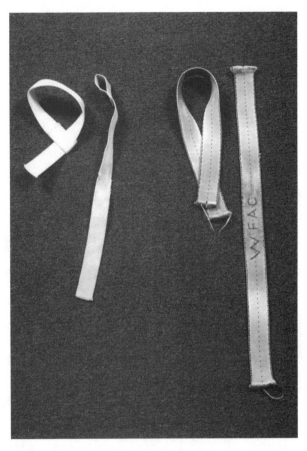

Figure 4-7. Lifting straps are a training aid that assists in removing grip strength as a limitation. Used inappropriately, they can prevent the development of improved grip strength.

Figure 4-6. The alternate grip can produce problems for some people, especially those with inflexible shoulders. The lifter above is left-handed, with the right hand in supination. This requires that the right humerus be in active external rotation, in contrast to the left side in passive internal rotation. This loads the shoulders and elbows differently, and has caused biceps tendon avulsions or ruptures for many strong deadlifters. It is interesting to observe that "normal anatomical position" is normal upright posture with no active contraction of any non-postural muscles, except the active external rotation of the arm into supination.

The hands are prone to callus formation as a normal part of training. All competitive lifters have them, and need them to protect the hands from blisters and tears. Skin adapts to stress like all other tissues do; skin thickens precisely where it receives the stress of abrasion and folding. Calluses are only bad if they are excessive, and gripping the bar incorrectly causes excessive callus formation. Most lifters do this, and have never considered the role of grip in callus formation. Heavy calluses tear frequently, usually at the top of the palm (and most often into the base of the ring finger, because ring wearing has already produced a starter callus there). A torn callus makes the rest of the meet a challenge, eased only by some lidocaine gel that the coach hopefully has in the meet bag. But if the bar is gripped correctly, callus buildup is kept minimal and the problem is not nearly as bad.

When setting the grip, if you place the bar in the middle of your palm and wrap your fingers from there, a fold forms at the top of your palm, right before the area where your fingers start. When the bar is pulled, gravity shoves this fold further down towards your fingers, increasing the folding and stress on this part of the skin. Callus forms here as a result, and the presence of the callus amplifies the folding problem by making the fold even thicker. If the bar is gripped further down towards your fingers to begin with, it can't slide down much because it's already there. This is actually the place the bar needs to be, since gravity will pull it there. And since it will hopefully stop there anyway, you might as well start like this. You also get the advantage of having less far to pull the bar – if it is further down in your fingers your chest is up higher, your position off the floor is easier, the further down your thigh it locks out, and the shorter the distance it has moved before being locked out. Put the bar where it's trying to go to, not where you think it needs to be.

Equipment can contribute to callus formation, and this applies to all the lifts. A bar with an excessively sharp knurl is an annoying thing to have to use in the weight room. Older bars usually have better knurls than newer bars: they are either worn smooth or made more correctly (it seems that companies decided to start making Texas-Chainsaw-Massacre knurls about 1990). Bad knurls can be improved with a big mill file and about an hour's work.

Chalk is important for hand safety. It keeps the skin dry and tight, making folding under a load less a problem. You should apply chalk before you start training every day, for all the lifts. If your gym is one of those that does not allow chalk, for reasons of cleanliness or whatever, you need to reevaluate your choice of gyms.

Gloves have no place in a serious training program. A glove is merely a piece of loose stuff between the hand and the bar, reducing grip security and increasing the effective diameter of the bar. Gloves make bars harder to hold on to. The ones that incorporate a wrist wrap prevent the wrist from getting used to training. The only legitimate use for a glove is to cover an injury, like a torn callus or a cut, where the workout is important enough to do with the injury and it cannot be done without the covering. A desire to prevent callus formation does not constitute a legitimate use. If your gym makes a lot of money selling gloves, you have another reason to look for a different gym. And if you insist on using them, make sure they match your purse.

Deadlifts are hard. Many people don't like to do them. Most people, even the ones who will squat heavy and often and correctly, will leave deadlifts out of the workout at the slightest provocation. This is the reason most powerlifters squat more than they deadlift – there was often no "time" to do them in the program. But doing them adds back strength, and back strength is necessary for the other lifts and for sports. So let's learn how to do them.

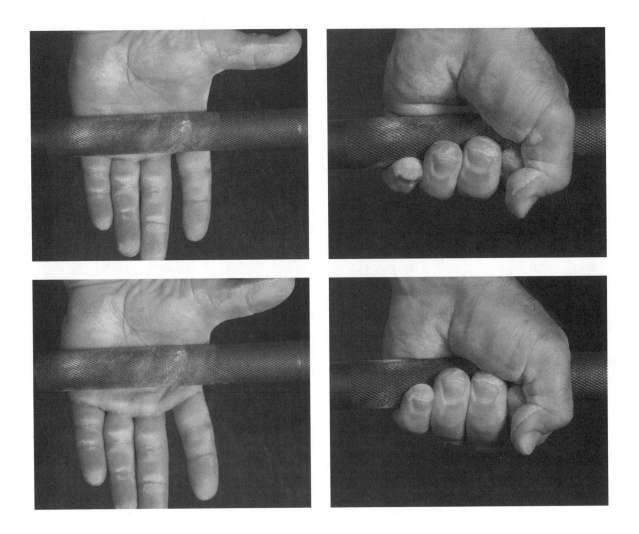

Figure 4-8. Gripping the bar correctly, well down into the hook of the fingers (top), will reduce the amount of callus development. Gripping the bar too high in the hand (bottom) will allow the bar to slide down into the fingers, folding the palm skin as it goes. This folding along the area between the distal palmar crease and the palmar digital crease causes the majority of the callus formation. If they become excessively thick, calluses can tear off during heavy lifts and ruin the rest of your day.

Learning to Deadlift

The bar should be loaded to a light weight relative to your capability. A light weight for a novice 55 year-old woman will be different than that for an 18 year-old 205 lb. athlete. Your gym should be equipped to load weights as light as 55 lbs., or possibly even lighter to accommodate people of all levels of ability. This makes it necessary to obtain 5 lb. plastic training plates that space a 45 lb., 15 kg., or even a 10 kg. bar off the floor to the same height as a standard plate. If there is no way to obtain these light plates, blocks can be used under 10 or 25 lb. iron plates, or the bar can be set in the power rack to the correct height; the small iron plates place the bar closer to the floor than most people's flexibility can accommodate in a correct starting position (fig. 4-9). Judgment must be exercised here; the starting weight must be light enough so that if your form is bad you cannot hurt yourself, just in case these instructions are not followed closely enough. So for some people 55 lbs. or lighter will be the starting weight, 40 kg. (88 lbs.) will work for most everyone else, and there is never a reason for anyone to start heavier than 135 lbs.

The stance for the deadlift is about the same as the stance for a flat-footed vertical jump, about 12-15 inches between the heels with the toes pointed very slightly out. Bigger, taller people with wider hips will use a proportionately wider stance. This stance is narrower, and thus more toes-forward, than the squat, because of the difference between the two movements. The squat is done from the top down, the hips lowered and driven up; the deadlift starts at the bottom, the feet pushing the floor, the back locked in place and the legs driving the bar up. The difference in stance is due to this difference in mechanics (fig. 4-11). (It might also be noted here that this is a natural stance angle for this stance width. The wider the stance, the more the toes will angle out, to match the femoral/tibial external rotation inherent in their angle at the hip, and vice versa.) The bar should be about 1 to 1.5 inches from your shins. This is enough room for the knees to travel forward to a position just in front of the bar as you lower into the starting position, but not so much that the bar is too far away to pull. This position will place the bar directly over the middle of the foot when the pull starts, the place over which the bar stays on its way up to lockout. Once this correct stance has been assumed, grip the bar, double-overhand, at a width that places your hands just wide enough that your thumbs clear your legs (fig. 4-12). Bar markings will vary, but with a standard Olympic bar, the grip will be one to two inches into the knurl, or about 20 inches between for most people. Bigger people will need to use a proportionately wider grip to match their stance.

Take your grip on the bar by bending over at the waist, and then bend your knees and lift the chest, as shown in figure 4-14. When this is done correctly, you will have assumed a relatively flat-backed position, depending on your flexibility. Make sure to keep the bar close to the shins. Basically, if you place the middle of your feet directly under the bar in the correct stance (this may take a second pair of eyes the first time), take your grip, drop your knees forward until your shins touch the bar *without rolling it forward out of position*, and then squeeze your chest up until your back is tight in extension, you should be in the right position to pull.

If I had a nickel for every scary deadlift I've seen at high school powerlifting meets, I actually wouldn't have more than about five dollars in nickels because I quit going to the damn things after I'd been to just three or four of them. I do not enjoy seeing the egos of coaches take precedence over the spinal integrity of athletes. Little skinny kids trying to open with 405, when their backs are not capable of staying flat with 225. Beautiful little 15-year-old girls stuffed into squat suits, low backs rounded into complete flexion on their opening attempts. Big, potentially strong kids doing the lifts with technique that passes for legal at a meet of this type, with weights that they cannot lift correctly – that is, in a way that satisfies the rules of biomechanics that govern safety and efficiency. I witnessed high squats in spinal flexion, hitched deadlifts in spinal flexion, and coaches and referees behaving as though this was Just Fine. It is truly amazing that more kids are not hurt in activities of this type, and that in itself tells us something about the nature of healthy human bodies and the actual injury potential of barbell exercises.

Mark Rippetoe, *Strong Enough?*

A deadlift requires the production of force from a dead stop. Thus, the name. Deadlifts differ from squats in more than just depth at the bottom: the deadlift starts with a concentric contraction and ends with an eccentric. The squat begins eccentrically, as the bar is lowered from lockout, and then returns to lockout with the concentric contraction, like the bench press. To review, an eccentric contraction occurs when the muscle lengthens under contraction, and a concentric contraction occurs when the muscle shortens during contraction. (Muscles don't "flex" - they contract. Joints flex and extend.) Sometimes referred to as the "negative," the eccentric phase usually lowers a weight while the concentric phase raises it. The stretch reflex occurs at the transition between lowering and raising, and many studies have shown that a muscle contracts harder concentrically when preceded by a stretch, the very thing provided by an eccentric contraction. Demonstrate this to yourself by trying to do a vertical jump without doing a dip to start the jump. Or try applying this principle to barbell curls by starting them from the top instead of from extended elbows at the bottom. The down phase, if used skillfully, makes the up phase easier. But a deadlift is not preceded by any loaded stretch reflex, no matter how much drama the lifter engages in before the pull. Much of the effect provided by the eccentric/concentric transition comes from the viscoelastic energy stored in the muscles and tendons that are elongating under a loaded trip to the bottom of the range of motion; if there is no loaded trip, there is no energy to store. The deadlift starts at the mechanically hardest part of the movement, and requires the lifter to generate the entire explosion necessary to break the bar off of the floor and get it moving up, without any help from a negative or anything else.

A   B

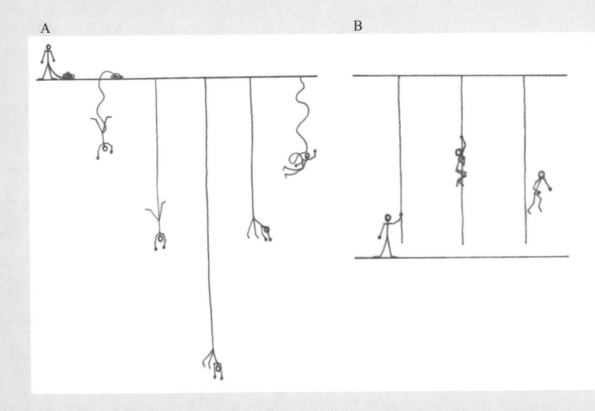

As in A above, the squat starts at the top, and as the weight stretches you down into the bottom position energy is stored during the stretch in the elongating muscles and connective tissue. It is then used to help increase the efficiency of the contraction that drives the weight up – the stretch reflex. In contrast (B) the deadlift starts in a position where these muscles and connective tissues are already elongated, with no way to store any energy in them. The downward half of the deadlift, if done slowly and if used as a loading phase for the next rep bounced off the floor, would function this way, but this defeats the purpose of the exercise.

Figure 4-9. Standard plate diameter provides a standard height for the bar above the floor. Different weights in this standard diameter allow people of different strength levels to pull from this standard height, 8 ½ inches or 21.5 cm between the bottom of the bar and the floor.

Figure 4-10. Starting position stance for the deadlift is heels approximately 12-15 inches apart with the toes pointed slightly out.

Figure 4-11. The differences in the stance of the deadlift and the squat are due to the differences in the mechanics of the two lifts. The vertical jump (A) starts from a foot position similar to a deadlift (B) because the depth of the hips is similar (D), and the task in both cases is a push against the floor. In contrast, the squat (C) involves lowering the hips to a point below parallel (E) and then driving them up, and the stance is designed to maximize the ability to get hip depth and use the adductors, glutes, and hamstrings to generate rebound out of the bottom.

Figure 4-12. The grip width should be just outside the legs when the feet are in the correct position. This allows the thumbs to just clear the legs on the way up.

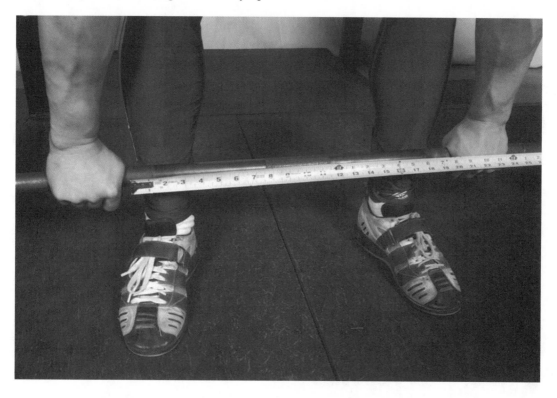

Figure 4-13. Grip width for most people of average height will be about 20 inches.

Figure 4-14. The process of assuming the start position. The grip is set, the hips are lowered, the chest is lifted, and the back is squeezed flat.

Figure 4-15. The correct finish position.

You are now ready to pull your first rep. Take a breath, make sure the bar is against your shins, look forward and slightly down, and pull the bar up your legs. At the top of the pull, lift your chest and pull your shoulders back. This gets you in a good position at the top. Seen from the side, this position will be anatomically normal, with both lordotic and kyphotic curves in an unexaggerated position, eyes looking straight ahead, hips and knees fully extended, and shoulders back. This is the position your body must assume to safely bear weight, and the correct back position during the pull represents the safe way to transfer the load from the ground to this upright position. Be aware of this good position at the top by identifying the key elements of it when you are there. Your chest is up, your knees and hips are straight, your chin is straight ahead, and your shoulders are back. Refer to figure 4-15 for this position.

Back injuries are fairly common in the weight room, and unfortunately this is a part of training with heavy weights. Both squats and deadlifts, as well as cleans and all other pulling exercises, can produce these painful, inconvenient, and time-consuming problems. But knowing what actually causes them can lend a whole new perspective on how necessary it is to prevent position errors that result in these injuries.

If you go to the doctor when you have a back injury, nine times out of ten she will tell you that "You just tore a back muscle. Take these drugs and quit lifting so much weight." This diagnosis reflects a lack of personal experience with these types of injuries, and a lack of understanding regarding how and when muscles actually get torn.

Torn muscle bellies bleed. This is because they are vascular tissues and a tear of any significance disrupts the connective tissue components of the muscle belly to the extent that the contractile and vascular components burst; blood begins to accumulate in the area of the tear, producing a hematoma. These look like large bruises, and go through the same processes that bruises do as they reabsorb and heal. Bad tears will leave a visible gap in the muscle belly. Minor tears hurt like hell too, but don't bleed enough to make a noticeable bruise. Little ones heal quickly, while a major tear can take several weeks.

The majority of muscle tears occur in the thighs and legs, with bench pressing accounting for quite a few torn pecs. These muscles are attached to long bones that either move heavy weights over a long range of motion or accelerate the bones themselves very quickly over a long range of motion. In the case of bench press and squat tears, the weight itself provides more resistance than the muscle can temporarily overcome and the rupture strength of the contractile tissue is exceeded. These tears can occur at any velocity of movement, even after sufficient warmup. More commonly, running injuries occur in which the contractile strength of either the agonist or the antagonist muscle exceeds the rupture strength of the opposing component. Hamstrings, quads, and calves are torn with unfortunate frequency, and this becomes more common as athletes age and lose both muscle and connective tissue extensibility.

The common feature of muscles that are the most subject to belly rupture is the job they do: they accelerate long bones around an angle. As such, they produce long ranges of motion and relatively high angular velocities. Contrast this to the job of the spinal muscles: they produce and hold an isometric contraction. They are postural muscles, and their primary function is holding a column of small bones in a constant position relative to each other. Their morphology reflects this task: the spinal muscles are long muscles, true, but they all have multiple origin and insertion points on a segmented bony structure that is designed to be itself held in place while its appendicular structures – the arms and legs – propel it through space. The vertebral column depends on stability for its structural integrity, and though it features a relatively limited amount of flexure, it must be held rigid as it bears load. Lifting weights requires this rigidity, and the postural muscles of the trunk provide it.

Back injuries often occur during lifting, and most usually when lifting incorrectly. But even when this does occur, the circumstances are markedly different to those in which a hamstring tears. A leg muscle tears during a long angular contraction, while a back injury occurs over a terribly small range of motion, so small that it would not be expressed even in centimeters. Even in the event of a complete relaxation of the entire lumbar musculature, not much movement has occurred, certainly not when compared to a sprint stride. This makes it highly unlikely that you will actually rupture a back muscle while picking up a sack of groceries, yet these low-force, low-velocity types of activities are precisely where most back injuries happen. In the absence of blunt trauma, true back muscle ruptures are quite rare.

Most back injuries are, unfortunately, spinal in nature. Think of them as joint injuries, like a knee injury. The intervertebral discs and facet joints are quite susceptible to intervertebral movement, the kind of movement that back muscle contraction is supposed to prevent. Strong back muscle developed through correct lifting technique is perhaps the best preventative for back injuries, since the habits formed while lifting correctly contribute to spinal safety just as much as the strength it produces. Knowing this, pay extra attention to form while learning to pull off the floor; it will come in handy. That's a promise.

Down should be the perfect opposite of up with respect to back position, the only difference being that the bar can go down faster. It is just as easy to injure the back setting the bar down incorrectly as it is picking it up incorrectly, and it is extremely common to set the bar down wrong, with a round back and the knees forward, even if you have pulled it correctly off the floor. More on this later.

Most people will not have the bar close enough to their legs, and many will bend their elbows on the way up near the top of the deadlift. Leaving the bar out away from the legs is due to the perfectly natural desire not to scrape the shins. Bending your elbows is due to the large section of the brain that says "All things are lifted with the arms." But these concerns are secondary to your low back position, the most important part of the lift. Everything else can be wrong with the deadlift and nothing really bad happens, but if your low back is round under a big load, safety is compromised.

So now is the time to learn the most important part of the deadlift, "setting" the back correctly. After you set the bar down, stand up without the bar and lift your chest. At the same time, arch your lower back by thinking about sticking your butt out. Refer to figure 4-16 and imagine a coach touching you on the chest, to cue your chest-up position, and touching you at the small of your back to cue your lumbar arch. The touch at your lower back gives you a point to rotate around as you stick out your butt, the net effect of which is to contract the erector spinae muscles under your conscious direction.

Figure 4-16. Become familiar with the position the back should assume during the pull. Lifting the chest towards the hand of a coach places the upper back into extension, and arching the lower back around a hand in contact with the muscle bellies of the lumbar spinal erectors puts the lower back in extension.

The position in which the lower back muscles – the *erector spinae* group – are placed in contraction so that the lower back is arched is referred to as *lumbar extension*. Now, you will probably not be able to maintain this degree of lumbar extension at the starting position with the bar on the floor – hamstring tension will pull your pelvis and lumbar spine out of this position to some extent, relative to your flexibility, and few people are so flexible that they can maintain absolute extension at the bottom (fig. 4-17). This is not desirable anyway. An over-arched lower back is in just as bad a position for the lumbar discs and their normal weight-bearing ability as a rounded one. The desirable position is an anatomically normal lordotic curve or normal

118

anatomical arch, but to achieve this it will usually be necessary for most people to concentrate on an exaggerated extension, since most people will test the limits of their flexibility to even get correctly arched. The point here is to learn to set your back and identify and control the muscles you must use to do this, so that the correct position can be developed quickly.

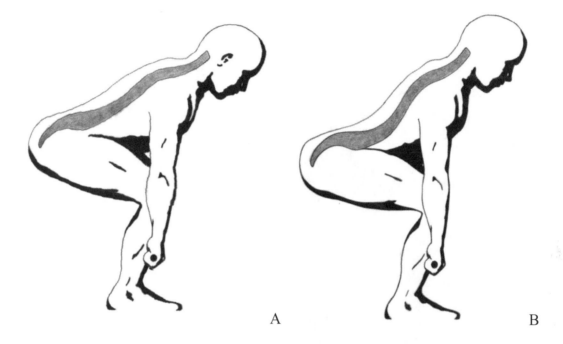

Figure 4-17. The correct starting position for the lower back is normal anatomical arch (A). A hyperextended lordotic curve (B) is both unnecessary and counterproductive, as well as being difficult for people of normal flexibility to attain. Just be aware that a hyperextended position is not actually desirable, but that it may be necessary for an inflexible person to *try* to hyperextend just to get into a correct arch.

Once you understand what your back must do, fix your eyes on a point that will put your neck in normal anatomical position, and pull a set of five. Think very hard and pay close attention to your form, concentrating especially on your low back position and keeping the bar close to your legs. If you're sure your form is good enough, add weight for a few sets until it feels like the next increase might be a problem, and that's the first deadlift workout.

The majority of the problems encountered in the deadlift will involve an incorrect lower back position. Most novice trainees that exhibit incorrect back position in the deadlift – a round lower back – are completely *unaware* of their back position. They are unable to identify the correct position, the incorrect position, or any position in between. This may be your problem if you struggle for more than a couple of workouts with your deadlift form. You may lack the "kinesthetic sense" – the ability to identify the spatial position of your body or a bodypart – required to perform the movement correctly. The cause of this may be related to visual perception: you can't see your lower back, and you haven't even attempted to look at it. You can tell you if your elbows are flexed or extended, but you have no idea if your low back is flexed or extended, probably because you haven't thought about it before, and this is because you can't see the muscles involved. Arms are in view, both in a normal field of vision and in a mirror, and it is natural to relate voluntary control to an observed, observable movement. In contrast, the lower back is behind you, and it would require a truly innovative mind to think of an excuse to look at the action of the lower back in a mirror from profile while picking up stuff in the garage.

Figure 4-18. The rounded lower back is the most common problem encountered for most people learning the deadlift.

Fixing low back problems requires placing in your mind an awareness of what the lumbar muscles do, what it feels like when they are doing these things, and what must be done to do them right every time. Repeat the action of lifting your chest and sticking your butt out several times to practice the voluntary contraction of these muscles. Just to be sure, get on your belly on the platform and do the drill described in the BACK section (page 38) of the squat chapter a few times too. Setting the back is essentially the opposite of a sit-up, which is an active flexion of the spine. Active extension of the spine activates the muscles on the other side of the torso, and thinking about it this way can help too.

Once you know what an extended low back feels like, you can get yourself into a good position at the bar by steps. Take your correct starting stance, set your back, and lower your hips into position a little at a time, going down until you feel your lower back break out of extension. Then come back up as high as you need to, to set it in extension again, and then try to get a little lower than the last time. In this incremental way you can eventually get into a reasonably good starting position at the bar.

Pulling Mechanics

The bar path in a heavy deadlift should theoretically be straight, because that is the most efficient way to move an object through space from one point to another, and vertical, because that is the direction in which gravity is pulling the barbell. Work is defined as force (the force of gravity acting on the mass of the loaded barbell) multiplied by distance (the measured distance the barbell has to travel), and can therefore be expressed in foot-pounds. The farther it has to move, the more work must be done to move it, and the shortest distance between two points is a straight line. Since there is no lateral movement necessary in a deadlift, the shortest distance between the starting point and the lockout point of a deadlift is a straight *vertical* line. A bar path that is perfectly perpendicular to the floor should be recognized as the physical model we try to approach; a good deadlifter gets very close. As with all other barbell exercises which involve standing with the bar in the hands or on the back, the bar never deviates much during its path from start to finish from the point where it is in balance: right over the middle of the foot.

The Deadlift

The deadlift places the bar in front of the legs, creating a different situation than exists in the squat, and to a lesser extent the press: the bar is not balanced on the shoulders directly over the mid-foot, with roughly equal mass on either side of the bar that can remain in balance during the lift. A deadlift must stay in balance with most of the body *behind* the bar. This creates a situation in which the center of gravity (COG) of the bar/lifter system must be considered. During the deadlift, this COG will vary slightly, and cleans and snatches are even more complicated than deadlifts due to their longer range of motion and increased musculoskeletal complexity. Light deadlifts actually balance differently than heavy deadlifts – the heavier the weight, the closer the COG of the system is to the bar, and the less important the imbalance in body mass behind the bar becomes. This allows a light deadlift to leave the ground from a position more forward of the exact middle of the foot than a heavy deadlift, and the same is true of a snatch or clean. But these variations all occur within the general confines of the middle one-third of the foot, and any movement that carries the bar either forward or behind this range of balance require a shift in foot position to compensate for it.

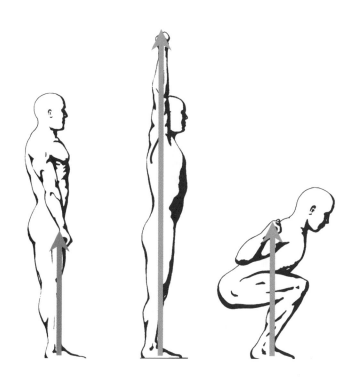

Figure 4-19. The position of the bar relative to the middle of the foot in all three main barbell exercises is the same. When the body moves the bar to or from a standing position with the bar parallel to the frontal plane of the body, the center of gravity of the system is in its best balance when the bar is directly over the middle of the foot – the geometric center of weight distribution against the floor. The heavier the weight the more nearly the COG of the system is in the same place as the bar, and the more critical this relationship becomes.

The perpendicular bar path will be the result of an initial knee extension. The hips are up above parallel in the starting deadlift position, and the correct starting position will facilitate the initial knee extension off the floor, felt as a push against the floor with the chest held up and the back flat. The deadlift uses force generated by the extension of the knees, and then the hips, to drive the bar off the floor to lockout. The force is transmitted up the rigid spine, across the scapulas to the arms and down to the bar. The scapula, a flat bone with a comparatively large surface area, interfaces with the rigid back as it lays against the ribcage, anchored in place by the extremely strong trapezius, as well as the rhomboidius and other muscles. (This is why the deadlift is such a good builder of traps, and why good deadlifters have bigger traps than other athletes.) The long bony ridge that runs down the length of the scapula, called the scapular *spine,* is the attachment point on the bone for the trapezius, and provides a large area against which the traps can pull. So the correct position from which to pull will be one where:

121

- the bar is touching the shins with the feet flat on the floor in a position that places the bar over the middle of the foot
- the back is in good lumbar and thoracic extension
- the spine of the scapula is directly over the bar
- the elbows are completely straight

This will be the correct starting position for everybody, and it will be the most efficient place for the bar to be when it leaves the floor on its way up. It is common to confuse the starting position with the *set* position, which is probably best described as the individual lifter's interpretation of the start position. The set position is where you try to put your hips before you start your pull, the action of setting the back angle immediately before you push the floor to start the transfer of force. Most people will take their grip, lower the hips into their set position, and begin the pull. This is accomplished with the greatest efficiency if the set position and the correct starting position are the same. An incorrect mental picture of the starting position and its mechanics can result in an inefficient set position.

It is interesting to note that the position of the bar in the back squat – right below the spine of the scapula – places it vertically above the same place it would be were it hanging from the arms in the deadlift, or a clean or snatch for that matter. In both movements the bar is over the middle of the foot for the entire range of motion. This duplication of mechanics occurs because of the common factors affecting the lifter/barbell system: gravity pulls straight down on the weight, and the force that overcomes it must be applied at a point as close to the weight as possible to avoid the introduction of torque, or turning force, that happens when there is distance between the two points. When the weight sits on the back, the bar rides directly over this point all the way down and up, when technique is correct. When the weight is in the hands in front of the legs, it also rides a plumb line to this point. In both cases, the center of mass of the lifter/barbell system is balanced over this point.

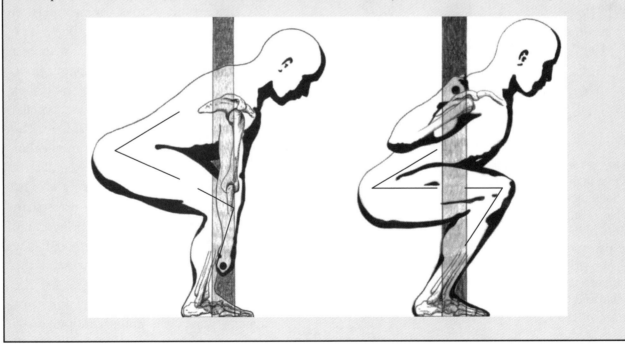

In the starting position, the shoulders will be in front of the bar, and the arms will *not* be perpendicular to the floor. The force transferred up the back is directed to the arms through the shoulder blades, and they lie at a slight angle forward, from the medial (spine) side to the lateral (arm) side. The upper arm articulates with the scapula at the most lateral end, at the ball and socket joint called the glenoid, and the front of the shoulder will be forward of the bar when the spine of the scapula is in the correct position vertically above the bar (fig. 4-20). The arms in this non-vertical position would, at the urging of gravity, very much like to swing out away from the shins to a vertical position. This would pull the center of gravity forward and cause problems, and fortunately this does not happen. The latissimus dorsi muscles have a major role in the deadlift: from the floor, the lat pulls back on the humerus to keep the arms from swinging forward away from the shins, and acts as an anchor on the upper part of the humerus to maintain the position of the bar directly under the shoulder blades until the bar crosses above the knees. The lats act in an essentially isometric way from the floor to the point where hip extension allows the arms to become vertical. At this point tension comes off the lats, and as the back becomes vertical, the arms drag the bar into the thighs as they assume an angle *behind* the vertical, opposite the starting position. During this entire process, force continues to be transferred from the hips and legs up the spine to the shoulder blades and down the arms to the bar, and the traps act as the anchor for this process.

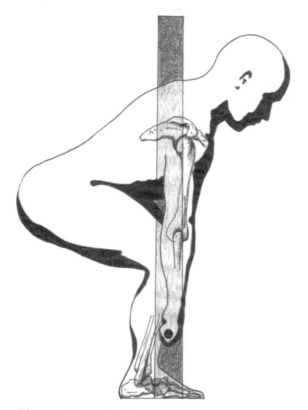

Figure 4-20. The skeletal relationships in the deadlift. The bar is touching the shins with the feet flat on the floor in a position that places the bar over the middle of the foot, the back is in good lumbar and thoracic extension, the scapula is directly over the bar, and the elbows are completely straight.

There are three angles to consider when looking at the deadlift, that result from this correct position: the angle at the knee, formed by the tibia and the femur, the angle at the hip, defined by the femur and the plane of the torso (assuming that the lumbar spine is locked in extension), and the back angle, that the plane of the torso makes with the floor (fig. 4-21). In a *correct* deadlift, the knee angle is the first to change as the bar comes off the floor, indicating that the quadriceps are working to extend the knee under load. The back should maintain the same angle with the floor as it keeps the scapulas over the bar until it passes the knees; the hamstrings "anchor" the pelvis so that this angle can be maintained (more on this later). The hip angle opens up only slightly as the femur gets more vertical. It is only after the bar clears the knees that the back angle, and consequently the hip angle, begins to change significantly (fig. 4-22). As hip extension begins to increase, the hip extensors – the glutes and hamstrings – become the predominant movers of the load, the quads having essentially finished their work of straightening the knee. The role of the back muscles during the pull is to hold the trunk rigid and the shoulder blades back in adduction so that force generated by knee and hip extension can be transferred up the back to the shoulder blades, across to the arms and down to the bar. Lockout at the top occurs when the knees and the hips reach full extension simultaneously, with the chest up and the shoulders back. All of the angles have straightened out, and the vertical line from the top to the bar has moved forward from the scapula to the point of the shoulder. If this pulling sequence is followed, the bar will come up the legs in a vertical path.

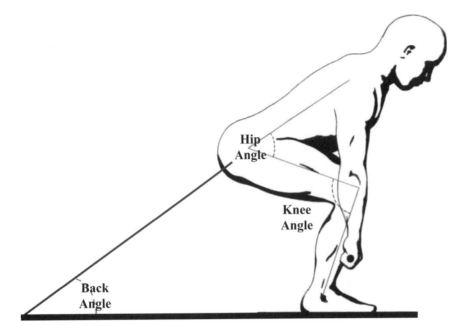

Figure 4-21. The three reference angles: knee angle, hip angle, back angle.

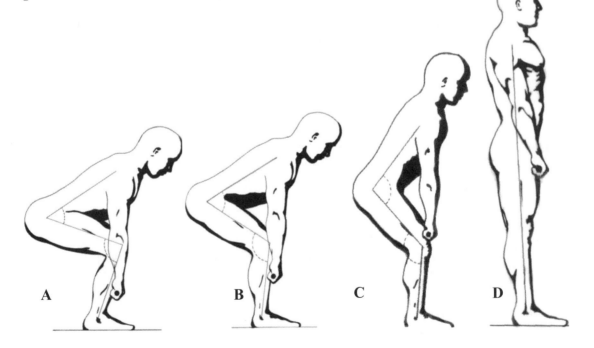

Figure 4-22. The correct sequence off the floor. A. Starting position. B. Knees extend, opening the knee angle. C. Once the bar is above the knees, the hip angle opens, carrying the bar up to the finish position, D.

If the back rounds off during this process, some of the force that would have gone to the bar gets eaten up by the lengthening erectors, and as the shoulder blades are pulled forward the load shifts forward to a mechanically bad position. If the weight is sufficiently heavy, the rounded back cannot be re-straightened and the deadlift cannot be locked out; the spinal erectors are designed to hold an extended position isometrically, not actively extend a flexed spine under load in a vertical position. The knees and hips are already extended – the knees in this position are straight and the pelvis is in line with the femurs – and their extensors cannot be used since they are already fully contracted.

Figure 4-23. A rounded back is difficult to straighten when the weight is heavy. The muscles that hold the spine in extension are postural and are not designed to change the relative positions of the vertebrae; their job is to maintain extension, not actively extend under compressive loading. If lumbar extension cannot be maintained, this position is usually the result. The hip and knee extensors have finished their job, and the low back cannot be straightened under load. Many heavy deadlifts have been missed this way.

The question of exactly what these three angles should be must be answered for each person individually, since it will depend on individual anthropometry. Tall people with long femurs, long tibias, and relatively short torsos will have a different starting position than short people with long torsos and short legs. Each person will have a different set of knee, hip, and back angles, but the correct starting position for everyone will have the previously discussed things in common: the shoulders will be slightly in front of the bar, since this is the position of the shoulder where the scapulas are plumb to the bar, the bar will be touching the shins, and the hips will therefore be in the position that best enables the knee extension that pushes the bar away from the floor. Of the three angles, the back angle will exhibit the most individual variability. The knee and hip angles are controlled by the lengths of the femur and the tibia, the collective lengths of which, are bent at the knee. Three inches added to the back would be nearly twice as important as three inches added to the legs, unless it is all added to only one of the bones. For example, our tall, long-legged person will have a more horizontal back angle, the back more parallel to the floor, than a person with short legs, who can easily get his chest up at a steeper angle to the floor.

Arm length must also be considered when analyzing these angles. Very long arms tend to mitigate the effects of a short torso, in that long arms allow for a more vertical back in a lifter who would otherwise be more horizontal, but this is true for all back lengths. Conversely, short arms and a short torso would make for a nearly perfectly horizontal back, and very little can be done to improve the mechanics of a start position for a person with this anthropometry. Arm length does not usually vary enough to cancel out the additive effects of all the other segments, since there are three segments that can be weird all together, but very short arms are not usually found on very good deadlifters.

Figure 4-24. The Travelsteads. Dwayne (left) is 6'5" with a very short torso, long legs and a slight kyphosis. Hunter (right) is, thankfully, more normally proportioned. Both are in the correct starting position.

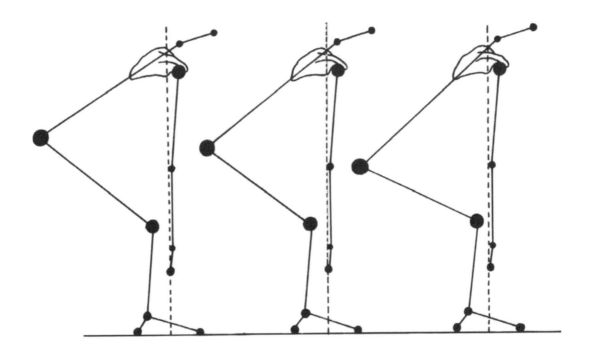

Figure 4-25. The effect of different variations of back/femur dimensions on back angle in the starting position. From left to right, back length increases as femur length decreases.

Most of the problems you will have with deadlift form can be analyzed with a good understanding of pulling mechanics. For example, the problem of lowering the bar with a round back, caused by unlocking the knees first: the down phase is the exact reverse of the pull – if the last thing that happens at the top of the deadlift is hip extension with a back locked in extension, the first part of lowering the bar *has* to be hip "un-extension" with a back locked in extension (fig. 4-26). This movement is eccentric hip extension, the "negative" part of the lift; the butt travels back with the lower back locked, closing the hip angle and using the hamstrings and glutes eccentrically, under contraction as they lengthen. As the bar slides down the thigh, further closing the hip angle, it reaches a point as it passes the knee where the bar is back to a position directly under the shoulder blades, and the knee angle begins to close more than the hip. As the bar is lowered past the knees, they bend and the quadriceps and hamstrings do their eccentric work as the bar gets to the floor. This sequence of movements, the opposite of the pulling-up sequence, allows the bar to drop down in a vertical line.

Any deviation from this order will not work. If the knees move forward first when lowering the bar, they will be in front of the bar, and the bar cannot go straight down since it has to go forward to get around the knees (fig. 4-27). Your knees can move forward only so far before your heels get pulled up and you start to fall forward, so you round your back to let the bar go forward far enough to clear your knees.

From off of the floor, if you attempt to extend your hips first the result will be a non-vertical bar path. This happens when you lift your chest first (different than "*keeping* the chest up" – keeping the back angle the same off the floor), opening the hip angle first and shifting the scapulas to a position behind the bar. If this happens, the bar will pull into the shins and follow their forward angle out around your knees, which have not pulled back out of the way. This actually occurs only with very light weights; heavy weights – being more affected by gravity, which acts vertically – like to move in straight lines. Since the bar stays under the scapulas, if you pull heavy weights chest-first you will be dragging the bar back into your shins, and the blood on the bar will tell you that this is wrong. But when the knee angle opens first, like it should, the shins get more vertical and move back relative to the front of the foot, allowing the bar to travel in a vertical path up the leg. If the knee angle changes first, the bar can move in a straight line up, the way heavy bars like to move. If you feel the weight go to your toes, or if your heels come up, you know what you're doing wrong. Get your weight back on your heels, off your toes, and pull the weight back toward your shins on the way up as you push the floor. This forces the bar back into the correct path that lets your knees straighten out and allows your quadriceps extension to start the deadlift correctly. It is also helpful to think about pushing the bar back into your legs with your lats, reinforcing the close-to-the-shin position a second way (fig. 4-29).

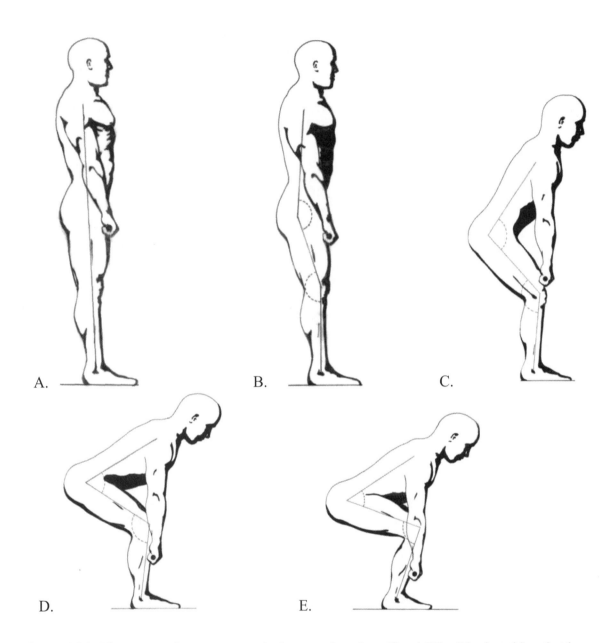

Figure 4-26. The correct down sequence is the opposite of up (fig. 4-22). The last thing that happens on the way up is the first thing that happens on the way down: hips unlock backwards and lower the bar to below the knees, then knees unlock and lower the bar to the floor.

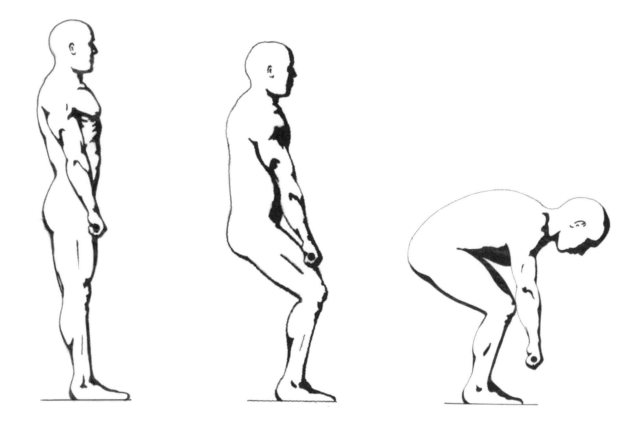

Figure 4-27. This is the wrong way to set the bar down. The knees have moved forward first, and this places them in a tragic position where kneecaps often pay a high price. And if the kneecaps somehow remain unscathed, the lower back might not.

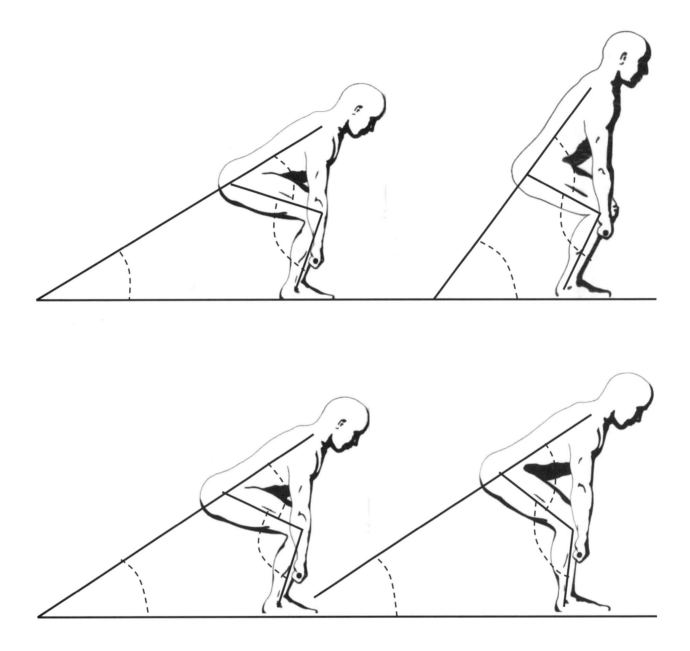

Figure 4-28. The order in which the angles open up off the floor is important to correct technique. When the hip angle opens first (top), the bar must travel forward to clear the knees, and usually the shins get scraped when this happens. The correct order – knees first, then hips (bottom) – allows for a vertical bar path.

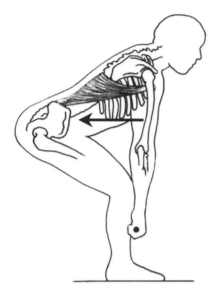

Figure 4-29. It may be necessary to think about the active use of the lats to hold the bar back against the legs. The lats do this anyway as a part of their job of maintaining scapular position directly over the bar, but if need be, actively think about using them to shove the bar back into the legs. This sometimes helps them discover the role they play in the movement, especially if the bar is often too far from the shins off the floor. Even the simple act of rolling the bar back to the shins to get in the correct starting position uses the lats, and this cue will be useful in fixing the problem.

When the weight gets heavy, it is common for the bar to come away from your shins before it even leaves the floor. When this happens, your hips will have lifted too, also before the load moves. Using our pulling model, it is apparent that when this occurs, the knee angle has opened, the hip angle has closed, and the back angle has become more horizontal, all before the load moves, giving the lats more work than they can do (fig. 4-30). In this situation, the muscles that extend your knees, i.e. your quadriceps, have done so, but have not moved any weight *while* doing so. In opening the knee angle unloaded – pushing your butt up in the air without moving the bar – they have avoided participating in the lift and placed the entire job on your hip extensors, which now have even more to do since they must move through more angle to extend. In addition, since your back angle is now almost parallel to the floor, your back muscles are in a position of decreased mechanical advantage: they have to stay in isometric contraction longer, rotate through more angle, *and* at a position of maximum torque. The quadriceps must participate in the deadlift properly in order for the movement to be safe and efficient.

The reason for this is not immediately apparent. Raising the hips before the chest is a common enough problem in the deadlift, the clean, and all other pulling exercises from the floor that we should analyze it here. The quadriceps straighten the knees, and if the back angle stays constant, the bar comes vertically up the shins. But it is the hip extensors – the glutes and hamstrings – acting as stabilizers during the initial phase of the pull, that maintain the back angle by exerting tension on the pelvis from the posterior, at their insertion points on the ischium and the ilium. If the spinal erectors keep the back flat, the hip extensors "anchor" the back angle by pulling down on the distal pelvis. The pelvis and the spine are locked in line by the erectors, so the hamstrings actually keep the chest up and the back angle constant. This enables the scapulas to stay over the bar, allowing the quad work of straightening the knee to lift the bar off the ground. During this phase the hip angle will open slightly, but the back angle should stay constant relative to the floor. It is only after the bar crosses the knee that the hip extensors begin to actually *change* the back angle by actively opening the hip angle. So, the function of the hamstrings and glutes changes during the pull: initially they act to maintain the back angle as the quads

131

straighten the knees, then they change the back angle as they extend the hips and finish the pull (fig. 4-31).

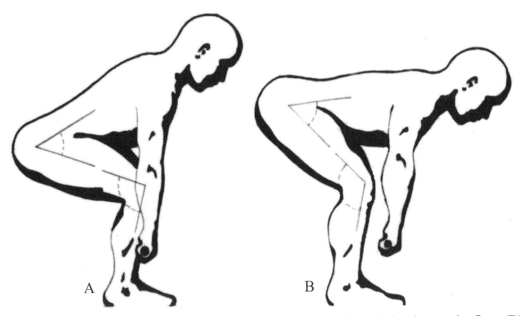

Figure 4-30. When the hip angle closes and the knee angle opens *before* the bar leaves the floor (B), the quadriceps have avoided their part of the work. This leaves the bar away from the shins, and the hamstrings and glutes to do all the work of lifting the weight (C). Technique errors that involve one group of muscles failing to make their contribution to an exercise are a common phenomenon in barbell training.

If the hamstrings fail to maintain the back angle, the butt comes up and the shoulders drift forward, allowing the quads to avoid their share of the work since the knees have extended but the bar has not moved. The bar, however, must still be pulled, so the hip extensors end up doing it all, and in a much more inefficient way. They should be working through both the initial phase of the pull *with* the quadriceps and through the lockout by themselves, instead of having to open the whole angle at the end of the pull. Either way, the hip extensors work, but their job is easier if the initial work is isometric and the last part is active concentric hip extension, instead of the whole movement being a long, mechanically hard hip extension.

The problem is not that the hamstrings are not strong enough – after all, they're strong enough to lock out the weight without the help of the quads when it's done wrong. The problem is one of motor learning, teaching the muscles to move the bones correctly, in the right order at the right time. The only way to correctly address this problem is to take weight off the bar and make sure you do the deadlift with proper form, with all the angles correct, so that all the muscular contributors to the pull learn to do their job in the right order.

An interesting thing happens when all the pulling mechanics are correct: the deadlift feels "shorter," like the distance the bar has moved is reduced when compared to an uncorrected, sloppy deadlift. It obviously hasn't, but the increased efficiency obtained from the improvement in pulling mechanics is significant enough that the perception is one of a shorter movement. This is larger due to the reduction in extraneous hip and knee movement, and a consequent reduction in the time the lift actually takes.

Most people are reluctant to keep the bar close enough to the legs during the pull, as well as when setting it down, and for that matter before the bar leaves the ground. This is often due to the fear of marring the beauty of the shins and thighs. In addition to the above analysis of the angles involved in the pull, consider this: the further the bar is from the place on the ground that the force is being applied, the longer the lever arm along the back from load to hips. This inefficiency gets multiplied quickly, and it doesn't take much distance away from your shins to drastically increase the effective weight of the bar. This is true both going up and coming down: if the bar needs to be rolled back to the shins very much between each rep, something is wrong with the way you set it down.

Torque, or rotating force, is at its maximum when applied at 90 degrees to the thing being rotated. Think about turning a nut with a wrench; a weird angle to the nut is not strong, and the strongest position is when your hand is at a right angle to the wrench. This is why a mechanic always wants to have enough room to get at right angles to a stuck bolt. The same is true for the deadlift: the force against the lower back is highest (and most efficient at keeping the bar where it is) when the back is parallel to the floor, and decreases as the chest gets higher and the back becomes more vertical. Turning inefficiency is precisely what we *do* want in the deadlift: the reduced ability of the weight to adversely affect back angle.

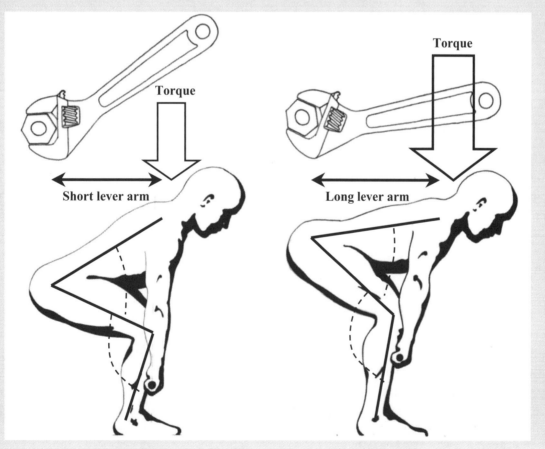

Torque also increases with distance away from the thing being turned. A grip on the wrench turns the bolt easier the further it is from the bolt. A longer wrench works better than a shorter one, and a long cheater-pipe slipped over the end of a wrench works even better than that. This fact applies to all situations where a weight is lifted by the back, i.e. pulling or squatting.

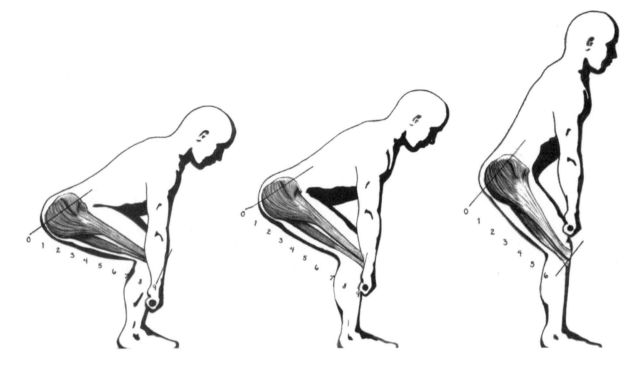

Figure 4-31. The hip extensors – glutes and hamstrings, and to a lesser extent, the adductors – work initially only to maintain the back angle as the bar rises from the floor. After the bar rises past the knee they continue to contract, but at this point they begin to actively open the hip angle.

One of the most common technique errors in the deadlift is a starting position that holds the back in a too-vertical position. This is a set position problem, a misunderstanding of the correct starting position that may have a couple of different causes. It may be due to confusion about the role of the back muscles in the deadlift. In an attempt to reduce shear, or sliding forces, between the vertebral segments, the idea might be to make the back as vertical as possible so that most of the force on the vertebrae becomes compressive rather than shear. But shear does not occur when the spinal erectors do their job and lock the vertebrae in place. This is why the deadlift is a back exercise. Strong erectors protect against this much more effectively than what is actually an unnatural pulling position ever could. When the back functions as a rigid segment, the only torque is that which affects the hips, produced by the lever arm formed by the distance between the load and the mid-foot.

It may be the idea that the deadlift is somehow just a squat with the barbell in the hands, and that driving with the legs is best accomplished with a more squat-like starting position. The deadlift is not a squat with the bar in the hands: it is a pull, a completely different piece of mechanics. And if it *was* a squat, you'd want to be as high as you could get, because you can half-squat more weight than you can from a deep position – you don't have to travel as far. It may be due to the idea that the weight on the bar should not be allowed to pull you forward, and *back* is therefore the direction the bar should be pulled; the bar cannot be pulled back *through* the legs. Or it may be that an observation of the Sumo-style deadlift as performed by competitive powerlifters has created an incorrect impression of the proper back angle in the conventional deadlift. Sumo technique employs a much wider stance, which places the shoulder blades plumb to the bar with a steeper back angle. In an attempt to assume this position with a close stance, the hips are lowered to a point where the angle is obtained, but only at the expense of placing the scapulae behind the bar. Since the bar cannot leave the floor in this position, when the pull starts the hips will rise up and the back angle will adjust itself to the point where the scapulae are plumb to the bar, and only then can the bar break off the floor. The problem with this is the tendency for the shins to pull back from the bar as the knees and hips adjust, leaving the bar out in front of the shins and forward of the mid-foot.

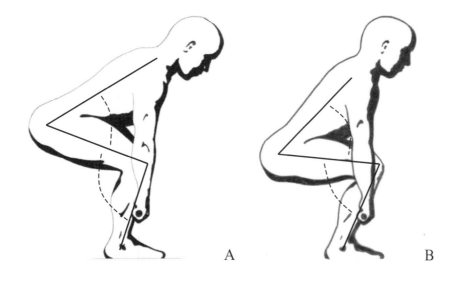

Figure 4-32. The correct starting position (A), and the position that often gets used instead (B). The correct position reflects proper pulling mechanics; from this position the bar can leave the ground and travel in a straight path up to lockout. The bar cannot leave the ground from the incorrect position with anything more than a warmup weight, yet many people think it is the correct position from which to pull. What actually happens is that the lifter "sets up" in position B, thinking that the bar leaves the ground from there, but the hips are raised into position A before the bar leaves the ground. Video analysis of any heavy deadlift (or clean or snatch) clearly shows that this is always the case. This shift from set-up to pull leaves the bar out in front of the shins as the knees pull back, producing a bar path that curves back toward the legs before it becomes vertical. The most efficient pull is a straight pull, and the closer to this model your pulling mechanics allows you to be, the better.

It is an error in understanding to try to assume a back position more vertical than the relationship between the scapula and the bar allows. The scapula will be plumb to the bar when it leaves the ground, and an artificially vertical back angle will decay as the pull is started, leaving the bar out in front of the shins when it finally clears the ground. The best position that can be assumed at the start is one already described, the bar over the mid-foot and the scapulae directly over the bar. The closer the distance between the point where the scapula is vertical to the bar and the point where the force is applied to the ground – the middle of the foot – the easier it is to pull, and the closest it can get to this place is touching your shins with the flat back at the correct angle.

Make sure the bar is touching your skin or your socks before it leaves the floor. It is not necessary to bump your shins with the bar, or scrape the meat off of them on the way up. Good control of the weight is necessary to avoid this, and it should be avoided or sores can get established on your shins that will be a problem for a long time – every time you deadlift you break the sore open and make a big mess on your socks or the bar. Sweats eliminate this problem, and allow the bar to slide up the thighs better as well.

The knurl of the bar might also be a problem if it extends in too close to the middle. A standard Olympic weightlifting bar has an opening in the knurl that is about 16.5" wide, as are most power bars, and this is usually sufficient to accommodate all but the tallest people. Some bars are manufactured with no thought given to the possibility that they might someday be used to deadlift. Don't use these bars. Find one that works correctly, or find a gym that has the proper equipment.

Foot placement has been discussed above. In a deadlift, you are pushing the floor, not lowering the hips as in a squat, and the stance is placed accordingly. If your feet are too wide, your legs will either rub your hands on the way up or force your grip out wider to avoid being rubbed. The wider the grip, the farther the bar has to travel. The grip and the stance are interrelated in that your stance must be set to allow the best grip, and the best grip for the deadlift is one that allows your arms to hang as straight down from the shoulders as possible in order to make the shortest possible distance from the floor to lockout for the bar. Too wide a stance necessitates too wide a grip and confers no mechanical advantage. If you're thinking that since we squat with a wider stance, we should pull with a wider stance, don't think that. We are not squatting; we are pushing the floor with the feet, an entirely different thing.

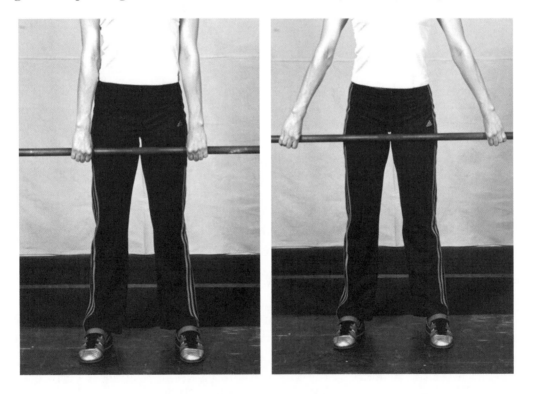

Figure 4-33. The difference in bar height produced by grip width. A narrower grip reduces the distance the bar has to travel.

Too narrow a stance is less harmful, but is rather pointless, and is not a thing encountered very often. There have been great deadlifters – Vince Anello and George Hechter come to mind – who pulled with a narrow stance, with heels nearly touching. This is called a "frog stance", and

Figure 4-34. Vince Anello's rather unique deadlifting stance. It worked well for him, with an official 821 lb. in competition, 880 in training.

some lifters can use it effectively. And a variation in toe angle is quite useful for some lifters, because a more toes-out stance enables a better knees-out position. This makes a better back angle possible – and as a result an easier placement of the scapulas over the bar and the bar over the middle of the foot – for the same reason that it enables better depth in the squat.

The easiest way to identify and reproduce the stance every time is to note the position of the bar and its knurling marks over the shoelaces as you look down at your feet. Use this landmark on your shoes to help quickly and consistently get to the same stance.

Figure 4-35. The stance can be easily duplicated every time by establishing a reference position for the bar against the shoelaces when looking down at your feet.

The Little Details

While we're on the floor here, breathing should be discussed. Inhale while the bar is on the floor, not while supporting a heavy weight at the top. Remember from our discussion during the squat the role of air and pressure in trunk support. This applies especially to the deadlift. Review this now, please, if you are not familiar with this concept.

A set of deadlifts should *start* at the floor, meaning that each rep begins and ends at the bottom, the back getting set and a new breath taken between reps while the bar is on the floor. Many people like to pull the first rep off of the floor, breathe at the top at lockout, and finish the set by bouncing the bar off the floor for the remaining reps. This is bad. It is easier to do the set this way, true, but easy and strong are usually opposing concepts. You need to develop the ability to set your back and control your position each time you pull the bar, because this uses precisely the skills and the muscles you are doing this exercise to develop. The point here, as is so often the case in the weight room, is not to simply *do* the deadlifts, but to *get strong by doing* deadlifts. They have to be done right, not just done. Also, any back position problems that develop during the set cannot be addressed when doing them with a bounce – the only place to do this would be at the top, and the back is under load at the top so the position cannot be reset there. If your back begins to round during the set, it tends to stay round or get worse unless it is reset, which must be done at the bottom when the bar is sitting on the floor and the back can move into the correct position unloaded.

One of the key features of the deadlift is that it requires the production of force from a dead stop. In contrast, a key feature of efficient squatting is the use of the controlled "bounce", which takes advantage of the stretch reflex that occurs at the transition between an eccentric and a concentric contraction. Any muscular contraction is more powerful if it is immediately preceded by a stretch, as always occurs when you jump. One of the reasons a heavy deadlift is so brutally hard is that it starts up out of the bottom without the benefit of the bounce that helps the squat change the direction of the force from down to up. Up to down without a bounce is quite a bit harder. If a bounce is incorporated into all the reps of a set of deadlifts except the first one, much of the value of doing them is lost.

There are a couple of ways to think about "setting" the back before the pull starts. For some people, it is sufficient to think about arching the lower back. This is, after all, most of what setting the back is about. But really and truly, you "set" the *entire torso* before you pull, and you may find it helpful to think about it in this way – squeezing low back and abs and chest all at the same time on a big breath, not as separate muscle groups but taken as a whole unit. This increases the effectiveness of the Valsalva and causes all the muscles participating in it to contract harder and provide more stability.

Eyeball position is often overlooked when assuming the starting position. If you look straight down at the floor when you pull, the bar will usually swing out away from your legs. It is easier to keep your chest up and upper back tight if your eyes are focused on a point on the floor (if you're in a big room) or on the wall facing the platform that places your neck in a neutral position. If the floor is your gaze point, look about 10 feet in front of you. Looking up is not any better for the deadlift than it is for the squat, as discussed at length in that chapter. Actually, looking straight down is not terribly detrimental to the squat, but it will make the deadlift harder most of the time. The function of correct eye gaze direction is to keep the neck in a safe, useful position during the movement, to aid in placing the back at the correct angle for the mechanics of the lift, and to provide a visual reference for balance purposes. *Up* never works well except for the bench press.

Arms must stay straight during the deadlift. There is no better way to produce a really decent elbow injury than to let 500 lbs. straighten out your elbows for you. The physics of this is not difficult to understand. The force produced by the hips and legs is transmitted up the rigid torso, across the scapulas and down the arms to the bar. Seen from the side, the shoulders will be in front of the bar and the arms themselves will not be vertical, because it is the *scapulas* that are vertically above the bar, not the glenoid joint of the shoulder that would make the arms vertical. Force is transmitted vertically between the scapula and the bar, and tension from the lats keeps the bar from swinging away from the legs until the knees are crossed, when the arms begin to assume a vertical position. As the chest is lifted and the scapulas retract at the finish of the pull, the arms shift to a position slightly behind the vertical because the bar is on the thigh in front of the shoulders.

In the same way the back must stay locked to facilitate force transfer, the elbows must stay straight during this whole process too. The bent elbow is a thing that can be straightened out, if the weight is heavy enough, and the straightening-out is done by force that should have gotten to the bar. Unlike a rounded back, a heavy deadlift can be finished with bent elbows, but there is large potential for injury. The elbow is flexed by the muscles of the forearm, the brachialis, and, in the supine arm, the bicep. If your elbows are bent, these muscles are working unnecessarily, since they add nothing to the lift, and in fact bent elbows actually increase the distance the bar has to travel by causing the bar to lock out at an unnecessarily higher position. It is important to convince yourself that your arms are not involved in the deadlift, and that straight elbows are the best way to pull. This will also be important when you learn how to power clean.

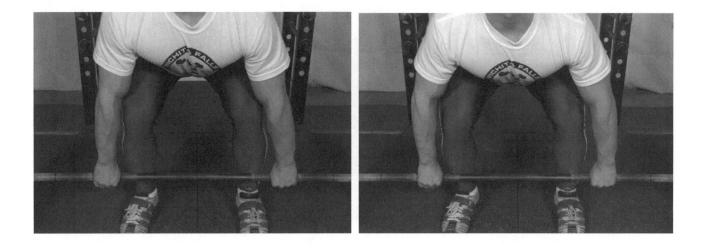

Figure 4-36. Bent elbows in the deadlift are the fault of the part of the brain that tells you that "All things must be lifted with the arms". The only function of the arms is to connect the shoulders to the bar; straight-arms must be learned early and well.

Once the bar has completed the trip up the legs, there are several ways to finish the deadlift, only one of them correct. The bar is locked out by lifting your chest, pulling your shoulders back, and bringing your knees, hips, and lumbar spine into extension simultaneously. Many people insist on exaggerating some of these things, causing them to perform the movement inefficiently and, if carried to the extreme, unsafely.

For instance, it is unnecessary to roll your shoulders up and back at the top, overemphasizing the shrug. The deadlift is not finished until the shoulders are back and the chest is up, and finishing this part of the movement is important. But the traps get sufficient work from heavy deadlifts without attempting to add additional trap work by exaggerating the shrug, and possibly causing a neck injury in the process. Heavy barbell shrugs are a good assistance exercise for an advanced lifter that knows how to perform them correctly, but novice deadlifters have no business trying to combine deadlifts with incorrectly performed barbell shrugs.

Likewise, it is unnecessary and unwise to exaggerate the hip-extension part of the lockout (fig. 4-37). Since it is virtually impossible to hyperextend your hip joint in an upright position with a loaded bar on the anterior side of the thighs, what actually happens is that you hyperextend the *lumbar spine*, sometimes as almost a separate movement after the deadlift is actually finished. This is a very dangerous habit to acquire: uneven loading of the lumbar discs is as harmful from the posterior as it is from the anterior.

Figure 4-37. An over-zealous lockout that produces lumbar hyperextension is both dangerous and unnecessary.

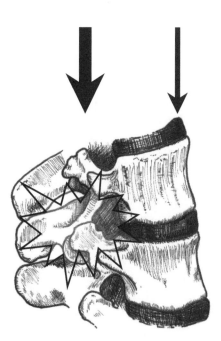

Figure 4-38. Unnecessary arching, as in Figure 4-37, asymmetrically loads the spine to the posterior, setting up the conditions that may result in disc injury.

Figure 4-39. Our very strong friend Phil Anderson has forgotten to lock his knees at the top. The fix for this is better coaching and a cue to "Stand up!" After total knee replacements at the age of 48, Phil deadlifted 525 – this time correctly.

Knees sometimes get forgotten in the rush to lock everything out from the hips up. Many contest deadlifts have been red-lighted because of failure to lock out the knees. This always produces a flurry of bad language from the lifter when the lights are explained to him, because anybody who can lock out a 622 lb. deadlift can also straighten out his knees the final 3 degrees. Once the deadlift is finished at the top, it requires essentially no work, only remembering to do it, to lock your knees out. Make sure you are finishing each deadlift with locked knees, and remind yourself occasionally to check them. This last little movement is an important part of the lift, even if a powerlifting meet is not the goal of your training.

Get in the habit of holding the bar locked out at the top for just a second before you set it down, so that a stable position is achieved first. If you are in the process of falling backwards as you attempt to lower the bar, there will be a significant wreck. The bar should only be lowered *after* it is locked out and motionless for just a second, indicating a correctly finished lift with the bar under control.

Setting the bar down fast in the deadlift is actually okay. Since the deadlift starts as a concentric movement, much of the effect of the deadlift is due to the hard initial position and the lack of help from a stretch reflex during the lift, as discussed above. Setting it down slowly will make it harder, and some people might benefit from the extra work, but the emphasis in the deadlift is picking up heavy weights. As the weight increases, bar speed will decrease with the difficulty. Setting it down slowly uses up too much gas that could be better used picking up your next rep. As long as some modicum of control is exercised, it can be dropped as fast as you are capable of doing safely, with the back in good position according to our previous analysis. Going down fast with poor control is, of course, hard on your kneecaps and shins. And depending on the type of plates being used and the nature of the platform surface, a poorly controlled bounce can cause problems. But in general, a deadlift can, and probably should, go down faster than it comes up.

A platform is a good thing to have in your weight room: multiple layers of plywood or particle board glued and screwed together, with rubber mats under the area of plate contact or the whole thing surfaced with rubber; horse trailer mats work just fine and are relatively cheap (fig. 4-40). Failing that, rubber mats placed under the plates on the floor will work, but the room really needs to be set up correctly to train the pulling movements. Bumper plates, a necessary expense for the clean and the snatch, can be used for the deadlift as well, but the more reasonably priced ones take up so much space on the bar (they are very *wide*) that iron plates will eventually need to be used as you get stronger. Your gym should be equipped for this. And if your gym is one of those places that doesn't allow deadlifting, find a better gym.

Figure 4-40. The basic components of a cheap and durable training platform. Three layers of 4 foot x 8 foot x ¾ inch plywood or particle board laid in alternate directions each layer, and covered with horse trailer mats provide a durable, inexpensive training station. It works well on a concrete floor. This particular platform has been in service in a commercial gym for 12 years.

Straps will be useful on occasion. Use the kind made from seat belts (it's probably best not to take the ones out of your car for this purpose), or other nylon-type strapping material, about 1 ½ inches wide. Cotton will not work, no matter how thick and strong it looks; it will tear at an inconvenient time. They can either be left as simple pieces of strap material, about two feet long, or the ends can be tacked together. Straps go around your hands, not your wrists. And do not use the kind with a loop sewed into one end, where the rest of the strap passes through the loop. These will continue to tighten on your wrist during the set. They are never really secure with a heavy weight, tend to wear out quickly and tear during a heavy set, and will never stay in adjustment.

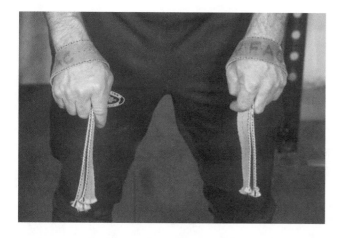

Figure 4-41. Our favorite straps are simple pieces of seat belt webbing or other 1 ½ inch strapping. They are 2 feet long, never made of cotton, and ride down on the hand – not the wrist.

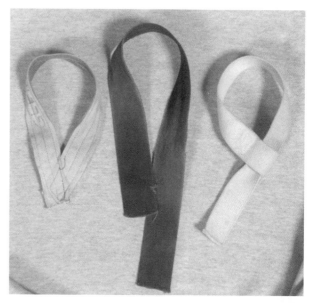

Figure 4-42. Several types of straps are commonly seen in the gym. The kind most commonly available commercially (right) are junk: the design does not work well, they do not last long, they hurt the hands, and they can break with heavy weight. The black ones in the center have been in use for 23 years, and have never failed.

Finally, this method of learning the deadlift is designed to be used in a sports conditioning program – it is not a powerlifting course. The sport of powerlifting has its own experts, and these guidelines are meant for general strength training purposes. The author was a moderately good deadlifter during his career in the sport, and learned many valuable lessons about strength off the floor during this time.

Among them is that not everybody needs to do heavy deadlifts. People with injured backs, that are prone to re-injury, and people that cannot learn to perform the movement correctly don't need to deadlift with maximum loads. It's better if you can, since functional back strength is best built with functional back work, and the heavier you pull the stronger you'll get. But if you are not powerlifting, you don't have to do limit singles. From a training standpoint there is little to be gained by doing 1 rep max deadlifts, and 1RM can be inferred from a 5RM if obtaining this information is somehow necessary. That having been said, deadlifts are still the best way to develop useful back strength. Apply yourself to learning them correctly.

Non-dominant Hand

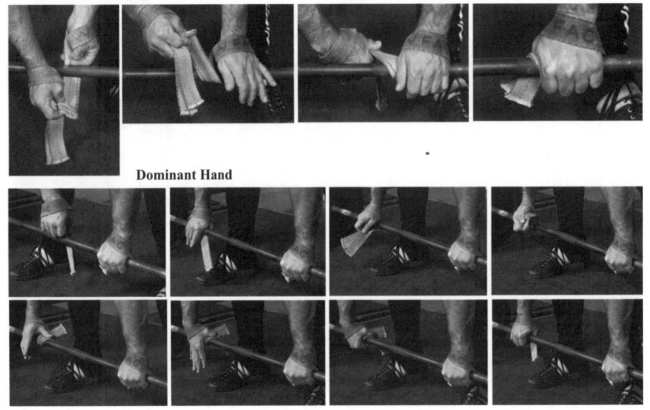

Dominant Hand

Figure 4-43. Using the straps is sometimes a challenge for novice lifters. Here's how it's done.

Figure 4-44. The deadlift.

"Loyalty to petrified opinion never broke a chain or freed a human soul."

Mark Twain

The Press

Figure 5-1. Bill Starr, the father of strength coaching, presses 350 in the gym.

Figure 5-2. Tommy Suggs demonstrates a moderate amount of layback in this 1968 National Championships photo. The press was eliminated from Olympic competition due to "judging difficulties" – a reluctance on the part of the international governing body to establish and enforce adequate criteria about layback. It is likely that the press was actually eliminated due to a desire to shorten the meet.

The Press is the oldest upper body exercise using a barbell. The day the barbell was invented, the guy who invented it figured out a way to pick it up and shove it over his head. After all, it *is* the logical thing to do with a weight.

Equipment has changed quite a bit over the past hundred or so years. We now have barbells that load with plates, racks to set our bars in that adjust to various heights so that we don't always have to clean them to our shoulders first, and even plates made out of rubber in case we need to drop the weight. But pressing the barbell overhead is still the most useful upper body exercise in the weight room.

Back then, the standard test of upper body strength was the Press, or more correctly, the Two-hands Press. The popularity of the bench press has changed this, to the detriment of athletes and lifters that never obtain the benefits of this more balanced exercise. Bench pressing, a contest lift in powerlifting, actually became popular among bodybuilders first, when large pectorals ("pecs," or maybe "chesticles") became the fashion in physique contests starting in the 1950's. Powerlifting incorporated the bench press as a standard contest lift in the mid-1960's, thus diminishing the importance of the overhead version of the press among those training primarily for strength. The final nail in the coffin was the elimination of the Clean and Press from Olympic weightlifting competition in 1972. The exercise has continued its decline in both popularity and familiarity, to the extent that today one is quite likely to hear a seated behind-the-neck press described as a "military press" by the personal trainers in big-box gyms.

So, a terminology lesson is in order. A "press" refers to a movement performed while standing, whereby a weight is extended to arms length overhead with the use of the shoulders and arms only. If a barbell is used in both hands, it is properly a two-hands press, although it is understood that the unqualified term "press" refers to a barbell press using both hands. Any deviation from this description warrants a qualifier. A Seated Press would be a two-hands barbell press done in a

148

Figure 5-3. Various pressing exercises. A. Press. B. Behind-the-neck press. C. Seated press. D. Seated behind-the-neck press. E. Bench press. F. Dumbbell press. G. Dumbbell bench press. H. Military press (heels together). I. Push press.

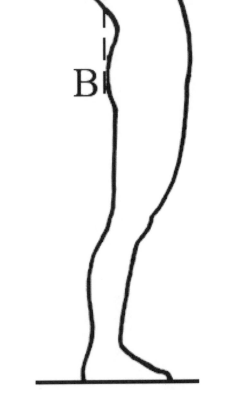

seated position (an exercise that requires a special bench to be performed, unless the lifter is capable of cleaning the weight and sitting down with it on his shoulders, and then lowering it to the floor after the set). A Dumbbell Press is a standing two-hands movement, unless the one-hand version is specified. Any press performed supine on a bench is a Bench Press, the barbell being understood as the equipment unless a Dumbbell Bench Press is specified. If the barbell is used behind the neck, this is part of the name. A Behind-the-Neck Press is a harder movement than a press; still harder is a Seated Behind-the-Neck Press. "Military Press" refers to the strictest form of the exercise. A Military Press is performed without any bend of the hips or back used to start the weight. The use of the legs as an aid in starting the bar off the shoulders means that a Push Press has been performed.

One of the reasons the Press was eliminated from Olympic weightlifting was the difficulty most judges had in bringing themselves to red-light an excessively weird press. Referred to by the term "Olympic Press," the extreme form of this movement was a "Continental Press," started from the shoulders by the use of a combination of a back flexion from hyperextension and a whipping of the hips. Some very adept practitioners could lean back to a point almost equivalent to a bench press, rendering the description of the lift as a "press from the shoulders" rather inaccurate. An inexperienced or unconditioned lifter attempting this movement ran the risk of a spinal hyperextension injury, although such injuries were not that common. Experienced, conditioned lifters had very strong abs. Figure 5-4 illustrates a method of judging the press that could have solved a lot of problems in 1972, had there been a serious desire to do so.

Figure 5-4. Judging criteria for the press. The position of the most anterior aspect of the armpit (A), the most posterior aspect of the buttocks (B), and the plane formed by a straight line between these two points. The movement of that plane to a position of "A" behind the vertical would constitute excessive layback.

The Press, performed in rather strict fashion (although not so strict as a true Military Press) is the most useful upper-body exercise for sports conditioning. This is primarily because it is not *just* an upper-body exercise. Except for powerlifting and swimming, all sports that require the use of upper body strength transmit that strength along a kinetic chain that starts at the ground. Any time an athlete pushes against an opponent, throws an implement, uses a racquet or club on a ball, or transmits force to an object, that force starts at the ground. The kinetic chain – the parts of the body involved in the transmission of force from the places where it is generated to the places where it is applied – starts at the ground and ends at the bar in the hands when performing a press. The kinetic chain in a bench press, in contrast, begins at the point on the bench where the upper back interfaces with it, and ends at the bar in the hands. Proficient bench pressers involve the legs all the way down to the ground, thereby adding to the length of the kinetic chain, but can still perform a significant percentage of their best lift with their feet up on the bench, or even up in the air. And even a very proficient bench presser, using the trunk in as efficient a manner as possible, is still lying on a bench, not balancing the load *and* using his entire body against only the ground as he presses.

Basic bench press performance is different from the press in that it is primarily an upper body exercise. It is an unusual thing in sport to actually place the back against an immovable object and use it to push against. The press involves the entire body down to the feet against the floor, using all the trunk musculature and the hips and legs to stabilize the body while the shoulders, upper chest, and arms press the bar overhead. The length of this kinetic chain, from overhead at full arms length down to the floor, is the longest possible for the human body. This distance, essentially a long lever arm, produces a lot of potential torque if it is not well controlled by the muscles at the core of the body. And this makes the press an excellent tool for training core stability.

Figure 5-5. The kinetic chain of the press compared to that of the bench press.

It differs also in that the bench press begins with an eccentric contraction, or "negative," while the press starts from the shoulders with a concentric contraction. The bench press has the advantage of using a stretch reflex out of the bottom to assist the concentric contraction, the up phase of the lift. In contrast, the press, like the deadlift, starts the drive up from the shoulders with the bar at rest; the hardest part of the movement is the first part of the movement. A multi-rep set can be modified so that the reps after the first can start at the top and utilize a stretch reflex off of the shoulders, but the basic movement – the one done with the heaviest weights – starts at the shoulders from a dead stop.

For an exercise to be useful as a conditioning tool for a sport, it must utilize the same muscles and the same type of neurological activation pattern as that sport. It need not be an identical copy of the sport movement. In fact, it has been demonstrated that if the motor pathway of the slower conditioning exercise is too similar to that of the faster sport skill, as in throwing a weighted basketball, interference with correct skill execution can result. It just needs to incorporate all the muscles involved in the skill in a coordinated way, so that strength is produced in the context of coordination. A sport such as football requires the use of all the muscles in the body, since force is generated against the ground by the hips and legs, transmitted up the trunk, and applied to the opponent through the arms and shoulders.

It is important to understand that the force is *not* produced solely and independently by the upper body. Shoulders and arms participate in the production of force, but they are completely dependent on the hips and legs to react through the feet against the ground as they work. In football, the kinetic-chain begins at the ground, since the feet move first; in pressing, it begins at the bar. But both movements transfer force along this kinetic-chain through the trunk, and its isometric function is the same in both. The press provides exactly the pattern of kinetic similarity required of a useful, applicable exercise (fig. 5-6). The bench press does not, but it does allow the use of heavier weights. We will do them both in this program, but we must realize the strengths and limitations of each.

As a general rule, the more of the body involved in an exercise, the better the exercise. The press produces strength in the trunk muscles – the abs, obliques, costals, and back, as well as the shoulders and arms. It trains the whole body to balance while standing and pressing with a heavy weight in the hands and overhead where the moment arm is the longest the body can produce. It uses more muscles and more central nervous system activity than any other upper-body exercise. And it produces force in a more useful direction than the bench press, in which force is directed at about 90 degrees away from the trunk. In football, most of the use of the arms is at an angle well above 90 degrees. The press, producing force vertically overhead, is not an exact match, but it is much closer to a useful direction than the bench press. If football players put their backs against solid objects positioned at an inclined angle and pushed against them, the Incline Bench Press would be a pretty good exercise. Some programs have switched to the incline for this reason, but this still ignores the important kinetic-chain element of the press.

It is in fact possible to press a lot more weight on the bench than standing with the bar in the hands. For simple upper-body strength, the bench press is the better exercise. Doing both enables the strength from the bench press to be applied in a more useful way for sports. But athletes that never do anything but bench press tend to have more shoulder problems than those who include overhead training. With all the pressing emphasis directed to the anterior side of the shoulder, the posterior gets relatively weak. Since it is possible to bench very heavy weights with years of training, this strength imbalance can be very pronounced. The posterior shoulder musculature includes the very important rotator cuff group (the external rotators), the muscles responsible for decelerating internal humeral rotation during throwing movements (fig. 5-7).

Figure 5-6. A comparison of the kinetic chain vectors of the press, typical football activity, and the bench press. Note that in the lineman's effort there are elements of both vertical and horizontal force application. The press strongly develops the ability to push through a range of directions while driving from the ground. The bench press is more limited in the applicability of the strength it produces, although it allows the use of heavier weights.

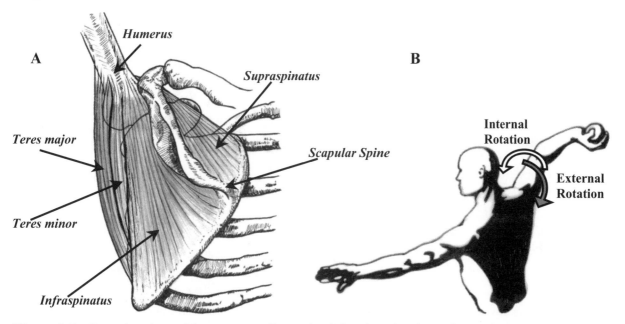

Figure 5-7. Posterior view of the rotator cuff muscles (A). They decelerate internal rotation of the humerus during throwing.

The rotator cuff basically consists of the muscles on and immediately beneath the shoulder blades, and although they do not work directly in a press, they are used in the movement and are strengthened. The bench press does not work them much, certainly not much in comparison to the loads being handled by the pectorals and anterior deltoids, which function as the main internal rotators of the humerus. If the internal rotators become strong enough to exceed the capacity of the external rotators to decelerate the humerus during a throw, injury can and often does occur. This problem is usually addressed in physical therapy with direct work on the rotator cuff involving very light isolation exercises. But 3 lb. dumbbell external rotations are not the only thing the rotator cuff muscles do. The press uses them isometrically to stabilize the lockout position at the top, and proper form ensures that they are active in this capacity. Rotator cuff problems can be addressed in training before they ever start by making sure that bench press work is balanced by an equivalent amount of overhead work. For every bench press workout there should be at least one press workout.

An absolutely wonderful thing about the press is its simplicity. It is a very easy movement to learn and perform correctly. But it is a very hard lift to do with a lot of weight; most people work for many years developing their ability to do it well. We'd better get started.

Learning To Press

The press starts at the rack with the empty bar. After a good shoulder warm-up, approach the bar. It should be set at the same height as for the squat, at about the middle of the sternum. The grip should be narrower than either the squat or the bench press, not much more than an inch or so wider on each side than the widest part of the shoulder, so that the forearms are vertical when viewed from the front or back (fig. 5-8). This vertical position ensures that the initial drive off the shoulders is directed straight up without any lateral rotation of the humerus that a wider or narrower grip would create. For most people this will put the index finger about an inch and a half out from the edge of the knurl on a standard Olympic bar, as in figure 5-9. The choice of equipment may not be up to you here, and most people will need to work with what they have, so make note that a standard Olympic weightlifting bar has a 16.5 inch (42 cm) space between the knurls (there is no standard center marking for a powerlifting bar). It might make things easier to mark your bar (if you can get away with it) to this standard so that you can use the same grip width every time. The thumbs should be around the bar with the weight as close to the heel of the hand as wrist, elbow, and shoulder flexibility permits (fig. 5-10). This position may be hard to maintain at first, but your flexibility in these joints will improve rapidly.

Take the bar out of the rack – The EMPTY BAR. The idea is to have the bar resting on top of your anterior deltoids, the meaty part of your shoulder, at the start of the movement. Inflexible people may not be able to get the shoulders far enough forward and up to put the bar in this position. Flexibility improves quickly, so just try to get it there as well as you can (fig. 5-11). Sitting on the delt is the ideal position; the movement can be done from a less than perfect position without any real problem. Now rotate your elbows forward and up so that your elbows are in front of the bar when viewed from the side (fig. 5-12). Very flexible people need not try to raise the elbows too high; this pulls the scapulae forward and produces a lack of tightness and stability across the shoulder blades that is not conducive to an efficient press. The idea is to have the elbows forward of the bar just enough that the forearm is vertical as it drives the bar up.

154

Figure 5-8. Grip width, just outside the shoulders at a position that makes the forearms vertical when viewed from the front or back.

Figure 5-9. Grip landmarks on the bar. Note the thumbs-around position. When the bar moves through space at the end of the arm, the thumbs are around the bar; if the bar rides on the back or the shoulders (as in a squat), no-thumbs is fine.

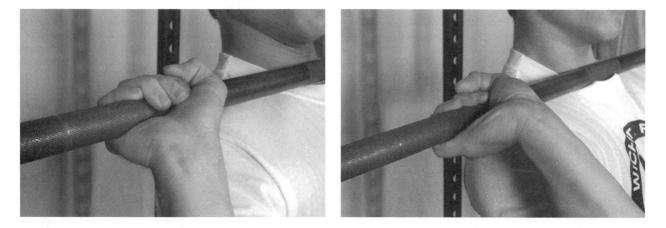

Figure 5-10. A. Correct positioning of the bar in the hand close to the heel of the palm, not back in the fingers (B).

Figure 5-11. The bar rests on the meat of the shoulder – the anterior deltoid – if possible. Flexibility quickly improves to allow this position to develop, even for inflexible people.

Figure 5-12. The elbows are in front of the bar. This places the bar in the correct position on the shoulders and provides for the correct direction of upward drive.

Stance in the press is not as precisely critical as with the squat. Take a comfortable stance, and you will usually end up with something that will work. Your heels will be about 10 to 12 inches apart. Much closer than this would be a balance problem, and much farther apart just feels weird.

Many initial position problems can be prevented with a correct positioning of the eyes. Look straight ahead to a point on the wall level with your eyes. (It is assumed that you are in a facility with walls.) Stare at that point for the whole set. It may be necessary to give yourself a point to look at. If you need to, draw a big dot on a sheet of paper and hang it up at the point that causes you to hold your eyes in the correct position.

Now lift your chest. This is actually accomplished by placing the upper part of the erector spinae in contraction. Think about lifting your sternum up to your chin. Refer to Figure 5-13 for this position. "Chest up" is really a back contraction, and the press and the front squat are the two best exercises for strengthening and developing control of these muscles. Lifting your chest improves the chances that the bar will move in the correct path during the press, and improves stability between reps due to the tightness produced in the upper back.

When your elbows are up correctly and your chest has been lifted, the bar is ready to press. The press is learned in two stages: first, you will put the bar where it is going to be in the finished position, and second, you will learn how to get it there correctly.

Take a big breath, hold it (our friend the Valsalva maneuver), and drive the bar up over your head. (The breath should be held until the bar is replaced on the shoulders.) The vast majority of people will press the bar up to lockout but in a position just in front of the forehead. Make sure that you have the bar directly above the back of your neck, a point that should line up the bar, the scapulas, and the mid-foot in a straight vertical line (fig 5-14).

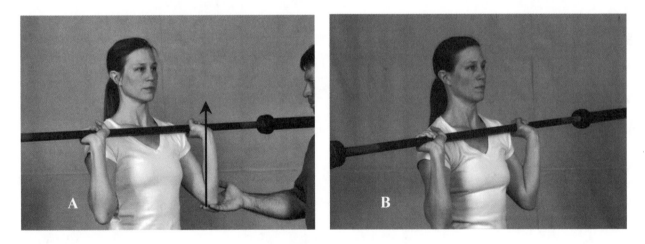

Figure 5-13. The correct upper back position (A), providing a firm platform from which to drive the bar. A relaxed upper back (B).

Once the bar is over your head correctly, the elbows must be locked and the shoulders shrugged up to support the bar. The elbows are locked by the triceps and deltoids and the shoulders are shrugged up with the trapezius, and both of these must work together to support heavy weights overhead. Imagine someone behind you gently pushing your elbows together and pulling them up at the same time, as illustrated in Figure 5-15. The combination of locking the elbows out and shrugging the traps up at lockout with the bar directly over the ears produces a very firm, stable position at the top and involves all of the shoulder girdle muscles.

After this position is correct, it is time to learn how to get under the bar. This involves making the bar path correct and establishing the proper movement of your body in relation to the bar. The bar moves from the point on the shoulders in front of the neck to the position above the neck and the scapulas, behind the starting position. This represents a lateral movement of a few inches (fig. 5-16), but bars like to travel in straight lines up and down, especially when heavy.

So the way to make up this backward distance is to lean back slightly, very slightly, and drive the bar up straight. As soon as it crosses the top of your forehead, get under the bar. Move your body forward under the bar and lock it out. Don't move the bar back. *You* move *your* body *forward* under the bar (fig 5-17). When you do this correctly, you will find that it is easier to lock out at the top, because the forward movement of the body straightens out the angle of the shoulder, thus driving up the distal end of the humerus and the attached forearm. Do this for a set of five, and rack the

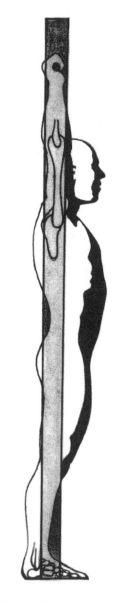

Figure 5-14. The skeletal landmarks of the press. The lockout position is correct when the bar, the scapulae, and the mid-foot lie in a vertical plane.

Figure 5-15. Cues for the lockout position. A. The bar is back in a position over the shoulder blades, a point that will be well behind the forehead. It may help to think of the bar being pulled back into this position from behind. B. The bar is then supported in this position with the triceps, deltoids, and traps. It may help to feel a gentle upward and inward squeeze on the humerus from either side to learn this position, along with a reminder to "shrug" the bar up.

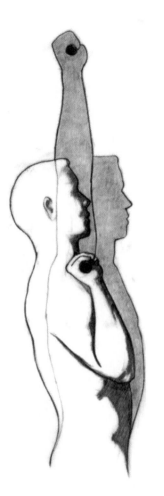

bar. At this point, the vast majority of people will have grasped the concept of getting under the bar, but will have made it very difficult by pushing the bar too far forward, away from the chin, thus increasing the distance back to the lockout position over the ears. Fix this on the third set, still with the empty bar, by thinking about keeping the bar close to your face on the way up. Aim for your nose as the bar leaves your shoulders. This should result in a nearly vertical bar path directly over the mid-foot, the body having accommodated to the physics of efficient work against gravity. You may hit yourself in the nose before you figure this out, but you will probably only do this once. Do a set of five and rack it. Start up in ten or twenty pound jumps until the bar speed begins to slow markedly on the fifth rep of the set, and call it a workout.

Figure 5-16. The lateral distance between the initial position of the bar on the shoulders and the final position overhead. This distance is covered by the movement of the torso as it drives forward after the bar crosses the level of the forehead on its way up.

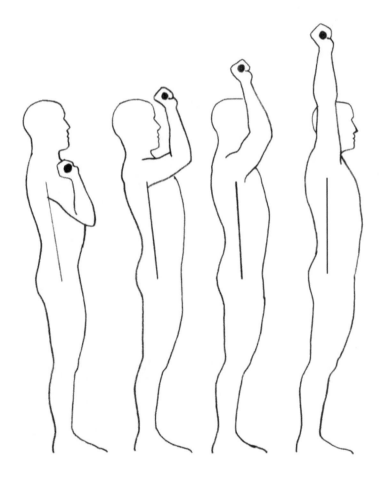

Figure 5-17. The torso drives forward as the bar drives up, taking the plane of the torso from slightly behind the vertical to slightly in front of vertical.

158

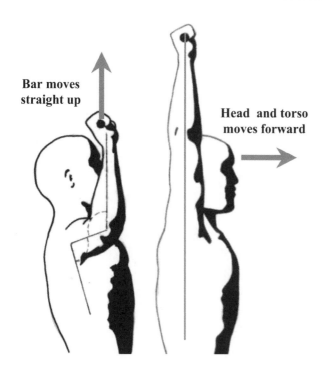

**Bar moves
straight up**

**Head and torso
moves forward**

Figure 5-18. The forward movement of the torso aids in the lockout. As the shoulder and the elbow extend, the forward motion of the shoulder drives the distal end of the humerus up, helping to straighten the elbow.

Faults and Corrections

A correct press will have certain characteristics at the start position and at lockout that are determined by the Universe. They have to do with balance and gravity, and how the muscles use the skeleton to solve movement problems.

In the starting position for the press:
- Knees, hips, and lumbar and thoracic spine are all locked in extension
- The bar rests on the deltoids or chest, depending on individual flexibility and body shape
- Elbows are in front of the bar
- The bar is directly over the mid-foot

At the top of the press:
- Knees, hips, lumbar and thoracic spine, and elbows are all locked in extension
- Scapulas are elevated (i.e., "active shoulders")
- The bar, the scapulas, and the mid-foot will be vertically aligned

During the trip up from the starting position to the top, the bar path should also be vertical and directly over the mid-foot. If it deviates from this position a little as it travels forward around the head, the center of mass is kept over the mid-foot by leaning back slightly, to the extent necessary to balance the bar deviation. This should be minimized by keeping the bar close to the face during the press so that the bar doesn't get so far away forward that it cannot be pressed efficiently. But the ideal is a vertical bar path, and the closer you get to it the fewer technical problems you'll have.

There won't be nearly as many problems with the press as there are with the squat or deadlift, because there are fewer joints actively participating in the movement of the bar. Most problems are either starting position problems or bar path problems.

As mentioned earlier, eye position is important for good body position. It is also the key to good neck positioning, and your cervical spine will appreciate the attention. If you are having problems of any kind, always check to make sure your eyes are looking at the right place. Or get someone else to check you during a set; it is often hard to remind yourself to do this after the bar is out of the rack. Correct eyeballs solve lots of problems with all the lifts in this program.

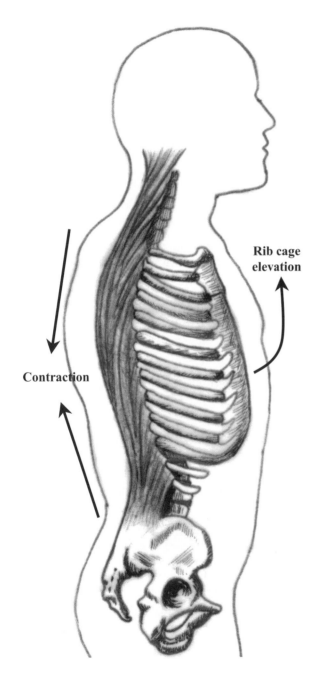

Rib cage elevation

Contraction

Figure 5-19. Lifting the chest is primarily a function of the upper back muscles.

The preferred torso alignment is nearly vertical, especially at first. The stronger and more skilled at pressing you become the more trunk movement you can correctly incorporate. Leaning back excessively is seldom a problem at first. It will not occur to most people that they can lean back to start the press until well after they have begun training the movement. Leaning back too much hurts the lower back, and this is where you will notice it first. It is usually accompanied by a shift onto the toes as the body keeps the bar over the mid-foot by shoving the knees forward to balance the backward lean. Quite often the elbows will also be too low, behind the bar, like you are trying to make a flat spot on your chest for the bar instead of putting it up on the deltoids correctly. Rotate your elbows up to the right position and you will usually stop leaning back. You may need to get someone to check your position during the press and tell you to "stand up straighter" as a position cue.

There are two types of upper back looseness that commonly screw up the press. Letting the chest cave in so that the upper back rounds is very common. Heavy weight on a military press is uncomfortable enough already, without exacerbating the problem with a lack of good support. Keeping the chest up is the way to keep the thoracic spine in proper anatomical position, and this is primarily accomplished with the upper back muscles. When the upper erector spinae contracts, it rotates the ribcage up, holding it in place against the load on the shoulders. Remembering to "lift the chest" is usually all that is required, but most will need to really focus on this every rep for a while. Most people's attention span is short under a bar, especially a bar on the front of the shoulders, and focus on technique – as with eye position – is more difficult the heavier the weight gets.

The other way to be loose is to let the shoulder blades slide forward, out of active retraction by the rhomboids and traps. The muscles that anchor the scapulae to the spine are the rhomboidius, which attaches the medial edge of the scapula to the spinous processes between the seventh cervical and fourth thoracic vertebrae, and the trapezius, which attaches to the spine of the scapula – the long bony ridge across the back of the shoulder – from the top of the neck down to the lower back. These are very strong anchors for a bone that is supported mainly by muscles; the only point of attachment the scapula has to the rest of the skeleton is at its rather flimsy articulation with the collarbone. These muscles are what keep the shoulder blades in position during the press, and if they are allowed to relax, which occurs when the bones slide up and forward, the press will not be supported from the posterior side of the chest and the potential for pressing inefficiency and injury goes way up. This is corrected by keeping the shoulder blades retracted and tight and the elbows not too far forward. In this position the shoulders are supported and the forearms can drive the bar straight up.

The traps are also a very important component of the press in that they provide for the "active shoulder" aspect of the lockout. When weights are supported overhead, the bar is held up by the arms, the arms are attached to the scapulas, and the scapulas hang from the trapezius muscles which attach to the spine from C1 through T12. So the traps form an important part of the attachment between the arms and the rest of the body. The bar is not held in lockout only by the arms; the entire shoulder – both anterior and posterior muscles, big ones like the traps and deltoids, and little ones like the rotator cuff muscles and neck muscles that attach to the scapulae and clavicles – as well as the triceps, holds up the bar. This aspect of lockout should not be underestimated, and it should be learned from the very first rep you do with an empty bar. Later, when you decide you cannot live without learning to snatch, the importance of "shrugging" the bar at lockout will become apparent: the bar simply will not stay overhead with only the support of the arms.

During the press the traps start off as scapula retractors, keeping the shoulder blades back and the upper spine supported, and then change to scapula elevators as the bar drives into a position directly over them at lockout. The vertical line from the bar to the floor that passes through the shoulder blades makes the traps an important part of the press lockout.

There are two different breathing patterns that can be used during the set. The first, which seems to be more useful for novices using lighter weights, is to breathe at the top of the press, at lockout. It has to be a quick breath, taken without relaxing anything that is supposed to be tight. It has the advantage of allowing you to rebound the bar quickly off of the shoulders, making the press analogous to the bench press with the stretch reflex at the bottom. This use of a stretch reflex is fine at first, but most lifters tend to outgrow this and adopt breathing at the shoulders between reps. This method requires that the lifter stay very tight, with chest up during the breath, a thing learned with experience. Breathing at the top allows a novice to handle heavier weights while learning the skills necessary to maintain control during the press, and will work better for flexible people who can get in a good forward lockout position to catch a breath. Breathing at the shoulders allows the more experienced lifter the luxury of a second or two of rest between heavy reps. Try both methods and see which works better for you.

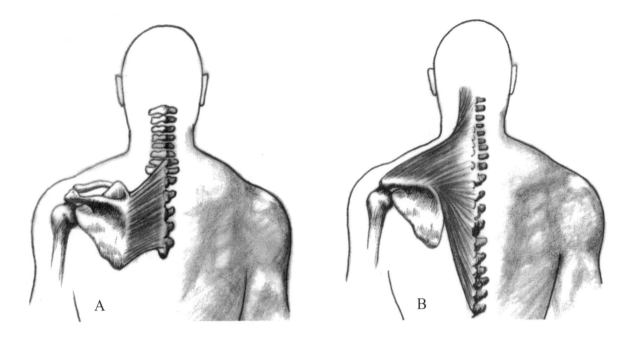

Figure 5-20. The muscles that maintain scapular retraction, the rhomboidius (A) and the trapezius (B). They provide the tightness that finishes the job started by "chest-up". The traps also provide lockout support by "shrugging" the scapulae up at the top, when the bar is directly over them in the finish position.

Three common bar path problems need to be investigated. Pushing the bar away, failing to get under the bar after it passes the forehead, and leaning back away from the bar are all different problems, but they all affect the press the same way. All three faults increase the distance between the bar and the shoulder, making the lever arm longer and decreasing the ability to overcome the force of the loaded bar. **The closer the bar is to the shoulders – and the face – the shorter the lever arm and the more efficient the press.**

The most common form problem with light weights is the bar out in front too far, away from the face, producing a curved bar path (fig. 5-21). Heavy weights like to move in straight lines, since they represent less work done than curved lines. This is true for all barbell exercises, from the simple press to the very complex snatch and clean and jerk. Heavy weights don't follow a curved bar path in the press, because heavy weight can't be pressed like this. If the bar curves out forward, you have to go backward so that the center of mass of the system stays balanced over the mid-foot. This erodes the position necessary for a powerful press, with the delts and triceps driving up on the elbows close to the body, in a position of increased mechanical efficiency with a shorter lever arm. It is sometimes the result of allowing the elbows to drop into a lower position that puts the forearms behind the vertical, instead of up where they should be. This is an easy thing to correct, if you catch it early. You just need to raise your elbows, and aim for your chin or push the bar toward your nose.

Leaving the bar out in front, not "getting under the bar," is a different problem, and most definitely will occur often at heavy weight. This occurs when the bar has been started perfectly straight up, but the lifter fails to move forward under the bar after it clears the head. Heavy weights tend to blur awareness of the fine points of technique, as anyone who has trained heavy

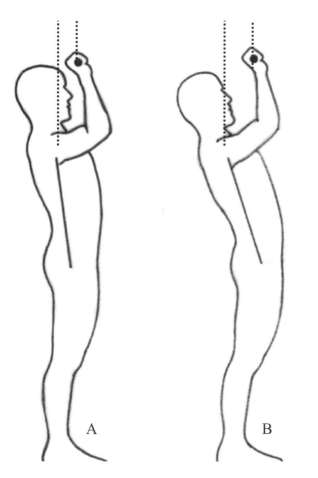

Figure 5-21. Pressing efficiency is strongly influenced by the mechanics of the pressing position: the shorter the distance between the bar and the shoulder, the shorter the lever arm. A. Driving up close to the face provides this good mechanical position. B. In addition to a curved bar path, pushing the bar away from the face radically increases the length of the lever arm between the bar and the shoulder.

knows. We depend on our training, which has embedded the correct motor pathway, and coaching – when we can get it – to keep our form good. Most often, when you miss a heavy press in front, you won't know why. Most often you didn't get under the bar. You must drill this movement pattern during the warmup sets so that it can be done without a lot of thought and conscious direction during the work sets.

There is another way to make the body get forward under the bar at lockout. As is so often the case in athletics, a thing can be conceived and understood in many different ways. As you become experienced as a lifter, you should get better at understanding the mechanics of what is happening under the bar, and be able to visualize solutions for movement problems you may be experiencing. The lockout of the press can be thought of as the shoulders moving forward under the bar, but it can be approached from the opposite direction and thought of as the hips moving *back* as the bar crosses the forehead. These are obviously two different ways to explain the same concept. If the lift starts with a slight back extension, lockout is facilitated when the back is straightened and the shoulder and elbow angles are driven up, as previously illustrated. Either the chest and shoulders moving forward or the hips moving back produces the same net effect relative to the bar; use the one that helps you best.

An emphasis on getting forward under the bar can result in a balance problem, noticeable as a tendency to be on the ball of the foot during the drive and lockout. A good connection with the ground requires that the weight be evenly distributed over the whole foot even as the bar is centered over the middle of it. Any shifting forward during the press must be done in the context of the entire body staying in balance under the bar. If the forward shift is sufficient to actually alter the center of gravity of the bar/lifter system, you will have to compensate by moving a foot or both feet forward to avoid losing balance. Getting under the bar comes from a shift in torso position, not from a shift affecting the body all the way to the ground. Excessive movement disrupts the kinetic-chain and the lift. It may be necessary to overcorrect yourself by trying to stay on your heels during the press in order to average out to the middle of your foot. Driving from the heels during the set will usually correct this immediately. It might be necessary to pick up your

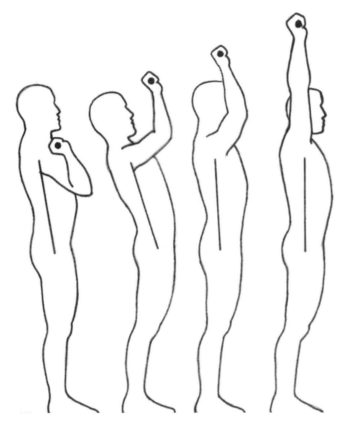

Figure 5-22. Pushing the bar away from the face produces pressing inefficiency and a curved bar path. The bar/lifter center of gravity will stay over the mid-foot, but at the expense of a longer lever arm produced by the increased distance between the bar and the shoulder.

big toes inside your shoes to get this done; this always throws the weight back on the heels, since it requires a huge effort to balance forward on the remaining four little toes.

Leaning back is a problem that gets worse as the weight gets heavier. Virtually everybody will do this after a few weeks of training as strength improves and you learn that the bar can be started from the shoulders with a hip drive. This movement becomes an important part of the lift as you gain experience, and is only a problem if it becomes excessive. Excessive is bad because it alters the movement sufficiently that the target muscle groups get left out, the desired anterior/posterior balance across the shoulder is lost, the longer lever arm makes the weight harder to lift, and extreme loaded hyperextension of the lumbar spine is dangerous. Furthermore, excessive is really a judgement call. If you consistently miss heavy presses out in front at a certain

Figure 5-23. Excessive layback is not the same as pushing the bar forward. Note the position of the bar over the correct places on the body, except that the torso is too far behind the bar, contributing to lever arm length and an excessive lateral distance to make up during lockout.

degree of lean-back, that much is probably excessive if the miss would not have occurred with a better back position.

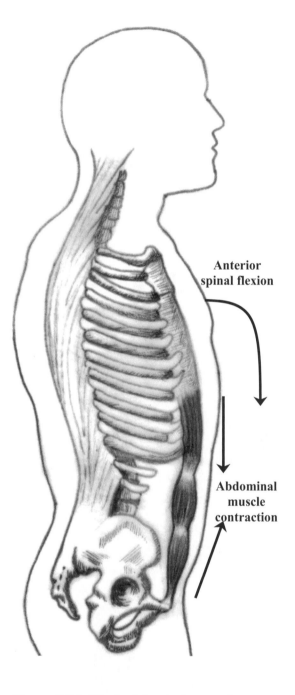

Anterior spinal flexion

Abdominal muscle contraction

Figure 5-24. Weak abdominal musculature can account for excessive layback. Very strong pressers have very thick sections of rectus abdominis.

Part of the problem may be weak abs. The rectus abdominis acts directly against lumbar hyperextension by providing tension between the ribcage and the pubis, counteracting lumbar hyperextension and increasing intra-abdominal pressure to reinforce correct lumbar curvature from the anterior side of the trunk. Weighted situps, or more specifically weighted Roman chair situps develop a strong set of abs.

Another common problem is that when the weight gets heavy, most people try to make the press into a *push* press, by starting the bar up with a push from the knees. This is a logical way to cheat − after all, the hips and legs are much stronger than the shoulders and arms. If a push press is the intended exercise, then it must at least be done correctly, with the bar resting firmly on the deltoids for a firm transfer of power to the bar, and a sharp dip and drive using hips and legs, not a slow push out of the knees. But if you are trying to do a strict press, then it must be done with strict form. If the weight is too heavy to do with strict form, take some off.

Some people are reluctant to admit they have too much weight on the bar, in the same way that they are prone to take too big an increase in weight each workout. Their ego interferes with their thinking, causing them to attempt to handle weights they cannot do with correct form. As with all exercises, correct form is necessary for real progress and for safety. The push press enables heavier weight to be handled, true, but the shoulders are doing less of the work while the triceps are getting better at locking out the bar. This is fine if kept in proper perspective: push presses make a good assistance movement for the press, but they are no substitute for it. Strict work with good form causes strength to be developed in the target muscle groups. More importantly, we need to learn how to bear down on a hard rep and finish it without cheating it, so that we develop the mental discipline to stay with a hard task and finish it correctly. This is one of those indirect benefits that can be obtained from physical education. If you learn nothing else from training, it is very important to learn that your limits are seldom where you think they are.

Figure 5-25. One of the better exercises for developing strong abs for the press. The roman chair situp is an old way to place a tremendous load on all the anterior trunk musculature.

Figure 5-26. The press.

The Power Clean

The power clean cannot be done slowly. There is therefore no confusion over the nature of the exercise. The power clean is used in sports conditioning because it increases explosion, and done correctly it is the best exercise for converting the strength obtained in the other exercises to power. Since the nature of the vast majority of sports is explosive, involving the ability to accelerate the athlete's body or an object, the ability to accelerate is pivotal in sports performance. The power clean is our most important tool in the war against inertia.

In his famous book "The Strongest Shall Survive," Bill Starr included the power clean in his Big Three, with the comment that "If your program only allowed you to do one exercise, this would be the best." The power clean has always been used by weightlifters as an assistance exercise for the clean, the more complete and more complicated version of the lift. The term "clean" refers to a way to get the bar clear of the floor "clean" to the shoulders. If this is accomplished in one movement, it is a clean; if in two (if it stops on the way up on the chest or a belt) it is referred to as a "Continental Clean." Heavier weights can be lifted in the Continental style, but a simple clean requires more power to make the bar complete its trip in a single effort. In the modern usage, the term "clean" refers to a full squat clean. It has not always been this way. The split clean – a style that made use of a forward/back split like that commonly used for the jerk in Olympic weightlifting – was used more commonly until the 1960's, when the squat style began to be favored due to the heavier weights that could be lifted with this front squat-based technique. The term "power" as a qualifier in front of an exercise refers to an abbreviated version of a more involved movement, the shorter version being harder to perform at the expense of reduced technique requirements. A "power snatch" is a snatch without a squat or split, the use of which reduces the distance the bar must be pulled. The "power jerk" is a version of the last part of the Clean and Jerk where the feet do not move. Likewise, the "power clean" is the version of the clean without a split and without too much front squat.

Figure 6-1. The power clean is a variation of the full squat clean – usually referred to as the "clean" – used in Olympic weightlifting. Bill Starr cleans 435 at the 1969 Nationals.

Figure 6-2. The split clean was commonly used prior to the 1980s, and is a useful competitive style for some lifters that lack sufficient flexibility to make the squat style advantageous.

The Power Clean

The clean requires pulling the barbell up fast enough and high enough, using power generated by the hips and legs, to catch it on the shoulders. As such, the faster it comes up the higher it will go, and the higher the bar can be pulled the more weight can be cleaned. As a corollary, the lifter can clean more weight if he can get better at getting under a bar not pulled as high. This is the purpose served by splitting and squatting: it shortens the distance the bar has to be pulled. Since our purpose is sports conditioning and not cleaning heavy weights per se, but rather generating as much upward explosion as possible, we will use the power version of the lift.

A few authorities have taken the position that the full squat clean is the superior version of the lift for most training purposes, arguing that going under the bar is accomplished more efficiently when the front squat is taught as a part of the lift from the beginning. This may in fact be the case, and if you want to squat clean when learning the movement, feel free. And a case can be made for the fact that the full squat clean is easier on the knees because the hamstrings and adductors get to help absorb the shock of the catch. But be aware of the fact that the front squat will likely interfere with your back squat form if you are learning both movements at the same time. They are radically different exercises, and the author is of the opinion that the front squat, even when used as a part of the clean, is best left to intermediate-level lifters to learn after good back squat technique has been nailed down by several months of training. This, in addition to the aforementioned power-production aspects of the two lifts, is the reason that power cleans are the recommended explosive lift for novices.

The term "power" has a very specific meaning in the study of mechanics. Power is defined as the amount of work performed per unit of time, and physicists measure it in joules per second, or watts. As a practical matter – and as we will use it here – power can be best understood as the ability to exert force rapidly.

More terms now: Velocity is the speed of an object, the rate of change in its position. Acceleration is the rate of change of velocity, the *increase* (or decrease, known as deceleration) in the speed. For an object to change speed, to *accelerate*, force must be applied to it, since the now-faster moving object has more *kinetic energy*. Strength is the physical ability to generate force. "Power" is the ability to generate that force rapidly. A more familiar term for this might be "quickness," especially when applied to movement of the body itself. For sports, just developing strength is not enough – you must also develop the ability to rapidly recruit the strength you build, so that you can accelerate better. A strong man might very well be able to apply enough force to a very heavy weight to get it moving, but a powerful man can get it moving more quickly.

The vertical jump is a valuable diagnostic test for power. It directly measures an athlete's ability to generate force rapidly enough to accelerate his bodyweight off the ground. It is used to predict this aspect of performance. Studies have shown that vertical jump performance is predictive of sports proficiency, that power clean performance is predictive of vertical jump performance, and that power clean performance is predictive of squat strength. Squat performance is predictive of squat jump performance, and squat jump performance is predictive of power clean performance. The power clean, by training the athlete to move a heavy weight quickly, is the glue that cements the strength program to sports performance.

One way to understand the concept of power in this specific situation is by comparing performances in the power clean and the deadlift. As we have already seen, the deadlift is a straight pull off the floor, standing up with the bar and stopping at arms length, whereas the power clean continues the pull on up through an explosive phase to a catch on the shoulders. A deadlift can obviously be done with a heavier weight than a power clean, if for no other reason than that it is a shorter movement. The power clean can be thought of as being done with a percentage of the deadlift. A very strong powerlifter can deadlift two to three times his power clean. (If he trains the clean at all. In the early days of powerlifting, most competitors had weightlifting experience or were coached by people who did.) So his power clean might be 40% of his deadlift. But a very powerful Olympic weightlifter might power clean 75% of his deadlift. This is a direct result of training specificity: the powerlifter is good at pulling big weights slowly, and the weightlifter is good at pulling moderate weights faster, and thus higher. But it could be that the weightlifter has not trained with sufficiently heavy weights to develop his deadlifting strength. Or it could be that the powerlifter has neglected to develop his power off the floor (sorry for the awkward sentence, due to the bad choice of name for the sport – it should be "strengthlifting," but I predict that my suggestion will not be adopted soon). Actually, the question is this: why is the higher-velocity weightlifter cleaning a higher percentage of his deadlift than the lower-velocity powerlifter? We shall soon see.

As evidence that strength and power are related, George Hechter incorporated power cleans and clean high-pulls (the partial version of the clean, where the bar is shrugged hard but not racked on the shoulders) into his deadlift training, by warming up his deadlifts with the explosive movements up to about 60% of his max single deadlift, and then deadlifting on up to his work sets. His best deadlift of 825 lbs. at a bodyweight of 242 is testimony to the effectiveness of this approach. The popular Westside method, developed by the amazing Louie Simmons, trains power production by using weights in the range of 50-75% of max in the squat, bench press, and deadlift with an emphasis on maximum acceleration during the reps. His lifters have rewritten the records in all weight classes as a result of his ingenious incorporation of the principles of power/strength production into the training of athletes whose emphasis has historically been training for strength. He has figured out a way to train the squat, bench and deadlift as if they were the Olympic lifts, by training them with weights that can be used at the velocity where maximum power is produced.

This range, 50-75% of 1RM, is where maximum power is produced. The range represents differences in the nature of the various exercises, whether the exercise is primarily an upper-body or lower-body movement, and the skill, strength, experience, and sex (women are able to use a higher percentage of 1RM explosively than men) of the individual athlete. At weights heavier than this, velocity drops off to the point where power begins to diminish; remember, power requires high velocity. But at very light weights the velocity is so high that maximum recruitment of muscle is not possible. This is due to several factors involving the physiology of skeletal muscle contraction, among them the fact that a very high velocity movement does not allow enough time for the nerves to recruit many of the components that contribute to muscle contraction. Like trying to throw a wiffleball, a very light weight moving very fast does not provide enough resistance to push against effectively. A baseball is pretty good to throw, because it's just about the right weight to throw hard and fast. Power is at a maximum when throwing a 16 lb. shot, due to the combination of weight and velocity. But a great big rock would be too heavy to allow for the production of much power, because of the very slow velocity even a very strong man could produce. So the load must be optimum for power production. Weights in the range of 50-75% are in the right range for weight training, for the speeds we use for total-body explosion.

As it turns out, the ability to produce force against a weight is dependent on the speed at which the movement is trained. What this means is that if heavy weights are lifted at a slow speed, the lifter gets good at lifting them *at that slow speed*. He does not get good at lifting them at a faster speed. So slow deadlift training will not make the clean move faster. And if a lifter gets good at pulling a weight fast, as in a power clean, he gets good at generating force at that faster rate of speed. The rate of speed that is trained is the rate of speed to which we adapt. But this rule only works well in one direction: strength developed at a slow rate of speed can only be effectively used slowly, but strength developed at a high rate of speed can be used at that high speed *and* at speeds slower than that. It is incredibly important to understand this. **High speed training with enough weight to make high power production necessary makes for useable strength at a wide range of speeds, from fast with moderate loads where the training takes place to slow with heavier loads, where the contest squat, bench and deadlift are done.**

Figure 6-3. The power clean contributes to the deadlift, and the deadlift contributes to the power clean. The power clean teaches timing and athletic synchronization of complex, multi-joint movement; the commitment involved in getting under the bar, the all-or-none that is sometimes lacking in a deadlift attempt; it trains the rate of motor unit recruitment, thus improving neuromuscular efficiency; and it teaches explosion, the mental cue for highly efficient motor unit recruitment. The deadlift develops the concentric and isometric strength involved in holding the correct position through the slower parts of a heavy clean, and the ability to hold the back rigid during the explosive hip extension that makes for an efficient second pull; it increases the total number of motor units that can be recruited in a contraction; it teaches and enables "grind" – the patience necessary to maintain position through a long effort; it disinhibits the nervous system against heavier weights, so that heavy cleans feel light in contrast to heavy deadlifts; and it develops the good old-fashioned ability to produce force. (From an idea developed by Stef Bradford, Ph.D.)

This is probably due to the way the central nervous system adapts to exercise, and the way it plugs in to the muscles. The most demanding way to use the muscles and the nerves that run them is explosively, with weights that require the production of maximum power. If muscles are trained to do this efficiently, the slower jobs, even with heavier weights, are a piece of cake.

So the next logical question is this: why do we need to squat and deadlift at conventional speeds – to develop strength at slow speeds – if we are training for explosive sports? The reason is that there are slow and isometric components in explosive movements that benefit from the strength developed at slow speeds. A clean has a slow phase off the floor that benefits from the strength it takes to maintain the position until the explosive phase, so deadlifts are useful for training the clean. The actual explosion at the top does not benefit from the slow strength developed in the deadlift and squat, but the whole of the lift does, from the pull from the floor, to the ability to hold the back locked, to the catch position, and final the support position at the top. Likewise, a tackle in football, while it has explosive components from off the ground till the moment of impact, takes on slow strength characteristics after contact is made. In fact, there are few examples in sports of movements that don't have both slow and fast components.

And since strength gained at a given speed translates down to slower speeds, but not up to faster speeds, the squat and deadlift at conventional speeds build strength at speeds slower than that at which they are performed. This speed range goes from the slow, like that with which a clean comes off the ground, down to zero velocity – an isometric contraction in the position-holding components of the immobile segments of the body in faster movements.

Both types of training are necessary and each contributes to the development of the other. It should be obvious that a man with a 500 lb. deadlift can clean more than a man of the same bodyweight with a 200 lb. deadlift, because of the great difference in the ability to produce force. But between two men that both deadlift 500 lbs., the one moving it faster is producing more force, is therefore stronger, and is training in a way that teaches his muscles and nervous system to produce even more force. Training faster with a given weight requires more force production, because acceleration requires force. And when the ability to produce force goes up, heavier weights can be lifted at all speeds, from the fastest speed trained on down. This is why the power clean makes the deadlift go up and the deadlift contributes to the power clean.

The weight that can be used for a heavy power clean, for most athletes, is the correct weight to use to improve force production. It is heavy enough to have to pull on hard, and by its very nature cannot be done without explosion. Unless it is moving fast at the top, it will not even rack on the shoulders. Its only drawback is that it is a technique-dependent exercise. Let's learn to do it.

Learning the Power Clean

The power clean is best learned from the top down. This means that the mechanics of catching, or "racking" the bar on the shoulders is learned first, and the emphasis in your mind is on the rack position from the beginning. It is important to learn that in the power clean speed becomes important at the top of the pull, not off the floor. The lower part of the pull, from the floor to the mid-thigh, serves to get the bar in the correct position for the explosive movement that racks the bar, and this part must be done *correctly*, not quickly, at least at first. From the mid-thigh on up the movement must get faster, but it cannot be done correctly if it has not started from the right place. By learning the top of the power clean first, and worrying about getting it down to the floor later, you assign the correct priority to the most important part of the pull. After all, the first part of the power clean is essentially a deadlift, which you already know how to do. When the top of the pull has been learned, we will slide down a little at a time into a deadlift, making the transition from half a movement to the whole thing.

The empty 20 kg. (45 lb.) bar will be correct for the vast majority, but some smaller kids and women may require a lighter bar, a 15 kg. women's competition bar, or an even lighter shop-built one to comfortably learn the movement. There is no point in adding weight to the bar at first, as you are learning the movement only. The empty bar is enough resistance to provide some ballast for the elbows to rotate around. A broomstick is too light to have sufficient inertia to stay in place during the turn, and even light weights on the bar at this point will interfere with focus on what the body should be doing.

Figure 6-4. The basic stance for the clean is the same position used for a flat-footed vertical jump.

Foot position will be about the same as for the deadlift, 12-15 inches apart, with toes pointed very slightly out, like the stance for a flat-footed vertical jump. This is the stance that allows most people to apply maximum power to the ground.

First, the position at the top, with the bar in the hands at arms length, with straight elbows, straight knees, and chest up is referred to as the **Hang Position** (fig. 6-5). A power clean done from this starting point is referred to as a "hang power clean." This position is assumed by taking the EMPTY bar off the floor with a correct grip and deadlifting it into position. The correct grip for most people will be about 21 inches between index fingers in a double-overhand grip, just a tiny bit wider than the deadlift grip and an inch or so wider than the press grip. This grip is wide enough to let the elbows rotate up unimpeded into the rack position, to be described shortly, and will obviously vary with shoulder width. Later, we will learn the hook grip, but for now a normal thumbs-around grip will be fine.

The next step involves getting the bar on the shoulders. From the Hang Position, with correct width grip, get the bar up onto your shoulders, any way you want to use right now. It should sit right on top of the frontal deltoids (the meaty part of the front of the shoulder), well off of the sternum and collarbones. This position is referred to as the **Rack Position** (fig. 6-7). The key to this position is the elbows: they must be up very high, pointed straight forward with the humerus as nearly parallel to the floor as possible. Some people will have trouble getting in this position due to flexibility problems. A grip width adjustment usually fixes this. Widen the grip a little at a time until the position is better. If the elbows are up high enough, the bar will clear the bony parts and sit comfortably on the belly of the deltoid muscles. The bar is not sitting in the hands, and the hands are not supporting any of the weight; the weight is resting on the shoulders and the hands are keeping it in position. This position is secure and pain-free, to the extent that you will never in your entire life be able to clean a weight that will be too heavy to hold like this. It is imperative that you understand that *this* is where the bar goes and *not* anywhere else – not

Figure 6-5. The Hang position.

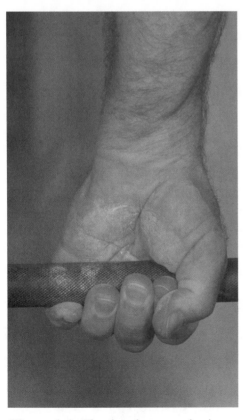

Figure 6-6. The thumbs-around grip used when first learning the power clean.

sitting on your chest, and not just carried in your hands. You must not stop with your elbows pointing at the floor (fig. 6-8).

It may take a couple of workouts to stretch your wrists out so that this position is tolerable. Wrist discomfort is the most common complaint among novices learning the power clean. It may help to actively stretch them out between sets, using the free hand to stretch the other wrist.

Figure 6-7. The Rack position, with chest up and elbows pointed forward.

Figure 6-8. The incorrect elbow position places the elbows directly under the bar, and the weight of the bar on the arms and wrists instead of the shoulders.

Get back in the hang position, and unlock your knees and your hips. This is accomplished by sticking your butt back as your bend the knees. Let the bar slide down your thighs to a position somewhere between a third and halfway down. This position we will call the **Jumping Position** (fig. 6-9). Your elbows will be *straight*, shoulders will be very slightly in front of the bar, knees and hips will be unlocked, the bar will not be too far down the thighs, and on the skin touching the thighs. In this position the spine of the scapula will be directly over the bar, and this is the position at which it rotates behind the bar as the pull is finished, the last and highest point during the pull at which it will be directly vertical to the bar.

Now, from the jumping position, jump straight up in the air with the bar hanging from the arms. Don't bend the elbows the first few times, but rather concentrate on the fact that you are jumping and leaving the ground. Jump high enough that you have to extend the knees and hips to do it. In fact, think hard about not bending the elbows as the bar slides down the leg to the jumping position. Most people will try to bend the elbows instead of letting it slide, but don't you be that person. Once the act of jumping with the bar in your hands is firmly embedded, jump and catch the bar on your shoulders in the rack position. Catch it in the same place you had it before, with your elbows up.

Figure 6-9. The Jumping position. Note the position of the bar in contact with the thighs. All cleans must touch this place on the thighs before the jump occurs.

Figure 6-10. The cure for incorrect elbow position. Lifting the elbows after an incorrect rack can be fixed by lifting them (or having them lifted) repeatedly enough that initially catching them in the correct position becomes reflexive.

Figure 6-11. The three basic positions in the power clean: The Hang position, the Jumping position, and the Rack.

Jumping is the key. The power clean is not an arms movement, at all, and if you first learn that a jump is the core of the movement, you will never learn to arm-pull the bar. The jump generates the upward movement of the bar, and later when your form is good the jump will be thought of as an explosion at the top of the pull, that will also produce the shrug inherent in cleaning the weight.

Put the bar back down to the jumping position and try it several more times. Each time be sure that 1.) you start from the jumping position with the bar *touching* the thigh and your elbows straight, 2.) you actually *jump*, and 3.) you rack the bar with your elbows up high. After you jump and catch the bar in the rack position a few times, check the position of the bar as it passes your chest. It should be close enough that it nearly touches your shirt. Start now to be aware of the path of the bar as it comes up through the top of the pull, and keep it close.

When you are racking the bar fairly well, begin to stomp your feet as you catch it. This might be poorly coordinated at first, but will improve very quickly as you time the stomp and the catch together. This is a very natural movement, and will add explosion to the jump and quickness to the catch, as you anticipate the faster foot movement required to stomp. Again, be *sure* that each pull starts from the jumping position, *touching the thigh with straight elbows*. This cannot be overemphasized, as the pull will be wrong if the jump starts from any other position.

During this process, you will find that your hands get tired, so rest them as needed. It is not productive to let fatigue interfere with concentration and good form. Take the time necessary to go through this critical process properly.

When you are consistently producing a good jump and rack, with the bar close and elbows in good position, slide the bar down below the jumping position and then come back up to it to do the jump and catch. Unlock your knees, shove your hips back, and slide the bar down to below the middle of your thighs, perhaps as low as the top of the knees. This movement should be done with the weight on the heels with the shoulders slightly out in front of the bar at the lowest point on the thighs, with straight elbows. The chest should stay up and the low back should stay locked in position. The bar slides down the thigh as the knees unlock, the butt goes back, and the shoulders go forward. Then return to the jumping position, jump, and rack the bar. During the entire movement, the bar must stay **on** the thigh, touching the actual surface of the leg as it moves down and up, until the jump. The elbows must remain straight during this sliding along the thighs; they do not bend until after the jump. After you do this movement above the knees a few times, lower the bar on down past your knees, and then bend your knees to finish the trip down to the mid-shin. It should be noted here that *from the point at which the knees unlock at the top they do not move forward as the bar is lowered to the knee, and that from just below the knee on down they* do *move forward*. **In other words, the hips lower the bar to the knees, and the knees lower the bar to the floor.** Coming back up is the exact opposite movement – straighten the knees until the bar clears them, and then return to the jumping position by dragging the bar up your thighs as you extend your hips (see fig. 6-12) and note the knee position during the movement). This movement prepares you to do the full power clean correctly, and integrates the lower part of the pull with the top part of the pull before they can be separated in your mind into two distinct things.

As you think about this new part of the movement, be sure that the bar stays in contact with the thighs as you slide it down, *that you slide it down by shoving the hips back*, and that you keep your chest up while you do this. And the elbows must stay straight until the jump. Be sure the bar is touching the thigh on the way back up, touching it as you jump, and that you rack the bar with elbows up high.

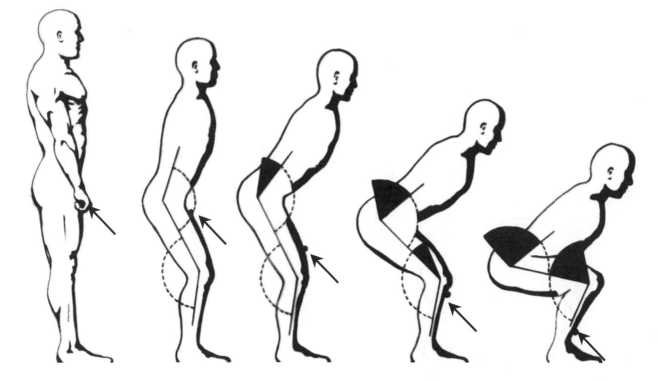

Figure 6-12. Learning to lower the bar correctly from the beginning will make it easier to pull from the floor correctly later. Note the progression from predominantly hip movement to predominantly knee movement after the bar passes the knees.

If at any time during this progression the form breaks down, stop. Go back and work it until it is correct. This method works from the top down, and if you leave a mistake in the middle of the power clean, it will cause problems that will have to be fixed later.

By the time you get the bar to the mid-shin position you are doing a power clean, since that is the height above the platform a bar loaded with regulation-diameter plates would rest. When the movement is correct from the hang, load the bar with the lightest plates you have (2.5 kg plastic plates are available to facilitate the correct spacing at weights light enough to practice the form) and start pulling the bar from the floor. And unfortunately, this critical step is where you will have problems, since most people forget about the jumping position here. *Don't let this be you.* Make sure the bar is in contact with the thigh and your elbows are straight as you jump into the rack position. **Do not clean without touching the thigh in the jumping position, and do not forget that the jumping position requires straight elbows.** It may be necessary to return to the jumping position many times while learning the clean, but eventually you will become dependent on the mechanical advantage obtained by doing it this way and in fact become unable *not* to touch the thigh on the way up.

So basically we have a movement that consists of a deadlift that turns into a jump and catch. But even though the two phases are learned separately, it is important to integrate these two movements into one. There should be no break in velocity between the pull from the floor and the jump and catch. In fact, the velocity gradually increases from the floor to the rack position. Don't *stop* to touch your thigh with the bar. If you slow down to touch, when the bar gets heavy you will lose momentum and miss the lift. Just brush your leg on the way up without slowing down to do it.

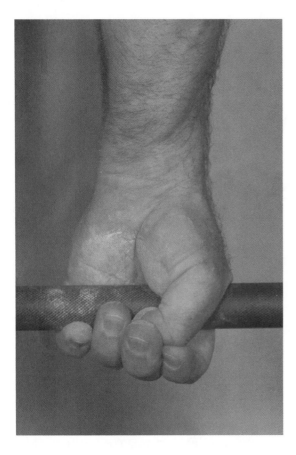

Figure 6-13. The hook grip. Note that the middle finger catches the thumbnail. The friction of the finger against the thumb is amplified by the weight of the bar squeezing the grip components together, and makes for a much more secure grip than can be produced by grip strength alone.

Within a couple of workouts, when the movement is good enough to worry about peripheral matters, start using the **hook grip**. The hook grip is critical in enabling heavy weights to be used. It should not be considered optional. This is a very important thing to get out of the way early, before much weight is being handled in the lift. It is accomplished by simply laying the middle finger on top of the thumbnail as the grip wraps around the bar, and letting the bar settle into the bottom of the "hook" made by the fingers, so that the bar rests in the fingers during the pull, not the tight fist. In the hook grip, the friction between the thumbnail and the middle finger provides a tremendous amount of security, enabling the forearm muscles that squeeze the grip tight to relax and thus enabling the elbows to rotate faster when the bar is racked. Most people will release the hook as they rack the bar, due to wrist flexibility, and this is fine. The hook will need to be reset for each rep.

Once the power clean is complete, from the floor with the hook grip, form problems can be addressed.

Figure 6-14. The power clean.

Correcting Problems

Olympic weightlifting coaches have spent a lot of time analyzing the clean and all its constituent elements, and even a cursory examination of this material would require more time and patience than the reader and the author combined possess. And it is not necessary for our purposes here. Most of this material applies to the full squat clean anyway, since that is the version of the lift almost universally used in modern Olympic weightlifting. There is actually a dearth of information specifically about the power clean in the literature.

There are just a few guiding principles that need to be in place. First and foremost, the bar *must* be close to the body all the way from the floor up until it racks. Second, the elbows *do not bend* until after the jump has occurred. And since the whole purpose of the exercise is power production, the movement must be done explosively. We will now examine a few specific problems that are commonly encountered, starting at the floor, and address them in as practical and simple a way possible. Just remember that acquiring a good understanding of the theoretical basis of the lift will help you analyze and correct the problems you encounter in the power clean, or in any of the other lifts as well.

Stance

The stance should be the same as that used in the deadlift. Your feet should be in the stance used for a flat-footed vertical jump, for the same reason. We are going to rapidly transfer force to the floor and this stance, heels 12-15 inches apart, is the best for this. Some people develop a taste for a wider stance, and as long as grip is not adversely affected that is fine. Grip and stance are related in that the grip is chosen to maximize racking efficiency and stance is chosen to fit just inside the grip. Since the bar must be close to the shins, the stance must be inside the hands so that the fingers clear the legs on the way up (fig. 6-15). The wider the grip, the wider the stance can be, and since no one can use too wide a grip (since it just doesn't work) the range of stances available won't include one much wider than about 15 inches between the heels.

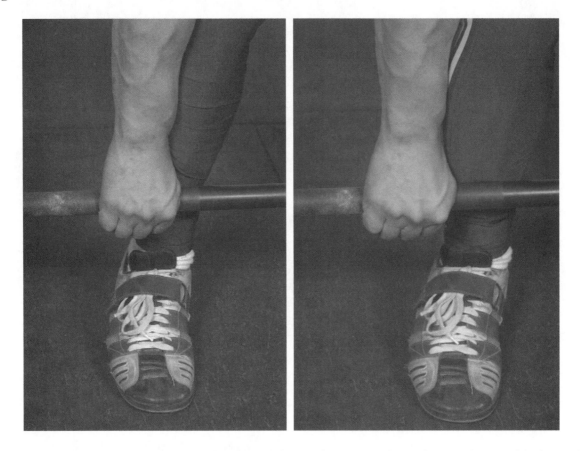

Figure 6-15. The grip width can vary (experienced lifters often use a wider grip than the one they learned with), but it must be wide enough to clear the legs on the way up to spare the skin on the thumbs (right).

Some very tall individuals with wide hips and shoulders will need a stance wider than this, but not many and not much wider. A wider grip is sometimes necessary for people with longer forearms, because the proportions produced by a long ulna and a short humerus make a good, high elbow position impossible with a normally close grip.

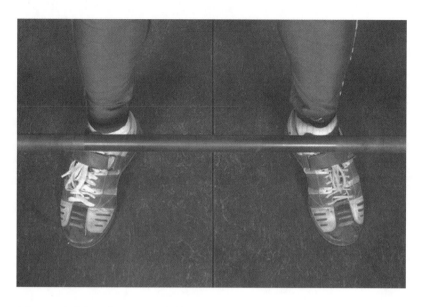

Figure 6-16. The stance width and toe angle for most people will look like this.

Figure 6-17. The position over the foot as seen from above as you look down at your feet. Memorize the details of this position – the place where the bar lines up with your shoelaces, the exact width and angle of the feet under the bar – so that it can be quickly assumed the same way each time.

Toes should point very slightly out (fig. 6-16). Most people will not have problems with an incorrect toe position, as it is uncomfortable to do it terribly wrong and most people will assume a slightly toes-out position at this stance width anyway. The slight angle out allows the knees to assume the correct angle, since feet and knees need to line up straight to prevent patellar tracking problems. Just make sure that your toes do not point dead-straight ahead, or out too much.

And the bar will be in position right over the middle of the foot, as in the deadlift (fig. 6-17). All major standing barbell exercises depend on this position for balance and even force transfer to the floor. Lining up the bar forward over the ball of the foot creates a situation that will have to be fixed after the bar leaves the floor, because the bar wants to ride the vertical line over the mid-foot, and if it doesn't leave the ground from this position some energy will have to be expended getting it there, or the pull will be inefficient.

Off the floor

We have discussed the mechanics of the pull off the floor in great detail in the deadlift section of this book. All of that material applies to the power clean and it is suggested that the analysis developed for the deadlift be applied here as well. It is important to be as efficient off the floor as possible, as any problems that develop at the top part of the pull can usually be traced to an incorrect starting position and subsequent bad initial pull off the floor.

The path the bar makes through space from starting position to racking position is a major factor in the efficiency of the lift. The bar path is observed by looking at the end of the bar from a position exactly perpendicular to the bar, just off the platform looking at the lifter from the side. Imagine that the end of the bar traces a line in the air during the lift. This line is the bar path, and it is very important to develop your ability to form an image of this line. Watch other lifters do the movement, and learn to translate the image formed of the bar path to your perception of the bar as it moves up from the floor to the rack position.

There are several advanced movement analysis instruments that record and interpret bar path information, but none is as immediately useful in real time as the experienced eye of a coach. The power clean is a complicated movement, and of all the lifts presented in this program, it benefits the most from the input of an experienced coach.

An ideal bar path is illustrated in figure 6-18 and will vary only slightly among individual lifters due to anthropometry. If correct position over the middle of the foot and the correct back angle are established, the bar comes off the floor in a vertical path as the knees straighten out. It follows an essentially vertical path until it reaches the jumping position, after which it curves slightly away as the elbows begin to rotate under the bar. At the top, the bar path will describe a little hook as the bar comes back and down onto the shoulders in the rack position. Individual body segment lengths and girths may vary among lifters, but this general bar path will be observed in every correct power clean.

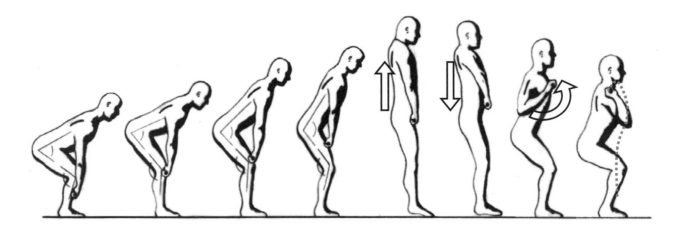

Figure 6-18. The bar path of the power clean. If the bar starts from a position over the middle of the foot, the bar should travel an essentially vertical path until the jump occurs at mid-thigh. This ideal vertical path will be altered if the start position is forward of the mid-foot.

Let's review the angles involved in the pull and see what varying them does to the bar path. The knee angle, hip angle, and trunk angle are the same for the power clean pull off the floor as for the deadlift. The correct starting position facilitates an efficient pull. For example, if your

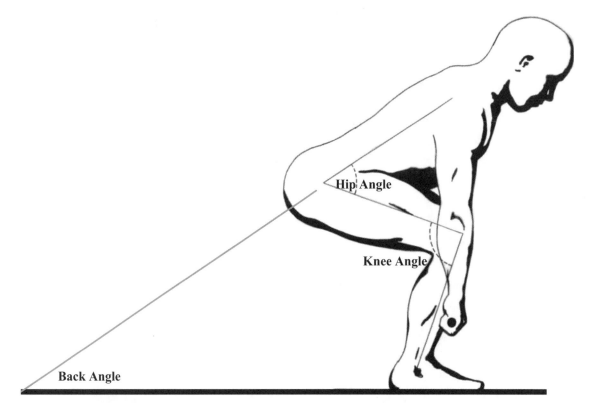

Figure 6-19. The angles for analyzing the power clean are the same as for the deadlift or any pull from the floor: the hip, knee, and back angles.

knees are too far forward, as when the knee angle is too acute or when you are on your toes, your back angle will be too vertical, placing the scapulas behind the bar and the thighs too nearly parallel to the floor. The bar cannot come up in a straight line, but rather must move forward to get around the knees. Pulled from the floor up around the knees this way, the bar is already too far out in front as it approaches the jumping position. This initial error is magnified as the bar ascends toward the rack position. Since the weight is too far out in front and you are forward on your toes, it is difficult to get the weight and the knees back far enough to correctly finish the clean in a good vertical jumping position. The bar stays forward, causing you to jump forward instead of *up*. This very common starting position error is corrected by raising your hips and pulling the bar back in to your shins, which puts the bar closer to the correct line of pull before it leaves the floor. Another approach is to think about keeping your weight back on your heels, or even raising your toes, as the bar comes off the floor.

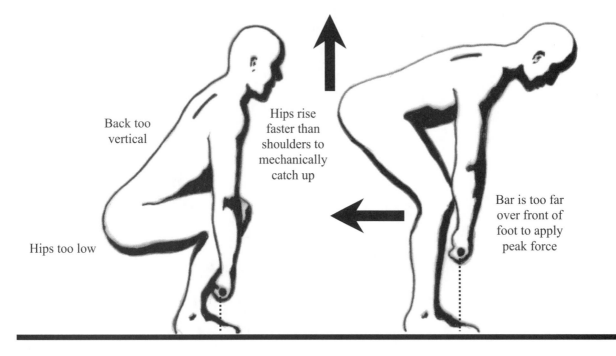

Back too
vertical

Hips rise
faster than
shoulders to
mechanically
catch up

Hips too low

Bar is too far
over front of
foot to apply
peak force

Figure 6-20. A starting position with the hips too low places the bar in front of the mid-foot position and leaves the bar too far away from the body throughout the pull. This introduces a forward component into the pull, and as a result, the rack.

Figure 6-21. A simple correction for a too-forward starting position (A) is getting your weight back over your heels, or even lifting your toes up inside your shoes (B). This brings the bar back over the mid-foot.

The other extreme, with the hips up too high, where the knee angle is too open, the hip angle is too acute, and the trunk angle is nearly parallel to the floor, presents a different problem. Here the quadriceps muscles of the thigh have essentially been removed from the lift, since their job of extending the knee has already been done before the bar leaves the floor. Since this happens before the bar moves, they contribute nothing to the first part of the lift. Again a starting position problem contributes to problems higher in the pull. Since the back is nearly parallel to the floor, this position places the scapulas in front of the bar. When the bar leaves the floor it swings out to get in position under the scapulas, leaving it too far from the legs. If the pull is rescued from this mistake, the knees are still too straight and the hips too flexed when the bar gets to the jumping position. The knees are too straight to jump efficiently since jumping requires knee extension, and the bar swings away from the body as the hip angle opens, in a "loop," a classic error in the clean where the bar goes out instead of up. This is also easily fixed by adjusting your starting position, by looking ahead, lowering your hips and using more "squat."

These examples represent the extreme variations in starting errors, and define a gradient that will be observed throughout people of differing anthropometry, skill, and talent. Most starting position errors will lie somewhere along this continuum. It is very difficult to detect the subtle variations in starting position by feel. Even elite weightlifters experience "form creep," where a good starting position erodes over several workouts into a bad one. The use of a video camera (if one is available) so you can see the relevant angles – or the eyes of an experienced coach – are *extremely* helpful for holding your clean technique together.

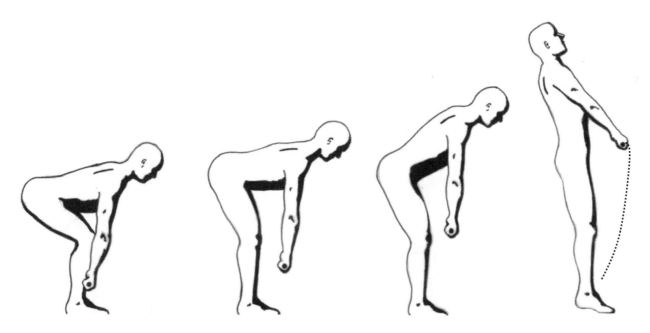

Figure 6-22. The hips-too-high starting position. Even with the bar in the correct place over the mid-foot, the scapulae will be in front of the bar in this position. This causes the bar to swing away forward to the normal pulling configuration with the bar plumb to the shoulder blades, leaving the bar out in front. The bar likes to be over the middle of the foot *and* under the shoulder blades, and much energy will be wasted trying to deal with it in any other position. In both this case and the example in figure 6-20, the bar ends up in a position too far in front of the ideal vertical bar path, but different position errors are responsible.

These next comments are possibly the most important to understand in the whole discussion of the pull from the floor. Remember from our initial instructions that the bar accelerates from the bottom to the top, getting faster as it gets higher. This means that the bar starts off the floor slow and gets faster as it comes up. The *entire purpose* of the lower half of the pull, the deadlift part, is to get the bar into the jumping position, so that the bar can be accelerated on up to the rack position. As such, it is far more important for the pull from the floor to be *correct* than it is for it to be *fast*. Remember this: the bar must be pulled correctly at the bottom and fast at the top. **Pull the bar slow and correct off the floor – fast and close at the top.** The off-the-floor errors mentioned above usually occur when you get in a hurry and jerk the bar off the floor. If you jerk the bar off the floor, you jerk yourself out of position. If you're out of position you can't hit the jump.

Any position error that is caused by being in a hurry off the floor will be magnified on the way up, as described above. Since the movement is so fast, there is no time to correct the error. But if the bar comes off the floor slowly, your proprioceptive skills – your ability to reference your position in space – have time to make the small corrections that might be needed to put the bar back in the right place before it begins moving so fast that a correction is impossible. Control of the bar position is the whole point of coming up slowly, so that the jumping position can be hit correctly every time.

Figure 6-23. Preparing to jerk the bar off of the floor (A) versus preparing to squeeze the bar off of the floor (B). The bent elbows and incorrect back angle ruin the pulling mechanics, and the jerk that follows as the slack comes out of the elbows worsens the situation.

Jerking the bar off the floor is the most common problem after the transition to the full power clean from the hang. From the starting position, many people bend their elbows a little and then jerk the slack out of the arms in an attempt to get the bar moving rapidly as it leaves the floor. This jerk is often accompanied by shoving the butt up in the air, as discussed above (fig. 6-22). This must be identified and dealt with the first time you do it. Pay close attention to the sounds you hear as you start the pull: if the plates and bar rattle, you have jerked it. Several things work to fix this. Think about "squeezing" the bar off the floor. Or think about "long straight arms." Or just "slow off the floor." Also make sure that your eyes are looking forward and not down, since eyes-down is often associated with hips-up. The idea is to maintain correct position while accelerating on up through the jump.

At the top

After the bar has been pulled up past the knees from the correct starting position, it will continue in a nearly vertical path until it reaches the jumping position. The jump is the power phase of the pull, in which the force that produces the upward acceleration peaks. Prior to this phase, the bar should stay over the mid-foot for the most efficient power production; after the jump starts, the bar path can deviate from vertical. Since force production is no longer occurring perpendicular to the floor, and the racking phase happens after the bar has stopped its upward acceleration, some deviation from vertical will occur at the top due to the actions that precede rotating the elbows into the rack. The jump itself pushes the bar slightly forward, and the shrug phase of the jump pulls it back in.

The shrug phase of the jump occurs with a movement of the torso in a slightly backwards direction, since shrugging on a bar in front of you has to be a little backward so that the shrug does not pull your body forward. The bar will go a little forward as this happens to keep the center of mass of the system over the mid-foot during this last part of the power phase and because the hips have extended very hard and pushed it slightly away. The point immediately previous to this deviation is actually where peak power is produced, and after the shrug power stops being produced as contact is lost with the ground and the bar is racked.

Figure 6-24. It is important that the bar be in contact with the thighs at the jumping position. The bar must move from this position upward with as explosive and vertical a jump a possible, and peak power directed correctly upward cannot be developed at this critical position if the bar is not in contact with the legs.

Any bar path deviation from directly over the mid-foot is a technique issue only if it occurs before the jump, in which case it adversely affects power production.

This middle part of the pull is the range in which the angle of the back begins to change. This change in angle produces the pre-jump acceleration of the bar. As the angle of the back becomes more vertical, the angular velocity of the back increases and the linear velocity of the bar hanging from the back increases as well. The bar needs to be on or very close to your legs during this phase, touching or nearly touching the skin all the way up, with straight elbows. The path is vertical because the knees and hips extend in a coordinated way that results in the load moving up in the most efficient trajectory possible – a straight line with as little forward or backward deviation (seen as lateral movement in the bar path) as possible. Any non-vertical bar movement will require you to do "extra" things at the top to catch it. The bar should be starting to accelerate through this phase, gaining velocity in anticipation of the jump that is about to occur.

During this section of the pull, forward movement of the bar is usually due to an incorrect start, as previously discussed. Starting errors are magnified as the bar goes up. If the bar feels like it is too far forward – if it is not touching your thighs all the way up – check your starting position again. You may need to think about using your lats to actively push the bar back into your legs on the way up. This will usually correct the fundamental position problem, since you can't actually use your lats to do this if you are in the wrong position.

As the bar approaches the mid-thigh jumping position, the most important part of the movement occurs. If you are correctly pulling the bar, it is accelerating as it moves up the thigh, sliding up your skin or your sweats. As it gets to the jumping position, about two-thirds of the way up the thigh, you should actually try to jump off the ground with the bar. The reaction with the ground during this explosion is the impulse that imparts momentum to the bar, and occurs at the point at which the scapulae rotate behind vertical to it. The knees, hips, and ankles extend simultaneously, with the knees and hips being the primary contributors to the force production. Active ankle extension is not really a huge contributor to the explosion; the calf muscles do contract and produce force, but the momentum of the knee and hip extension is what actually carries you up onto your toes at the top of the pull. An active attempt to perform a hard plantar flexion will not add much to most

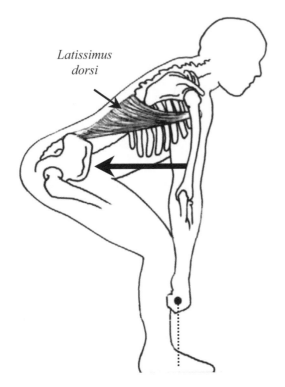

Latissimus dorsi

Figure 6-25. The most important concept in the understanding of pulling mechanics is the relationship between the skeletal components and the musculature as the pull is executed. Note the positions of the bar, the mid-foot, the scapulae, the spine, the knees, and the hips. Then note the muscular actions involved in maintaining these relationships during the pull. The lats are the key to keeping the bar in the correct position relative to the skeletal components, and their conscious activation can solve many position problems.

190

people's clean, and may actually slow it down by cluttering up the jump with another task.

The bar accelerates on up in response to the burst of force generated by this extension and is transmitted up the back, across the scapulae, and down the straight arms to the bar. The shrug will then happen as a natural consequence of this upward extension when the clean is learned as a jump with the bar in the hands. As the bar comes up high enough that the elbows must unlock, they begin to rotate up into the rack position. The clean is finished as the elbows complete their rotation by coming to a position pointing forward.

An interesting thing to note about this phase of the pull is the movement of the knees. As the knees extend in the initial pull from the floor, the shins have become vertical, placing the knees back enough to allow the bar to come up in its vertical path. After the bar clears the knees and as it slides up the thighs, the knees will come forward a little to a position back under the bar as the hips extend. This puts the back in a more vertical position to facilitate the jump with the bar hanging from the arms. Then the jump occurs, and the knees and hips extend explosively. So the knees actually extend *twice* – once off the floor and again at the top during the jump – allowing the quadriceps to contribute twice to the upward movement of the bar. Olympic weightlifting coaches refer to this as the "second pull", although second *push* (against the floor) might be more descriptive. This movement will occur as a natural physical consequence of getting into the jumping position and the bar touching the thighs as the jump occurs. Learned this way, the second pull requires no conscious direction, and no time will have to be spent learning it separately. That is why you should ensure that the jumping position is learned early and thoroughly.

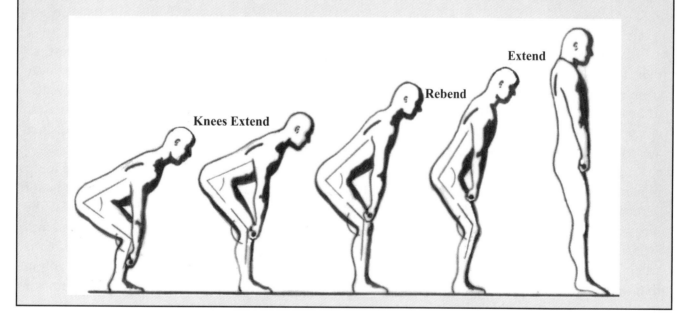

One way to ensure that the jumping position is used correctly every time is to establish a marker for its successful execution. If you actively try to touch the same place high on your thigh with the bar each rep, and develop the ability to feel the contact point and control it, you will gain a large measure of conscious control over the finish of the power clean. Bar contact on the thigh is necessary for correctly meeting the jumping position, and if that contact is used as a cue, the jump is much more likely to be correctly performed. Using this bar contact as a cue can also increase the speed of the clean, by hitting the thigh harder and thus using more power during the jump that causes the contact. It can also be used as a diagnostic tool, clothing permitting, by looking at your thigh to see where the red mark from the bar contact is. Pulling errors can be identified by seeing where the mark is on the thigh in relation to where it should be for the most efficient jump.

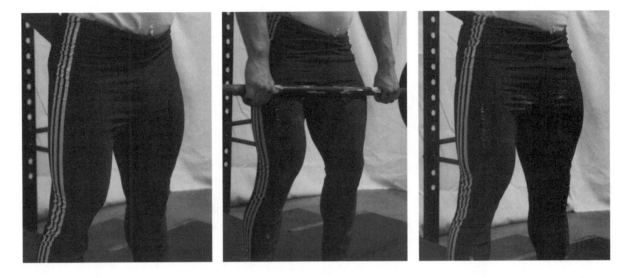

Figure 6-26. Chalk is a handy tool for many jobs in the weight room. In this case it allows the contact of the bar against the thighs to be identified and gauged at the jumping position.

After the bar leaves the jumping position, it is important that it stay close to the chest, so that it doesn't have to travel very far to get back into the rack position. If the bar heads away from the body between the jump and the rack, the distance between the bar and the shoulders has to be closed. This is done by either pulling the bar back in to the shoulders in the trajectory that is referred to as a "loop," or by jumping forward to meet the bar. Neither of these is efficient, since any force that directs the bar anywhere other than straight up to the shoulders is wasted.

A loop should be corrected by first determining how the bar is going forward. If the jump is started early, i.e. too low on the thighs, the bar will loop forward due to a trunk angle that is not vertical enough. If the bar is to go straight up, the back must be vertical enough that most of the hip extension is already over before the jump takes place, or the remaining hip extension will swing the bar away (fig. 6-27). This fault is determined by observing where on the thigh the bar is when the jump occurs, using the mark-on-the-thigh technique. If you have a jumping position that starts consistently too low on the thigh, think about waiting longer before you jump, or touching higher on the thigh as you jump.

If the loop occurs because you are forward on your toes during the lower pull off the floor, your heels will be "soft" against the floor and your knees will be forward as the bar passes them. In this case, it loops because the bar is headed forward from the ground up, as the bar path will show on your video or to your coach (fig. 6-28). Get back on your heels to start the pull, and make sure you keep your heels down until the jump occurs with the bar well up on the thigh.

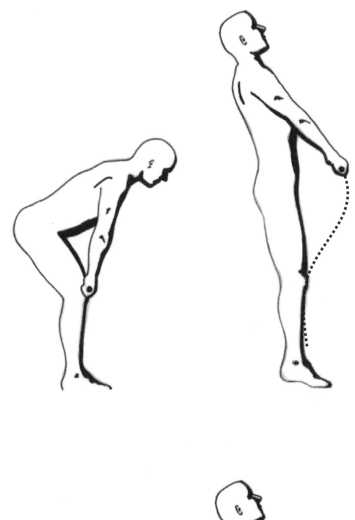

Figure 6-27. If the jump starts early, i.e. too low on the thighs before the bar gets high enough, the bar swings away forward. This happens due to the back angle: the finish of the pull depends on the angular velocity of the rigid back generated by hip extension, and if the back is not sufficiently vertical, the force of the jump will be directed along a non-vertical path.

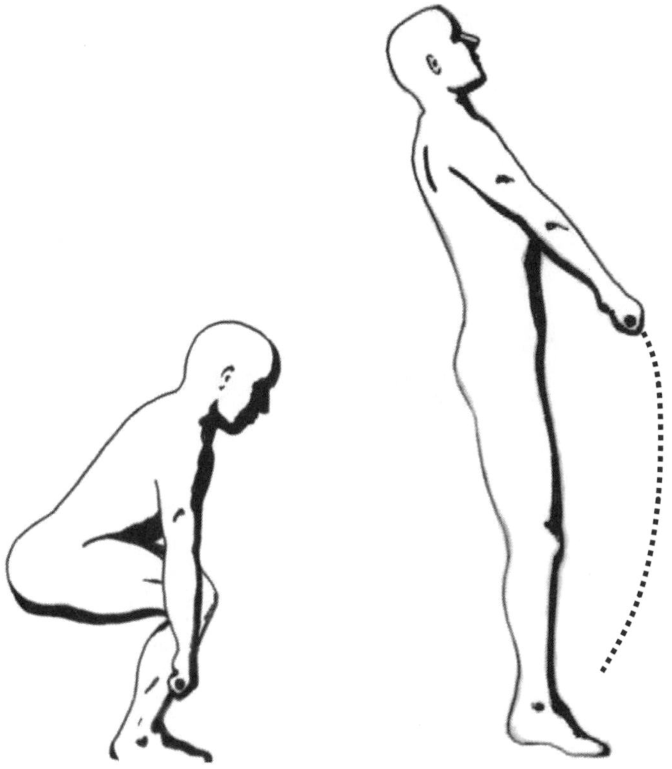

Figure 6-28. Trajectory error originating below the knees. This occurs only when the start position is especially bad, with the heels "soft" – not planted firmly – against the floor, the knees forward, and no attention paid to touching the thighs at the jumping position.

If you somehow manage to loop the bar from the correct jumping position, you may be "banging" it away with the bar contact on the thigh. This is caused by a lack of shrug from the traps that keeps the bar close to the body on the way through the top part of the pull. You can think about shrugging the bar at this point if you need to, or you can make the bar touch your shirt on the way up. Keep the bar close enough to you that you feel it on the way up as it passes your chest, and you will have shrugged it.

Actually, if you try to touch your shirt on the way up, this will usually correct the errors made at the bottom. This is an excellent example of "correction displacement," where sufficient attention focused on correcting an error later in a sequence of movements unconsciously causes the correction of the initial problem earlier in the sequence. If you manage to touch your shirt with the bar before you rack it, you will have to get back on your heels to do it, since the shirt is more "back" toward the heels than forward towards the toes. This trick comes in handy many times in the weight room, and throughout athletics.

Figure 6-29. Touching the shirt on the way up keeps the bar closer to the ideal vertical bar path. Thinking about getting it there can unconsciously correct the pulling errors that lead to the problem: the bar cannot swing away forward when you are pulling towards the shirt, and the hips and knees cannot get in a position to swing it away if you are doing what it takes to keep it close from the start of the pull. This NOT the same thing as using the arms to raise the bar up to the shirt, as discussed below.

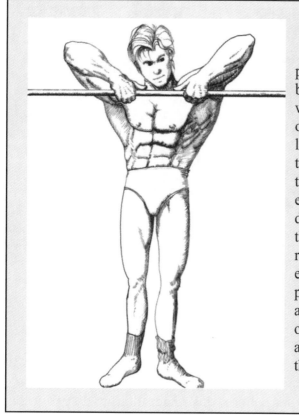

A common error during the jumping phase of the power clean is the use of the arms. There is a bodybuilding exercise known as the Upright Row, where the bar is raised to the chin with a narrow double-overhand grip. Most people have, deep in their brains, a little bundle of brain material that tells them that all things must be lifted with the arms, especially if these things are going to be lifted above the waist. And embedded in your mind is a picture of a bodybuilder doing an upright row. It is a slow movement that uses the arms and deltoids, and though it bears a superficial resemblance it has absolutely nothing to do with our explosive power clean. After the bar leaves the jumping position, no thought whatsoever should be given to the arms. None. **N-O-N-E.** The arms should be conceived of as pieces of rope that attach the shoulders to the bar, and the bar gets to the shoulders through the action of the jump, and the jamming forward of the elbows.

Bent elbows and round backs

The bending of the elbows as the bar leaves the floor is a habit that must be addressed as early as possible in the process of learning the power clean. We have mentioned several times above that the elbows *must* stay straight until the jump occurs. You should know not to bend the arms early, since you have learned this in the deadlift, and the lower part of the power clean is a deadlift. So again, the function of the arms is to transmit the pulling power generated by the hips and legs to the bar. Power is transmitted most efficiently down a non-elastic medium, like a chain, as opposed to a medium that stretches, like a spring. A chain transmits all the power from one end to the other, while a spring absorbs some of the energy as it deforms. When the bar is pulled from the floor with bent arms, the bent elbow is essentially a deformable component, a thing that can straighten out, thus preventing some of the pulling force from being transmitted to the bar. The little variances in the degree of elbow bend result in an unpredictable amount of force transfer to the bar, and thus in an unpredictable bar path. If the bar path varies with each clean, bent elbows are often the problem. And once elbows are bent, they cannot be straightened out during the pull; that would require the forearm, bicep and brachialis to relax, which they will be reluctant to do even if there was time for you to think about it and do it.

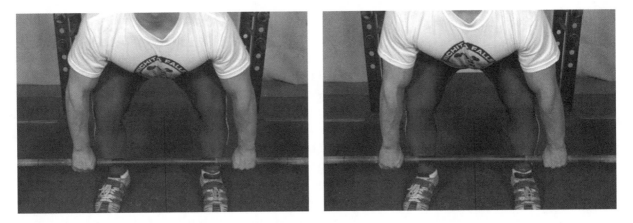

Figure 6-30. Bent elbows just absolutely suck. They are one of the most persistent, hardest to correct, and most detrimental of bad habits that a lifter can acquire. Make it a priority to learn and keep perfectly straight elbows.

The same is true for the low back. The back is the transmission to the hips/legs engine, and force generated against the ground travels up the back, across the scapulas, and down the arms to the bar. If the low back is not locked in hard, absolute extension, it is not as tight as it could be. A round back is a deformable component in the same way that bent elbows are, and will result in the same unpredictable bar path that is the inevitable consequence of unpredictable force transfer. If form problems are occurring without any set pattern, this might indicate that your low back is not as tight as it could be. Tight hamstrings could be the cause, but often it is merely a case of inattentiveness to this important position requirement.

Figure 6-31. The spine during the pull should be in absolute thoracic and lumbar extension (A). Any softness in the chest-up position or lower-back arch (B) reduces the effectiveness of the back as the transmitter of force from the hips and legs to the shoulder blades and on down to the bar.

At the top, your elbows might bend because you are trying to curl or upright row the bar with the arms. Your elbows can rotate very fast – blindingly fast, in fact – if the muscles of your arms are relaxed and provide no resistance to the rotation. The very second you tighten the forearms, biceps and triceps as you attempt to use these muscles to move the bar, you slow the movement down. After the bar is racked, this tightness causes the elbows to stop at the point where these muscles reach the end of their range of motion in contraction, which leaves the elbows pointing down and the bar sitting on your sternum. (This is another good reason to use the hook grip. The hook makes for a secure grip without the need to squeeze the bar with the fingers, thus contracting the forearm muscles.)

Rack position

After the elbows rotate and jam up into position, pointing forward, the bar is said to be in the rack position, or "racked." The upward rotation of the elbows causes the deltoids to come into a contracted position that puts them at a higher level than the sternum, permitting the bar to sit comfortably clear of the chest. At this point, most lifters will have relaxed the grip somewhat, and some will have released the hook. It is okay to release the hook, or even to let the last two fingers drop off the bar if it facilitates a good rack position. It is not okay to completely let go of the bar, although this does occur with some very inflexible lifters. The most important factor in the rack position is the elbow position and its effect on the deltoids, making a place for the bar to sit.

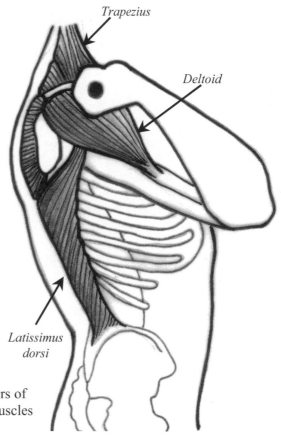

Figure 6-32. The rack position, on the meat of the deltoids. The hook grip can be released during the rotation of the elbows.

Figure 6-33. In the rack position the bar is supported on the deltoids by the elevated elbows, while the traps, the upper fibers of the spinal erectors, and the rhomboids, lats, and rotator cuff muscles support the scapulae and the spine.

197

This is actually the position of the bar for a correct Front Squat. The correct rack position is the one that allows the most weight to be supported on the deltoids. In the correct position, the bar sits on the contracted deltoids. The delts hold the humerus up high, keeping the weight off the sternum. The ribcage is held up by tension in the upper back musculature, and the entire trunk is rigid in isometric contraction and further supported by a Valsalva maneuver. In this position, as much weight as you can ever clean can easily be supported.

The pull stops during the racking phase. "Stops" means that the muscular force generated during the pull ceases being applied to the ground. As soon as the feet shift position out of the pulling stance and begin the stomp, you have stopped pushing the floor. If you hadn't, your feet could not move. When force stops being applied to the bar, it stops accelerating, and Mean Old Mr. Gravity causes its velocity to drop to zero and start back down almost instantly. It is during this reversal in acceleration that the racking position is assumed. The movement is a shrug of the shoulders instantly followed by jamming the elbows up and forward to catch the bar on the deltoids. The movement is fast, as it must be if the bar is to be caught before it falls too far.

Figure 6-34. The transition between the pull and the rack happens very quickly. Immediately after the jump occurs and the final acceleration is imparted to the bar, the direction of the movement of the body changes from up to down before the rack position is assumed. This transition must happen quickly; the instant force stops being applied to the bar and gravity ceases to be overcome by the pull the weight decelerates, goes to zero upward velocity, and starts back down, and the rack must occur before the bar falls too far. Some downward bar movement is inevitable, but it must be minimized before the acceleration of gravity results in high momentum that will be more difficult to control.

Most people will catch the bar with their elbows pointing at the floor. This is due to either a misunderstanding of the concept of the rack position, a lack of flexibility, or too narrow a grip for the length of the forearms. A sufficiently flexible trainee should be physically able to get the elbows in the correct position, although you may be reluctant to do so for various reasons. If you rack the bar wrong a few times and feel it bump your sternum because your elbows were down and the deltoids were not up enough to space the bar away, you may become gun-shy and try to hold it up with your hands, exacerbating the problem. Rack the bar once and then move your elbows up into position, very high so that the bar comes up off of the sternum. In this way you can see where they should be and feel why. If you can't do this, you need to stretch, or adjust your grip to a width that facilitates the position.

Many times, a lack of wrist and tricep flexibility prevents the quick, complete rotation necessary to rack the bar. Wrist flexibility is the more obvious of the two, but tight triceps also prevent the elbow from coming up high enough to permit a good deltoid contraction. Both can be stretched and worked on for an extended range of motion, using the bar or a stick in the rack.

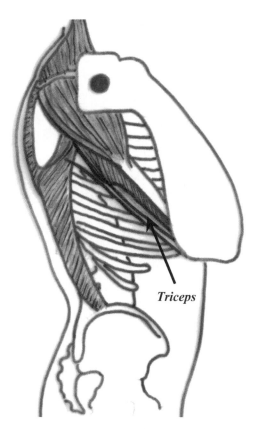

Figure 6-35. Tight triceps can cause the lack of flexibility required to rack the bar correctly, limiting the ability to push the elbows forward and up.

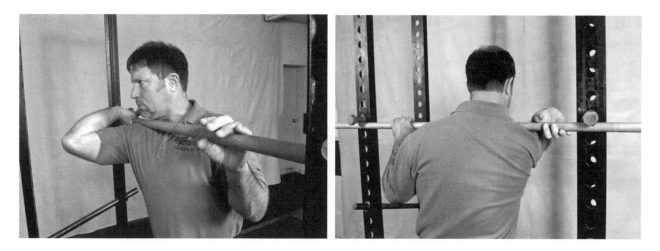

Figure 6-36. This stretch in the power rack enables the training of racking-specific flexibility.

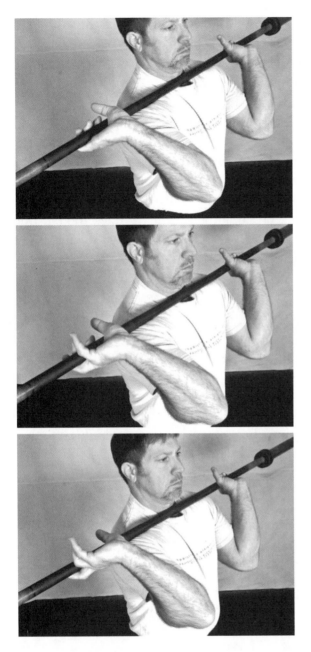

If your flexibility is not sufficient to permit the full rotation of the elbows into a good rack, the fingers must go. They are the expendable part of the chain, and after the pull has stopped their function as the last element of force transfer to the bar is over. This concept is sometimes the source of the confusion – the hands do not hold up the bar, and they stop being critical to the clean after the elbow rotation starts. So the fingers can do what they want to as the bar is racked. They can hang on, or they can release to the extent that only the index, middle, and ring fingers are in contact with the bar.

If your flexibility is sufficient but you still cannot rack the bar quickly, you may just be reluctant to let go of the bar enough to permit the elbows to come up. All that is necessary is a little relaxation of the hand, and a willingness to quickly rotate all the way up into position a couple of times to see how it feels to do it right. Several mental tricks can help with racking speed. Imagine slamming your elbows into the hands of your coach, as in figure 6-38. Sometimes it helps to aim your shoulder at the bar, or to hit the bar with your shoulders, like you're trying to strike a blow even as the elbow comes up. The crucial concept here is that the bar is not racked until the elbows point forward, and that stopping the elbow rotation before it reaches this position is not acceptable.

Figure 6-37. Under ideal circumstances, the best grip for the rack position is with four fingers under the bar (top). Flexibility limitations may make it necessary to use fewer fingers, but the most important consideration is elbow position. Do what is necessary to get the elbows up.

Figure 6-38. A target for your elbows can help with learning to rack the bar.

Just after the shrug and at the same time as the elbows begin to jam forward, the feet stomp the floor. This foot movement causes everything happening around it to time out better. It feels better when the feet stomp and the bar racks at exactly the same time, and your body will time the rack to coincide with the stomp. Then, if the stomp is fast, it pulls the rack along faster with it. The simultaneity of the two events is fairly automatic, and not too many people will stomp out of phase with the rack because it just feels too weird. So the stomp actually sharpens the timing of the racking movement. A certain amount of knee bend will accompany the stomp, necessary to cushion the catching of the weight. Catching the weight with perfectly straight knees is not desirable, and actually doesn't occur very often since it also feels too weird. The stomp thus makes the movement quicker, while at the same time cushioning the catch.

The feet will stomp into their same footprints, or just a little wider. Just a little means a couple of inches per side wider. Some people will shift their feet out to a position wider than a squat stance. This "spider-in-heat" position is used in an attempt to drop lower under the bar, in lieu of pulling it high enough. You don't get a good stomp going this wide because the angle is not conducive to stomping and the distance covered is so great that it takes too long. Stomping is quick, lateral splitting is not. Fix this when you do it by stomping into your correct starting position footprints several times without the bar. And focus on this foot position during the clean with a lighter weight that can be racked properly. A lateral split is a bad thing to choose as a habit: it is dangerous, hard to control, and ineffective. The purpose of the power clean is pulling the bar high – we don't want to make it easier to get under the bar, we want to pull the bar higher. And if we *were* going to make it easier to get under the bar we would use the standard squat version of the clean, not a weird bastardized mutation thereof.

Figure 6-39. A lateral split is very common among novices and high school athletes that have never been corrected. It is often associated with other racking technique problems, such as bad elbow position and leaning back. It is corrected by giving the feet a job to do: stomp your feet back into your footprints or just a little wider.

After you rack the bar, recover back to a fully upright stance with elbows still in the rack position. Don't develop the habit of putting the bar down before a full recovery, and good control of the bar and the final position has been established. If you're in a big hurry to put it down after you rack it, you might soon find that you've gotten in a big hurry to rack it and start racking it wrong. Disaster follows close on the heels of such things. Finish each clean correctly.

All Olympic weightlifters have heard the words, "Finish the pull!" This cue is used when the bar gets heavy and understanding it is crucial to completing any type of clean or snatch. If the racking movement starts before the jump has put all available force into accelerating the bar that critical last bit, the bar fails to travel to its full height and the rack must be accomplished at a lower position than it would be if the pull had been finished. This usually means that the bar is caught in a position more forward than up, or not racked at all. An unfinished pull indicates that the last part of the pull, the jump and shrug, has been done inefficiently or incompletely. Finishing the pull will be a necessary skill to learn, and will be something that you work on doing well every time you train the clean for the rest of your training career.

After the rack

After the clean is racked and recovered, the bar must be dropped safely, without destroying you or your equipment. The method used here will depend on the equipment. If a platform and bumper plates are available, as they should be, the bar can be dropped from the rack position in a controlled manner. Care should be taken to keep the bar from bouncing away from where it is dropped by keeping it level on the way down. Your hands should not leave the bar while it is dropped until just before it gets to the floor: bars that are released at the top and allowed to free-fall are much more likely to bounce unevenly than bars that are tended as they drop.

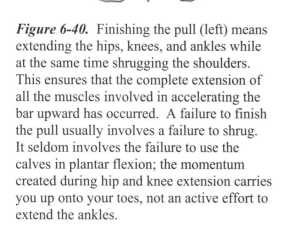

Figure 6-40. Finishing the pull (left) means extending the hips, knees, and ankles while at the same time shrugging the shoulders. This ensures that the complete extension of all the muscles involved in accelerating the bar upward has occurred. A failure to finish the pull usually involves a failure to shrug. It seldom involves the failure to use the calves in plantar flexion; the momentum created during hip and knee extension carries you up onto your toes, not an active effort to extend the ankles.

Figure 6-41. Bumper plates are designed to make the explosive lifts safer for the lifter and easier on the bar and platform; they absorb the shock of the drop so that the bar can be lowered by dropping rather than through the use of an eccentric effort, as was necessary before the invention of the equipment. But they must be used correctly so that the bounce can be controlled. As a general rule, don't let go of the bar until it is at the level of the knees.

If bumper plates are not available, the task becomes harder. The bar must be released from the rack and caught at the hang, and then lowered to the floor, to prevent damage to the barbell and the floor. This can be tricky, since it really hurts to actually drop the bar right on the thighs. The bar has to be released from the rack with enough grip on it to be able to slow it down before it hits the thighs. It is decelerated with the traps using a movement that is the opposite of the shrug used during the jump. It needs to stop here under control before being lowered on down to the floor. And if metal plates are used, it would be prudent to use rubber mats to protect the floor. But really, get some bumper plates. They are important enough to consider necessary.

As with almost everything we do in the weight room, eye position is important for balance and stability, and neck safety. Eyes should be focused slightly down on a fixed position on the floor in front of you. This keeps the cervical vertebrae in a more normal anatomical position. Failure to consistently focus the eyes on a fixed spot will usually result in a wandering bar path, due to the resultant slight variations in back angle in the starting position. This will not be a problem until the bar gets heavy, but if you start to miss heavy cleans, remind yourself about your eye position. It's easy to forget about, and one of the easier things to fix.

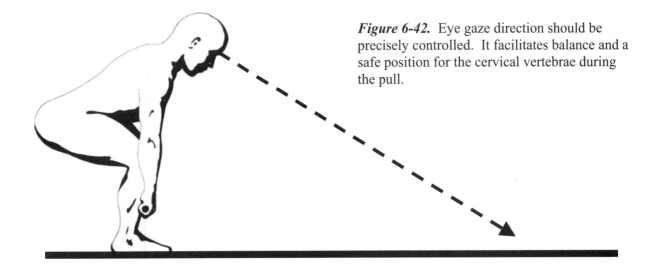

Figure 6-42. Eye gaze direction should be precisely controlled. It facilitates balance and a safe position for the cervical vertebrae during the pull.

Power cleans are not like squats or deadlifts, movements that can be ground out to a bone-on-bone finish through perseverance and hard work. A deadlift can be locked out even if it is a little out of position by just pulling harder. The movement is slower and there is time to fix minor form problems with more strength before the pull is over. The clean takes less than a second to do, and if it is not right, it doesn't rack. Cleans can be racked only if all the contributing factors are there: strength, power, and technique. Since the clean is a much more mechanically complicated movement, it is more sensitive to each contributing factor than the slow movements are. This is evidenced by the experience common to all lifters, where 100 kg. is good for many attempts but 105 *just will not rack.* Finishing the pull collates all the factors involved in the pull, and causes them all to come together at the right time to contribute to racking the weight. The slow movements rely on *absolute strength* – the simple ability to generate force in the correct position – at their limit capacity, while the quick lifts utilize the ability to apply maximum power at exactly the right time, in exactly the right place. These are two distinct skills, producing different types of training stress, and resulting in two different types of adaptation. Recognizing this difference between the slow lifts and the explosive lifts is fundamental to your understanding of barbell training.

Useful Assistance Exercises

The squat, bench press, deadlift, press, and clean form the basis of any successful, well-designed training program. But there are other exercises that can assist these five and improve certain aspects of their performance.

There are, quite literally, thousands of exercises that can be done in a well-equipped gym. Bill Pearl, in his classic text *Keys to the Inner Universe* includes cursory descriptions of 1621. Not all of these exercises are useful for strength training purposes, because few of them actually contribute to the performance of the core barbell exercises.

This is important for a couple of reasons. Your training priorities, which should depend on your advancement as an athlete, should involve strength, power, or mass. No matter how long you train, how strong, explosive, or big you get, your training will always be tied to the performance of these basic movements or their derivatives. The fact that resources – time, recovery, the patience of family and friends – are always in shorter supply than we'd like makes the efficiency with which your goals are accomplished an important consideration. The best assistance exercises are those that contribute directly to the performance of the basic movements that produce the most benefit.

Not that the basic movements need much help. They are complete exercises in and of themselves, since they all involve lots of muscles moving lots of joints in anatomically correct, functionally useful ways. But after a certain period of time, usually several months after serious training begins, the stimulation provided by the simple execution of the basic exercises alone is not enough to produce sufficient stress to cause further adaptation. This is not due to any deficiency in the basic exercises, but to the trainee's ability to successfully adapt to the stress these exercises provide. It is a natural result of training that progress slows down after progress has been made, and progress is why we train. These topics are discussed at great length in *Practical Programming for Strength Training*.

For example, an excellent way to improve a stuck bench press is to add chin-ups to the workout. Chins add enough work to the triceps, forearms, and upper back that the contribution of these muscle groups to the bench press is reinforced for the trainee that needs a little extra work. And this work is done in the context of another multi-joint functional exercise. A less efficient way to accomplish the task would be to add a tricep isolation movement like cable triceps extensions, a movement that when done with strict form leaves out lats, scapula retractors, forearms, posterior deltoids, biceps, and grip strength. Since the bench press uses all these muscles, why lose the opportunity to train them all together at the same time, the same way they function? (The lying triceps extension is an example of an exercise that actually is more beneficial when performed with what would conventionally be interpreted as less-than-strict form. When a lying triceps extension is done with heavy weight and a pullover preceding the extension, it uses a lot of lat, grip and forearm work.)

Assistance exercises work by either 1.) strengthening a part of a movement, like a partial deadlift – a rack pull or a halting deadlift – or 2.) are variations on the basic exercise, like a stiff-legged deadlift, or 3.) are *ancillary* exercises, which strengthen a portion of the muscle mass involved in the movement in a way that the basic exercise does not, like the chin-up. All assistance exercises of value can be assigned to one of these three categories.

Partial Movements

The deadlift, as mentioned earlier, can be a brutally hard exercise. When done with very heavy weights, as a very strong trainee would need to use, deadlifts can become very hard to recover from in a reasonable period of time. A limit set of five in excess of 500 lbs. might require a week or more for adequate recovery for the next workout, and in the meantime squats have suffered as well. When your deadlift gets strong enough that heavy sets of five create more stress than can easily be recovered from within the timeframe of your training, it might be good to alternate two assistance exercises instead of the deadlift. Halting deadlifts come from the floor up to the top of the kneecaps, and cover the bottom part of the movement, and rack pulls are done from below the knees up to full lockout at the top. The combination of the two covers the entire pull, while at the same time producing less recovery demand than the full movement.

The halting deadlift is done from the same stance as the deadlift with a double overhand grip. The first part of the deadlift is a knee extension, and the halting deadlift emphasizes this part of the movement. A brief review of pulling mechanics might be useful here; refer to chapter 4 if necessary. The knee extensors function to move the load up from the floor, the hamstrings and glutes maintain the back angle while this happens, the spinal erectors keep the spine rigid in extension so the transfer of force from the knees and hips to the bar can occur efficiently, the traps transfer this force to the scapulae from which the arms hang, and the lats keep the arms from swinging forward so that the load stays in position under the shoulder blades during the trip from the floor to the top of the knees and back down. Haltings really work the whole arrangement of pulling muscles, but in a way specific to the first part of the pull, before the back angle begins to change. The amazing part of this exercise is how much work the lats get while doing their isometric job of holding the weight back under the shoulder blades.

Take a normal deadlift stance and a double-overhand grip of the same width as for a deadlift. Lift the chest and lock the back into extension, and then drag the bar up the shins until the patellas are just cleared, and then set it down. Don't worry about setting it down slowly, since the work on a halting is supposed to be mostly concentric. It is very helpful to think about 1.) pushing the floor with your feet, and 2.) pulling the bar back into your shins as it comes up. Breathing is the same as for the deadlift; take a big breath before you pull and hold it until you set the bar back down. Start with 135 lbs. and take reasonable jumps up to your work set weight.

Haltings will not be done in the same workout with the deadlift, so you will not be warm when you start them as you might be with a smaller muscle group assistance exercise that would be done after the core movement, and they should be warmed up just like a deadlift. They are used for higher reps, but due to their shorter range of motion work sets of 8 reps will use heavier weights than a deadlift work set of 5, possibly as high as 85% of 1RM. At this load, one work set is plenty.

A few details should be discussed. Haltings seem to respond well to higher reps, and sets of eight make a good place to start. Breathing takes place at the bottom, and is the biggest problem during the exercise due to the bent-over position; the last reps of a long set are no fun when you're out of air, and you can't really get a good breath in the start position. The grip is a straight double-overhand, or clean, grip, as mentioned earlier. Supinating one hand for a heavy single deadlift is a necessary evil in a meet, but multiple reps with one shoulder in internal rotation and the other in external rotation produce an asymmetric shoulder stress. Haltings are very good

Figure 7-1. The bottom (left) and top (right) position of the halting deadlift.

for developing the grip, since you won't be using your 1RM deadlift weight for them, and the clean grip is harder than the alternate grip, so use it as a grip exercise too. If you get strong enough that your grip strength is exceeded, then you can either use straps, or switch your alternate grip – change the supine hand each rep. This change is a little trouble, and straps are fine if your grip is otherwise strong enough, i.e. you don't normally have any trouble hanging on to heavy deadlifts.

Some attention will have to be paid to keeping the bar against the shins on the way up. Haltings are best thought of as a push against the ground with the feet and almost as a row at the top as the bar breaks over the knees. Lifting the chest a tiny bit right at the top helps cue the lats, as does pushing the bar back into the shins and knees as the bar nears the top.

Rack pulls are the other half of this pair. They are done from inside the power rack, from level pins set at a point somewhere below the knee. How far below the knee the rack is set determines the amount of overlap that the halting and the rack pull have with each other. Just below the patella is probably not enough, while down to mid-shin defeats the purpose of dividing the whole pull into two movements. Three or four inches below the joint line is about right. The point of the halting deadlift is to work the initial drive off the floor, which depends heavily on the quads for the drive and the hamstrings to anchor the back angle; the rack pull should use as little quadriceps drive as possible, just enough to the carry the bar past the knee, with the main emphasis on hip extension – hamstrings and glutes, and above all, a flat back while this happens.

The rack pull stance will be the same width as the deadlift, but with the shins very close to the bar, much closer than the start position off the floor, with the bar directly over the mid-foot. The bar should be in the position it would be were it deadlifted to that height off the floor. This will make the shins almost, but not quite perfectly, vertical. The shoulders should be in front of the bar, and it is very important that they stay there until the bar is well up the thigh. The back must be locked hard in both lumbar and thoracic extension – the chest is up, and the lower back is arched, the position described earlier with the deadlift. It is easier to get in this position higher up the shin since less hamstring tension is pulling on the pelvis/lumbar lock at this point. As with the halting deadlift, the rack pull is performed with a clean grip, usually strapped due to the heavy weights used and the friction of the bar against the thigh on the way up.

Figure 7-2. The start, middle and finish of the rack pull.

From the starting position the bar is pulled up the thigh, in constant contact with the skin, the shoulders out over the bar, the chest up, and the knees held in position with no forward movement. When the bar is high enough up the thigh that the scapulas have moved behind the bar, the hips are extended forcefully – "shoot the hips" is a good cue for this movement. The finish position is the same as for a deadlift, with shoulders back, chest up, knees and hips straight, and eyes straight ahead. No exaggerated shrug is necessary or useful; the hips are shoved forward into extension with the chest held up, and this is all that needs to be done at the top. Breathing is also the same as for the deadlift, a big breath taken before the pull each rep. Sets of five work well for rack pulls. The weights that can be used are amazing, due to the shorter range-of-motion, and it is not uncommon to do a 5RM rack pull with very close to 1RM deadlift weight. Again, they should be warmed up with the same progression as a deadlift.

The rack pull bears more resemblance to the position of a clean pull at the top of the "first pull" phase than a deadlift in that it keeps the shoulders out over the bar longer than a deadlift. The scapulas begin to rotate behind the bar shortly after it rises above the knees in a deadlift; a rack pull, like a clean, keeps the shoulders forward and the scapulas out over the bar longer, until the bar is a little further up the thigh. This is because the knees start out in such a straight position, to minimize the use of the quads, that only hip extension is available to move the bar; the deadlift has saved a little quad extension to use after the bar clears the knees, placing the back in a more vertical position when the bar is lower on the thighs. This means that the back must be held locked in extension in a more horizontal position up higher on the thighs than a deadlift. For this reason, rack pulls just plain murder the lumbar erectors.

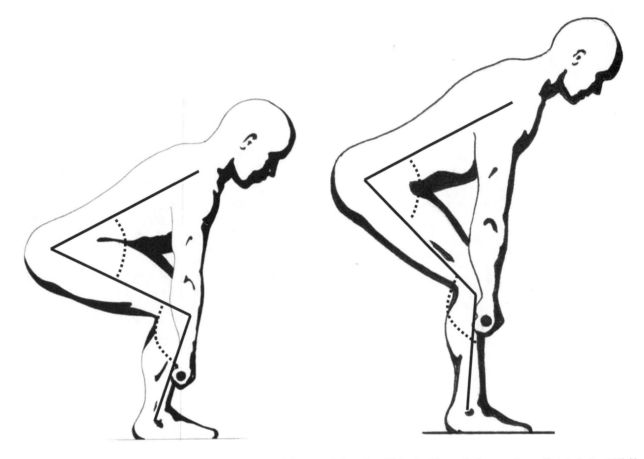

Figure 7-3. A comparison of the start positions of the deadlift (left) and the rack pull (right). While the deadlift uses an initial knee extension to start the bar off the floor, the rack pull begins at a point up the shins where this would have already occurred; vertical shins and the absence of quadriceps involvement is the key feature of the exercise.

As simple as this movement sounds, it is very easy to do wrong. Most people will allow their knees to come forward as soon as the bar passes them, making the back angle more vertical and dragging the bar back up the thighs along an angle – and supporting some of the weight on the thigh – instead of keeping the bar path vertical. Any time the knees move forward under a load, the hamstrings have allowed it to happen, whether the movement is a squat or a pull. **Any closing of the knee angle in any context involves a shortening of the hamstring, because one end of the hamstring is attached to the tibia immediately below the knee, and when the knee bends that end of the hamstring has come closer to the other end.** This will either be due to an active hamstring contraction that causes the knee to flex – the distal function of the muscles (not the case here) – or a passive shortening of the muscles in the form of a relaxation of the contraction from the hip-end of the chain – the proximal function. This is what happens when the knees move forward; the hip angle opens when the knee angle closes as the knees move forward under the bar. (This is illegal in the deadlift in a powerlifting meet, since the bar will actually go down a little during this knee shift, and it is referred to as a "hitch".) Your body wants to do this for the same reason the second pull on a clean works: you get a second opportunity to use the quads to straighten out the knee if you re-bend it. But unlike a clean, the rack pull is specifically used to strengthen the hamstrings, and they must be made to do their job as intended, to pull the hips into extension while the back holds flat. It is important to stay out over the bar, keep the knees back, keep the bar on the legs, and extend the hips only after the bar is well up the thigh.

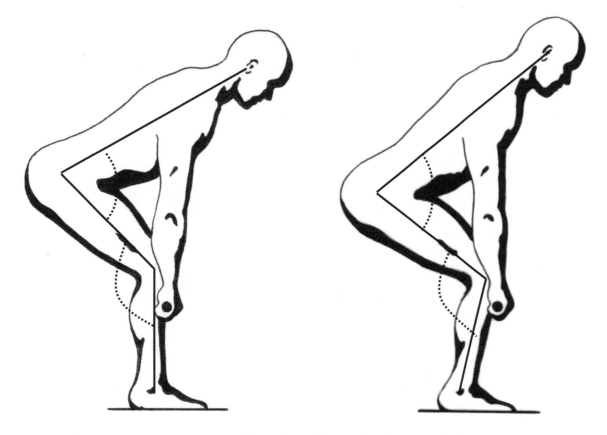

Figure 7-4. The most common error in the rack pull involves the starting position. Correct position (left) uses a vertical shin with the shoulders well out over the bar, eliminating nearly all quadriceps involvement and producing a movement that depends almost entirely on hip extension. Any deterioration in this strict position that allows the knees to drop forward dilutes the hip extension by shortening the hamstrings and adding in a knee extension component.

The rack pull obviously depends on the power rack, and its design is critical for this, and all the other exercises that can be done in one. The rack should have a floor; it should not be merely *on* the floor, with you standing on something that is not also holding the rack down. A heavy plywood floor inside the rack attached to the frame ensures that the weight of you *and* the loaded bar standing on the floor are always acting to stabilize the rack, so that when the bar is set back down on the pins the rack does not move. Your position between the uprights will be determined by the depth of the rack. Shallow racks are a pain in the ass; rack pulls are the test of a power rack's design, and if the dimensions are wrong it can be very hard to use. The rack should be deep enough that some play front to back is no problem. Drift during the set will occur no matter how careful you are, and if the uprights are so close together that you keep bumping them when you move a little, the quality of the set will suffer. If the rack is too deep, the pins will have too much "bounce" because the long span between front and back uprights requires a longer, and therefore springier, pin. The bar bouncing around on the pins is also disruptive during the set.

A good rack will be at least 16 inches deep. And if the rack is not wide enough, it can make loading the bar a problem. A narrow rack will allow an unevenly loaded bar – which they all are while being loaded – to tip. This, and the fact that a narrow rack is potentially very hard on the hands when racking the squat, makes 48 inches outside to outside a very handy width for a power rack. The holes in the uprights should be on three-inch centers or closer. This allows for fine enough adjustment in heights that it is useful for all exercises inside the rack, as well as for squatting and pressing outside the rack.

Barbell shrugs are a type of rack pull that starts up above the knee, at about the point where the hip shoots forward at the very top of the deadlift. They can be done with very heavy weights, up to 100 lbs. over your PR deadlift, due to their very short range of motion and good leverage position. In fact, if they are to be effective they must be done very heavy. But they are an advanced exercise, and not everybody should do them. The fact that they are done heavy means that a novice lifter unadapted to heavy weights, in terms of bone density, joint integrity, and motor control, can become very injured very quickly even doing them correctly. (An impatient friend of the author broke the spinous process off of C6 doing these prematurely.) Rack shrugs are best left for competitive lifters that have trained for a couple of years, and there is no real reason for athletes that are not powerlifters or weightlifters to do them at all. They are included here for the sake of completeness, lest anyone think that they do not exist

If you are sure you're ready, set your rack pins at mid-thigh and load the bar inside the rack to 135 lbs. A shrug is done like the top part of a power clean and the best warm-up for a shrug is racking the bar on the shoulders with 135 from this high position. This establishes the correct movement pattern for the subsequent heavier sets, and weeds out the novices: if you cannot easily hang clean 135, you have no business doing heavy shrugs. After a couple of sets of 5 at 135, add another big plate and try to clean it for 5. If you can, good; if you can't, you have shrugged it. The mechanics of the movement should be the same as the second pull of the clean, the heavier weight limiting the ability to rack the bar on the shoulders but with the rest of the movement intact. As the weight goes up the bar will travel less and less, until for the last couple of warmups and the work set the elbows do not even unlock and only the hips, knees, and shoulders move.

The point of this heavy load is to make the trapezius finish what the hips and legs have started. The key to the movement is the snap that must be used to make the traps fire at the top. The bar will start up slowly from the pins with the chest up, the low back locked VERY tightly, and the elbows straight, and then the shoulders are shrugged back explosively, as if to touch the top of the traps to the back of the skull. Now, this does not mean that the head moves back – it means that the traps shrug back and up, not forward towards the ears. No attempt is made to hold it at the top. For each rep the bar is caught in the finish position of the deadlift and lowered back to the pins. Each rep starts and is returned to the pins; this distinguishes a proper barbell shrug from incorrect versions in which all reps start from the hang. The start from the pins, using hip and leg drive to propel the bar up into the trap shrug is what allows the enormous weights to be used, and causes it to be such an effective exercise.

Heavy shrugs make the traps grow; there is no doubt about it. At lighter weights, sets of 5 at the 1RM deadlift, they are good for cleans, and at heavier weights they prepare the traps for the top of the deadlift and the brain for the feel of very heavy weight. They will always be done with straps, at all weights heavier than 135, due to the snap that must be present at the top when the traps shrug the bar. One heavy set after warmups is enough; sets across are extremely stressful due to the heavy skeletal loading inherent in supporting this much weight, even for the brief time it takes to complete a rep. Likewise, barbell shrugs should be used conservatively in the schedule, maybe once every two weeks in the appropriately designed program.

Figure 7-5. The barbell shrug. Each rep starts on the pins and ends at the hang position before it is set down for the next rep.

These same principles – using portions of the parent exercise as assistance exercises – can be applied to squats and presses, although not as effectively, due to the differences in the fundamental nature of the exercises. The deadlift starts from the floor, without a stretch reflex (or stretch-shortening cycle), making it very different from a squat in more ways than just the location of the bar. The hip and knee angles in the squat are more acute than at the start of the deadlift, and this longer range-of-motion is a terribly critical difference in the two, since the added ROM just happens to lie within the most mechanically disadvantageous part of the human anatomy. The only thing that mitigates this mechanically hard position is the stretch reflex rebound out of the bottom provided by the hamstrings and adductors. Squats that start from a dead stop, removing the assistance obtained from the stretch reflex, are quite useful when performed from different positions, just below parallel, well below parallel, and just above parallel. The pause makes the drive up very, very hard; a below-parallel paused box squat for 5 reps might only be 60% of 1RM. If you strengthen the squat at these positions from a dead stop, the explosion you must generate to start up from the bottom without the benefit of the bounce makes for a stronger squat when the bounce is added back in. The term "partial" when applied to squats refers mainly to the use of a non-standard technique that selectively focuses on a portion of the whole squat, and not really to the depth, since most of these methods will involve a full range of motion.

Partial squats are done two ways, off a box or in the power rack. Box squats are an old training method that has worked effectively for several generations of lifters. The box is set up on the platform behind the lifter, another footstep back from the regular foot position for safety in backing up. The box can be an actual box, built of wood or metal like a plyometric jump box, or it can be a stack of bumper plates. It should always be adjustable, non-slip against the platform or your butt, and hell for stout. The stance is generally the same as the squat, perhaps a little wider to allow the adductors to stretch a little more and increase their contribution from the dead-stop. Take the bar out of the rack and step carefully back to a position that allows a firm contact with the box as your hips reach back at the bottom. This will vary a little with the box, but in general your heels will be very close to the front edge of the box. The radius of stacked bumper plates will allow your heels to be a little behind the front of the plates. The squat itself will be an exaggeration of the correct form, with lots of attention paid to getting the hips back, the knees out to the sides, and enough forward lean to stay in balance with this extreme hips-back position. As you approach the box, slow down so that you don't slap the box with your butt. The purpose here is to load the box carefully, to avoid compressing the back. Pause for a second or two and drive the hips straight up hard. **Do not exhale at the bottom**. Air is support, and if you ever in your life need support, it will be at the bottom of a box squat. This exercise can be used for varying numbers of reps and sets, depending on the effect desired. The box can be varied in height from several inches below parallel to an inch or two, no more, above. The deep versions use light weights, as mentioned earlier, and the high box version can be done with weights greatly exceeding a 1RM squat (this alone should indicate how important it is to squat below parallel; high squats are much easier to do with lots more weight because they are not a full range-of-motion exercise, and yes, an inch or two *does* make this much difference).

A version of this exercise, known as the "rocking box squat" (developed at Westside Barbell in Culver City, California in the 1960s) has the weight leaving the feet briefly as you rock back very slightly, coming back onto the feet and driving the hips up hard off the box. Louie Simmons at the modern Westside Barbell has mastered the use of this exercise and others like it. But this should be kept in mind: **box squats are an advanced exercise with a huge potential for injury if done by inexperienced or physically unprepared trainees.** The risk of spinal compression between the box and the bar is very high, and high school coaches should know better than to allow it. Please do not do them if you are not prepared, and this statement most definitely constitutes a disclaimer.

The other way to do partial squats is inside the power rack with the pins set at a height that produces the desired depth when the bar on your back touches the pins at the bottom. There are, fascinatingly enough, two ways to do these. The easy way is to set the pins at the desired depth, set up the hooks inside the rack, take the bar out of the hooks, squat down and either bounce the bar off the pins (the easy way) or dead stop on them and then come up (the better way). This permits you to get tight and store some elastic energy on the way down to the bottom. The hard way is to load the bar on the pins, squat down under it and get in position *at the bottom,* and then squat the bar up from what is most assuredly a *very* dead stop. This is really a challenge at the lower reaches of depth, and is hard with even light

Figure 7-6. Box squats can be done with different equipment. Use what you have, as long as it is sturdy.

weights. As with box squats, they get easy at rack heights much above parallel, with so much quadriceps and so little posterior muscle involved that they become only good for producing sore knees.

Bouncing the bar off of the pins is the much easier of the two methods, because the pins add to the rebound that your hamstrings and adductors should be providing. The weight really should be lowered to the pins, dead stopped, and then driven up, making them harder. The dead-stop from the pins provides the same opportunity to work initial explosion out of the hole that box squats do, without the risk of any spinal entrapment compression. It is easier to get tighter at the bottom if you have had the whole trip down to the box or the pins to do it; it is hard to get in an efficient position to squat if you have to do it while wadded up at the bottom, unable to stretch down into the bottom from the correct position assumed at the top. There are advantages and disadvantages to each method, but by the time you're ready to do partial squats, you'll have a feel for which one will work best for you. Just remember: *partial squats are not for novice trainees.*

Figure 7-7. Two ways to do squats in the rack. The bottom start (left) with the bar resting on the rack pins requires that the concentric contraction be started from the hardest position of the movement from a dead stop, greatly increasing the difficulty and decreasing the weight that can be used. The top start (right) allows a bounce off the pins at the bottom, and can be used with much heavier weights.

Notice that these options do not include a half-squat, which would be done from approximately the angles seen at the start of the deadlift. The half squat is an arbitrary position to start or stop, since there is no anatomical reason to do so; the full squat works because the hamstrings and adductors achieve full stretch at this depth, but nothing good occurs at half-squat depth. The positions from which the squat can be trained with useful assistance exercises are all very close to the position of full range of motion. Training from the bottom up to the middle and then going back down can be useful (the top half of the squat is very easy if the bottom is strong, since it's the mechanically easy part anyway; conversely, training the top will not strengthen the bottom), as are all the variations that work from the bottom with a pause to kill the rebound. But unlike the deadlift, it is not very productive to divide the squat into an upper and lower component and then train each separately. The top does not need the work and half-squats are hard on the knees, and the bottom is the hard part of the squat anyway; there is not an easy part of a deadlift, and both halves can successfully be worked separately.

The press, like the deadlift, starts from a dead stop – on the shoulders – at least for the first rep of a set and for a 1RM. Partial presses from different pin heights in the rack can be very useful assistance exercises. Dead-stop explosion can be worked from every position the rack permits to be set and loaded, from eyeball level to lockout, to overhead support work starting from locked-out elbows. The bench press, at least the touch-and-go version used in training, can be worked the same way as the squat inside the rack, the dead-stop assistance versions adding to the effectiveness of the rebound when the regular bench movement is resumed. The limitation of this partial movement training for pressing exercises is the shoulder. Shoulders are easier to injure and more susceptible to overuse than knees and hips, and dead-stop exercises with heavy weights tend to beat the joint up pretty badly if used too often or at excessive volume. But if you don't get carried away by the glamour of the heavier weights that are possible because of the shorter range of motion, partial benches can make you very strong.

For presses, set the pins at the desired position, from chin level (just off the shoulders) on up, even as high as slightly below lockout, and press the bar off the pins with your standard press grip, keeping the bar close to your face with good elbow position and chest up. Tighten up against the bar before it leaves the pins, taking all the "slack" out of your elbows and shoulders before you try to make it move up. The higher the pins, the heavier the weight can be. The heavier the weight, the greater the instability at the top, the harder it becomes to prevent excessive layback, and the more stress the shoulders will receive. Resist the temptation to do lots of sets with weights heavier than you can press, especially the first time you try this. Pin positions in the middle of the movement where most people get stuck – the point about the top of the forehead where the transition from delts to triceps is trying to occur – is a good place to apply this kind of work. And as a general rule, any partial exercise is quite useful when used to strengthen the sticking points in its parent movement, and most of them were developed specifically for this purpose. Reps can vary from sets of 3 to 10, but don't get carried away with the volume. Sets across from a dead-stop will beat your shoulders up, so pick a weight, do it for the number of reps you want to use, and then adjust the weight next workout if you picked it wrong.

The bench press can be used the same way, with the bar loaded on pins set at the desired height above the chest. The flat bench should be carefully centered so that it accommodates the correct position under the bar, with your head on the bench and your chest and elbows in the same place under the bar and in the same position that they would be in had you pressed it off your chest to this level. As with the press, take all the slack out of your elbows and shoulders before you push the bar up off the pins; this is important for correct mechanical execution and to prevent excessive dynamic shock to the tendon insertions on your humerus, which can get badly inflamed from this stress. Sets of 5 work well for both presses and bench presses, but again, just use *one heavy set*. These are very stressful, and you *will* develop tendinitis if you do too much work on partial exercises that allow the use of heavy weights.

Figure 7-8. Pressing from different positions within the range of motion inside the rack.

It is also possible to start either pressing movement from the finish position at the top by setting the hooks inside the rack at this height, unracking the bar and then lowering it to the pins, pausing and driving back up, as with the rack squat. And as with the squat, a bounce off the pins defeats the purpose of the exercise; its value lies in that it allows sticking points to be worked from a dead-stop. The pause must be controlled to keep the bar from getting out of position on the pins. This version is not commonly used, but it could be. More common is the board press, which uses varying thicknesses of lumber laid directly on the chest to make up the spacing for the partial. The board press does not require a power rack, but does require the assistance of a spotter for the placement and removal of the board. Many versions of all these exercises have been developed by many people over the years and used with varying degrees of success. The key is good form, an understanding of the function and desired result of the exercise, and the judicious use of load.

So it appears that for all the basic exercises – the ones that use a rebound as well as the ones that start from a dead stop – partial movements from a dead stop are useful. For the deadlift and the press, they mimic the mechanics of the parent movement by training the dead-stop start from different positions within the range of motion. For the squat and the touch-and-go bench press they make you generate all the upward motion without the help from a stretch reflex. Either way they are beneficial.

Figure 7-9. Rack bench presses allow for the use of heavier weights at different heights above the chest. They must be respected for the amount of stress they can produce if overused.

But partial movements are not substitutes for the parent exercises. The full movement is the primary work, and the partial versions function as assistance. If they were capable of replacing their parent exercises, they would have already. The full movement, by definition, involves muscles and neuromuscular details that the partial movement does not, and is therefore inferior to the whole parent exercise in its ability to improve performance. Even the deadlift is better than its partial derivatives; there are technical aspects to the deadlift that need to be practiced, and only experienced lifters should substitute haltings and rack pulls for the bigger, harder movement. For all these partial exercises that allow the use of heavier weights or harder positions, the point is to apply more or more-specific stress than the parent exercise can produce. They must be used sparingly, under appropriate circumstances, by trainees experienced enough to understand how and why.

Squat Variations

There are a couple of variations of the basic barbell squat that should be discussed. Front squats and high-bar position, or Olympic, squats are very important and commonly used assistance exercises. They are not pieces of the back squat, but rather alternative versions of the parent movement that can be used as a substitute if need be. Opinions differ, and in the interest of full disclosure they are herein described.

The Olympic squat is preferred by many coaches over the low-back position described in this book. This could be because the high bar position is much easier to teach, since most people will put the bar on top of the traps unless made to do otherwise. It is an easier position to get in for people with inflexible shoulders, and some older trainees with chronic shoulder problems have no choice but to squat this way. The high-bar position is easy to identify, and coaches dealing with lots of trainees may prefer to just let them carry the bar high, regarding the question of bar position as an insignificant issue in the grand scheme of things. The reasons for a preference for using the low-bar position having been discussed previously, it will be assumed that the high-bar position is the alternate version, and that there is a compelling reason for using it over the low-bar.

Some of these reasons might be related to shoulder flexibility. Olympic squats are preferable to no squats at all, and there are people who just cannot get the bar on their backs any other way. There are people with shoulders so inflexible that the high bar position with a very wide grip is the only way the bar can be carried. Shoulder flexibility this bad sometimes improves, and sometimes, especially for older trainees, it doesn't improve much at all, especially if it is due to bony changes within the joint capsule.

Some people may decide that Olympic squats are useful since they are harder to do. The high bar position requires that more attention be paid to keeping the chest up, which depends on upper back strength. The longer lever arm against the hips produces more torque – rotational force – that tends to bend you over (the lever arm is the distance between the point where the force is applied and the point where the force produces movement; the longer the lever arm, the greater the leverage, like the grip on a wrench). This must be countered by keeping more upright to minimize the effects of the longer lever arm. The more vertical the back is, the less torque will be produced: in a system in which the force is produced by gravity, the closer to vertical the force is applied the less of the force is converted to torque. Torque is 100% of the force when applied at 90 degrees – your back bent over parallel to the floor – and 0% of the force when applied parallel to the lever arm, when the back is vertical, where it is all compression. The closer to vertical the back is, the smaller the effects of the longer lever arm. This more upright position is also required if the squat is to stay in balance, since any squat is in balance only when the bar is over the middle of the feet. But the more upright the back, the less hamstring involved in the movement, since the hip is already extended in this position. All these position requirements and leverage disadvantages make the Olympic squat harder than the low-back version. The low-back position is recommended for novices since they have enough problems already, but if it is decided that a change is in order for a more advanced trainee, the high-bar version might be just what is needed. If this is your situation, use the high bar position as your standard squat and refer to chapter 2 for the rest of the info on the exercise.

The front squat is a completely different exercise (fig. 7-10), different enough from the back squat that it should not be used by novices still trying to learn that movement. The front squat uses a different model than the back squat, in that the hips are not the emphasis when thinking about how to do it. The differences in the two movements are entirely due to the bar position (fig. 7-11). In order that the system is in balance the bar must stay over the middle of the foot, while it is in the resting position at the top and as it travels down and up through the whole range of motion of the exercise. The back squat will thus be done with a back angle of somewhere between 25 and 45 degrees forward of vertical to permit the bar's vertical position over the foot. Since the bar sits on the anterior deltoids in the front squat, with the elbows up and the hands trapping the bar in place, the required back angle is nearly vertical. This extremely upright position places the bar over the feet, and keeps it from falling off the shoulders. Front squats are missed when the weight is too heavy to squat, or too heavy for the back to stay upright enough to hold the bar in place. In either instance, the bar falls away forward.

Figure 7-10. Three views of the front squat. Note the very steep back angle and the position of the bar over the mid-foot.

Anytime a new movement is introduced, be conservative with the weight you use the first time you do the exercise. This is a lesson you will learn eventually anyway, so you might as well learn it now. Anytime a new exercise is tried, you will be working with a movement pattern or a piece of equipment that you have not used before. Even if you are using a partial range of motion from a familiar exercise, that piece of the movement has not been used by itself before. It has previously been used in the context of the whole movement, and pulling it out to work separately is a different mechanical task than the whole movement. It is sufficiently different that you have chosen to do it that way instead of the other way. In either case, you are not adapted to the new exercise, and as a result it will make you sore, perhaps very sore. This may be due to the simple fact that you are doing a different number of reps with the assistance exercise than you use for the parent movement. A rep range to which you are not adapted will make you sore too.

But a brand new movement pattern has the potential to go beyond simple soreness. It is one thing for unadapted muscles to get sore, and quite another thing for unadapted joints to get sore. Sore joints usually mean inflammation, if not outright structural damage. Sore muscles mean inflammation too, but muscle bellies are vascular – supplied with lots of vessels and capillaries that carry blood to help them heal quickly – whereas joints are not. Joint soreness is a much more serious matter than muscular soreness or even muscular injury.   Joint problems can persist for years, while muscle belly injuries will heal in a matter of days or weeks. And lots of sore joints start on the day you try something new with as much weight or as many reps as you can do with it.

This is not to suggest that you be a weenie. It is to suggest that you be intelligent and prudent with new exercises, so that you don't end up being an involuntary weenie later. This is especially important if you are an older trainee. Start a new exercise with a good warmup, and only go up as heavy or to as many reps as you would consider being equivalent to a heavy warmup set, leaving something on the bar for next time. This way, there can be a next time soon enough that you can proceed to make progress on the new exercise, instead of having to wait for something to heal.

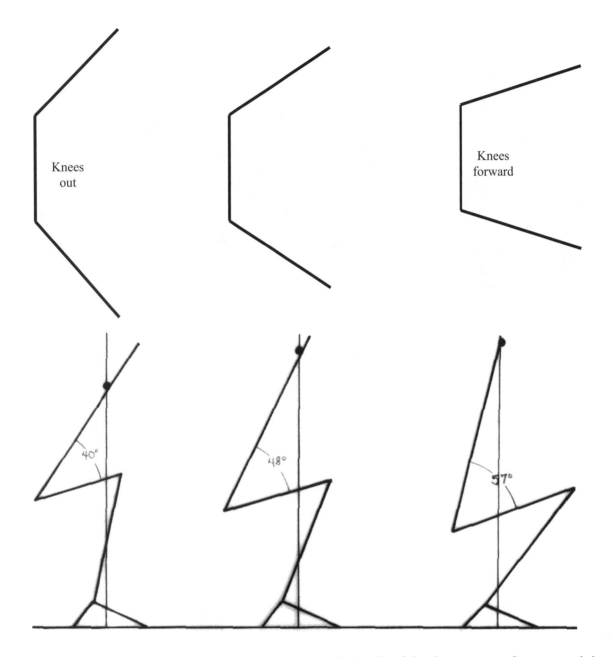

Figure 7-11. The relationship between bar position on the back of the three types of squats and the resulting back, knee, and hip angles.

The position of the bar determines the best way to drive up out of the bottom. The back squat uses a "hips" cue, which enables a more forceful, deliberate initial hip extension. The idea is to drive the butt straight up out of the bottom, which is a way to more effectively make the glutes, hamstrings, and adductors fire. This hip drive is possible because the back is at an angle which permits it; driving the butt up with the bar on the back just requires that the chest be maintained in position, preserving the back angle.

This does not work for the front squat. When the back is at an angle, the hips present a "surface" – the top of the glutes, the sacrum, and the lowest part of the lower back – that a coach can touch with the hand and identify to the trainee. A hand can actually be placed on this area and the trainee told to "push it up", a neuromuscular cue that greatly improves the efficiency of the contraction of the muscles that produce the movement. The front squat has the hips directly under the bar, or as nearly so as possible, a position which presents no surface for cueing. There is no area close to the hips that presents a surface that can be driven up. The column of the torso stops at the chest and shoulders, and these, along with the elbows, are the surfaces that get cued. A focus on the chest, shoulders, and elbows – driving them up, even as the bar is lowered – preserves the vertical position that is so critical to finishing a heavy front squat. This is in stark contrast to the back squat, both in position and in the way the movement is visualized. The differences are great enough that they should not get confused, but they quite often do, and for this reason the front squat is best left untaught until the back squat movement pattern is undisturbable.

Since the front squat has such radically different form, you might expect that it produces a different result than the back squat. The vertical back position of the lift seems like it would result in a more direct compressional load on the spine than the back squat's inclined angle would produce. This is partially true. The lower back is in a nearly vertical position, but the upper back has a much tougher job because the load it is holding up is further away. The bar in a back squat, low bar or Olympic, sits right on top of the muscles that are holding it up. The front squat places the bar all the way across the depth of the chest, which in a bigger guy might be 12 inches away. This is a much longer lever arm than no inches at all and presents a mechanical challenge to the muscles that maintain thoracic extension (it is very common to get pretty sore between the shoulder blades when first starting the exercise). So while the lower back is vertically compressed, unless you are flexible enough to be capable of actually leaning back a little with the bar on your anterior delts your thoracic erector muscles have a lot of work to do. What actually happens is a gradual shift from compression to torque from low back to upper back, so things are not as simple as they may seem. The load on the lumbar spine in the front squat is friendlier (partly because it will be lighter) as long as the upper erectors are able to maintain position, and for this reason many people find it easier on the low back to front squat. And anything that gets too heavy gets dropped automatically before death can occur.

And since the knees are so much further forward than they are at the bottom of the back squat, the hamstrings are not as involved in the hip extension. This is because the vertical back position and its relationship to pelvic position, along with the acute angle of the tibia, place the hamstrings in a position where the origin and insertion are closer together – a position of contraction. A knees-forward back-vertical position at the bottom produces a more acute knee angle, an already shortened hamstring, and a more extended hip. If the hamstrings are already contracted, they cannot contribute much to hip extension, because they are not in a position to contract much further. But the hip extension must still be done, so the glutes end up doing most of the job without the help of the hamstrings. Then the knees-forward, vertical-back position puts the quads in a position to do most of the work after the initial hip extension. This is true for high-bar Olympic squats as well, but especially so for the front squat.

225

The Olympic squat has been the preferred form of the exercise for Olympic weightlifters for decades. This seems to be largely a matter of tradition and inertia, since there are compelling reasons for using the low-bar position for weightlifters too. Since the squat is not a contested lift in weightlifting, and since Olympic lifters front squat to directly reinforce the squat clean anyway, the reasons for doing it in training for weightlifters must involve other considerations. The squat makes you strong, and weightlifting is a strength sport; even if it is terribly dependent on technique, the winner is still the one that lifts the most weight. The high-bar position may be harder, but the low-bar position is easier on the lower back, uses more muscle, allows more weight to be lifted, and consequently prepares the lifter for heavier weights.

It is also more applicable to the mechanics of Olympic weightlifting than the high-bar squat. The low-bar position, with the weight sitting just below the spine of the scapula, is the same as the mechanics of the position in which the bar is pulled off of the floor. As the discussions of pulling mechanics in the deadlift and power clean chapters have illustrated, the shoulder blades are directly above the bar when it leaves the floor, and they stay there until the back changes position when the bar rises above the knees. (This is true for both the clean and the snatch, with the snatch being done from a position even less similar to the Olympic squat than the clean.) Low-bar squats done utilizing this same relative position will train the movement pattern more directly than the high-bar version, which places the back at a higher angle due to the higher position of the bar on the traps, and the scapulas *behind* the position they are in during a pull. And they do it through a nice, long range of motion due to the fact that the squat goes deeper than the start position of either the snatch or the clean and jerk.

For both the low-bar squat and the pull from the floor, the relationship between the load and the spine is essentially the same: the load transfers from the spine to the bar at the level of the scapula. Both also share the essential requirement of the maintenance of the correct back angle off the floor. Neither the squat nor the pull will tolerate either bending over or rounding of the back during their initial phase, and the chest must be kept up during both movements. If the back angle is kept constant for both, which it must be, they are very similar movements, more similar than a high-bar squat and a pull of any type. If an argument is to be made for squatting with a form specific to the motor pathway requirements of the sport, the low-back position would be that form. And if an argument is made that the squat need not be similar, the low-bar squat still makes more sense, because it is easier on the back and can be done with heavier weights.

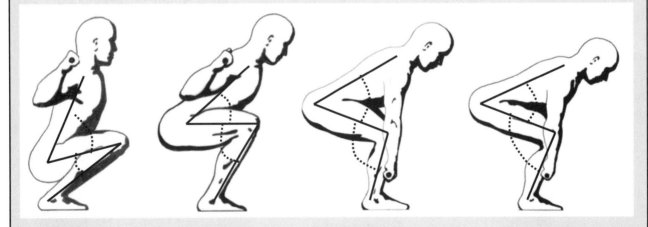

The progression from the high-bar "Olympic" squat through the low-bar position advocated here, the clean-pull start position, and the snatch start position. There are more similarities between the low-bar squat and the pulls in back angle, knee angle, hip angle, and scapular position.

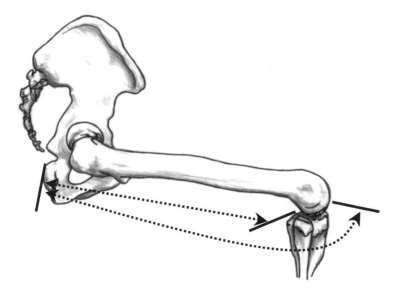

Figure 7-12. The effect of tibia angle on hamstring tightness. The more acute the knee, the shorter the hamstring; this is the function of the hamstring in knee flexion. But when the knee angle becomes more acute *without* an active hamstring contraction – as it does when the knees passively travel forward on the way to the bottom of the squat – the hamstrings lose the opportunity to contribute to *hip extension*, because they are already shortened.

So the primary difference between the back squat and front squat is one of degree in terms of the amount of involvement from the contributing muscle groups. But the primary reason for the difference is the position in which the system is in balance – the bar in both cases must be over the middle of the foot, and the correct back angle is the one that keeps it there.

Learning the front squat is best done from the power rack or squat stands. The bar is set at the same position as for a back squat, the level of the mid-sternum. The grip is a very important component of the front squat, more so than in the back squat. The grip must allow the elbows to come up high enough that the shoulders can support the load while the back remains vertical during the movement. The grip width will depend largely on individual flexibility, and will vary between trainees and during the individual trainee's career as flexibility is acquired through stretching or lost due to injury. In general, the less flexibility a trainee exhibits, the wider the grip will need to be. Also, some people have

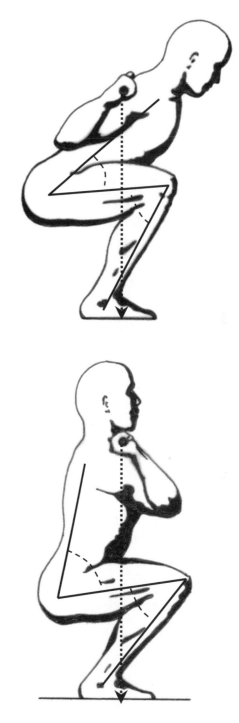

Figure 7-13. The differences in the back squat and front squat are determined by the position of the bar. The resulting angles and their effects on the biomechanics of the movements are responsible for the different training effects of the two exercises.

227

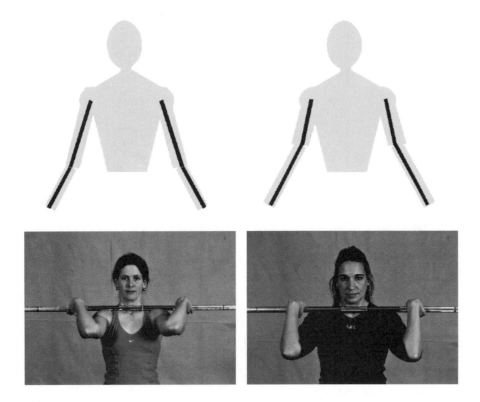

Figure 7-14. Differences in forearm length relative to the upper arm affect elbow position in the front squat and the clean. Long relative forearms shove the elbow down lower. This effect can be compensated for by widening the grip.

long forearms relative to their humerus length and find it hard to elevate the elbows with what would otherwise be a normal grip width. Adjust it as necessary so that the elbows can be raised as high as possible.

The weight of the bar should be taken on the shoulders, with elbows in the elevated position and shoulders tight, before the bar is unracked. The weight sits on the meat of the deltoids, and if the elbows are not in the up position before the weight is unracked, they'll never get there. Even though we will be starting, as usual, with an *empty bar,* this is an important thing to learn first. This position is maintained by lifting both the elbows and the chest as high as possible, from the time the bar is unracked until the last rep is finished. Think of touching a hand held above your sternum to cue this movement, which is accomplished with the upper back muscles.

Figure 7-15. The cue for lifting the chest. The hand is the target.

Take the bar out of the rack and step back a couple of steps to clear the hooks (when the bar is loaded, preferably with bumper plates, a miss will be dropped away forward and no spotters will be involved, so the distance from the rack must be sufficient that the bar can fall without hitting anything but the floor). Your stance will be essentially the same as for the back squat, heels at shoulder width and toes out at about 30 degrees. The stance for a front squat is more variable and can be a little wider or narrower, more on this later. Once the stance is assumed, lift your chest and elbows, take a big breath to support this position, and squat. The vertical position of the back is retained on the way down by forcing the knees forward and out, keeping the chest and elbows up, and possibly even by thinking about leaning back slightly. The bottom of the front squat is quite easy to feel, since some contact between the calves and the hamstrings will occur. There is no pause at the bottom, and the ascent starts with an upward drive of the chest – not the elbows. Elbows *stay* up, chest is *driven* up, since merely raising the elbows will not positively affect the upper spine, the whole point of the "chest up" cue. As the chest is driven up, the hips rise vertically underneath it, maintaining the vertical position and keeping the bar – up high on the delts – from rolling forward and down. The elbows-up position traps the bar between the fingers and the neck, but the weight is on the delts, not the hands. At no time during the movement is the back relaxed at either the bottom or the top; the spine must be consciously squeezed tight and held in position vertically, more of a challenge in the front squat due to the bar's position in front of the neck and the consequently greater torque against the upper back.

The differences in bar position and hamstring function between the front and back squat necessitate a different set of cues for each version. The back squat depends on hip drive, and it is cued at the sacrum, as mentioned previously. Chest and elbows are the focal points for attention in the front squat. "Big Air" is critical to chest position, as is the strength of the upper part of the spinal erectors, which get sore when this position is trained hard the first few times. Thinking about leaning back on the way down may produce a feel for the position if it does not interfere with balance. Most people can grasp this concept without falling backwards, so try it if you need to. It might also be helpful to picture a slick firepole against your back, from neck to butt, that you slide down and slide back up, to reinforce your upright position during the movement

Some people have proportions that make the front squat difficult. A short torso with long legs is a bad combination for good front squat form, and little can be done about this. In extreme cases it may be best not to perform the exercise if correct form cannot be maintained due to an anthropometric problem that cannot be solved (fig. 7-17).

Front squats are usually done in sets of three, due to the greater sensitivity of the exercise to form deterioration. Volume is accumulated with multiple sets across.

Figure 7-16. An upright torso for the front squat is necessary, and this is one way to visualize the situation.

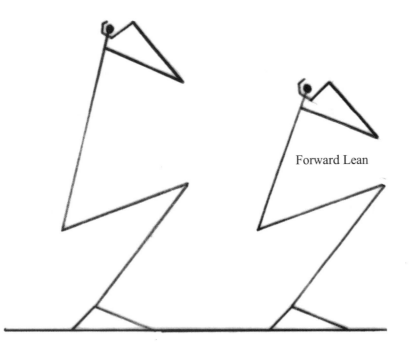

Forward Lean

Figure 7-17. Anthropometry affects the ability to assume an efficient position in the front squat, as it does with all barbell exercises. The front squat suffers from a short torso and long legs (right).

Breath control is terribly critical in the front squat. More leverage against the upper back – the result of the increased distance of the bar from the spine – results in more rotational force that must be countered. The support provided by increased intrathoracic pressure is often the difference between holding a heavy last rep in place and dropping it in the floor. A big breath keeps the chest up, the shoulders up, and the elbows up by tightening the entire upper body. Each rep will need a new breath at the top, maybe just a top-off for the previous breath so that tightness is not relaxed.

As mentioned previously, a missed front squat will fall away forward off the shoulders. This is unavoidable, since if you are training hard you will eventually miss a front squat, so it might as well be prepared for by practicing it occasionally during the warmups. The possibility exists that unless you are used to getting away from the bar as it falls – putting enough distance between you and the bar that it won't hit you on the way down – you might drop it on your knees or lower thighs. This is usually prevented by most people's sense of self-preservation, but it is prudent to have at least practiced it a few times.

One of the problems associated with front squats is related to bar placement. If the throat is pushed on too hard by a bar taken too far back on the shoulders, the result can be a blackout. It is caused by an occlusion of the carotid arteries by the pressure of the bar. This is dangerous because of the fall that will occur if you allow yourself to pass completely out before doing something about it. If you feel your perception start to change – and you'll know it when it happens – either rack the bar while you can or drop it safely on the platform and take a knee so that you don't have as far to fall if the blackout continues to develop. An uncontrolled blackout can cause severe head injuries if you hit the racks, the bar, or the plates on the way down. The blackout itself is harmless, and is corrected by moving the bar away from the throat a little. Once the buzz diminishes, the set can be resumed with no trouble as long as the correction is made. But if you manage to blackout once, you will find that you're more prone to it for the rest of that workout, so be careful when making your correction to the rack position.

There is a version of the front squat, referred to around here as the California front squat, that involves the arms crossed in front, the right hand on the left shoulder and vice-versa. This form involves less wrist flexibility than the standard hand position, and proportionately less security on the shoulders. It is not as safe at heavy weights, and since we train with heavy weights, we don't use it. And if you need to drop the bar in the event of a miss, the crossed-arm position makes the drop awkward and hard to control.

The standard position is derived from the clean, the movement typically preceding the front squat in Olympic weightlifting, in which the bar is trapped against the shoulders by the upraised elbow jamming the hand and the bar *back* into the rack position. The crossed-arms position relies entirely on the elbow position and completely loses the stability effect provided by the hands. Doing front squats this way is tantamount to just holding your hands out in front of you with the bar balanced on the delts. And if you need to drop the bar in the event of a miss, the crossed-arm position makes the drop awkward and hard to control.

There is an argument to be made for cleaning everything you're going to front squat, and California front squats contribute to the argument. You can front squat more weight the right way, and that sounds like a good idea to most of us.

Bench Press Variations

The bench press is such a popular exercise that it's no surprise there are lots of variations of the basic version. Selectorized bench press machines that control the bar path have long been a feature of the multi-station machine; bars have been developed that allow the weight to travel past the top of the chest, down to where the shoulders aren't supposed to go; machines have been invented that allow each side to work independently of the other (like dumbbells, only way more expensive); the pec-deck takes the triceps out of the exercise – just wonderful; a way to work fewer muscles at one time is always very useful. None of these are particularly helpful advances in exercise technology. The bench press is a valuable exercise because it couples heavy potential load with the motor control aspects of barbell training, and these devices remove some of this benefit. The most valuable variations preserve the benefits while allowing different aspects of the movement that might need additional work to receive it. They are of two types: variations in the grip width and variations in the angle of the shoulder during the press.

231

The grip can be either wider or narrower than standard. The narrower the grip, the more inclined towards the middle the forearm is at the bottom, the sooner the elbow stops traveling down as the bar touches the chest, and therefore the shorter the range of motion of the humerus, even though the bar travels farther. The less angle the humerus covers as it travels down, the less work the chest muscles do; the more angle opened up by the elbow, the more work done by the triceps (fig. 7-19). A medium grip – with the forearms vertical at the bottom – uses the longest range of elbow motion, and a very wide grip involves a shorter range of bar and elbow motion because the bar touches the chest before the elbows can travel down very far. With a wide grip, the triceps extend the elbow over a shorter angle, and the pecs and delts end up doing more of what work gets done. So, bar travel is at maximum when the arms are vertical at lockout, and elbow travel is at maximum when the forearms are vertical at the bottom. It is for this reason that wide-grip benches have the reputation for being a chest exercise. More weight can be done due to the shorter range of motion, and that weight is done without much help from the triceps, so the chest gets most of the work.

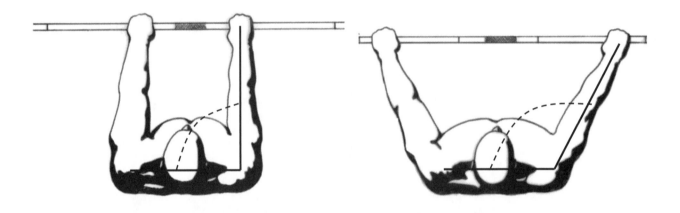

Figure 7-18. A comparison of the start positions of the close grip and the standard grip bench press. Range of motion of the bar is at maximum when the arms are vertical in the lockout position.

The close-grip version is not really just a tricep exercise, though it seems to have that reputation. The large elbow angle the tricep opens provides more stimulation for that muscle group; the pecs and the delts are performing the same function – adducting the humerus – but over a different range of motion, since the humerus is more vertical at lockout but not as deep at the bottom with the closer grip. Less weight can usually be done close-grip than with the standard grip due to the decreased contribution of the pecs and delts out of the bottom, but not much less. Compared with the wide grip, the narrow grip is much harder in terms of total weight that can be used, due to the range of motion and less pec/delt involvement, while the wide-grip is a shorter movement that produces less work and permits heavier weights to be used. It omits some of the tricep work while relying much more on pec and delt. On the other hand, the close-grip version uses lots of tricep, less of the pec and delt work, and is harder. If your primary interest is in moving the heaviest weight, as a powerlifter needs to do, the widest grip legal for the meet is the one to use. If your interest is in the greatest amount of muscle stressed to cause an adaptation, a medium grip is the most useful. And if you need to get more tricep work, a close grip is useful for that.

The greatest effect comes from the closest grip you can tolerate, and this will be controlled by your wrist flexibility. On a standard power bar, the knurl ends at between 16 and 17 inches, and this makes a good place to start. After a bench press workout, take about 50% of your 1RM out of the rack with a grip set so that your index fingers are on the line formed by the edge of the knurl. The exercise is performed the same way as the standard bench press, with the same breathing, back set, foot position, and tight upper back. Rack the set, wait a little and do another set with the grip one finger-width narrower on each side. Continue to narrow each set of five one finger-width until the wrist begins to complain at the bottom, and then widen back out one finger-width. This may have to be adjusted out a little as the weight goes up, because what doesn't hurt with light weights may very well be painful at heavier weights.

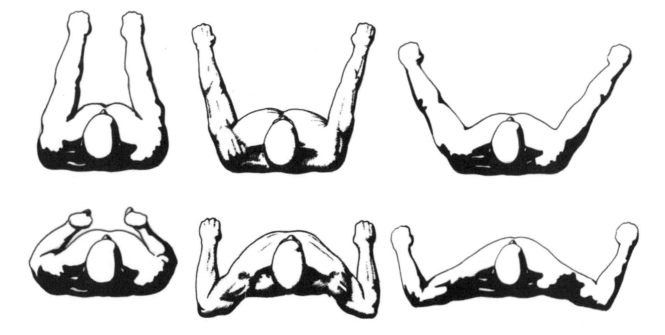

Figure 7-19. A comparison of the top and bottom position of the close grip, the standard grip, and the wide grip bench press. The longest range of motion is with the grip that allows the forearms to be vertical at the bottom. Any other forearm alignment causes the bar to touch the chest before full range of motion is reached.

Close-grips are usually used at higher reps, but this is merely tradition, and there is no reason that it must be done this way. Since they use a lighter weight than the bench press, they can be done after a bench workout, or they can be used on a separate day as a light day exercise. Care must be taken to hold the bar very tightly; the wrist position makes for a less secure grip than the conventional bench press, and it has been known to fail on the way up when the wrists "twitch" inconveniently. Close-grips are also famous for reaching failure rather suddenly, with the last completed rep giving little indication that the next one will be a partial. As a general rule, exercises that depend on less muscle mass or fewer muscle groups tend to fail more abruptly in their bar path than exercises that use more muscles. Learn to recognize this situation if you train by yourself, and rack the bar at the right time so you don't get pinned.

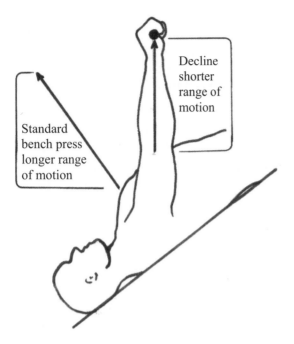

Figure 7-20. A comparison of the ranges of motion of the bench press and the decline bench press.

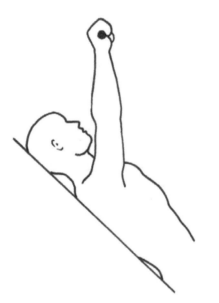

Figure 7-21. The position of the bar in the incline bench press, directly over a point just below the sterno-clavicular articulation, the point where the collarbones meet the sternum. This will be very close to the chin on the way down.

The other way to usefully vary the bench press involves the angle at which the humerus approaches the chest, controlled by the angle of the bench on which the exercise is performed. This angle determines the quality and quantity of pectoral and deltoid involvement in the press. There are two variations from horizontal: the decline, where the head is lower than the feet, and the incline, where the head is higher than the feet.

The decline press is a rather useless exercise because the angle of the body in the decline position shortens the distance the bar can travel, decreasing the amount of work done with respect to the distance the load moves. This has the effect of increasing the weight that can be used in the exercise by decreasing its difficulty. This leads to inflated perceptions of one's ability, and is essentially masturbation, much like that which is possible with a 30° leg press or a half-squat. It gets recommended for its effects on the "lower pecs"; dips perform this function much more effectively, while at the same time involving more muscle mass, more balance and coordination, and more nervous system activity, as discussed below. Declines are dangerous because if their point of contact on the lower sternum gets missed, the next stop is the throat. Couple this with a heavy weight and a lousy spotter, and you might have a really, really bad "chest" workout.

On the other hand, the incline can be a useful bench press variation. It should be said that if you are doing both bench presses and presses, everything that the incline press accomplishes is redundant; there is no aspect of shoulder and chest work that these two exercises do not more than adequately cover. "Upper pecs" are quite thoroughly involved in the press, and in fact the bench press uses the whole muscle belly, so there is no need to attempt an isolation of this portion of the chest musculature. But many sports involve the use of the arms at an angle somewhere between 90 and 180 degrees from the torso, and it is felt by some that this angle should specifically be targeted for resistance training. The incline bench

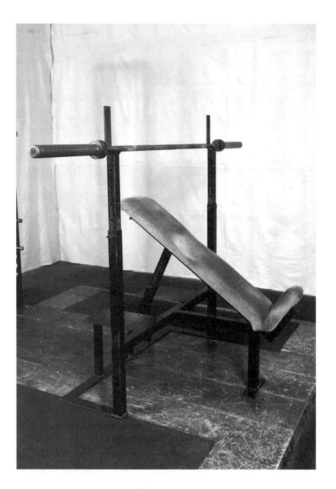

Figure 7-22. A useful type of incline support bench.

press does this, albeit at the cost of the body being supported at this angle while the work is being done, something which never occurs during the sports in question (see the discussion of this in chapter 5).

But limitations are what make them "assistance" exercises – if they were perfect, they'd be major exercises and have their own chapter. The incline is useful in some cases, as long as it's done correctly; it is easy to cheat, and pointless when cheated. Most commonly, the effects of the angle of incline are blunted when the trainee raises the hips up off of the incline bench, thus making the torso more horizontal. If a flat bench is what you want to do, just do it on the bench press. Indeed, this is a good reason to just bench press and press; most people will allow their greed to overwhelm their sense of propriety here, and too much weight will be loaded for the limitations of the inclined position, causing the hips to bridge just to get the last rep back in the rack. The incline is an *assistance* exercise – don't use so much weight that it has to be cheated, because this defeats the purpose of doing them. Keep your butt on the bench.

Most incline benches are made to be adjustable, so that the incline can be varied according to individual preference. They are made with support uprights for the bar, like a bench press bench, and the supports are also adjustable to enable the bar to be unracked at a position that matches the angle of the bench. (Fixed-position incline benches are available from some manufacturers, with neither the angle nor the uprights adjustable.) They also have a seat built into the frame so that a secure position can be maintained without the feet becoming too critical. It would actually be better if the feet were more involved, since this would extend some, although not all, aspects of the kinetic chain down to the floor. You occasionally find very old benches built this way, with a foot plate at ninety degrees to the bench, but they are not the industry standard now.

When doing the exercise, select an angle of between 30 and 45 degrees from vertical. Flatter angles are too similar to the bench press, and steeper angles are too similar to the press, with the disadvantage of having the angle held immobile in a position that is very hard on the shoulders. One reason the press might be a better choice is that the stress of a tough rep can be accommodated with some adjustment of the back position, whereas the incline bench nails you into a fixed position that might exceed the capacity of the fatigued shoulder joint.

The uprights should support the bar at a position that allows it to be taken out, the reps completed, and racked with a minimum of elbow extension but no danger of missing the racks.

235

This means that they should be set as high as possible, so that the elbows are nearly straight and that when they are straightened the bar clears the hooks by a couple of inches. If the supports are too low, too much work has to be done getting the bar out, and more importantly, too much work will have to be done getting it back in at a time when lots of control might not be possible. The easiest rack position will vary with your bench, and some trial and error will be involved.

The position of the shoulders and back against the bench, the elbow position, the eye position, breath control, grip, and foot position are all the same for the incline as they are for the bench press, while the differences are related to the angle. The shoulders are squeezed together for a tight position, and the back is arched into a brace between the seat and the point of contact on the shoulders. The elbows stay directly under the bar for the whole movement; they control the bar path as they do for a bench press. The eyes focus on the stationary reference of the ceiling; they do not follow the bar. Breath is held during each rep, with air movement only occurring between reps at the top. The grip is the same as that used for the bench, the thumb around the bar which rests on the heel of the palm. The feet are firmly planted against the floor as a brace for the position against the bench. The bar path will be straight, but instead of touching the mid-sternum the bar will touch right under the chin, just below the point where the collarbones and the sternum meet, the sternoclavicular articulation; this is a slightly longer range of motion than a flat bench press. This is because the elbows' position directly under the bar will place the bar at this point of contact on the chest at this angle of approach. The starting position at lockout over the chest will be the point where the bar is directly above this point on the chest, where the locked-out arms are vertical, and from the side it will appear to be almost directly over the chin.

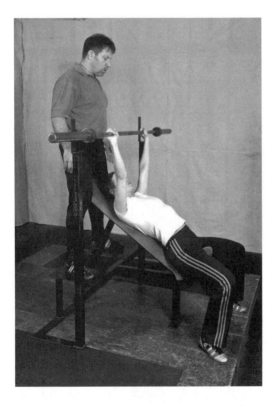

Figure 7-23. The correct spotting position for the incline bench press.

Most of the differences between the incline and the bench press are positional. The two are basically executed the same way. The chest is up, the back is tight, the drive is to the point of focus on the ceiling, the feet are planted to connect firmly with the floor, and "big air" supports the chest.

If the incline is to be spotted, the equipment must be compatible. Most good benches have a spotter platform built into the frame. This allows the spotter to be at a level sufficiently above the lifter that if there is a problem the bar can be pulled up safely from a position of good leverage. A spotter standing on the floor cannot be depended on to help, and if heavy weights are to be used the equipment must allow for correct spotter position. Likewise, if you feel as though two spotters are necessary for the weight you're doing, you should either use a lighter weight or do a different exercise, because two spotters cannot safely spot an incline and heavy 1RM attempts on the incline bench press betray a poor understanding of the purpose of assistance exercises.

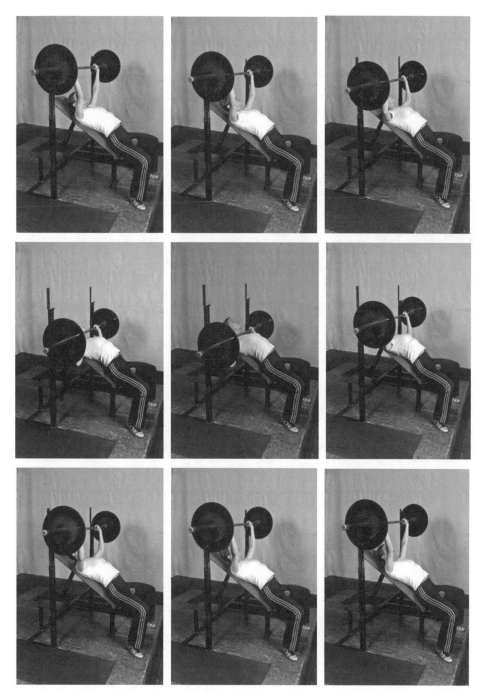

Figure 7-24. The incline bench press. Note the vertical bar path and the position of the bar over the clavicles.

Deadlift Variations

As legend has it, once upon a time the incredible Romanian weightlifter Nicu Vlad visited the US Olympic Training Center. Vlad was strong, probably as strong as any human being has ever been at a bodyweight of 220: word on the street has it that he front squatted 700 lbs. for a double. So when Vlad performed an exercise that no one had seen before, it quite naturally got a lot of attention from people not as strong as he was. The exercise involved taking the bar out of

237

the rack from the hang position, stepping back to clear the rack, and then lowering the bar down to mid-shins and raising it back to the hang. This looked like a deadlift, but one that started at the top instead of the bottom, so naturally it had to have a new name. The term "Romanian Deadlift" has been applied to it since then, although its name translated from the Romanian is probably something different (if it even has a Romanian name: the exercise has been developed since that day entirely in the USA, and may simply have been Vlad's way of dealing with unfamiliar equipment). It is referred to by the initials "RDL."

Figure 7-25. The great Nicu Vlad: the importer, as legend has it, of the Romanian deadlift. Vlad was pretty damn strong.

The RDL has two important characteristics that distinguish it from its parent exercise. It uses very little quadriceps due to the fact that the knee starts off nearly straight – unlocked, but not very – and pretty much stays that way, so that the quads don't have an opportunity to actively extend the knees during the movement. The RDL is specifically intended as a hip extension exercise, and the quads are not supposed to be involved. All the work that occurs through the range of motion of the exercise that would normally be shared between knee extensors and hip extensors is done only by the glutes and the hamstrings. The lower back muscles keep the lumbar spine locked in line with the pelvis, and the hamstrings – at their attachments on the bottom of the pelvis, the "ischial tuberosities" – cause rotation around the hip joints when they pull the pelvis and the back of the knee together, making the hamstrings the prime movers during the exercise.

But more important is the difference in the fundamental nature of the two movements. The deadlift starts with a concentric contraction as the bar is pulled from the floor, and the eccentric phase is not really emphasized since the lift is essentially over after it is locked out at the top. In contrast the RDL is like the squat in that the movement starts with an eccentric contraction, the "negative," that precedes the concentric. The bar starts from a position of knee and hip extension, the bar is lowered down into flexion and a stretch-shortening cycle initiates the concentric contraction back into extension.

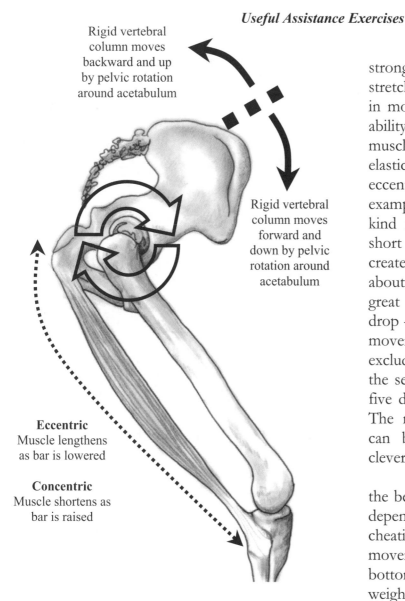

Rigid vertebral column moves backward and up by pelvic rotation around acetabulum

Rigid vertebral column moves forward and down by pelvic rotation around acetabulum

Eccentric
Muscle lengthens as bar is lowered

Concentric
Muscle shortens as bar is raised

Figure 7-26. The function of the hamstrings in the RDL is that of pure hip extension, both eccentric and concentric.

Any concentric contraction is stronger when it is preceded by this stretch reflex, due to increased efficiency in motor unit recruitment as well as the ability of the elastic components of the muscles and connective tissues to store elastic energy developed during the eccentric phase. A jump is the best example of this; every time a jump of any kind is performed, it is preceded by a short drop of the hips and knees that creates a stretch reflex in the muscles about to contract for the jump. It takes a great effort of will to jump without this drop – it is such a normal part of human movement that it is very difficult to exclude. It also explains why bouncing the second through fifth reps of a set of five deadlifts off the floor is so popular. The majority of weight room exercises can be "cheated" with the use of a cleverly-applied stretch reflex.

But for the RDL – and the squat, the bench, the jerk, and maybe the press, depending on how it's done – it is not cheating, but an inherent part of the movement. The "bounce" out of the bottom of the RDL enables rather heavy weights to be used in the exercise despite the fact that the quads have been excluded from helping with the movement. RDLs take advantage of the stretch reflex just to the extent that it affects the hip extensors. The fact that the quads are excluded makes the movement quite a bit different from the deadlift or any partial version of it or any other pull, so it really is a separate exercise.

The RDL starts in the rack with pins set at a position a little lower than the level of the hands in the hang position. This rack position allows for an easy, safe return to the rack in the event of a slipping grip that might lower the position of the bar between start and finish. With a clean-width grip, take the bar out of the rack and step back just far enough to clear the pins. Assume the same stance you use for a deadlift, with heels 12-15 inches apart, toes pointed very slightly out. The chest is up, eyes are focused on a point on the floor about ten feet in front.

The whole point of the RDL is that the back stay locked in extension while the hip extensors work. Unlock the knees so that a little tension comes into the quads, but no more than enough to lower the bar an inch or two down the thigh. Once this is done very little knee angle change should occur, although their position over the feet will change slightly. This position will place the knees above a point about halfway between the toe and the instep. Lift the chest up and arch the low back into a tight lock, trying to maintain this position for the whole movement. Start the bar down the thigh by shoving the hips back, allowing the hips to come into flexion, the bar never leaving the skin of the legs. At the same time push the shoulders forward, out in front of the bar to the familiar pulling position where the scapulas are vertically above the bar. As the bar approaches the knees shove them back too, shifting the shins into a vertical position. Drop the bar down past the knees, staying in close contact with the shins, as low as possible without unlocking the lower back. Stop just before the back begins to unlock – a position you will identify on the first few reps – and start back up. The stretch at the bottom should help turn the weight around without any pause. On the way up, keep the bar on the legs and the chest and back locked in position. Breathing is at the top, a big breath taken for every rep.

Figure 7-27. The RDL start position. The bar is walked back out of the rack just far enough to clear the pins.

The emphasis on driving everything back is very important; the use of the hips instead of the knees is what engages the hip extensors and excludes the quads. It helps to think about the weight shifting back to the heels, the knees moving back, the bar being shoved back to stay in contact with the legs, the butt moving back; in fact, everything moves back except the shoulders, which slide forward, out over the bar. The shins must come to vertical before the bar reaches the knees, or even a tiny bit behind the vertical; the knees must never move forward at all after the initial unlocking. Any forward knee movement puts the quads in a position to contribute to the movement by extending the knees on the way back up, canceling out the hip-extension effect desired.

The RDL has many things in common with the rack pull in terms of its mechanics. Both properly exclude knee extensor function in favor of posterior chain development, and both focus on the top half of the pull. The rack pull starts concentric and ends with the negative, like the deadlift, and the RDL uses rebound. In this way, the RDL is like the "squat version" of the rackpull.

Figure 7-28. The Romanian deadlift.

The most common error will be the knees forward problem. There will be a lot of temptation to relax the tension on the knees at the bottom; the hamstring tension builds all the way down and is not relieved until the muscle is shortened, either by having done the work of extending the hips at the top, or you relaxing your knees forward at the bottom. If you shorten the hamstrings by allowing the knees to drop forward – thus flexing the knees and causing the two ends of the muscle to come together, and taking the tension off from the bottom – then the quads do the work that the hamstrings should have done when they extend the knee during the recovery to the top.

Remember from the discussion of pulling mechanics in the deadlift chapter that the shoulder blades stay vertically above the bar during the pull, due to the geometry of the spine/scapula/humerus relationship. The bar hangs vertically below the scapulas, and this means that the arms are inclined back from the shoulders at a slight angle, with the lats pulling back on the humerus to maintain this vertical relationship. The lower the bar goes down the legs without a

241

knee bend, the more angle the arms must assume to keep the bar under the scapulas, and the more work the lats must do to maintain this position. At a very low position on the shin, this angle becomes quite extreme, contributing to the difficulty involved in doing a strict RDL very far below the knees. In fact, if you touch the floor at the bottom of an RDL, you probably did it wrong with a light weight.

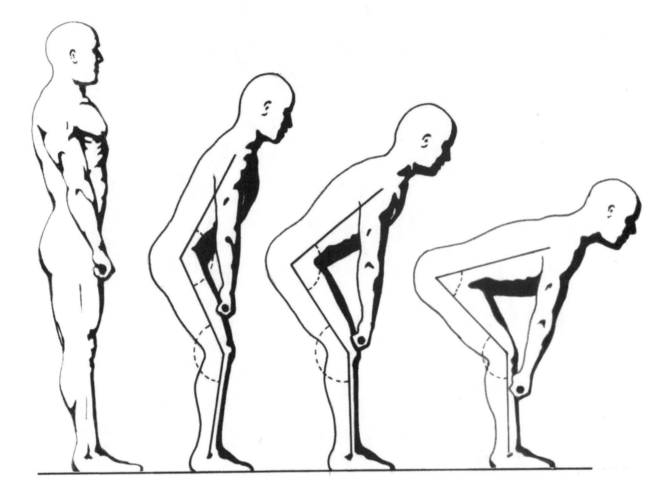

Figure 7-29. The progression from top to bottom position in the RDL.

Also common is the failure to hold the back rigid, in absolute extension. One of the main benefits of the RDL is the isometric work it provides for the erectors, as they hold the spine rigid while the hamstrings produce hip extension. This is a rather hard position to hold, and it requires a lot of concentration to keep the chest up and the low back arched with no looseness, while sliding the hips back, the knees back, the bar back, the heels down, and the shoulders forward. For a slow exercise, the RDL is technically difficult because it is very easy to do wrong. If the back rounds or the knees come forward, less work is being done by the targeted muscle groups and the movement feels easier. But done correctly, with the back locked into rigid extension and no knee extension involved, it is perhaps the best assistance exercise for deadlifts and cleans, because it works the very things that cause heavy deadlifts to be missed.

The best cues for good form on the RDL are "chest up," "arch the back," and "knees back," with an occasional reminder to keep the weight on the heels. The chest cue will remind you to keep the thoracic spine in extension, while arching the back usually gets interpreted by most people as a low back cue. The knee cue keeps the quads out of the movement, but it can also cause the bar to fall away forward and it may be necessary to cue the lats by thinking "push the bar back."

When RDLs are done heavy, a double overhand grip should be used. The shoulder asymmetry that results from an alternate grip is not desirable for this exercise, and the bar cannot be pulled back into the legs with the lats effectively using a supine hand. The weights that will be used for heavy RDLs are not really heavy relative to the deadlift, most people being able to use between 65% and 75% of their 1RM deadlift for the exercise, so it will not usually be a problem to just use a plain old double overhand grip. A hook grip or straps should be used if grip strength is insufficient, but the hands need to both be in the prone position. Being an assistance exercise, RDLs are done in the range of 5-10 reps.

The stiff-legged deadlift (or SLDL) is possibly a more familiar exercise in most gyms, as a result of the fact that many people do the deadlift wrong and it ends up looking this way accidentally. The SLDL is essentially an RDL off of the floor – without the stretch reflex – with a couple of other differences. Since the SLDL starts on the floor, it will most likely involve a longer range of motion than the RDL, which is supposed to stop at the point where the low back unlocks due to limitations in hamstring extensibility. Most people can't do a strict RDL all the way down to the floor with the bar loaded with 17 inch plates, so you will have to do the SLDL with enough knee bend to allow the back to get into good position to start. The amount of knee bend will obviously depend on individual flexibility; the point of the exercise is stiff-legs, so use as little as necessary.

Figure 7-30. The conventional deadlift start position (left) and the stiff-legged deadlift start position (right), as demonstrated by a person with very good hamstring extensibility.

Second, the bar will be further away from the shins in the starting position off the floor than it would be at the bottom of an RDL. This is due to the nearly-vertical shins that extended knees create, and the resulting relationship between the scapula and the bar. No matter what pull from the floor you are doing, the bar wants to leave the floor from a position where the scapulas are vertically above it, and as the weight increases the bar will tend to ride directly above the mid-foot. If the knees are pulled back away from the bar to make the knees straight, the bar still stays directly beneath the shoulder blades and over the mid-foot as it leaves the floor. Basic pulling mechanics dictates that this is always the case unless the weight is very light. This means that the bar will be in the air away from the shins until the scapulas begin to rotate back behind the bar, which usually happens just above the knee. This is also why most people cannot get an RDL – which is supposed to stay on the legs – all the way down to the floor, since the lower it goes with extended knees, the more it wants to swing out away from the shins to stay under the scapulas.

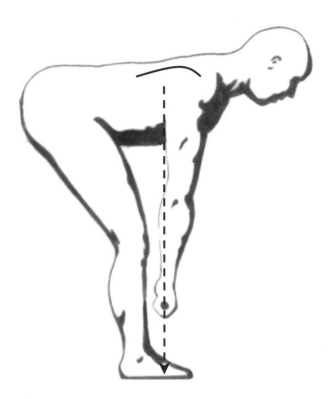

Figure 7-31. The starting position for the stiff-legged deadlift.

With this in mind, take your regular deadlift stance; the bar will have a tendency to be forward of correct position with light weights, but will pull back in closer as weight is added. The regular double-overhand clean grip is used, for the same reasons mentioned above for the RDL. Unlock the knees and set them in position hard, as straight as your flexibility permits with a flat back. Set the chest up, take a big breath, and pull. The bar will come onto the legs just above the knees, and the pull is then locked out like a regular deadlift at the top. Again, each rep is replaced on the floor, reset and pulled from a stop; it is a deadlift, not an RDL, and each rep starts from a dead stop.

Both SLDLs and RDLs are versatile exercises and can be applied to your training in many ways. They can be done in a variety of rep ranges, depending upon the desired effect. Used as a sub for the deadlift on a light day, sets of 5 work well, and in fact can be used for sets across unlike the deadlift since they do not produce the stress that the full movement is known for. For back-off work following deadlifts, they can be used for sets of 8-10 reps to accumulate extra volume. And high-rep sets of 20 RDLs can be an interesting addition to your training.

Despite the fact that both the RDL and the SLDL can produce extreme hamstring soreness in the short term that can interfere with the normal range of motion of the knees, both provide an excellent way to increase the extensibility of the hamstrings over time. They are excellent stretches, and are often used with light weights as warmups for the deadlift and the squat.

Figure 7-32. The stiff-legged deadlift.

245

Another variation on the deadlift is to do the exercise while standing on blocks. This increases the amount of work done by adding the height of the block to the range of motion (the same effect can be obtained by using smaller than 17 inch diameter plates). In doing so it also adds more knee extension – and therefore more quadriceps – to the exercise. By making the bar farther away, it requires more knee and hip flexion at the bottom to assume the start position, and the more acute angles require more hamstring extensibility to assume the start position with an extended lumbar spine. This makes it more difficult for inflexible people to get in a correct start position, so not everybody can do them. And the fact that the shin will be in a more inclined position at the bottom also means that the bar will be shoved further forward than mid-foot if the block is very high, or if a decent back angle is maintained. This makes the start awkward, mechanically difficult, and likely to become a SLDL if care is not exercised. It also tends to limit the weights that can be used.

If you can, be aware of the fact that a deadlift on blocks is an even more stressful movement than the full deadlift for obvious reasons, so treat them with respect. No sets across with max weights because they are an assistance exercise; use them at sub-max loads to accumulate work, and to make the deadlift easier off the floor.

Figure 7-33. Deadlifting from blocks (right) increases the range of motion of the movement. Note the more acute hip and knee angles while the back angle is maintained.

The goodmorning is sometimes thought of as a squat variation, since the bar is taken out of the rack like a squat and carried on the traps. But since it functions as a back and hamstring exercise, with no more knee extension than an RDL, and with lots of elements of pulling mechanics in the movement of the bar, a case can be made for considering it a deadlift variation. Goodmornings get their name from the rather tenuous similarity between their appearance and that of a subordinate individual greeting his superiors in the a.m. They are an old weight room exercise, largely unused today, but are worthy of consideration as a way to strengthen your pull.

The bar sits on top of the traps in a goodmorning, like the bar position in a high-bar squat. Basically, a goodmorning is performed by bending over with the bar on your neck until your torso gets to parallel with the ground or lower and then returning to an upright position. The mechanics of the movement are similar to that of the Romanian deadlift in that the whole thing is essentially a hip extension that begins with an eccentric contraction like a squat – an RDL with the bar on your neck. The difference involves the position of the weight relative to the scapulas and to the middle of the foot. The RDL hangs from the arms, meaning that the load leaves the spine at the scapulas; the goodmorning sits on the traps, so the load is carried at about the C7 level, adding three or four inches to the length of the lever arm affected by the weight. And in the RDL the bar stays over the middle of the foot like a pull, with a vertical bar path; the bar in the goodmorning will describe an arc as it is lowered. This is because the distance from the bar to the hips along the back is longer than the distance from the hips to the unlocked knee, and when the bar is lowered it will travel forward on the way down (fig. 7-34). This will place it in a position forward of the mid-foot with light weights (even if the bar is placed in the low-bar squat position), and as the weight gets heavier – and as the resulting center of gravity of the bar/lifter system gets closer to the bar – the bar will get closer to the mid-foot. The necessity of attempting to balance the system means that the goodmorning will place the hips further back at the bottom of the movement than they are at the bottom of the RDL even though the bar is in front of the toes. This is why the goodmorning allows for more direct stress on the hip extensors; it is a very hard exercise because the hip extension is not assisted by any knee extension. But at the same time it must be remembered that this weight is sitting *on your neck*. Any work done by the hip extensors must be transmitted along the spine, and the leverage against the smaller cervical and upper thoracic vertebrae will be very high. Be careful about using lots of weight and generating high velocities; the goodmorning is an assistance exercise, not a primary lift, and it must be respected for both its usefulness and its potential for injury. The smartest of the strongest men in the world never use more than 225 lbs. for the goodmorning, and since it is just an assistance exercise, they use sets of 8 to 10 reps. Done correctly, goodmornings make the back stronger; done incorrectly, they can make the back injured. Use good judgement when deciding how much weight to use. There will never be a reason to use more than 35% of your squat for sets of 8-10, and there is no reason to do them at all until 35% of your squat is 95 lbs.

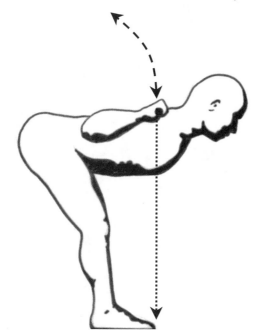

Figure 7-34. The flat-backed goodmorning lowers the bar to a position forward of the mid-foot, unlike the pulls. This increases the load on the hip extensors.

There are two ways to do goodmornings: flat-back and round-back. Flat back goodmornings are the most like the RDL. The knees are unlocked, the chest is up, the low back is arched, and the bar is on the traps with the hands pulling it down into the neck to keep it from rolling or sliding up at the bottom. (It is important to stabilize the bar against the neck and keep it from sliding, especially when using a bar with a center knurl; it will most assuredly dig a ditch in your neck if it moves.) The movement basically consists of sliding the hips back to lower the bar down as far as hamstring flexibility permits before the low back rounds off. The idea is to keep the back in extension the whole trip down and up, and the parallels to the RDL should be clear. Your flexibility will determine your depth, and the goodmorning improves hamstring length; there is not a much better stretch than a strict flat-back goodmorning. Breath control is extremely important here, since spinal support and protection is so critical to the safe performance of this exercise. A huge breath at the top held for the entire rep ensures greater spinal support.

The round-backed goodmorning is a completely different exercise. It deliberately employs less-than-optimum mechanics in order to strengthen the back against the inevitable occurrence of bad mechanics during a fatigued deadlift attempt. There are many situations, either at work or during competition, where lifting must take place under circumstances that prevent an ideal extended-spine position, and it may make sense to train for this eventuality. Strongman competition, for example, involves stone lifting, where a large mass that cannot be placed in a position that allows the spine to be flat must be lifted off the ground to an upright position. The entire trip from the ground to hip and knee lockout has to be done with the back in flexion. Or a situation may arise that requires you to lift an odd object that has no respect for your finely-developed sense of correct kinematics. Some round-backed lifting prepares you for this inevitable situation, and when planned and executed on your terms instead of the universe's, it can be made a productive adjunct to normal pulling and back work.

Round-backed goodmornings are a relatively safe way to introduce this position in the context of a controllable, increasable barbell exercise. They are probably better than round-backed deadlifts because of the tendency to use lighter, safer weights for them, and the lack of interference with the correct movement pattern in what is already a lift that is prone to errors. But since round-backed movements would have to be considered advanced exercises, and therefore not really indicated for inexperienced lifters, the advantages of round-backed goodmornings over round-backed deadlifts are not really germane; advanced lifters should have no trouble separating two styles of deadlifting from each other. The important point is that round-backed lifting is not always bad, and that goodmornings done this way are a good introduction to this aspect of conditioning.

Take the bar out of the rack as for a flat-backed goodmorning, and start down by dropping the hips back. Immediately drop the chest, rolling it down towards the knees. It is usually possible to go lower than the flat-backed form permits, since the adequate hamstring flexibility to maintain lumbar extension is not the limiting factor. Come back up by first lifting the chest and then rolling the spine into extension from the chest down to the low back, timing it to coincide with the return to the starting position. This will be difficult to do with heavy weights, especially at first, so don't go heavy until you can do so correctly. As with flat-backed GMs, higher rep sets of 8 to 10 work well. Round-backed goodmornings are an optional, advanced exercise, and the technical requirements for doing them safely and correctly may be above

Figure 7-35. Round-back lifting trains the back for situations where perfect lifting mechanics are not possible. Stone lifting is a good example of this, as is the round-back goodmorning.

the novice lifter's ability. No one's feelings will be hurt if you don't do them at all, but if you use them do them right, and light.

Figure 7-36. The flat-backed version of the goodmorning.

Press Variations

The first thing that usually comes to mind when thinking of different ways to press overhead is the behind-the-neck version, and its close relative the Bradford Press, which involves changing positions from front to back during the press. When the bar is behind the neck, the shoulders are put in a position that is not particularly advantageous under a heavy load. This position is right at the edge of the shoulder's range of motion, and puts a lot of stress on the ligaments that hold the shoulder together.

The shoulder joint is formed by the articulation of three bones, the *clavicle* or "collarbone", the scapula, and the humerus. The head of the humerus is the ball, and the *glenoid fossa* of the scapula is the socket of this ball-and-socket joint. The glenoid is a rather stingy little cup, not a nice deep socket like the acetabulum of the pelvis, and depends much more on ligamentous support for its integrity than the hip does. The net effect of this arrangement is a joint that is less stable at the edge of its range of motion than might be desired. The behind-the-neck press places the humeral head in just about the worst position it can assume under a load. If it is to be used in a program safely, it has to be done with such light weights that it becomes almost a waste of time if strength is the goal.

A better exercise is the push press. It is more than just cheating the press with your legs. The push press uses momentum generated by the hips and knees to start the bar up, and then the press is finished with the shoulders and triceps as you normally would. The movement begins with a stretch reflex, where the knees and hips unlock, the extensors lengthen a little and then immediately contract forcefully into lockout. This sharp extension provides enough drive to get the bar off the shoulders on its way up. It is not really a "push" so much as it is a bounce, since the knees and hips do not unlock and then stop in the unlocked position. It is exactly as though you are trying to bounce the bar up off of the shoulders.

This bounce requires that the bar be resting on the meat of the deltoids when this upward force gets there. If the bar is being held in the hands – resting on the palms or fingers instead of seated firmly on the shoulders, like a press should be carried – then the force of the bounce gets absorbed in the elbows and wrists instead of being transmitted to the bar. The solid connection between the bar and the shoulders allows the full effects of the hip and leg drive to carry the bar on up. A full breath before each rep braces the torso and makes the push more solid.

More weight can be done with a push than a strict press, and for this reason a heavy set of presses might get finished with a push press or two. A better approach might be to keep the two exercises as separate as possible in your mind, choosing your press weights carefully enough that a set of five presses does not turn into a set of two presses and a triple push press. After the last set of presses is done, extra work might be added in the form of two heavier sets of push presses. Or better yet, push presses could be used as a completely separate exercise on a different day, either after bench presses or as their own upper body exercise for that day.

Figure 7-38. The push press.

In addition to the same problems that affect the press, the push press has its own that derive from the involvement of the knees and hips. The most common is the tendency to dip forward onto the toes during the push. The bounce must be from the whole foot, and not the toes, or the bar/lifter system gets displaced forward. If the dip has a forward component, the motion of down-and-forward turns into up-and-forward, instead of straight down and straight up. This causes you to have to "chase' the bar as it goes forward on the way up, diluting your shoulder drive. This is fixed by making sure your dip is to your heels, and the easiest way to ensure a heels dip is to raise your big toe inside your shoe before each rep. This causes your weight to shift back onto the heels, and once you get used to the way this feels the toe dip will stop without having to cue the big toes each rep. This is a handy trick to learn, especially if you have entertained the possibility of any Olympic weightlifting; the dip that precedes the split jerk is essentially the same as the push press dip, and if you fix it now it will not be a problem later.

Figure 7-39. The tendency to dip to the toes instead of staying flat-footed introduces a forward component into the upward motion. This can be controlled by thinking about keeping the weight on the heels during the dip.

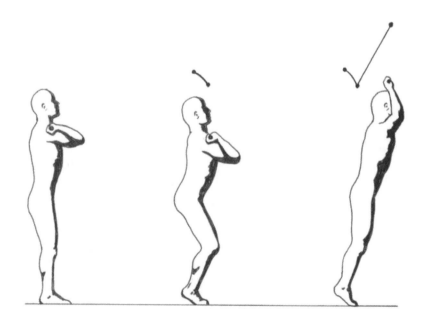

Figure 7-40. A toes-dip introduces a forward component into the push press. This can result in enough movement that a foot shift will be required to save the press.

Figure 7-41. A toes-dip (left) increases the stress on the knees during the push press. A balanced dip distributes the load between the knees and hips.

Push presses can be hard on the knees, believe it or not. The knee extensor tendons are subjected to some rather high forces during heavy push presses, and this is especially true if you are dipping to your toes. Stay out of your knees as much as possible to minimize the abuse. Knee wraps may help, but good form helps the most.

Just so you won't think it's been forgotten, assistance exercises for the power clean fall squarely in the bailiwick of Olympic weightlifting, and are outside the scope of this book. Those of you that are interested are encouraged to contact a competent weightlifting coach and develop a relationship with the sport. There is no better way to use barbells to train for power production.

Ancillary Exercises

Not every assistance exercise necessarily duplicates a portion of a parent movement. There is no chin-up-like motion in any of the five major lifts, yet chins are a terribly useful exercise. They are multi-joint, they involve the movement of the whole body, they work many muscle groups, and they are dependent on a complete range of motion for their quality – all characteristics of the major exercises. In contrast, it is difficult to do a wrist curl wrong. And really, who cares if you do? Good ancillary exercises contribute to functional movement the same way the major lifts do: they work several joints at one time through a range of motion that, when made stronger, contributes to performance in sports and work.

Ancillary exercises have traditionally been performed for higher reps than the core lifts. This is not necessarily a hard-and-fast rule; some of these movements are very valuable as strength exercises in and of themselves. Some lend themselves better to this than others: weighted chinups and dips are quite useful at lower reps and heavy weights, whereas heavy weighted back extensions can be rather hard on the knees. Each one has its own specific applications and fits into each individual trainee's program in different ways.

Chins/Pullups

Possibly the oldest resistance exercise known to the human race is the pull-up. Arboreal primates use this movement in the process of locomotion, and since we've been standing on the ground it's been difficult to resist the temptation of grabbing a branch overhead and putting our chins up over it. And you should be strong enough to do that; the pull-up is not only a good exercise, it's a very good indicator of upper body strength. If you can't do very many chin-ups, your press and bench press will increase as you get stronger on this very important exercise.

Chin-ups and pull-ups are most famous for their effects on the latissimus dorsi muscles, the "lats," but they are equally important for the other muscles of the upper back – the rhomboidius, the teres major, the serratus groups, and the rotator cuff muscles, as well as the forearms and hands. Chin-ups even work the pecs if done from a diligent dead-hang, and abs if enough reps are used to get them fatigued.

For purposes of this discussion, the term "pull-up" will refer to the version of the exercise with the hands prone, while "chin-up" or just "chin" refers to the supine hand position. The major – and significant – difference between the two is the bicep involvement in the chin-up and the lack of it in the pull-up. The addition of the biceps makes chin-ups a little easier than pull-ups, as well as adding the aesthetic elements of arm work to the movement. Pull-ups are harder, and they probably emphasize lat involvement more since the absence of the bicep means that something else must do its work. Both can be done either strict or with a hip-initiated action called a "kip" that increases the number of reps that can be done. Some work of each type is useful, but if you're not strong enough to do more than a few reps strict, the kipping version may be your default style (after you learn how to do it) until you develop the strength necessary for the strict versions. Once your strength permits, weights can be added to strict chins an pull-ups for increased workload. The more your trunk moves, the more trunk muscles are involved, and this is why abs can get sore. But any version of the chin-up/pull-up, where the whole body moves, is better than the machine version of the exercise, the "lat pulldown," where only the arms move.

Chin-ups are a better introductory exercise, due to their easier nature. We'll use a bar set at slightly above the level of the up-reached fingertips while standing flat on the floor. When hanging from this level, your toes should just touch the floor. This is, of course, an ideal height, and your equipment may be lower or higher. The crossbar at the top of a power rack works well, as might a bar set high in the rack pins. If you are fortunate enough to train in a gym enlightened enough to have provided chin bars, enjoy them, for they are not common. But it is not hard to make do, and most training facilities will have a place for the innovative trainee to chin.

Figure 7-42. The chin-up (top) uses a supine grip, and the pullup (bottom) done in the power rack uses a prone grip.

The grip will be palms-facing you, about shoulder width apart. Grip width can vary several inches depending on elbow flexibility; the more easily the hands can supinate, the wider the grip can be. The wider the grip for the chin-up, the more bicep, since this increases supination and bicep involvement. Likewise, the wider the grip, the greater the external rotation of the humerus; the closer the grip, the more internally rotated the humerus, the more abducted the scapulas and the less involved the scapula retractors and posterior delts will be. This may not be a practical variable to manipulate due to the joint stress it causes, but certain shoulder injuries can be affected by grip width for this reason. A shoulder-width grip is good for our purposes, and presents no problems for most people. Hand chalk makes for a better grip and fewer calluses, and is a good idea.

The movement itself is obviously simple: take your grip, and pull your elbows "down," which results in you leaving the ground. Each rep starts from a dead-hang, with straight elbows, and is complete when the chin clears the bar. It is terribly common to see partial chins, which should be called "foreheads" or "nose-ups," and are usually accompanied by less-than-straight elbows at the bottom. The same rules apply to pull-ups, if and when you decide to do them.

Breathing during the set takes place at the bottom. Each rep begins and ends there, at complete elbow and shoulder extension, and the breath should be taken and released in this position. A more complete breath can be taken here, where tension on the ribcage is lower. The increase in intrathoracic pressure provides a more stable skeletal platform for the muscles pulling the body up.

Figure 7-43. The jumping chin-up, used to strengthen for a complete chin-up later.

Figure 7-44. A correct chin-up (top) starts with straight elbows and ends with the chin well over the bar, as high as possible. An incorrect chin-up (below) starts with bent arms and displays an incomplete range of motion.

Figure 7-45. Chin-ups assisted by the used of resistance bands in your handy-dandy power rack.

But what if you can't do a complete chin-up? Lower the bar a little (or raise the floor, possibly an easier thing to do) and use a jump to get the movement started until you're strong enough to do it strict (fig. 7-43). Be sure to lower yourself under control to get the most out of the negative, and always use only as much jump as necessary. Or resistance bands can be used in the rack to assist until the movement is strong enough to do with only a jump.

Kipping chin-ups/pull-ups are a derivative of the jumping version.   The movement is performed using the momentum of a slight swing preceding the pull, when the swing is converted into an upward roll of the hips, translating the swing energy into upward movement. The kip distributes the movement over more muscle mass, using the abs, hip flexors, and lower back in addition to the lats and arms, so that more muscle mass is used in the exercise and more reps can be done. The strict versions concentrate the effort on less muscle mass and work it harder.

Figure 7-46. The kipping pull-up.

Weighted chins and pullups are an excellent source of heavy non-pressing work for the upper body. Plates are suspended from a chain on a belt, or a dumbbell can be held in the feet for the resistance if not much weight is to be used. A good rule of thumb is that when 12-15 bodyweight reps can be done, it is probably time to start doing some of the work weighted, possibly alternating higher-rep bodyweight workouts with lower-rep weighted workouts. Several sets across are appropriate for chins and pull-ups, either weighted, unweighted, or assisted.

Dips

The parallel bar dip is a movement borrowed from gymnastics. It consists of lowering the body down and then driving it back up from a position supported between and above two parallel bars by the arms. It is a good substitute for the bench press if it cannot be done for some reason, and is far superior to the decline bench press, which there is no good reason to do. If the "lower pecs" and triceps are the object of your desire – the apple of your eye, as it were – then dips are your exercise. They are better because, like any good exercise, they involve the movement of lots of your body besides the lower pecs and triceps. In this case, they involve the movement of your *entire* body; dips are like pushups in this respect. They are better than pushups because they can be weighted and performed alone, while pushups cannot be weighted conveniently even with two people involved.

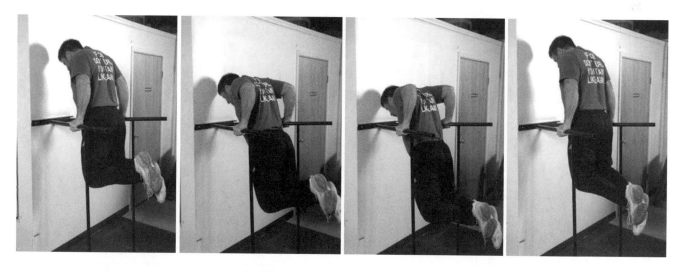

Figure 7-47. Parallel bar dips, performed on a dip station.

The quality of an exercise increases with the involvement of more muscles, more joints, and more central nervous system activity needed to control them. The more of the body involved in an exercise, the more of these criteria are met. When the whole body moves, a more nearly ideal state is achieved, with lots of muscles and nerves controlling lots of joints, and the central nervous system keeping track of lots of different pieces of the body doing many different things, hopefully correctly. By this logic, pushups are better than bench presses since they involve the movement and control of the entire body. But they are very difficult to do weighted, especially alone, because of the problems with loading the human body in this position. Were it possible, a good weighted pushup device would be in use today.

It has long been assumed that the bench press solved the problem, when in fact it hasn't. The only thing moving in the bench press is the arms: the bench is to the pushup what the lat pulldown is to the pull-up. But the bench does allow the same approximate movement to be loaded. Without adding weight, it is difficult for a fit person to train a pressing motion moving in the anterior direction without using very high reps, which are not always appropriate for every training goal. Dips address both problems, allowing heavy weights to be used while the entire body moves during an upper body exercise.

Unweighted dips are harder than pushups because the whole body is moving, not just the part that doesn't get supported by the feet. And for the more advanced trainee dips are very easy to use weighted, by hanging plates or other objects from a belt, or by holding a dumbbell between the feet (an option with only works well for light weights). The anterior aspect of the movement is provided by the slightly inclined torso position, a function of the fact that the forearms stay vertical during the whole movement. Vertical forearms dictate that the shoulder will travel forward relative to the elbow as the body is lowered. If the mass of the body is to be distributed evenly during the movement relative to the position of the hands on the bars, i.e. half of it in front of the hands and half of it behind the hands, then the body will have to assume an inclined position during the movement. The angle of the spine will never approach parallel to the ground, since the legs pull it down toward the vertical. The legs constitute the majority of the mass hanging from the shoulders; people with short legs or less leg mass will hang at a less vertical angle at the bottom. But there is enough angle to provide for a tremendous amount of pec involvement, primarily the lower part of the muscle belly.

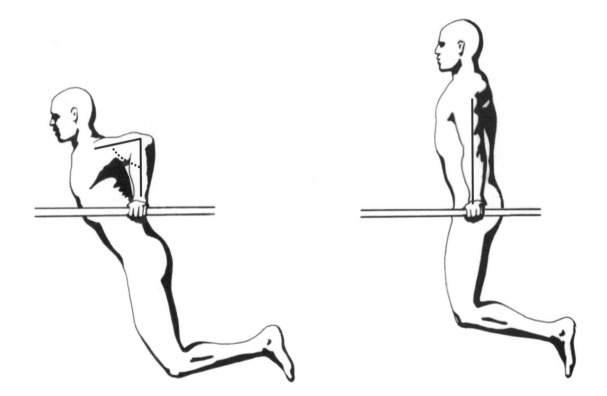

Figure 7-48. The bottom position of the dip, with the humerus below parallel, and the top, with fully extended elbows.

Figure 7-49. The dip station shown above and in figure 7-47, that permits a variety of grip widths.

Heavy weights can be used in this exercise, and it has been used by many powerlifters to maintain bench strength while a shoulder injury heals, one that the bench aggravates but that dips do not. It can be used unweighted for high reps or weighted just like the bench would be trained. The whole-body effects are felt more as weight increases, with very heavy efforts producing fatigue throughout the trunk and arms.

Dips are best done on a set of dip bars, a station designed for this purpose; most modern gyms do not have a set of parallel bars as might be found in a gymnastics studio, or previously, most gyms. Parallel bars will usually be between 24-26 inches wide, and the most comfortable ones will be made out of 1 ¼ or 1 ½ inch pipe or bar stock. They are between 48 and 54 inches high, tall enough to allow the feet to completely clear the ground at the bottom of the dip. They really, really need to be stable, either attached to a wall or built with enough base that any possible amount of wobble during the movement will not tip the bars. A non-parallel station, with the bars at a 30-degree angle allows for a variety of grip widths that can more closely approximate the press, bench press, or jerk grip without adversely affecting the neutral hand orientation. But in a pinch (or a motel room), two chairs can serve as a dip station if they are stable when turned back to back.

Figure 7-50. Dips can be done between two chairs if other equipment is not available, or if you are traveling.

261

To perform the exercise, jump up into position, setting the grip in the chosen position first. Hold yourself up with locked elbows. Take a big breath and hold it, and start down by unlocking the elbows and leaning forward a little, and continue down until your shoulders are below your elbows. This position is easily identified by someone watching you; the humerus will dip below parallel as the shoulder goes below the elbow. This ensures a complete range of motion – a good stretch for the pecs – and provides a way to judge the completeness of the rep, a way to quantify the work and compare performances between two people, thus serving the same purpose it does in the squat. Drive the body up out of the bottom stretched position until the elbows are locked out, raising the chest into position directly above the hands on the bar. Exhale at the top after the rep is finished, and when a breath is necessary be sure to take it only when locked out at the top. Don't exhale during the rep; the pressure provides ribcage support that is important for effective control of the body while it is moving.

The two most common errors in performing dips involve the completeness of the movement. Most people, when not being yelled at about it, will cut the depth off above parallel. This is because it is easier to do a partial dip than a full dip, just like a squat. A partial dip does not carry the injury potential that a partial squat does. But partial dips are not as valuable as deep dips for the same reason that a half squat is less than adequate: they work less muscle mass. If you're going to go to the trouble of loading a dip belt to do them weighted and then cheat the depth, you are just wasting training time and kidding yourself about how strong you are, *just like when you cheat any other exercise.* Do your dips deep, with a lighter weight if necessary, so you don't miss the actual benefit of the exercise.

The other problem is a failure to lock the elbows out at the top between reps. This is not the heinous crime that cutting off the depth is, because it is usually unintentional. Tired triceps don't always know they are not completely contracted. The chest-up position at the finish helps cue the elbow lockout, because it pulls the mass of the upper part of the torso behind the hands so that the triceps can extend the elbows against a more evenly distributed load.

And gentlemen, when doing weighted dips with a chain and a belt, be sure to arrange the chain and plates in such a way as to minimize the chance of damage to the important structures that are in unfortunate proximity, in the event of a loss of control or a swinging plate.

Figure 7-51. Weighted dips, done with a dip belt and plates.

Barbell Rows

Most people associate rows with machines that place you in a position to do them. The most valuable rowing exercise is the one that makes you assume the position and maintain it throughout the set. This way, you get the benefit of moving the bar through the whole range of motion, and the stability work involved in holding your back in the right position to do it. As with all beneficial barbell training, the more work you have to do during the exercise, the better the exercise.

Barbell rows start on the floor and end on the floor, each and every rep. The bar does not hang from the arms between reps. Each rep is separated by a breath and a reset of the lower back. Starting from the floor enables the hamstrings and glutes to help get the bar moving, so that the lats and scapula retractors can finish a heavier weight than they could from a dead hang in the arms. Done this way, the exercise works not only the lats, upper back, and arms – the muscles typically associated with rowing – but the low back and hip extensors as well.

When rowing from the floor, the most critical factor in technique is the position of the lower back. The lumbar spine must be held in extension, just like it is in a deadlift and for exactly the same reason. A major difference between rows and deadlifts is the fact that the back angle changes as the bar comes off the floor; the knees are already extended and are not really involved much, so the hip extensors contribute to the initial pull from the floor by raising the chest through the locked back, transmitting this force to the bar. The finish occurs as the elbows bend and slam the bar into the lower ribcage area. The bar will leave the floor from a position directly below the scapulas, just like a deadlift; unlike a deadlift, the back angle will never become vertical, and in fact will not rise much higher than where it is just after the bar leaves the floor, just above horizontal at the shoulders.

Approach the bar with a deadlift stance, maybe not quite as close; light weights can be pulled through the air to the belly over a curved bar path as you warm up, but as the weight gets heavier standard pulling mechanics will prevail and the bar will operate vertically over the mid-foot as in all heavy pulling exercises. As weight is added, the bar will adjust itself to the correct position over the foot whether you want it to or not. The grip can vary quite a bit, but about the same as the bench press width is perhaps the best place to start. A hook grip is useful at heavier weights, or straps can be used. Eyes should be fixed on the floor in front of your position a few feet, not looking straight down but also not attempting to look straight forward, which would place the neck in too extended a position.

From the correct stance, take the grip on the bar, take a big breath, raise it from the floor with straight elbows to get it moving, and continue it on up by bending the elbows and slamming the bar into the upper part of the belly. This movement leads with the elbows, and you should think about slamming the elbows into the ceiling. The most important part of the technique of the barbell row is the back position while the bar movement takes place: the spine must be locked into extension, with the chest up and the lower back arched the whole time the bar is moving. After the bar contacts the belly, it is lowered back to the floor, the air is exhaled and a new breath taken, and the back is reset before each rep. Don't attempt to hold it against the belly at the top or lower it too slowly; the barbell row is like the deadlift in that the work is intended to be mainly concentric. Since heavier weights will essentially be dropped, bumper plates are good to use for rowing, or use rubber mats under your standard iron plates.

Figure 7-52. The barbell row. Each rep starts and stops on the floor.

The row requires that the bar be started off the floor with a hip extension, not a knee extension. With light weights the arms alone can perform the row, but as you approach work set weight hip extension will become more important. The knees will be almost straight, just unlocked, before the bar moves up, so that there is little chance the quads can be used anyway. The movement starts with the chest coming up, with straight elbows raising the back angle slightly as the bar leaves the floor, a movement performed with the hamstrings and glutes acting on the rigid back held in isometric contraction by the erectors. This initial hip extension starts the weight up, and the elbows catch the momentum and carry the bar on up with a shoulder extension and scapula retraction. The lats, triceps, biceps, forearm muscles, posterior deltoids, and smaller muscles around the shoulder blades are the prime movers here. The trunk muscles that stabilize the spine enable the trunk to act as a rigid platform against which the force can be generated. The hamstrings and glutes, after their initial action off the ground, act to anchor the pelvis, and therefore the lower back, during the final rowing motion generated by the upper body. As is so often the case in complex human movement, muscles change actions during the course of the activity, starting off with one function and ending with another, and the function of the hip extensors during the barbell row is a good example of this.

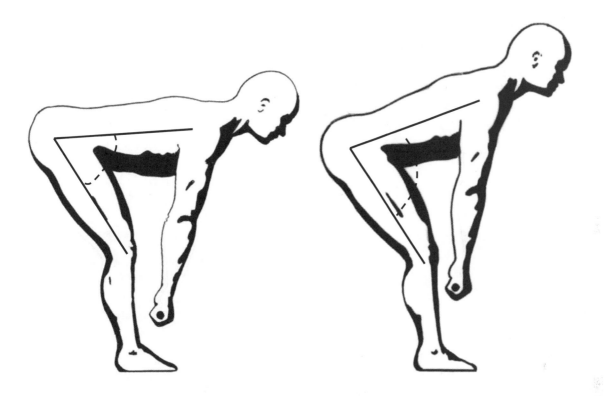

Figure 7-53. The barbell row starts off the floor with a hip extension. Just before the elbows begin to bend the back angle will have become more vertical.

Rows are not useful at weights so heavy that form is hard to maintain. The finish position when the bar touches the belly is controlled by the some of the same factors that limit a clean, in that a weight that can be rowed correctly may only be 15 lbs. lighter than a weight that cannot be rowed at all. A row that is not finished will not engage the range of motion that is unique to the exercise and might as well be called a partial SLDL. For this reason, sets of five or more reps are used, since weights that can only be rowed for a triple probably cannot be done correctly anyway. Much better to get good reps with a lighter weight for sets of 5, 8, or 10 and do several across than to lose the benefit of the exercise with a weight that is too heavy.

The first few reps will only use a slight – maybe less than ten degrees – amount of hip extension, but as the set progresses and the upper body becomes fatigued more hip extension gets thrown in to get the reps finished. Be sure to continue doing rows and not deadlifts. The back should never get much above horizontal, and if the chest comes up too high on the last reps, the bar is hitting too low, the range of motion for the target muscles has shortened, and the weight is too heavy.

As the weight gets heavy, there will be a pronounced tendency to allow the chest to drop down to meet the bar, completing the rep from the top down instead of from the bottom up. When this becomes excessive, the weight is too heavy. And excessive is a rather subjective concept here. It might be decided that no chest drop is allowable, in which case heavy weights cannot be used in the exercise. Or it might be decided that as long as the chest can be touched with the bar, the rep counts. This degree of variability is one of the things that distinguish an assistance exercise from a primary exercise: if a large degree of variability is inherent in the performance of an exercise, it cannot be judged effectively or quantified objectively. For this reason, the barbell row makes a very good ancillary exercise but a very poor contest lift.

A variation on the standard barbell row is to supinate the grip, thus adding more bicep to the exercise. This reverse-grip row is irritating to the elbows in inflexible people; the rather extreme degree of external rotation of the humerus combined with the completely supine hand is irritating to the forearm muscles' insertion points on the elbows during elbow flexion with a heavy weight. It can produce tennis or golfer's elbow very quickly, so if you decide to try this version of the movement start with light weights and work up to your heavier sets cautiously the first time or two. And use a narrower grip than you would for the prone grip version to minimize the grip position problems.

Figure 7-54. The supine grip used for the barbell row. This lifter also uses the hook grip.

It is interesting that when the bar hits the chest right below the xiphoid process, the humerus lines up across the back with the thickest part of the lats, where the fibers are parallel to the bar and perpendicular to the spine. A lower strike point on the belly fails to take advantage of this alignment.

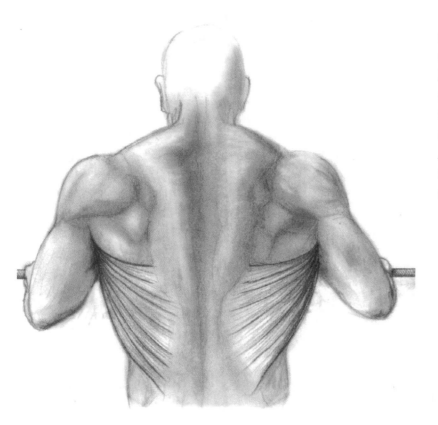

Figure 7-55. Seen from above, the lats working across the back where the fibers of the muscle bellies are roughly parallel to the bar.

Glute/Ham Raises

There are a couple of ancillary exercises that require special equipment which are useful enough to make it worth locating. The Roman Chair is an old piece of gym equipment that can be found in one form or another in most training facilities. It was developed by the famous physical culturist Professor Louis "Attila" Durlacher in the late 1800s from a device known as a "Roman column" that served a similar function. It is a very basic bench (a bench has no parts that move during an exercise; a machine does) that supports the foot from the top while supporting the thigh from below, allowing for a horizontal leg-supported position. The Roman Chair is used while both facing up for abdominal work and facing down for back work.

Abs done on this bench are called Roman chair situps after the device. The back exercise has been for many years referred to as a "hyperextension," although that term specifically refers to a position that most joints don't like to be placed in, and is therefore preferably termed simply a "back extension." You may hear this term used for the exercise, from time to time, but it is losing its place as more people become more familiar with biomechanical terminology.

The exercise itself is a very good way to directly work the spinal erectors in a concentric/eccentric contractile mode. The normal function of the trunk muscles is stabilization of the spine using an isometric contraction that allows little or no relative movement of the vertebrae. But they can be effectively strengthened using active motion of the spine with this exercise, which functions like a reverse situp by using the erectors to extend the spine from a flexed position over a broad range of motion. The fact that the spine is extended in a position parallel to the floor is a function of the simultaneous hip extension, which the glutes – all of them, the maximus, medius, and minimus – and hamstrings perform in coordination with the spinal extension.

The back extension is performed by assuming a face-down position in a Roman Chair with the middle of the thighs on the front pad and the back of the legs just below the calves and just above the heels, right on the Achilles tendon, jammed up into the back pad or roller pad, the body held parallel to the floor. The knees are kept very slightly unlocked but not bent, with just a little tension from the hamstrings to protect the knees from hyperextension. The movement is a resisted spinal flexion – just let your chest drop down toward the upright of the bench, until it is perpendicular to the floor – and then an active spinal extension, raising the chest, followed by a hip extension which kicks in the glutes and hamstrings to finish the exercise with the torso parallel to the floor. It is important to lead up with the chest, making it draw the back into extension – a full arch at the top of the movement. It works the spinal erectors, the glutes, and some hamstring.

Figure 7-56. A simple type of Roman chair bench.

Figure 7-57. Back extensions (left) and Roman chair situps (right).

The glute/ham bench is a modified Roman Chair that allows the back extension to be carried on up into a bodyweight "leg curl." They are becoming more popular as more people figure out the high level of utility of this exercise. The finish position in the glute/ham raise is with a *vertical* torso. It thus includes all the elements of the back extension with lots and lots more hamstring involvement added in. The modification that allows this added movement is a plate welded onto the frame right behind the back roller. This plate gives the foot a place to push against, allowing a knee flexion to occur which carries the torso and thighs on up to the vertical position. The hamstrings can do this with the plate against the feet because they have the help of the gastrocnemius, which cannot contribute to knee flexion unless its *proximal* function is facilitated by blocking its *distal* function against the plate.

Muscles that cross two joints can affect movement around either joint. The proximal function is that which is performed by the joint closest to the center of the body, and the distal function is performed on the other end of the bone, the one furthest away. Most of the joints in the body are moved by muscles that also attach across another joint. The hamstrings are perhaps the most classic example, since they both extend the hips and flex the knees. (The glute/ham raise causes them to do both, making it a very valuable exercise.) The gastroc is another example of this type of muscle; it attaches to the calcaneus, or heel bone, by the Achilles tendon, and to the lateral and medial epicondyles of the femur, behind the knee, as it splits into a right and left head. It both extends the ankle (referred to as "plantar flexion" in this particular instance) and flexes the knee. The other major calf muscle, the *soleus*, shares the Achilles tendon with the gastroc but attaches proximally to the tibia and therefore does not cross the knee.

Figure 7-58. A glute/ham bench, a modified adjustable Roman chair with toe plates for the full range of motion exercise.

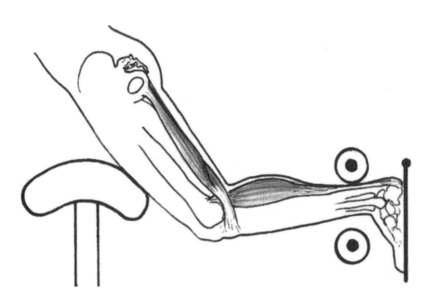

Figure 7-59. The glute/ham raise is essentially a back extension followed immediately by a bodyweight leg curl. The knee flexion is completeable because the feet are blocked by the plate, enabling the calf muscles to contribute their proximal function to knee flexion. Without the plate, a full knee flexion into an upright position (as in fig. 7-60) is not possible.

The glute/ham bench takes advantage of this anatomy and gives the foot a surface against which to push. The heel is trapped up against the roller by the weight of the body out in front of the forward pad, levering it up, and the foot is held against the plate by the tension of the calf. The plate blocks the ankle extension so that the contraction of the gastroc is transmitted to the femoral insertions, causing the knee to flex. The movement is essentially a back extension until the torso is parallel to the ground, where the hips have extended as well as the spine. Then the foot pushes the plate and the knee flexion adds to the upward momentum generated by the back extension, carrying the torso on up to a vertical position, with the knee flexed at 90 degrees, the back and hips in extension, and the chest up.

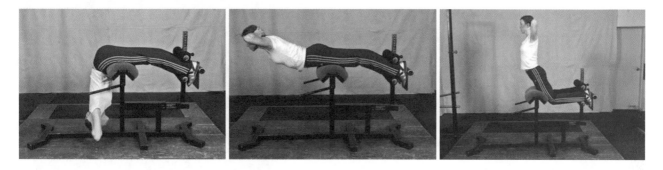

Figure 7-60. The glute/ham raise.

The glutes engage more strongly here than they do in a simple back extension. They help generate momentum through the transition between the back extension and the knee flexion. Depending on the individual, the glutes may not be particularly perceptible as they work in the exercise, because of the huge contribution of the hamstrings working over a much longer range of motion, and the fact that the glutes contract very efficiently over a shorter distance, since their origin/insertion points are not that far apart.

The poorer the conditioning of the athlete, especially with regard to the squat, the more perceptible the glutes will be in this exercise. And the poorer the conditioning, the less likely the trainee will be actually able to do an entire set of 10, or even a complete rep. Glute/ham raises are hard at first, but get stronger very quickly as the movement pattern and the associated neuromuscular efficiency improves.

The movement is performed in essentially the same way as a back extension until the spine reaches the full arched position, which must occur in a coordinated fashion or the timing will be off. The knees then kick in to finish raising the chest up all the way to vertical. The best cue for this is the chest: think about raising the chest up fast and hard, and the hamstrings, calves, and glutes will do their job at the right time. The hands are held either crossed on the chest, the easier way, or with fingers locked behind the head, the harder of the two since more mass is further away from the fulcrum at the thighs on the front pad. Glute/hams like to be done at higher reps; 10 to 15 for three to five sets works best.

In this exercise, you are lifting the part of your body that is in front of the pad with muscles located behind the pad, and the more mass in front of the pad the harder the job is to do. Most glute/ham benches are adjustable between front and back pads for this reason, and the difficulty of the movement can be adjusted accordingly. The front pad should be set far enough back that the crotch clears the pad, for rather obvious reasons, and to make the exercise hard enough to get

enough work out of it. But be careful about adjusting the back pad so far forward that the front pad is too close to the knees. This does increase the difficulty, but it also increases dramatically the amount of shear force on the knees, which are, after all, only held together by the cruciate ligaments, the capsular ligaments, and muscular tension. Specifically, in this position the knees are supported by tension from the hamstrings and by the posterior cruciates, and the closer to the knee the front pad is, the more stress on the knee. More advanced lifters can carry weight behind the neck or on the chest to increase the work if necessary. It is much better to add load with weight than with leverage in this exercise.

Do not allow the knees to bend prematurely – when the thighs slide or roll down the pads – before the back extension has been completed. Remember: anytime the knee bends, the hamstring shortens. If you allow this to happen before the back extension phase of the movement is finished, you have 1.) contracted the hamstring without making it do any actual work, since it hasn't contributed to the lifting up of the torso, and 2.) you have placed it in a position of partial contraction where it cannot contribute a full contraction to the exercise after the back extension phase has finished. Don't let your knees slide down from the thigh pad before the chest is up and the hips are extended. It ruins the effect of the exercise.

When you first start doing them, glute/ham raises may be very hard. Typically, an untrained person cannot do a complete rep all the way up to vertical. This is fine, just come up as high as you can for each rep of the set, even though that height will deteriorate as the set goes on. The exercise gets strong very fast, as mentioned before, primarily because you learn how to do it more efficiently very quickly. Within six or seven workouts, most people are capable of performing at least one complete rep. When several sets can be done all the way up, add load after a warmup set by holding a plate to the chest or a bar behind the neck.

During a back extension or a glute/ham raise, the torso is the portion of the body that moves.

Figure 7-61. A reverse "hyperextension" machine, well used for many years.

272

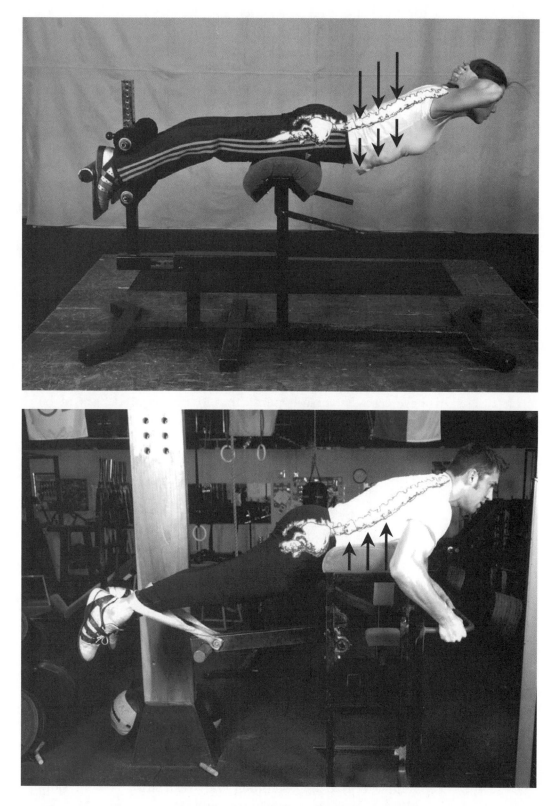

Figure 7-61. The glute/ham raise vs. the reverse hyper. Spinal shear in the GHR carries force across the spinal column, and countering this shear is an element of the exercise. In contrast, the table of the reverse hyper supports the spine, effectively eliminating the shearing force. This is an important consideration in the use of these exercises in rehab.

Conversely, if the torso is supported by a bench and the legs move up and down, providing the resistance for active lumbar flexion and extension, the exercise is the reverse of the back extension (or "hyperextension") and is referred to as a reverse hyperextension, or "reverse hyper" for short. They are to back extensions what leg raises are to situps. Reverse hypers are a good exercise if you have access to the equipment. The problem is that reverse hyper tables, like glute/ham benches, are rather specialized pieces of equipment that not every gym has on the floor. Reverse hypers can be improvised with other equipment once you understand the simple mechanics of the movement, but this allows only the bodyweight version which must be done for high reps. To do them effectively with weight, a special machine is required. This exercise is one of the few machine exercises that can make a significant contribution to functional back strength. It is multi-joint in that the hip and the lumbar vertebrae move together. But like the glute/ham it is not actually a functional movement because the back muscles normally stabilize the spine isometrically, and special equipment is required before they can be exercised concentrically.

Reverse hypers are valuable for another important reason: they are a very good rehab exercise for certain types of back injuries that the shear force inherent in a glute/ham raise tends to aggravate. The spine is supported along the whole length of the lumbar and thoracic by the table, which prevents intervertebral movement. In contrast, the glute/ham raise leaves the spine hanging in the air, supported by the legs from one end and pulled on by gravity from the other. This produces a "sliding" force between the individual vertebrae, which can irritate injured intervertebral discs. In these cases, reverse hypers can allow an injured back to be worked very hard, strengthening muscles that need to be strong if function is to return to the injured area.

Curls

Since you're going to do them anyway, we might as well discuss the right way to do curls. Curls are performed to train the biceps, a muscle that commands an inordinate amount of attention from far too many people. But that is the nature of things, and who are we to question so fundamental a matter? Effective curls require an awareness of the biceps anatomy and a willingness to diverge from the conventional wisdom regarding technique.

The biceps muscles (technically the biceps brachii, or "arm" biceps is distinct from the biceps femoris, one of the hamstring muscles) is one of the many muscles of the body that crosses two joints. Like its partner the triceps, the biceps crosses both the elbow and shoulder joints, and therefore causes movement to occur around both joints. The chin-up illustrates a combination of elbow flexion and shoulder extension. But so does the pullup, the difference being the prone versus supine grip. The elbow flexion during the pullup is performed without much bicep involvement, while the biceps are heavily involved in the chin-up.

This is due to the anatomy of the elbow. The distal end of the biceps attaches to the *ulna*, the longer of the two forearm bones and the one that forms the point of the elbow, the olecranon process, where the triceps tendon attaches. Standing with your arms at your side, palms facing your legs, the ulna is behind the *radius*, the shorter topmost bone of the two. *Supination* is the term given to the palm-upward rotation of the hand, and the palm-up position of the hand is referred to as *supine*. The primary supinator of the hand is the biceps, because when the forearm supinates, the ulna rotates in and up relative to the radius, and the biceps pulling on the ulna produces this rotation. In fact, if the biceps is in full contraction, the hand is supine. The pullup, performed with a prone grip, utilizes very little biceps – and therefore proportionately more tricep and lat – while the chin-up uses lots of biceps. The elbow flexion part of the pullup is accomplished by the other elbow flexors: the brachialis and the brachioradialis, and some of the smaller forearm muscles.

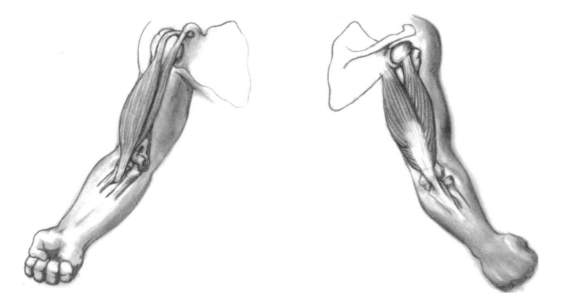

Figure 7-62. Both the biceps (left) and the triceps muscles cross the elbow and shoulder joints, causing movement around both.

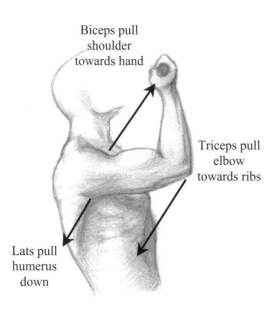

Biceps pull shoulder towards hand

Triceps pull elbow towards ribs

Lats pull humerus down

Figure 7-63. Chin-ups are an example of an exercise involving elbow flexion, a distal bicep/forearm function, and shoulder extension, a lat/proximal tricep function.

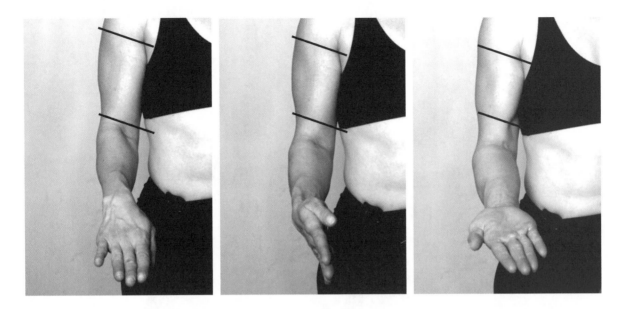

Figure 7-64. The effect of forearm supination on bicep contraction. The biceps brachii is the primary supinator of the forearm, and the biceps are not in complete contraction unless the forearm is fully supinated.

The biceps also performs the movement known as *shoulder flexion*. Anatomical movement descriptions can be at times arbitrary, and flexion in the shoulder joint is defined as forward and upward movement of the humerus. The biceps contributes to this movement because the proximal attachments (yes, there are two; thus the name) are located on the anterior (forward) side of the scapula, the main bone of the shoulder joint. Since the tendon attachments cross the joint, they move the joint, and shoulder flexion is therefore a bicep function.

Elbow flexion, along with shoulder extension, is used whenever anything is grasped and pulled in to the body. This is why chin-ups and pullups are such functional exercises: they duplicate this very normal motion under a load. In fact, elbow flexion is normally accompanied by shoulder extension; this is the way the arm is designed to work. And this is why elbow flexion with an immobile shoulder requires special equipment: the preacher curl was invented for the purpose of providing a way to work the biceps in isolation. The isolation of a single muscle group that moves a single joint seldom contributes significantly to other more complex movements which include that muscle group. A good definition of "functional exercise" is a normal human movement that can be performed under a scalable, increasable load. By this definition, no exercise that requires a machine or specific device to perform it can be a functional exercise. And if a muscle is isolated in an exercise, its tendon attachments are too; this has a bearing on the injury potential of these types of exercises.

Examples of shoulder flexion are harder to find, since raising things overhead is generally accomplished with a prone hand and a pressing motion that relies primarily on deltoids and triceps. Shoulder flexion with a supine forearm is pretty much the exclusive domain of exercise. But the biceps do perform this function, and since that is the case, it should be incorporated into biceps training so that this function gets worked. So, curls should involve shoulder flexion.

Barbell curls allow for both elbow flexion and shoulder flexion, they utilize a normal function of the arms, and they do not require specialized equipment (the bar being considered non-specialized; a big rock could be used if necessary). So barbell curls could be considered a functional exercise, in the strict sense of the definition.

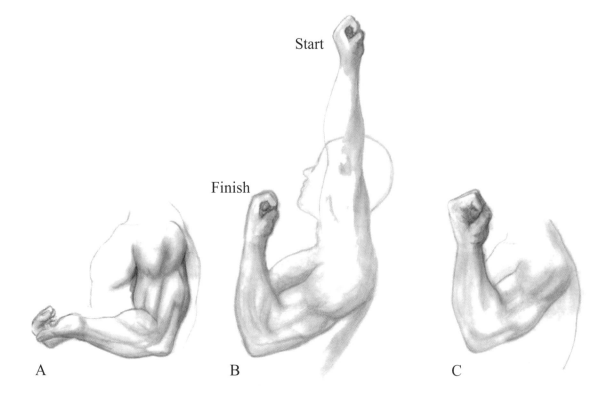

Figure 7-65. Three ways to work the biceps. A. Elbow flexion in isolation: a strict curl. B. Shoulder extension with elbow flexion: a chin-up. C. Elbow flexion with shoulder flexion: a barbell curl as described in this book.

There are as many ways to do curls as there are muscle magazine authors. If you're going to spend time doing them all, you have missed the point of this book. Let's assume you haven't, and that you want the best way to work the most bicep in the least time. That way is the barbell curl, done with a standard olympic bar. It is performed standing (since it cannot be performed seated) and is best done out of a rack set at the same height it would be for the press.

Approach the bar with a supine grip, the width varying between somewhat closer than shoulder width and several inches wider. The wider the grip, the greater the degree of supination that will be required to maintain that grip, and the greater the supination, the more the bicep will be contracted at full flexion. Depending on individual flexibility, a grip just wider than the shoulders will allow the full effects of the exercise to be expressed (this will be about the same grip used for the chin-up, for the same reasons).

This version of the barbell curl starts at the top, with the elbows in full flexion, as opposed to the more common method of starting at the bottom with an extended elbow. When the bar is lowered to full extension and then raised back into flexion without a pause at the bottom, the biceps get the benefit of utilizing a stretch reflex to contract harder, thereby allowing the use of more weight. Breathing is only at the top, with none of the supportive pressure released at the bottom. The elbows are kept against the ribcage and start from a position in front of the bar. The weight is lowered eccentrically in an arc, away from the body with the elbows maintaining their position against the ribs, in front of the midaxial line that separates front from back. As the elbows get almost straight at the bottom, the elbows slide back into a position behind this line. The elbows never straighten completely, since this would mean that tension is off the biceps, but they get close. Some tension is necessary to initiate the concentric flexion that comprises the essence of the movement, and a perfectly straight elbow makes this very hard and inefficient.

The upward phase starts with the elbows sliding back forward as the bar describes the same arc upward that it did on the way down. Elbows stay against the ribs the whole way up; this keeps the hands in supination by maintaining the supine position of the hand. A good cue for this position is to think about pushing the medial pad of the palm – the part just above the wrist on the little finger side of the hand – into the bar, like this is the only part of the hand in contact with the bar. This will require the wrist to be in a neutral position, neither flexed nor extended but in a position that keeps the metacarpal bones of the hand in line with the forearm. Drive the bar back up to the starting position keeping the hands supine and the elbows on the ribs. During this upward phase, the elbows will move forward to return to their position in front of the bar, producing shoulder flexion in addition to elbow flexion. It is common to see the elbows leave the ribcage and assume a position in line with, or even outside, the hands on the bar. This involves the deltoids in the movement, and takes away from biceps involvement. Keep the elbows close to the ribs and make them slide forward on the way up.

During this movement, it will be very difficult to maintain a perfectly upright posture, if any weight at all is used, since the system must balance over the middle of the foot, and that will require some backward lean. The heavier the weight, the more the lean. It is neither necessary nor desirable to try to stay strictly upright. If you are training for strength, heavier weights must be used, and physics of a heavy bar in front and you in back cannot be circumvented. What should not occur is any knee flexion and extension at all, or an excessive amount of upward movement out of the bottom initiated by the hips instead of the elbows. "Excessive" is a judgement call. Cheat curls are a legitimate exercise, depending on what you want out of the movement. If a heavy weight is started with a little hip extension and finished with a substantial amount of unassisted elbow and shoulder flexion, that is probably legit. But if you start it with hips *and* knees and then dive under it to receive the bar in full elbow flexion, you are doing a reverse-grip clean, defeating the purpose of the exercise, risking several different injuries, and inviting criticism from more experienced lifters.

Figure 7-66. The barbell curl. Note the starting position at the top with the elbows in flexion.

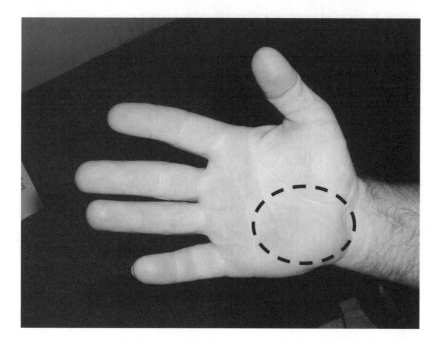

Figure 7-67. The medial chunk of the palm is the key to ensuring maximum supination during a curl. Push the bar up while thinking about using this part of the hand.

Most gyms have an EZ Curl bar, a cambered bar intended for doing curls as an alternative to using a straight bar. The EZ Curl car was invented by some poor bastard back in the early 1970s that probably didn't make a dime off of the thing. It apparently ended up with the one of the big magazine publishers who also happens to sell equipment, and who started marketing it as their own device. Typical situation.

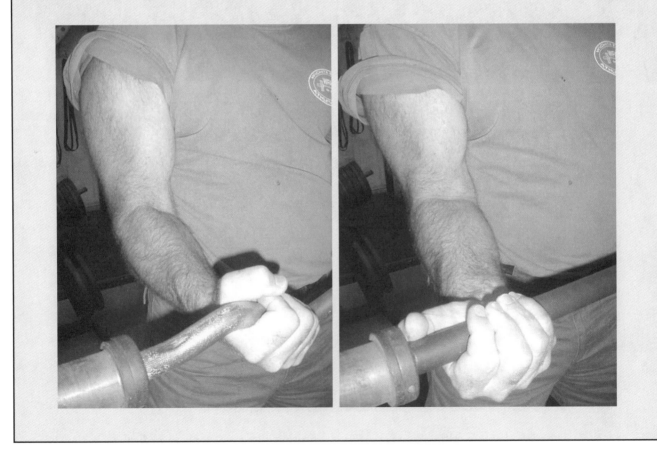

The problem is that it doesn't work. EZ Curls are not nearly as effective as straight-bar curls for recruiting bicep contraction. This is because the degree of supination of the forearm and hand directly affects the amount of bicep in contraction, as discussed earlier. The EZ Curl bar does in fact take the stress of supination off of the wrists and elbows, but it does so at the expense of a quality bicep contraction. The camber of the bar is specifically intended to decrease the supination of the forearm, and anything less than full supination results in a less-than-complete biceps contraction.

But the EZ Curl bar works fine for the lying triceps extension. The triceps is composed of three muscle origins that share a common insertion on the olecranon process of the elbow, and the angle of the hand on the bar makes no difference to the quality of the triceps contraction. The more prone grip afforded by the EZ Curl bar is more comfortable for this exercise too, but does not in this case reduce the effectiveness of the exercise.

There are lots of useless assistance exercises which contribute nothing to the performance of the major exercises, nothing to the performance of sports activities, and which in fact may do worse than merely waste time. Exercises that utilize only one joint, which usually require machines to do, are non-functional in the sense that they do not follow a normal human movement pattern. They also quite often predispose the joint to overuse injuries, and the vast majority of weight room injuries are produced by these exercises. This is not only by default, since it is obvious that in a world where most people only use machines that most of the injuries will occur on machines. Isolation exercises cause tendinitis because human joints are not designed to be subjected to the stress of movements where all of the shock, torque, and load is exclusively applied to one joint. The knee did not evolve on the leg extension machine. There is no movement that can be performed outside the modern health club that involves *only* the quadriceps; the only way to isolate the quads is to do an exercise on a machine designed for that purpose. This is a function that hundreds of millions of years of vertebrate evolution did not anticipate. The knee is the home of many muscles, all of which have developed while working at the same time. Any exercise that deviates from the function for which the joint is designed contributes very little to the function of that joint, and is a potential source of problems.

Exercise machines have made several people a lot of money, and while there's absolutely nothing wrong with that, they have been a very large diversion from more productive forms of training. The pendulum swings, and barbell training is once again being recognized as the superior form of exercise. Glad we could help.

"There is one thing more wicked in the world than the desire to command, and that is the will to obey."

W.K. Clifford

"One can resist the invasion of an army, but one cannot resist the invasion of ideas."

Victor Hugo

Programming

It is May 15, and you decide that this year you are going to get a suntan – a glorious, beautiful, tropical suntan. So you decide to go out in the back yard (to spare the neighbors and innocent passers-by) to lay out at lunchtime and catch a ray or two. You lie on your back for 15 minutes and flip over to lie on your belly for 15 minutes. Then you get up, come in and eat lunch, and go back to work. That night, your skin is a little pink, so the next day you just eat lunch, but the following day you're back outside for your 15 minutes per side sunbath. You are faithful to your schedule, spending 30 minutes outside every day that week, because that's the kind of disciplined, determined person you are. At the end of the week, you have turned a more pleasant shade of brown, and, heartened by your results, resolve to maintain your schedule for the rest of the month. So, here is the critical question: what color is your skin at the end of the month?

If you ask a hundred people this question, ninety five will tell you that it will be really, really dark. But in fact it is exactly the same color as it was at the end of the first week. Why would it be any darker? Your skin adapts to the stress of the sun exposure by becoming dark enough to prevent itself from burning again, and it adapts *exactly and specifically* to the stress that burned it. Your skin does not "know" that you want it to get darker; it only "knows" what the sun tells it, and the sun only talked to it for 15 minutes. It can't get any darker than the 15 minutes makes it get, because the 15 minutes is what it is adapting to. If you just got darker every time you were exposed to the sun, we'd all be really, really dark, especially those of us who live in a sunny area, since we all get out of the car and walk into the house or work several times a day. The skin does not adapt to total accumulated exposure, but to the *longest* exposure. If you want it to get darker, you have to stay out longer, in order to give the skin more sun exposure than it has already adapted to. The widespread failure to comprehend this pivotal aspect of adaptation is why so few people actually understand exercise programming.

Exercise is the same thing as getting a tan – a stress imposed on the body that it can adapt to, but only if the stress is designed properly. Lots and lots of people come in to the gym and bench 225 every Monday and Friday for years, never even attempting to increase the weight, sets, reps, speed, or pace between sets. Some don't care, but some are genuinely puzzled that their bench doesn't go up, even though they have not asked it to. Your bench strength doesn't adapt to the total number of times you've been to the gym to bench, or your sincerest hope that it will get stronger. It adapts to the stress imposed on it by the work done with the barbell. Furthermore, it adapts to *exactly* the kind of stress imposed on it. If you do sets of 20, you get good at doing 20's. If you do heavy singles, you get better at doing those. But singles and 20's are very different, and you don't get better at doing one by practicing the other. The muscles and nervous system function differently when they do these two things, and they require two different sets of skills and abilities, and thus cause the body to adapt differently. The adaptation occurs in response to the stress, and *specifically* to that stress, because the stress is what causes the adaptation. This is why calluses form on the hand where the bar rubs, and not on the other parts of the hand, or on the face, or all over your body. It can obviously be no other way.

An awareness of this central organizing principle of exercise physiology is essential to program design. If a strength program is not designed to get you stronger, you don't get to call it a strength program. It is just an activity. To get stronger, you must do something that requires that you be stronger to do it, and this must be built into the training program.

Programming

Many millions of words have been written on the subject of program design, and it is perhaps the major topic of discussion in exercise science circles. This book will take a very simple approach to the problem of programming for novices, and then leave it to the individual, and other sources, to provide programs that challenge and improve.

The less experienced the athlete, the simpler the program should be. The stronger you become, the more susceptible you become to **overtraining**, a condition produced by the body's inability to adapt to the stress level applied. Rank novices are not strong enough to tax themselves beyond their ability to recover, because they are so thoroughly unadapted to stress; they have made almost no progress on the road to the fulfillment of their athletic potential. Rank novices can be trained close to the limit of their ability every time they train, precisely because that ability is at such a low level. But that changes rapidly, and as you progress through your training career, the program should get more and more complicated as a result of the changing nature of your adaptive response. The intermediate trainee has advanced to the point where the stress required for change is high enough that when applied in consecutive workouts exceeds the capacity for recovery within that period of time. Intermediate trainees are capable of training hard enough that some allowances for active recovery must be incorporated into the training program, but progress still comes faster for these athletes when they are challenged often by maximum efforts. Advanced athletes are working at levels close enough to their genetic potential that great care should be taken to ensure enough variability in the intensity and amount of exercise that overtraining does not become a problem. These principles are illustrated in Figure 8-1, and discussed at length in *Practical Programming for Strength Training* (The Aasgaard Company, 2006).

So, as a general rule, you need to try to add weight to the work sets of the exercise every time you train, until you can't do this anymore. This is the basic tenet of "progressive resistance training." Everyone can do this for a while, and some people can do it for longer than others, depending on individual genetic capability, diet, and rest. If you are challenged, you will adapt, and if you are not, you won't. For as long as possible, make sure that you lift more weight each time.

Before you even get through the door of the weight room, you should already know every thing you will do while you are there, the order in which it will be done, how much weight it will be done with, and how to determine the next workout based on what you do today. No one should ever arrive to train not knowing exactly what to do. Wandering around the gym, deciding what looks fun, doing it until the fun stops, and then doing something else **is not training**. Each training session must have a definite achievable goal, usually an increase over the previous workout in the amount of weight lifted, or another definable objective based on the previous workout.

Strength in each exercise will progress differently, due to differences in the amount of muscle mass involved, and the sensitivity of the movement to technique problems. The deadlift, for instance, improves rather quickly for most people, faster than any of the other lifts, due to its limited range of motion around the hips and knees, and the fact that so many muscles are involved in the lift. In contrast, the press goes up rather slowly due to the smaller muscles of the shoulder girdle. The more muscle mass involved in an exercise, the faster the exercise can get strong and the stronger it has the potential to be.

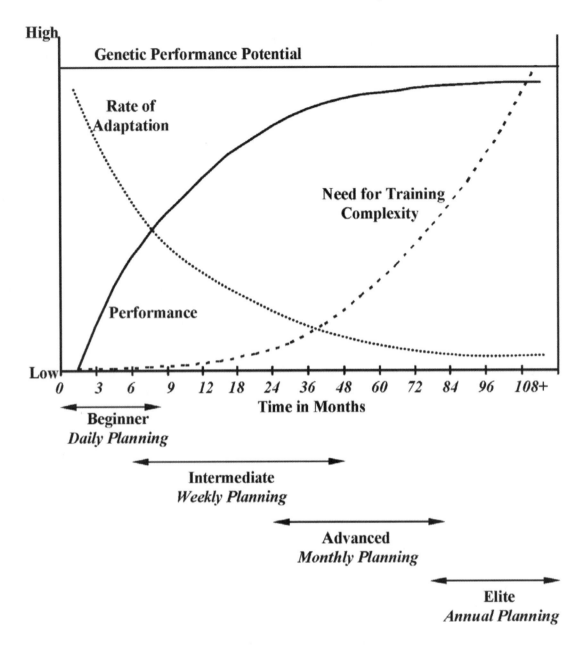

Figure 8-1. The generalized relationship between performance improvement and training complexity relative to time. Note that the rate of adaptation to training slows over a training career.

In a trained athlete, the deadlift will be stronger than the squat, the squat stronger than the bench press, the bench press and the power clean close with the bench usually a little stronger, and the press lighter than the other four. This distribution holds for the majority of athletes, and is predictive of what should happen. For example, if you bench more than you deadlift, something is out of whack. You may have a grip problem, an injury, or a motivational discontinuity, e.g. a strong dislike for the deadlift. In any case, this situation should be addressed lest a strength imbalance cause problems for other lifts.

The differences in the nature of the lifts must be considered in all aspects of their use in the weight room.

Figure 8-2. In order from left, strongest to weakest, the continuum of potential strength gains for the basic barbell exercises. The deadlift, squat, bench press, and press actively involve incrementally decreasing amounts of muscle mass. Other factors affect the power clean; although it involves a large amount of muscle mass, the technical requirements of the lift place it somewhere between the bench press and the press in strength and improvement potential.

Learning the lifts

The squat should be learned first, since it is the most important exercise in the program and its skills are critical to all the other movements. The squat should be your introduction to the training program. When you begin this program, if you have been taught the movement wrong you will have to de-program yourself (the worst-case scenario), or you will never have been shown it at all (the best case scenario since no incorrect motor pathways exist that need to be fixed). It is much harder to correct an incorrect movement than it is to learn a new one, as any sport coach will attest. The problem is particularly evident in the weight room, where correct technique is the essence of everything we do, and a stubborn form problem resulting from prior incorrect instruction can be costly in terms of time and slowed progress.

Assuming that you have time to learn more than one exercise the first day (and you should arrange things so that you do), the next exercise would be the bench press. The squat has fatigued the lower body, and the bench press allows it an opportunity to rest while another skill is introduced. The bench is usually easy to learn, especially in the absence of preconceived notions acquired from pictures in the muscle magazines or helpful buddies. Fewer problems will be encountered while learning the bench press, since fewer muscles and joints are involved in the primary aspect of the exercise and there is less that can go wrong.

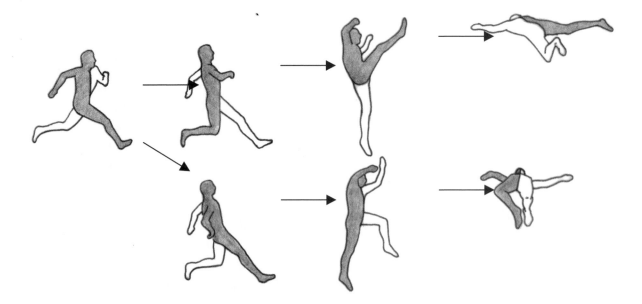

Figure 8-3. The relationship between similar movements and their motor pathways. Both high jump techniques work, but the Western Roll (top) is less efficient than the Fosbury Flop (bottom). Early in the approach the motor pathways of the two techniques are very similar, and they diverge before the takeoff stride and become increasingly dissimilar thereafter. The period of divergence, where similarity is the greatest, is the most sensitive to overlap and interference, were the two techniques practiced together. The more similarity between techniques, the greater the potential for motor pathway confusion. A weighted bat, for instance, is swung more slowly than a standard-weight bat, and practice with heavy bats can interfere with a normal swing. The same would be true for heavy basketballs. The more divergent motor pathways become, the less likely they are to overlap and interfere. It is therefore essential to learn complicated movements correctly since correct and incorrect movements often have similar motor pathways, and repetition of incorrect movement patterns can imbed the wrong motor pathway.

The deadlift will be the last thing to learn the first day. The mechanics of the correct pull from the floor are crucial to the clean, and for that matter to manual labor-type skills that are a part of life. The deadlift is where you learn to set the lower back, and doing this at the conclusion of the first day, after the squat, will solidify the concept of back position and make it more understandable to your body and to the mind. If the squat that first day has been difficult or has taken a long time, or if you are older or very deconditioned, the first deadlift workout might just be an introduction with light weight. This prevents excessive soreness after the first session, which would definitely compromise the second one. The next deadlift workout can be heavier, and the target weight more easily and accurately determined after recovery from the first squat workout has occurred.

The other two lifts are learned at the next workout, provided there were no major problems encountered. Start the second workout with the squat, and then learn the press. The bench press may have produced a little soreness in the pecs, but not usually in the triceps, and pec soreness will not interfere with the press unless it is excessive. Pressing provides the same break for the lower body between exercises that the bench press does, since you will be power cleaning next. The press is slightly more complicated than the bench press, and introducing it after the bench serves to allow a graduated increase in complexity.

The power clean, being the most mechanically challenging of the exercises, should be introduced last, and only after the deadlift is correct off the floor. If that occurs the first workout, the clean can be learned the second time. If more time is needed to correct the deadlift, take it. Introducing the power clean too early will produce problems, since the lower part of the movement depends on the deadlift being fairly automatic.

Workout order

For novices, and in fact for many more advanced trainees, a very simple approach to training should be taken. Effective workouts need not be long, complicated affairs. Many people are under the impression that progress in the weight room means learning more ways to curl, the basic one or two not being sufficiently numerous. Progress means more strength, not more exercises. It is not necessary to do many different exercises to get strong — it *is* necessary to get strong on a very few important exercises, movements that train the whole body as a system, not as a collection of separate body parts.

So, in keeping with this philosophy, the following novice workout is offered in Table 8-1.

Essentially, you squat every workout and alternate the bench press and press, and the deadlift and power clean. This schedule is for three days per week, allowing a two-day rest at the end of the week. It will mean that one week you press and power clean twice, and the next week bench and deadlift twice. The workout should be done in the listed order, squatting first, the upper body movement second, and the pulling movement third.

1	2
Squat	Squat
Bench Press	Press
Deadlift	Power Clean

Table 8-1. The teaching order of the first two workouts. The series is repeated in this order, and forms the basis of a novice barbell training program.

This allows the squat to get everything warm for the next exercise (a thing it will do well), then the upper-body exercise allows the legs and back to rest and recover for the pulling movement to be done next, with any assistance exercises to be done saved for last.

People without access to bumper plates may choose to use the barbell row instead of the power clean. This is not a terrible substitution, but be aware of what you're giving up if you do. Cleans are important to the deadlift in that they add an element of power to the pull off the floor, and in the long run this contributes to strength in that pull. The row is a different movement entirely, and contributes to deadlifting only in that it works the hip extensors and provides isometric work for the low back. If you are avoiding the clean because you don't want to have to learn how to do it, it is suggested that this might not be the best way to approach your training.

Most Olympic weightlifting coaches will use a workout order that places faster movements before slower movements, so that the explosive lifts, the snatch, clean and jerk, and their variations, are performed before the strength exercises like the squat and the pressing movements. This makes perfect sense if the competitive lifts are the emphasis of the program. This program uses the power clean as the explosive movement, but since none of the exercises in the program are approached as competitive lifts, doing the power clean as the last exercise in the workout is just as productive for our purposes. If you want to emphasize the clean for some reason, that is fine, provided sufficient warmup is done first. A major advantage to doing the squat first is the superior warmup it provides to all the subsequent movements, and if cleans are done first, some squats should probably be incorporated into their warmup.

For most people, and for quite some time, this schedule will work well. Any supplemental exercises added to this should be chosen very carefully so as not to interfere with progress on these five crucial movements. Remember: if progress is being made on these exercises, you are getting stronger and your objective is being accomplished.

After you progress beyond the novice phase, this workout, with very few additions, can still be used. The variety is introduced into the programming of each lift, and variations are made in the workload. Even for more advanced trainees, it is still unnecessary to add lots of different exercises to the workout, as the purpose is always served when the strength level increases on the basic lifts. Any assistance exercises that are added must be kept in their proper perspective; they are there to help make the basic lifts get stronger, not as an end in themselves. The press, for example, will always be more important than tricep work, and if tricep exercises interfere with pressing or benching, they are being misused.

Warmup sets

Warmups serve two very important purposes. First, warmups actually make the soft tissue – the muscles and tendons, and the ligaments that comprise the joints – warmer. General warmup exercises, like walking fast or jogging, riding an exercise bike (a better method, due to the greater range of motion the knee is exposed to during the exercise, better preparing it for the squat), or using a rowing machine (the best, due to its range of motion and full involvement of the back and arms as well as the legs) serve to increase the temperature in the tissue and mobilize the synovial fluid in the joints. Specific warmups, like the unweighted and empty bar sets of the barbell exercise itself, also serve to warm, mobilize, and stretch the specific tissues involved in that particular movement. This is important for injury prevention, since it is more difficult to injure a warm body than a cold one.

The elevation of tissue temperature is very important, and requires that several variables be kept in mind. The temperature of the training facility should be considered as a factor in this phase of warmup. A cold room interferes with effective warmup, while a hot room aids it. Winter months and summer months produce different warmup requirements for most athletes, who will usually arrive at training feeling different in August than in January. A healing injury needs extra warmup for the affected tissues. And the age of the trainee affects warmup requirements as well. Younger people are less sensitive to a lack of warmup than adults, and the older the adult the more time needed for pre-workout preparation.

The second function of warmup is especially important in barbell training: it allows you to practice the movement before the weight gets heavy. Light warmup sets, done first with the empty bar and then progressively heavier until the work sets are loaded, serve to prepare the movement pattern itself, so that when the weight gets heavy attention can be focused on pushing hard instead of how to push. The motor pathway – the neuromuscular adaptation to a complicated movement pattern – must be prepared every time it is used, whether throwing a baseball or doing a squat. The warmup sets prepare the motor pathway at the same time as they prepare the tissue for the upcoming heavier work. While the first sets are being done, form errors can be addressed and fixed, and good form can be practiced, so that when the work set is done your conscious attention can be more focused on driving the load and less on form.

It is foolishness to neglect warmup. Many school programs, in a jam for time, omit most of this crucial part of the workout. The coach in charge of a program that does this commits *malpractice* by doing so. Please heed the following rather strong statement: **if your schedule does not allow time for proper warmup, it does not allow time for training at all.** It is better to omit strength training from your program than risk the probable injuries that will result from lack of warmup. Yes, warmups are *that* critical.

Warmups will vary with the lift being warmed up. The squat, being the first lift of the workout and by it's nature a total-body movement, should be carefully and thoroughly prepared with a couple of empty bar sets, and then as many as five sets between those and the work sets. This ensures that the initially cold body is warm before any heavy work is done. The next upper-body movement will have the benefit of some advance preparation, and, in the absence of an injury, can be warmed up adequately with only three or four sets. The deadlift, being a simple movement, requires mainly tissue preparation, and this has occurred during the squat, provided that the pressing hasn't taken so long that you have gotten cold. The power clean, being a more complex movement, will require more warmup for technique purposes. Assistance exercises, if they are done, will be done last with already-warm muscles and joints, and will require only one or two warmup sets.

Any area that is injured will require additional warmup. If the injured area does not respond to the warmup sets by starting to feel *much* better after two or three sets with the empty bar, a decision will have to be made about whether to continue with light sets or to wait until the area has healed better.

First, some terminology clarification. A **work set** is the heaviest weight or weights to be done in a given workout, the sets that actually produce the stress which causes the adaptation. **Warmups** are the lighter sets previous to the work sets. **Sets across** refers to multiple work sets done with the same weight. The work sets are the ones that provide the training effect – they are the sets that make strength go up, since they are the heaviest. The warmup sets serve only to prepare the lifter for the work sets; they should never interfere with the work sets. As such, they must be planned with this in mind. The last warmup before the work set should never be so heavy that it interferes with the work set, but heavy enough to allow you to feel a heavier weight before you do the work sets. It might consist of only one or two reps even though the work sets are five or more reps. For instance, if the work sets are to be 225 x 5 x 3, then 215 x 5 would not be an efficient choice for a last warmup; a better choice would be 205 x 2, or even 195 x 1, depending on your preference, skill, and experience. Since the focus is on completing all the reps of the work sets, the warmups must be chosen to save gas for the heavier sets.

As an example of the importance of proper warmup, let's examine the effects of a bad warmup carried to the extreme. There is an old workout "method" still floating around weight rooms and gyms all over the world, known as the Pyramid. For the bench press, it would go something like 135 x 10, 155 x 8, 175 x 6, 185 x 5, 195 x 4, 205 x 3, 215 x 2, and 225 x 1. By the time the last set is finished, you might feel like you've had a pretty good workout. The problem is that by the time you have done 6390 lbs. of work before the last set at 225, the chances of ever increasing this last single are slim. By the time you reach what should be a work set you are used up, since all of your warmup sets have essentially been work sets too. The warmups didn't prepare you to increase your work sets, so you will never lift any more weight than you did the last time you did this workout, and you are therefore quite thoroughly stuck. If the warmup sets fatigue instead of prepare, they are not warmups and strength cannot increase.

As a general rule, it is best to start with an empty bar (45 lbs.), determine the work set or sets, and then divide the difference between them into even increments. Some examples are provided in Table 8-2. Most people will need to select three to five warmup sets, depending on the work set weight; extremely heavy weights may require more increments to get warm so that the jumps are not too big. If additional warmup is desirable (as with a cold room, older trainees, or injured lifters) multiple sets can be done with the empty bar and the lighter sets. This provides the benefits of the warmup without the fatigue of too much work at heavier weight before the work sets.

As the warmups progress from the empty bar up through heavier weights, the time between the sets should increase a little. As a general rule, the time between sets should be sufficient to recover from the previous set, so that fatigue from the prior set does not limit the one about to be done. The heavier the set, the longer the break should be. This type of training requires that all of the reps of each work set be completed, since the program is based on lifting more weight each workout, not completing each workout faster. A strength program is designed to make people stronger, i.e. able to exert more force and lift more weight. Some training programs used in bodybuilding rely on the fatigue produced by short breaks between sets, and these programs specifically increase muscular endurance. Although endurance increases as a function of increased strength, it is not a parameter specifically targeted by this program at the novice level. More benefit can be obtained by lifting heavier weights, through efficient timing of sets to allow for recovery, than by trying to decrease the time between the sets and thereby allowing fatigue to limit the ability to exert maximum force.

Exercise Squat	Weight	Repetitions	Sets
	45	5	2
	95	5	1
	135	3	1
	185	2	1
Work sets	225	5	3

Bench Press	Weight	Repetitions	Sets
	45	5	2
	85	5	1
	125	3	1
	155	2	1
Work sets	175	5	3

Deadlift	Weight	Repetitions	Sets
	135	5	2
	185	5	1
	225	3	1
	275	2	1
Work sets	315	5	1

Press	Weight	Repetitions	Sets
	45	5	2
	75	5	1
	95	3	1
	115	2	1
Work sets	135	5	3

Power Clean	Weight	Repetitions	Sets
	45	5	2
	75	5	1
	95	3	1
	115	2	1
Work sets	135	3	5

Table 8-2. Example warmup/work set distributions.

Programming

The time between sets will vary with the conditioning level of the athlete, in a couple of different ways. Rank novices are not typically strong enough to fatigue themselves very much, and these people can go fairly quickly, just a minute or two, between sets, since they are not lifting much weight anyway. The first two or three sets can be done as fast as the bar can be loaded, especially if two or more are training together. More advanced trainees need more time between the last warmups and the work sets, perhaps five minutes. If doing sets across, very strong lifters may need 10 minutes or more between work sets.

Work sets

The number of work sets to be done after the warmups will vary with the exercise and the individual. The squat benefits from sets across, usually three sets for novice trainees, as does the bench press and the press. The deadlift is hard enough, and is usually done after a lot of squatting, and one heavy set is usually sufficient. The power clean can be done with more sets across, since the weight is lighter relative to the squat and deadlift, and the limiting factor is usually technique, not absolute strength.

Multiple work sets cause the body to adapt to a larger volume of work, which comes in handy when training for sports performance. One school of thought holds that one work set, if done at a high enough intensity, is sufficient to stimulate muscular growth. For novices, several problems with this approach immediately present themselves. First, inexperienced trainees do not yet know how to produce maximum intensity under the bar, and will not know how for quite some time. Second, if they don't know how to work at a very high intensity, more than one set will be necessary to provide sufficient stress to cause an adaptation to occur – one set will not provide enough. Third and most importantly, one intense set adapts the body to work hard for one intense set, since exercise, as we know, is extremely specific. Except for Sumo and a couple of others, sports do not usually involve one relatively brief intense effort, but generally involve repeated bouts of work. A sets-across routine more closely mimics the effort usually involved in sports, and is therefore more useful as a conditioning tool.

In fact, one of the most effective intermediate strategies for the squat, bench, and press is five sets across of five reps, done once a week as one of the three workouts, increasing the weight used by very small manageable amounts each week.

How many reps should a work set consist of? It depends on the adaptation desired. Five reps is a good number for most purposes, but an understanding of the reasons for this is essential, so that special circumstances can be accommodated correctly.

When trying to understand the nature of any given set of variables, it is often helpful to start with the extremes, the limits of which can reveal things about the stuff in the middle. In this case, let's compare a one rep max squat, or 1RM, to a 20RM squat and look at the different physiologic requirements for doing each. Credit for this explanation goes to Glenn Pendlay, in a conversation we had several years ago that yielded perhaps the most useful model of adaptation to exercise ever developed.

The single most important contributing factor to the successful heavy one-rep attempt is the ability of the muscles involved to produce force. The heavier a weight, the more force required to move it, as should be obvious. The one-rep set doesn't take very long to do, so muscular endurance is not a factor, and neither is cardiovascular capacity, for the same reason. Even a bone-on-bone limit attempt doesn't take more than a few seconds. The only thing the muscles must do is produce sufficient force to overcome the pull of Mean Old Mr. Gravity on the bar as it moves through the range of motion of the lift one time. So, in response to 1RM training, the body adapts by getting better at producing high amounts of force, one rep at a time. It does this by adjusting the components of the system that produce the force: the nervous system, the neuromuscular system, and the muscles themselves, specifically the components of the muscle that actually produce the contraction.

There are other adaptations that are secondary to the main ones, but they all involve helping the body perform a brief, intense effort. Psychological adaptations enable the fear of the heavy weight to be overcome. The heart adapts by getting better at working with a huge load on the back, and the blood vessels adapt by becoming capable of responding to the demands of increased peak blood pressure. The tendons thicken to better transmit force, and the ligaments thicken and tighten to hold the joints together under the load. The skin under the bar gets thicker, the eyeballs get used to bugging out, and new words are learned that express the emotions of success/failure with a new PR squat. But the primary adaptation is increased force production.

On the other hand, a heavy set of 20 reps is an entirely different experience, one of the most demanding in sports conditioning. A set of 20 squats can usually be done with a weight previously assumed to be a 10RM, given the correct mental preparation and a certain suicidal desire to grow or die. The demands of a 20RM, and therefore the adaptation to it, are completely different. A 20RM is done with about 80% of the weight of a 1RM, and even the last rep is not really heavy, in terms of the amount of force necessary to squat it. The hard part of a set of 20 is that the last 5 reps are done in a state resembling a hellish nightmare: making yourself squat another rep with the pain from the accumulating lactate, an inability to catch your breath, and the inability of your heart to beat any faster that it already is. The demands of a 20RM involve continued muscle contraction under circumstances of increasing oxygen debt and falling muscle pH, as lactic acid accumulates faster than it can be removed by the bloodstream.

In response to this type of stress, the body gets better at carrying lactate away from and supplying oxygen to the muscles. These adaptations are primarily cardiovascular in nature, since the main source of stress involves insufficient blood flow. The heart gets better at pumping blood under a load, the vessels expand and become more numerous, and the lungs get better at oxygenating the blood – although not in the same way that a runner's do. The main muscular adaptation is also essentially vascular, in that a denser bed of capillaries is produced, to provide oxygen and carry away lactic acid. The contractile part of the muscle tissue gets better at working under the acidic conditions produced by lactic acid accumulation. Psychologically, 20RM work is very hard, due to the pain, and people who are good at it develop the ability to displace themselves from the situation during the set. Or they just get very tough.

It is essential to understand that the 1RM work does not produce the lactate stress that the 20RM work does, and that the long set of 20 reps is not heavy in the same way that the 1RM is. They are both hard, but for different reasons. Because they are so completely different, they cause the body to adapt in two completely different ways. These extremes represent a continuum, with a heavy set of 3 more closely resembling 1RM in its adaptation, and a set of 10 sharing more of the characteristics of a 20RM. Sets of five reps are a very effective compromise for the novice, and in fact even for the advanced lifter more interested in strength than muscular endurance. They allow enough weight to be used that force production must increase, but they are not so heavy that the cardiovascular component is completely absent from the exercise. Sets of five may be the most useful rep range you will use your entire training career, and as long as you lift weights they will have an important application.

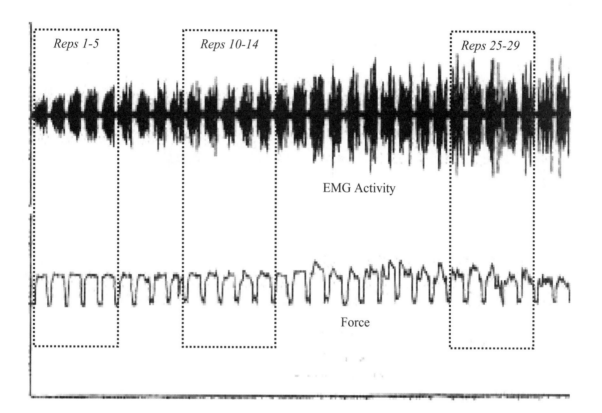

Figure 8-4. Sets of 5 reps are optimal for learning barbell exercises. It is apparent from electromyography (EMG, top), a recording of neuromuscular electrical activity, and force plate data (a measure of muscular force generated, bottom) that there is a progressive loss of motor coordination as reps increase. In reps 1-5 the muscle is firing in a coordinated manner, with tight, uniform EMG waves and consistent force production. By reps 10-14 there is a loss of motor coordination, with erratic EMG wave and force continuity. By reps 25-29 EMG activity is highly random and force production has deteriorated. Using more than 5 reps per set during the learning phase of a new exercise will usually make correct technique harder to reproduce and master. Note that the peak level of force production is the same on rep 1 and rep 20, although control has begun to degrade; a 20-rep set is not really "heavy," but it sure is long and hard.

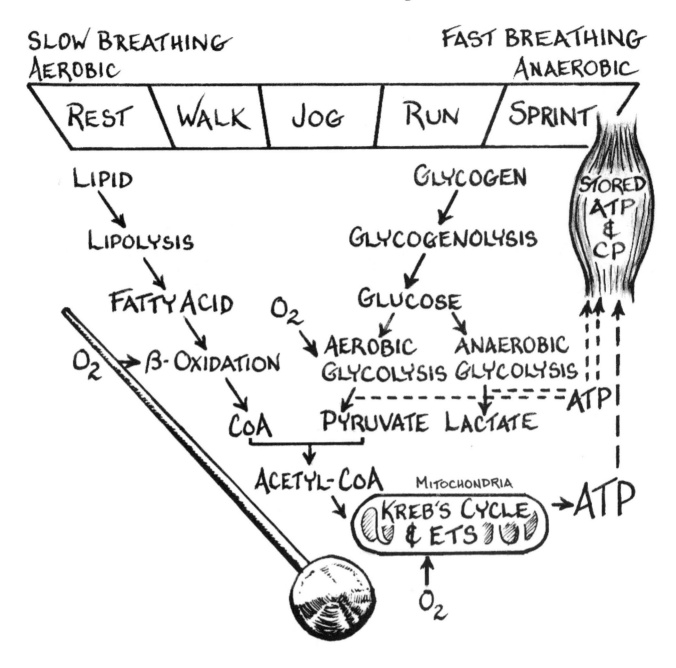

Figure 8-5. The metabolic speedometer. How hard and how long we exercise directly affects which metabolic pathways our bodies use to fuel the activities. All physical activity lies along a continuum, from rest to all-out maximal effort. All activities are powered by the ATP already present in the muscle, and all bioenergetic activity acts to replenish these stores. Low-intensity exercise depends on cardiopulmonary delivery and muscular uptake of oxygen, the ready availability of which enables the body to utilize aerobic pathways and fatty acids as substrate. These aerobic processes take place inside the mitochondria within the muscle cells. As activity levels and energy requirements increase, the ability of the heart and lungs to deliver oxygen and facilitate sufficient levels of aerobic metabolism to meet the increased demand for ATP is exceeded. Weight training or other forms of high-intensity training exists at the anaerobic end of the continuum, utilizing substrate that does not require added O_2. The diagram above represents the relationships between the energy substrates and the metabolic pathways in which they are used in different types of exercise. With the exception of short-duration all-out maximal effort, no activity uses only one metabolic pathway, so the scale above represents a sliding scale of continually increasing intensity of activity.

Programming

Back-off sets

It is occasionally useful to increase work volume by doing additional sets after the work sets are completed. These sets are done with a lighter weight, and are referred to as **back-off sets**. They can be done with the same number of reps, or a higher number, depending on the reason for doing them or the effect desired. If there were technique problems with work sets, a couple of back-off sets with 80% of the work set weight and 150% of the work set reps is a useful way to practice form. The weight is light enough to permit focus on just the technique without worrying about actually completing the last reps, and heavy enough that they have to actually be pushed with a little enthusiasm. The higher number of reps allows for more practice with the movement. Back-off sets must be done with as nearly perfect form as possible, since technical problems are the usual reason for doing them.

Sometimes it is desirable to just get some more work with heavier weight. If the work sets were doubles or triples (sets of 2 or 3 reps), it might be necessary to use back-off sets to increase the work volume. Or it might be that heavy singles are being done, either for testing purposes or for work volume as sets across, and heavy back-off sets would then be used to make up the actual training volume that day.

Training volume is calculated by multiplying the weight on the bar times the reps: 315 x 5 = 1575 lbs., the volume, or tonnage, for the set. Heavy singles, even though they're heavy, don't add up to very much volume. Sets of 10 do. Five sets of 5 do too. Compare singles across, 225 x 1 x 5 = 1125 lbs., with the corresponding set-of-5 capacity of the same trainee, 195 x 5 x 5 = 4875 lbs., and you can see the situation clearly.

Progression

The effective training of novices takes advantage of the fact that untrained people get strong very quickly at first, and this effect tapers off over time until advanced trainees gain strength only through careful manipulation of all training variables. Novices can, and should, increase the weight of the work sets every workout until this is no longer possible. In fact, novices get strong as fast as the workout makes them, and what was hard last time is not hard today. They can adapt so quickly that the concept of "maximum intensity" is hard to define. If a kid gets strong as fast as his work sets increase, a 10 lb. jump is not really heavier relative to his improved strength. The key to maintaining this rate of improvement is the careful selection of the amount of weight that we increase each time.

Work set increases will vary with the exercise, your age and sex, your experience, and the consistency of your adherence to the program. For most male trainees with good technique, the squat can be increased 10 lbs. per workout, assuming 3 workouts per week, for three or four weeks. When you miss the last rep or two of your last work set, the easy gains are beginning to wane and 5 lb. jumps can be taken for a while. For very young kids, older trainees, and most women, 5 lb. jumps are sufficient to start with, and then smaller jumps will be required, as will the lighter barbell plates (lighter than the standard 2 ½ lb. plates) that make smaller jumps possible. If it is important for women and kids to make progress – and why would it not be? – it is important to have the right equipment to train correctly. It may be necessary to make the plates, or to have some 2 ½'s milled down, but it is necessary, so get it done. Small plates are available from various sources on the web, and baseball bat weights will usually fit the bar quite well. It will be useful at some point for everybody to have access to light plates, since progress on the lifts will eventually slow to the point where they will be useful for even advanced men. Don't be afraid to take small jumps – *be afraid to stop improving.*

Some very talented, heavier men can take bigger jumps of 15 or 20 lbs. Anything more than this is usually excessive, even for the most gifted athlete, since an increase of 60 lbs. per week in the squat is not going to be realistically sustainable for very long. Don't be in a big hurry to find your sticking point early in your training progression. **It is always preferable to take smaller jumps and sustain the progress, than to take bigger jumps and get stuck early.** Getting stuck means missing any of the reps of the prescribed work sets, since the weight cannot be increased until all of the reps have been done as prescribed. **It is easier to not get stuck that it is to get unstuck.**

In the bench press, the muscles are smaller, so the increases will be smaller. If the first workout has properly determined the initial strength level, 5 lb. jumps for most men are possible for a while, assuming we are alternating bench presses and presses. Some talented, heavier men can make a few 10 lb. jumps, but not many. Older guys, the very young, and women will need to start with small jumps, and the special light plates are particularly important to keep making progress on the bench. Do not be afraid to slow the increases down to very small jumps on the bench; remember that an increase of even 2 lbs. per week means a 104 lb. increase in a year, not a shabby thing, especially for a lighter, older trainee.

The press will behave similarly to the bench press, since the muscles involved in moving the bar are small relative to the squatting and deadlifting muscles. The press uses lots of muscles, true, but you can only press what the triceps can lock out, and no chain is stronger than its weakest link, as the saying goes. The same jumps used for the bench can usually be used for the press, although the press will start off at somewhere between 60% and 80% of the weight used in bench press. Since we are alternating the two exercises, they will stay about the same weight apart as they increase.

The deadlift will progress faster than any of the other lifts, since the start position, basically a half-squat, is very efficient mechanically, and since virtually every muscle in the body is involved in the movement. Most men can add 15-20 lbs. to the deadlift each workout for a few weeks, with the very young, women, and older guys taking a more conservative approach. This being the case, the deadlift will start out with heavier weights than the other lifts, and should eventually be stronger and get stronger faster than the other lifts. A trainee who benches more than he deadlifts needs to quit missing his deadlift workouts. But since the deadlift involves more muscles and more weight than the other lifts, it is easier to overtrain and should not be trained using sets across. It is really easy to get really beat-up doing a lot of heavy deadlifts. One work set at the intensity of a real work set is usually quite sufficient to maintain improvement.

It is interesting that the power clean behaves more like the bench press than the squat or deadlift, in terms of the way it increases over time. The reason for this involves the biomechanical nature of the movement, and the factors limiting its progress. The power clean is explosive and technical, and involves more than just absolute strength. It is limited at the top of the movement by the ability to get the bar on the shoulders, and the higher the bar goes, the smaller the muscles involved in making it rack, and the more dependent it is on good technique having generated enough momentum to get it high enough to rack. It is sensitive to fatigue and the amount of work done prior to it. With this in mind, the power clean will move up maybe 5 lbs. per workout for most men. Women, younger and older trainees, and those with technique problems might only make 5 lbs. every other workout, or might need to introduce smaller plates earlier in the progression.

Assistance exercises, which are by their nature inefficient isolation-type exercises, make very slow progress. Anybody claiming rapid gains on tricep extensions or barbell curls is not utilizing particularly strict form, and should be criticized for such foolishness.

When these smaller jumps can no longer be sustained, a trainee can be considered an intermediate, and the fun begins with more complicated manipulation of training. This variation in training exercises, loads and intensity for purposes of ensuring continued progress is referred to as **periodization**. It is unnecessary for rank beginners, since they get strong as fast as the weight can be increased every workout, and it is indispensable for advanced lifters, who cannot continue to make progress without it. Intermediates are, like the name says, somewhere in between, with some degree of training parameter manipulation necessary to allow for continued, albeit slower, progress. Programming beyond the novice phase is beyond the scope of this book, and is dealt with in detail in *Practical Programming for Strength Training* (Aasgaard, 2006).

And all these guidelines apply only to committed trainees who do not miss workouts. Failure to train as scheduled is failure to follow the program, and if the program is not followed, progress cannot predictably occur. If you have to miss a couple of workouts due to severe illness, or possibly the death of a parent, spouse, or good dog, allowances can be made, and the last workout completed should just be repeated set for set. But if you continually miss workouts, you are not actually training, and your obviously valuable time should be spent more productively elsewhere.

Likewise, trying to increase the weight faster than prescribed by the program and by common sense is also failure to follow the program. If you insist on attempting unrealistic increases between workouts, it is your fault when progress does not occur. Ambition is useful, greed is not. Most of human history and the science of economics demonstrates that the desire for more than is currently possessed drives improvement, both personally and for societies. But greed is an ugly thing when uncontrolled and untempered with wisdom, and will result in your program's progress coming to an ass-grinding halt. The exercises must increase in weight in order for progress to occur, by definition. But if you allow yourself to succumb to the temptation of 10 lb. jumps on the bench press, or 50 lb. increases on the squat, just because the plates were handy (or the right plates were inconvenient), you are going to get stuck. Too much weight on the bar is just as bad as no increase in weight at all, or for that matter, missing workouts. Take the time and care necessary to ensure that the right weight gets on the bar and gets lifted the right number of times the right way.

It is understandable that you want your program to show results. But please understand this, if you miss everything else in this entire book: **stronger does not necessarily mean more weight on the bar**. Resist the temptation to add weight at the expense of correct technique – you are doing no one any favors when you sacrifice form for weight on the bar. Progress stops, bad habits get formed, injuries accumulate, and no one benefits in the long run.

Mark Rippetoe CSCS

Onus Wunsler

$\left.\begin{array}{l} \text{C2 Rower} \quad 5\text{min} \\ \text{Situps} \end{array}\right\}$ warmup everyday

A
_____

Squat

Press

Deadlift
alt. with
PowerClean

B
_____

Squat

Bench Press

Back Extensions

Chins

Figure 8-6 *(this page and facing page).* An example of the first few days of a typical beginner's program.

2/5	2/7	2/9	2/12	2/14	2/16	2/19
Mon.	Wed.	Fri.	Mon.	Wed.	Fri.	Mon.
Situps	Situps	Situps	Situps	Situps	Situps	Situps
BWx12	BWx14	BWx16	BWx18	BWx20	BWx5	10lbsx13
					10lbs.x12	

Squat (2/5)
45x5x3
65x5x2
85x5
105x5
125x5
140x5x3

Squat (2/7)
45x5x2
75x5
105x5
135x2
160x5x3

Squat (2/9)
45x5x2
95x5
125x5
155x2
175x5x3

Squat (2/12)
45x5x2
95x5
135x5
165x2
185x5x3

Squat (2/14)
45x5x2
95x5
135x5
165x2
195x5x3

Squat (2/16)
45x5x2
95x5
135x5
175x2
205x5x3

Squat (2/19)
45x5x2
95x5
135x5
175x2
215x5x3

Press (2/5)
45x5x2
65x5
75x5
85x5
90x5
95x5x3

Bench Press (2/7)
45x5x2
65x5
85x5
105x5
115x5
125x5
135x5x3

Press (2/9)
45x5
65x5
80x5
90x2
100x5x3

Bench Press (2/12)
45x5
75x5
105x5
125x2
140x5x3

Press (2/14)
45x5
65x5
85x5
95x2
105x5x3

Bench (2/16)
45x5
75x5
105x5
125x2
145x5x3

Press (2/19)
45x5
65x5
85x5
100x2
110x5x3

Deadlift (2/5)
40kg x5x3
50kg x5
135 lbs. x5
165x5
195x5

Back Ext. (2/7)
BWx10x3

Chins (2/7)
BWx5
BWx4
BWx3

Power Clean (2/9)
40kg x2x4 hang
40kg x3x2 full
45x3
50x3
55x3x5

Back Ext. (2/12)
BWx10x5

Chins (2/12)
BWx5
BWx4x2

Deadlift (2/14)
40kg x5
135 x5
185x2
225x5

Back Ext. (2/16)
BWx10x5

Chins (2/16)
BWx6
BWx4x2

Power Clean (2/19)
40kg x3x
45x3
50x3
55x3
57.5x3x5

Nutrition and bodyweight

A program of this nature tends to produce the correct bodyweight in an athlete. That is, if you need to be bigger, you will grow, and if you need to lose bodyfat, that happens too. It is possible, and quite likely, that skinny kids on this program will gain 10-15 lbs. of non-fat bodyweight in the first 2 weeks of a good barbell training program, provided they eat well. "Well" means 4 or so meals per day, based on meat and egg protein sources, with lots of fruit and vegetables, and lots of milk. Lots. Most sources within the heavy training community agree that a good starting place is one gram of protein per pound of bodyweight per day, with the rest of the diet making up 2500 – 5000 calories, depending on training requirements and body composition. Although these numbers produce much eyebrow-raising and cautionary statement-issuing from the registered dietetics people, it is a fact that these numbers work well for the vast majority of people that lift weights, and have done so for decades.

One of the best ways to move in the direction of these numbers is to drink a gallon of milk a day, most especially if weight-gain is a primary concern. A gallon of milk per day, added to the regular diet at intervals throughout the day, will put weight on any skinny kid. Really. The problem is getting them to do it. It is currently a fad, at this writing, for boys to think they need a "six pack", although most of them don't have an ice chest to put it in. The psychology of this particular historical phenomenon is best left to others to investigate and explain. Aesthetics aside, *heavier* is eventually necessary if *stronger* is to occur, and once most people see that weight gain actually makes them look better (amazingly enough), they become less resistant to the idea.

Milk works because it is easy, it is available, it doesn't need any preparation, and it has all the components necessary for growing mammals, which your trainees most definitely are. There also seems to be something special about milk that the equivalent amount of calories, protein, fat, and carbs can't duplicate in terms of growth enhancement. It may be the fact that milk has been shown to have very high levels of insulin-like growth factor 1 (IGF-1), a peptide hormone that has been shown to have some tenuous relationship to accelerated growth in mammals. But that research is far from conclusive; suffice it to say that people who drink lots of milk during their novice phase get bigger and stronger than people who don't. This time-proven method works for everybody that can digest milk – though the lactose intolerant may not be able to take advantage of its benefits without supplementing with lactase, the enzyme needed for the breakdown of this milk sugar.

Weight gain occurs the same way strength gains occur – fast at first, then more slowly as training progresses. It is possible for genetically favored individuals, for example a broad-shouldered, motivated kid 5'10" weighing 140 lbs., to gain as much as 60 lbs. in a year of good steady training, good diet, and milk. This is actually not that unusual a result for this type of trainee. (When it occurs, there will always be talk of steroids, because this is human nature; as a general rule, anybody stronger than you is taking steroids.) What is unusual is finding a genetically gifted athlete *that will actually do the program – all of it*. It is far more common to see 20 lb. increases in bodyweight over a 4-month period, with only a very few diligent ones doing much better. But most people that will eat even a little better than they did before will gain several pounds the first few weeks.

Fat people (not used here disparagingly) see a different result entirely, as their bodyweight doesn't change much for the first few months. What they notice is looser pants in the waist, legs and hips staying about the same, shirts that are much tighter in the chest, arms, and neck, and faster strength increases than their skinny buddies. Their body composition changes while their bodyweight stays close to the same, the result of a loss in bodyfat due to their increasing muscle mass.

Equipment

A lot of money has been wasted on weight rooms and gyms since the 1970s. Commercial exercise machines, as a general rule, are expensive, single purpose devices, delivering one exercise per footprint on the floor at a high price per square foot of training space. Home gym equipment is usually multi-station, using various elastic media to provide adjustable resistance for a variety of silly exercises. Barbells, on the other hand, are cheap. They can be used for lots of different exercises. The bench press, a single purpose device, is not an absolutely necessary piece of equipment, since the exercise we use it for can be done with a flat bench and a power rack. All of the exercises in this program can be done with a minimum of equipment, which allows for the better use of resources. Instead of the hundreds of thousands of dollars spent on an average 15-station circuit of machines, a third that amount could be spent on the best barbell room in the world, with bumper plates, good bars, and platform space to accommodate lots of lifters, all in the same space. At home, a good free-weight gym can be built in the garage for the price of three years gym dues. You may decide to build your own gym, and the following guidelines can apply to your garage or any gym you might decide to join.

The training facility should be organized around the power rack. The rack should have a floor built into it, and a platform attached to it, such that the inside floor of the rack is perfectly flush with the surface of the platform. An 8 x 8 foot platform works well, providing plenty of room for every purpose it will serve. The rack/platform unit will use about 96 square feet, and in this space all the exercises in this program can be performed. A bench

Figure 8-7. A simple and functional platform/rack/flat bench station. All basic barbell exercises can be done using this equipment.

press/bar assembly uses about 36 square feet if this is available separately. The layout of the room around this equipment must take into consideration the amount of space necessary to load and spot the bars used on the stations.

The power rack is the most important piece of equipment in the room, second only to the plate-loaded barbell as the most useful piece of gym equipment that has ever been invented. All five primary exercises can be done with a good rack, barbell, and flat bench. It should be wide enough between the uprights to just safely accommodate the bar without a lot of extra room between the sleeves and the uprights (about 48 inches). The wider the rack, within safe limits, the more easily it can be safely used by taller, bigger lifters, thus accommodating everyone. A 7 ½ to 8 foot tall rack allows the crossbar at the top to be used for chin-ups and pull-ups by tall trainees. The depth of the rack may need to accommodate squatting inside it occasionally, and for most people an inside dimension of 16 inches works well. The base depth should be greater (about 48 inches), for tipping stability. It should be fitted with a heavy plywood floor, reinforced with a welded crossmember or two. The floor will extend all the way to the edge of the rack base, so that it can be made flush and continuous with the platform surface. It should have a hook assembly for the bar to hang from outside the rack. It should have four heavy pins that cross the depth of the rack from front to back with 4 inches or so extra on each side. These pins and hooks will adjust in height using holes drilled in the channel iron that forms the uprights of the rack. The closer together the holes are, the finer the adjustments can be for lifter height; 3 inches center to center is good, 4 inches does not work well. The holes should extend from top to bottom. The entire rack should be correctly welded together, with no bolted components to loosen.

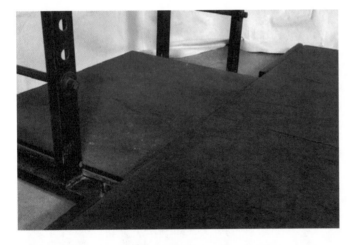

Figure 8-8. The rack should have a floor flush with the surface of the platform, so that squatting outside the rack is safe when racking and un-racking weights.

Figure 8-9 (right). The best power racks are heavy. This one is of welded construction, uprights of 4 inch channel with holes drilled on 3 inch centers, heavy 1¼ inch pins and chin bar, heavy plywood floor reinforced with channel, and heavy bolts for hooks.

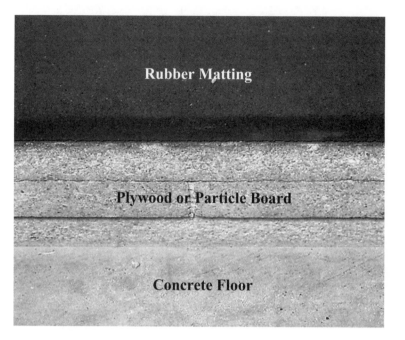

Figure 8-10. The layers of an inexpensive and durable platform.

Figure 8-11. A standard upright support bench for the bench press. Note the safety hooks at the lower position on the uprights.

Plywood is the least expensive and most convenient material for the platform. It is relatively cheap, very tough, and six sheets make a perfect 8 x 8 foot platform. The layers are alternated so that the seams do not penetrate the whole platform, and the unit is made very strong when the layers are glued and screwed together. Rubber horse trailer mats finish the surface, making it virtually indestructible. The thickness of this assembly is about 3 inches, assuming ¾ inch plywood and ¾ inch rubber. The rack and the platform surface need to be flush to eliminate the trip hazard, and invariably the rack will need to be shimmed, since racks and platforms usually won't match. Shim the floor under the rack with rubber, plywood, or some other dense, flat stuff to make the dimensions agree. Custom platforms are available from several sources; these are usually designed for the Olympic lifts and will be expensive but good-looking. They are unnecessary, but nice if the budget permits.

An upright support bench for the bench press should be sturdy as hell, fully welded with no bolted joints to loosen, and may or may not have adjustable hooks. If the hooks are not adjustable, the fixed hook should be about 19 inches above the surface of the bench. It should always have wide uprights, about 48 inches apart, to minimize the risk of loaded bar imbalances. The surface of the bench, with the padding compressed, will be 17 inches, the width will be 12 inches, and the length 48 inches. The feet of the bench should not interfere with your foot placement. It should be built in such a way that it does not tip back when heavy weights are racked hard. There should be no obstruction for a center spotter standing at the bencher's head. Some benches are equipped with safety hooks fixed below the top hooks, to allow a stuck solo bencher a way to get the bar off him without having to dump it on the floor or wait till Search and Rescue arrives. If these are present, they should be right above chest height, about 9 inches – 10 inches above the bench.

Figure 8-12. A flat bench can be used with power racks as a bench press station, as in figure 8-7. It should be as sturdy as an upright support bench.

Most commercial gyms will have bench press benches, since having them frees up the power racks (assuming they have power racks, or know how they're used) for other exercises, but again, they are not actually necessary since the power rack and a flat bench can be used for bench presses. Your garage gym will not need anything but a flat bench, which should have the same dimensions and simple construction as the support bench without the uprights. Too much padding will increase the effective height of the bench, not good for shorter lifters and annoying to taller ones that have used proper equipment before. Too wide a bench is a bad problem at the bottom of the movement, where it interferes with the shoulders and arms as the bar touches the chest.

Most benches are upholstered with vinyl for ease of cleaning. This material wipes off well, but fabric upholstery lasts many times longer, especially auto upholstery fabric. Fabric also provides better traction for the back during lifting. It can be cleaned with a shop vac, and stains can be removed with mineral spirits and a rag.

Bars are the place to spend money, if you have it. If you don't, raise it somehow, because cheap bars are dangerous, unpleasant to use, and a bad investment. Cheap bars will bend. Even expensive bars can bend under the wrong circumstances, if they are dropped loaded across a bench, for instance. But cheap bars will always bend, even under normal use. A good bar should be properly knurled and marked, should be put together with roller pins or snap rings, not bolts, and should require little maintenance beyond wiping it off occasionally. It should be made to international competitive specs, not because you'll be competing internationally (although you might) but so that it will accommodate the different brands of plates that all weight rooms eventually accumulate. Above all, a good bar is made of excellent steel, which will not deform with normal use. Expect to pay $250 or more for a good bar. There are lots of cheap imported bars available for less than $100. They are junk. Do not buy them. And do not hesitate to send back a good bar that bends under normal use, since they are not supposed to do that. A reputable company will replace a bar that fails, since their manufacturer will stand behind them in this event. If they don't, tell all your friends.

All real weight rooms are equipped with standard barbell plates with a 2 inch center hole. The little plates with a 1 inch hole are referred to as "exercise plates," and are not useful since no good bar is commercially produced for them. Standard barbell plates come in 2.5, 5, 10, 25, 35, and 45 lb. sizes. Of these, all are necessary except the 35s. Any loading that involves a 35 can be done with a 25 and a 10, and the space saved on the plate racks can be used for additional, more useful plates. Metric plates are 1.25, 2.5, 5, 10, 15, 20, 25, and occasionally 45 kg., with smaller plates down to 0.5 kg. used in weightlifting competition. Good plates are milled to be close to the weight named on the casting, and should be well within a half pound, or 0.25 kg. Metric bumper plates go up to 25 kg., and bumper plates are available from a few sources calibrated in pounds. Bumpers are useful for power cleans, and save a lot of wear and tear on bars and platforms. All plates bigger than 25 lbs., or bumper plates 10 kg. or bigger, should be 17.5 inches (45cm) in diameter.

Figure 8-13. Standard Olympic plates are the best choice. They come in a wide variety of denominations and construction. Metal plates as light as ¼ lb. are very useful, and bumper plates up to 25 kg. (55 lbs.) allow heavy bar loads with fewer plates.

Plate racks are available in two main styles, and A-frame tree and a tray. If the A-frame is used, it should have two pins on each side so that 45's or other full-diameter plates can be loaded on the bottom and smaller plates loaded on the top pins. Such a rack can accommodate more than 650 lbs. of standard barbell plates. The pins themselves should be made from at least 8 inches of 1 inch rod, so that the 2 inch hole in the plate fits over it with an inch of slop. This is very important for ease of racking the plates – if the pins are made from 2 inch material, both hands will have to be used every time a plate is racked. This can get to be annoying. Tray-style racks are easy to use since there is no center pin, but usually do not hold as many plates as an A-frame rack. They work well for bumper plates, and can be made longer for them since the load of rubber plates is less dense and heavy in the middle of the frame.

Figure 8-14. Plate racks are essential for weight room organization. An A-frame plate rack (left) and two types of tray racks are available commercially, or can be manufactured by clever, talented lifters.

Collars are usually thought of as necessary safety equipment in the weight room. While collars are important on occasion, it is much more useful to learn to keep the bar level so that plates don't slide off the bar. Plate slide is often a problem when squatting, since walking a bar out of the rack unavoidably involves some side-to-side movement when stepping back. Collars are useful when squatting, but are less important when benching and pressing since the bar theoretically stays level during the movement, and only one step out of the rack is used in the press. In the event of an uneven extension, collars are quite handy. If it becomes apparent that you have problems with uneven extension it would be prudent to use them. It would also be good to correct this error if possible. Collars are useful in the deadlift, since they help keep sloppy plates from "walking" down the bar during the pick-up/set-down cycle. The same holds true for the clean, although bumper plates aren't as bad about this as standard plates unless they are old and worn out.

Collars come in many designs, from inexpensive spring clips (which are very serviceable and reliable unless worn out or sprung), to expensive, very sturdy plastic types, to set-screw sleeve types, to adjustable competition collars. Springs work fine for most training purposes. If security is a problem, two can be used on each side.

Figure 8-15. The most common type of inexpensive spring collars is available from most sporting goods stores. They can be doubled-up for extra security.

Chalk should be provided in the weight room, by either the gym or you. It increases traction between the bar and the hand, reducing the likelihood of lost bars and grip accidents. It reduces callus formation, since stress against the skin of the palm and fingers is a function of the movement of the bar against it, and callus forms in response to this stress. It should be kept in a chalk box in a strategic location in the weight room. If the gym does not provide the chalk, for whatever misguided reason, you should bring your own, in a plastic bag or a can that stays in your gym bag. It can be purchased at most sporting goods stores, or ordered over the internet. If the gym is nice enough to provide the chalk, be nice enough back to use it sparingly; don't bathe in it, drop chunks on the floor, put clouds of it in the air, or otherwise waste it. Gyms that provide chalk have decided that training is more important that their housekeeping concerns, and you should appreciate the rarity of this attitude.

Each trainee should have proper clothing, i.e. a t-shirt, stretchy sweats or shorts, and a pair of shoes suitable for squatting and pulling. Some facilities provide belts, but not many, and you'll probably want your own anyway. One of the wonderful things about strength training is that minimal personal equipment is actually necessary, especially compared with other sports. The money spent on shoes is about the only significant expenditure the trainee has to make, belts being cheap and quite share-able between buddies.

Another thing each trainee should have is a training log – a journal to record each workout. No one can remember all the numbers involved in all the exercises in this program. It might be that the numbers for a couple of weeks of workouts can be remembered just fine, but a person's entire training history contains valuable data that should be recorded for future use. This is information that will be used each workout and over the course of your training career to determine the nature of problems and to analyze productive training periods. Training information should be written in a format that can be easily read by both you and any coach you might have, since you will have to consult it on a regular basis. A composition book works just fine, and the price is certainly right. A spiral tears up too easily in the gym bag. The best training book would be a bound ledger, with enough pages for years' worth of training notes. All people who are serious about their training write down their workouts.

Figure 8-16. All lifters who are serious about their training record every workout in a training log book. Commercially produced books are available, but composition books or money ledgers work just fine. Your training log is a part of your workout equipment, and is a necessary tool for progress.

Speaking of gym bags, get one, put all your stuff in it, and keep it with you. That way you'll always have your shoes, belt, chalk, training book, band-aids, tape, Desenex, spare shoelaces, extra shirt, towel, knee wraps, straps, and lucky troll doll. Don't worry about making a fashion statement with your bag. Just get one and take it with you every time so that I don't have to spot you a towel.

Soreness and injuries

There are two more things that everyone who trains with weights will have: soreness and injuries. They are as inevitable as the progress they accompany. If you work hard enough to improve, you will work hard enough to get sore, and eventually you will work hard enough to get hurt. It is your responsibility to make sure that you are using proper technique, appropriate progression, and safe weight room procedure. You will still get hurt, but you will have come by it honestly – when people lift heavy they are risking injury. It is an inherent part of training hard, and it must be prepared for and dealt with properly when it happens.

Soreness is a widely recognized and studied phenomenon. Despite the fact that humans have experienced muscle soreness since literally the Dawn Of Time, its cause remains poorly understood. It is thought to be the result of inflammation in the basic contractile unit of the muscle fiber, and the fact that it responds well to anti-inflammatory therapy tends to support this theory. Since muscular soreness has been experienced by so many people for so long, many misconceptions about it are bound to develop, and they have. What is certain is that lactic acid (a transient by-product of muscle contraction) has nothing to do with it.

Soreness is usually produced when the body does something to which it is not adapted. An good example of this would be your first workout, if not properly managed. Another example would be your first workout after a layoff, which can, if handled incorrectly, can produce some of the most exquisite soreness a human can experience. More on this later. Any time a workout program is changed, either by increasing volume or intensity or by changing exercises, soreness normally results.

The onset of the perception of soreness is normally delayed, anywhere from 12 to 48 hours, depending on the age and conditioning level of the athlete, the nature of the exercise being done, and the volume and intensity of the exercise. For this reason, it is referred to in the exercise literature as DOMS, or delayed-onset muscle soreness. It has been many people's observation that certain muscle groups get sore faster and more acutely than others, and that certain exercises tend to produce soreness while others, even when done at a high level of exertion, produce very little.

The part of the rep that causes most of the soreness is the eccentric, or "negative" phase of the contraction, where the muscle is lengthening under the load rather than shortening. This is thought to be due to the way the components of the contractile mechanism in the muscle fibers are stressed as they stretch apart under a load. And this explains why some exercises produce more soreness than others. Exercises without a significant eccentric component, like the power clean, in which the weight is dropped rather than actively lowered, will not produce nearly the soreness that the deadlift will. Deadlifts, like squats, benches, presses, and many assistance exercises, have both an eccentric and concentric component, where the muscles involved both shorten and lengthen under load. Some sports activities, like cycling, are entirely concentric, since all aspects of correct pedaling involve the shortening of the muscles involved and completely lack any eccentric component. Cycling, and resistance training assistance exercises like sled pulling, are therefore capable of being trained very hard without resulting in much soreness. Since soreness is inflammatory, it is likely that the harder an athlete can train without producing high amounts of muscle inflammation – and the attendant unfriendly hormonal responses – the better for recovery.

Soreness, unless it is extreme, is no impediment to training. In fact, many records have been set by sore athletes. If you are not training hard enough to produce occasional soreness, and therefore having to train while sore, you are not training very hard. Waiting until soreness subsides before doing the next workout is a good way to guarantee that soreness will be produced every time, since you'll never get adapted to sufficient workload frequency to stop getting sore. Extreme soreness that interferes with the normal range of motion must be dealt with on a case-by-case basis, and a decision made about whether or not to train through it after it has been warmed up carefully and thoroughly. But in general, if the warmup returns the movement to the normal range of motion, the workout can be done. Some allowances might have to be made if it is determined that the soreness is the result of an accumulated lack of recovery from the preceding several workouts.

In contrast to normal soreness, which by its nature is delayed for hours after the workout, injury could be defined as something that happens to the body that is immediately perceived as pain, and that persists after the movement has stopped. If pain occurs immediately in response to a movement done during training, it should be assumed to be an injury and should be treated as such. It is extremely important to develop the ability to distinguish between injury pain and normal soreness, since your health and long-term progress depends on it.

When you return to training after some time off, your de-trained condition must be considered. Depending on the duration of the layoff, different approaches are taken. If it has been just a few (fewer than 5 or 6) workouts missed, repeat the last workout you did before the layoff. You should be able to do this, although it may be fairly hard. This approach results in less progress lost than if significant backing-off is done, and the following workout can usually be done in the order it would have been had the layoff not occurred.

If the layoff has been a long one, a couple of months or more, care should be taken when planning your first workout back. If you have been training with weights for long enough to get very strong, adaptations have occurred in more than just your muscles. The nervous system and its relationship to the muscles – the "neuromuscular system" – has adapted to training by becoming able to recruit motor units more efficiently, and it is slower to detrain than the muscles it enervates. It remembers very well how to lift weights even if the muscles are out of condition. This neuromuscular efficiency is quite useful when you are in shape, but when detrained it allows you to lift more than you are actually in condition to do without incurring adverse effects. Spectacular soreness, as mentioned earlier, will result unless restraint is used in determining your volume and intensity. Heroism is not demonstrated when a guy comes back after a year's layoff and tries to repeat his PRs that day – foolishness is. Unless you have absolutely nothing else important to do for several days afterward, exercise good judgement when doing your first workout back in the gym.

A whole lot of people are under the erroneous impression that weight training is harmful for younger athletes, specifically the pre-pubescent population. Pediatricians are a wonderful group of people on the whole, but very often they are woefully uninformed regarding the data pertaining to the injury rates of various sports activities. They are also reluctant to apply some basic logic to an analysis of those numbers.

The table below lists the injury rates of various sports. Note that organized weightlifting activities, at 0.0012 injuries per 100 participation hours is about 5100 times safer than everyone's favorite organized children's sport, soccer, at 6.2 injuries per 100 player hours. Gym class, at 0.18, is more dangerous than supervised weight training. Yet even at this late date it is common for medical professionals to advise against weight training for kids. The most cursory glance at the actual data renders this recommendation foolishness.

So why does this mythology persist, and how did it get started? Most often cited as the primary concern is the chance of epiphyseal, or growth plate, fracture, leading to growth asymmetry in the affected appendage. The entire body of the sports medicine literature contains six reports of growth plate fracture in kids associated with weight training, none of which was specific enough in detail to determine whether the injury occurred under the bar (or if there even *was* a bar), if it occurred as the result of a fall due to faulty technique or improper instruction, or as the result of injudicious loading. And even in these six isolated examples, not one subsequently displayed *any* long-term effects that would indicate that a growth plate injury does not heal just like any other injury.

The most intensely lame argument of all is that weight training stunts a kid's growth. *But hauling hay does not?* Such nonsense is not really worthy of response.

Here's the bottom line: weight training is precisely scalable to the ability of the individual lifter. Soccer is not. We have 11 lb. bars – or even broomsticks – for kids to start lifting with, but a full-speed collision on the field with another 80 lb. kid is an inherently unscalable event. This logic also applies to every group of people that might be viewed as a "special population" – the frail elderly, people with skeletal and muscular disease, the completely sedentary, the morbidly obese, and the lazy (sorry, couldn't resist). Note that women are not listed as a special population: they are *half* of the population. Anyone who claims that women are sufficiently different in terms of physiologic response to exercise that the principles of basic barbell training do not apply to them is thinking either irrationally or commercially. In fact, the adaptation to weight training is *precisely* the adaptation that these special populations need, and unless they are also cardiac patients aerobic-type long slow distance exercise is only a tiny bit more useful than playing chess.

Blind obedience to the uninformed opinion of a professional who should know better represents lost opportunity, not helpful advice. For lots of marginally gifted kids, weight training is often the difference between a scholarship opportunity and a prohibitively expensive advanced education. People who could have benefited from improved strength, bone density, balance, coordination, flexibility, and confidence have instead done what they were told, and have not benefited at all. Not all expensive advice is worth the money.

Sport or Training Activity	Injury Rate	Sport or Training Activity	Injury Rate
Soccer	6.2	Squash	0.1
Rugby	1.92	Tennis	0.07
Basketball	1.03	Badminton	0.05
Track-and-Field	0.57	Gymnastics	0.044
Cross-country	0.37	Weight Training	0.0012
Track-and-Field	0.26	Powerlifting (competitive)	0.0008
Physical Education	0.18	Weightlifting (competitive)	0.0006
Football	0.1	Volleyball	0.0004
Data are injuries per 100 participation hours			
From Hamill, B. "Relative Safety of Weightlifting and Weight Training"			
Journal of Strength and Conditioning Research 8(1):53-57, 1994.			

Credits

Photographs

All photographs by Torin Halsey unless otherwise noted.

Photographs of Bill Kazmaier, Rickey Dale Crain, Pat Casey, Doug Young, Mel Hennessy, Jim Williams, Mike Bridges, Mike MacDonald, and Ronny Ray for figure 3-1 and of George Hechter and Jon Kuc for figure 4-2 courtesy of Mike Lambert and Powerlifting USA magazine.

Photographs of Bill Starr and Tommy Suggs for figures 5-1, 5-2, and 6-1 courtesy of Bill Starr.

Photographs of Nicu Vlad for figure 7-25 by Bruce Klemens.

Photograph of Kevin McCloskey on page 49 courtesy of Dan Herring.

Photographs for figures 2-57 and 4-24 by Stef Bradford.

Photograph of Phil Anderson for figure 4-39 by Treva Slagle.

Photographs for figure 2-63, 4-35, 6-4, 6-9, 6-17, 6-31, 7-33, 7-35, 7-50, 7-51, 7-64, 7-67 and the photograph of Mark Rippetoe's massive biceps on page 280 by Lon Kilgore.

Thanks to our models: Carrie Klumpar, Justin Brimhall, Ronnie Hamilton, Josh Wells, Stef Bradford, DeLisa Moore, Sean Street, Nic Teaff, Carla Nichols, Dwayne and Hunter Travelstead.

Illustrations

All illustrations by Lon Kilgore unless otherwise noted.

Concept for figure 2-56 by Becky Kudrna.

Concepts and illustrations for figures 6-3 and 7-14 by Stef Bradford.

Figures 8-1, 8-5 from Practical Programming, Aasgaard Company, 2006.

EMG and force diagrams for figure 8-4 courtesy of Jaqueline Limberg and Alexander Ng of Marquette University.

Index

Index

A

abductors, 15
absolute strength, 204, 293
acceleration, 9, 34, 169-170, 172, 189, 198
    definition of, 169
acetabulum, 29, 239, 249
Achilles tendon, 268-269
ACL, see *anterior cruciate ligament*
active shoulders, 159
adductors, 9, 10, 12, 15-17, 35, 39-40, 41, 43, 48, 134,
    169, 216-219, 224
aerobic pathways, 296
alternate grip, 107-108, 210, 243
Anderson, Phil, 141
Anello, Vince, 136-137
angle of attack, 83, 88
ankle extension, 190, 271
anterior cruciate ligament, 11, 12, 227
anterior deltoid, 67, 82, 87, 154-155
anterior superior iliac spine, 45
anthropometry, 5, 15, 42, 80, 184, 187, 229
arm length, 125, 228
ASIS, see *anterior superior iliac spine*
ATP, 296

B

back angle, 16, 18, 31, 122-127, 131-135, 184-185,
    188, 193, 209-210, 212, 222, 224, 226-227, 246,
    263-265
back arch, 38, 89, 93, 196, 263
back squat, 12, 42, 43, 122, 169, 221, 222, 224-229
back-off sets, 297
bar path, 55, 57, 74, 85, 97, 120,127, 130, 135, 157,
    159, 160, 162-164, 184-185,187, 189-190, 192,
    194, 195-196, 204, 212, 231, 233, 236, 247, 263
barbell curl, 30, 112, 277-279, 299
barbell shrugs, 140, 215-216
baseball, 170, 290, 297
behind-the-neck press, 150, 249
belt, 52, 58, 59, 168, 262, 309
bench press shirt, 57
bench shirt, 104
bicep tendons, 82, 107
biceps brachii, 276
biceps femoris, 34, 274
blackout, 52, 230
bodybuilders, 3, 148, 195, 292
Bolton, Andy, 104
box squats, 216-218
brachialis, 139, 195, 275
Bradford press, 249

bridge, 67, 85, 92-94, 235
Bridges, Mike, 66
bumper plates, 96, 142, 203-204, 216, 228, 263, 289,
    303, 307-308

C

California front squat, 231
callus, 19, 109, 110, 255, 284, 308-309
Casey, Pat, 66
center knurling, 68, 247
center of gravity, 121, 163, 164, 247
cerebrospinal fluid, 54
cerebrovascular accident, 50
cervical spine, 23, 90,160
chalk, 19, 109, 192, 255, 308-309
chest up, 25, 39, 63, 127, 156, 229, 242
chesticles, 148
chin, 24, 27, 116, 156, 158, 236, 255, 256
chin-up, 208, 252-257, 274, 275, 277
circuit, 3, 4, 5, 303
clavicle, 82, 249
clean and jerk, 162, 168, 176
clean pull, 212
close grip, 232-233
collars, 308
compression, 217, 218, 225
concentric, 81, 87, 112, 132, 138, 142, 152,171, 218,
    238-239, 263, 267, 278, 310
continental clean, 168
continental press, 150
core, 8-9, 67, 151
correction displacement, 194
Crain, Rickey Dale, 66, 105
cranium, 52
CSF, 52
cue, 17, 25, 63, 118, 131, 141 160, 171, 191, 192, 202,
    210, 211, 224, 225, 228, 229, 242, 243, 251, 262,
    271, 278

D

decline press, 92, 234, 259
deltoids, 19, 33, 67, 81-82, 154, 156, 159, 160, 161,
    165, 173, 195, 197-198, 199, 208, 228, 264, 276,
    278
dips, 234, 253, 259-262
distal function, 46, 213, 269
dive-bombing, 41
DOMS, 310
double overhand grip, 107, 173, 209, 243, 244
dumbbell press, 149-150

dumbbells, 52, 67, 77, 231
Durlacher, Professor Louis "Attila", 267

E

eccentric, 29, 81, 87, 112, 127, 138, 152, 203, 238-239, 246, 267, 278, 310
elastic energy, 41, 58, 87, 112, 217, 239
electromyography, 17, 295
erector spinae, 35, 36, 118, 156, 160
explosion, 112, 168-172, 177, 178, 190, 216
eye position, 38, 71, 74, 160, 204, 236
eyes, 27, 41, 70, 73, 74, 96, 116, 119, 138, 156, 160, 189, 204, 211, 236, 239, 263

F

fatty acids, 296
femur, 10-16, 34, 38, 40, 42, 48, 49, 84, 94, 123, 125, 126, 259
flat bench, 67, 68, 219, 236, 303, 306
flexibility, 4, 13, 20, 32, 34, 42, 43, 48, 50, 51, 60, 80, 95, 107, 111, 118, 119, 154, 155, 159, 168, 173, 180, 199, 200, 222, 227, 231, 233, 244, 247, 255, 312
flexion, 10, 25, 33, 35, 36, 45, 46, 120, 150, 165, 190, 203, 227, 238, 248, 266, 268-271, 274-278
foot angle, 30, 48
football, 152-153, 172, 312
force plate, 295
force production, 172, 189, 190, 294, 295
form creep, 187
frog stance, 136
front squat, 12, 29, 31, 156, 168, 169, 198, 221-222, 225-231, 237
full squat, 8, 9, 11, 12, 17, 22, 34, 50, 169, 181, 218

G

G-forces, 52
gastrocnemius, 269
gaze, 24, 74, 139, 204
glenoid, 123, 139, 249
glottis, 50, 51, 53, 104, 109
gloves, 109
glute/ham raise, 267-274
glutes, 10, 17, 24, 35, 37, 40, 41, 92, 114, 123, 127, 131, 132, 134, 209, 211, 224, 225, 238, 263-265, 268, 271
good mornings, 246-248
gravity, 4, 29, 32, 79, 84, 109, 120, 122, 123, 127, 158,

gravity (*Continued*)
159, 198, 222, 274
Gravity, Mean Old Mr., 198, 294
grip width, 20, 33, 71, 78, 115, 136, 137, 154, 173, 182, 227, 231, 255, 261
groove, 74
gym bag, 309

H

half squat, 11, 38, 106, 218, 219, 234, 262, 298
halting deadlift, 208-211
handoff, 100-101
hang position, 173, 176, 177, 238, 239
hang power clean, 173
Hechter, George, 66, 105, 136, 170
Hennessy, Mel, 66
Hepburn, Doug, 66
high-bar position, 19, 29-31, 221, 222, 226, 246
hip angle, 123-124, 127, 130, 131, 134, 185, 187, 113, 224, 226
hip drive, 15, 18, 23, 24, 35, 38, 39, 164, 224, 229
hip extension, 17, 34-36, 39, 43, 85, 92, 123, 127, 132, 171, 192, 193, 211-213, 224, 225, 227, 238, 239, 242, 246, 247, 264, 265, 268, 278
hip flexors, 45-46, 257
hip sled, 55
hitch, 213
hook grip, 173, 180, 197, 243, 263, 266
horse trailer mats, 142, 305
humeral angle, 81
humerus, 67, 78-84, 88, 108, 123, 153, 154, 157, 159, 173, 183, 198, 219, 228, 232, 234, 241, 249, 255, 260, 262, 267, 275, 276
hydrostatic column, 51
hyperextension, 23, 29, 140, 150, 164, 165, 267, 268, 272, 274

I

incline bench press, 152, 234, 235-237
intervertebral disc, 35, 117, 274
intra-abdominal pressure, 53, 98, 165
isometric contraction, 77, 92, 104, 117, 131, 198, 267

J

Jones, Arthur, 3
jumping position, 176-177, 179, 187-195

K

Kazmaier, Bill, 66
kinesthetic sense, 29, 34, 37, 119
kinetic chain, 60, 87, 91, 94, 95, 98, 151, 153
kinetic energy, 58, 169
kipping, 253, 257, 258
knee angle, 15, 30, 31, 38, 39, 43, 45, 50, 93, 123, 124,
    127, 131, 132, 185, 187, 213, 216, 225, 226, 227,
    240, 246
knee wraps, 58-59, 252, 310
knurl, 20, 31, 68, 69, 109, 111, 136, 137, 154, 233,
    247, 306
Kono, Tommy, 9
Kuc, John, 66, 105
kyphosis, 126
kyphotic, 36, 71, 116

L

lat pulldown, 3, 253, 260
latissimus dorsi, 67, 82, 123, 253
lats, 81, 82, 85, 123, 127, 131, 139, 190, 197, 208, 209,
    210, 241-243, 253, 257, 263, 264, 267, 275
leg extension machine, 3, 85, 281
leg press, 17, 55
lever arm, 19, 20, 133, 134, 162, 163, 164, 222, 225,
    247
leverage, 81, 83, 215, 222, 230, 236, 247, 272
longissimus dorsi, 33
looking up, 23, 26, 27, 70, 138
loop, 187, 192, 194
lordotic, 36, 71, 116, 118, 119
low-bar position, 29, 31, 43, 221, 225, 226, 247
lumbar hyperextension, 140, 165
lumbar vertebrae, 35, 274
lying triceps extension, 208, 281

M

McCloskey, Kevin, 49
McDonald, Mike, 66
mid-foot, 26, 29, 31, 106, 121, 134, 156, 157, 159, 162,
    164, 183, 184, 186, 187, 189, 190, 211, 223, 244,
    246, 247, 263
military press, 148, 149, 150, 160
milk, 302
Milo, 3
mirror, 29, 32, 41, 119, 120
mitochondria, 296
motor pathway, 152, 163, 287, 288, 290
motor unit recruitment, 77, 171, 239

muscle spindles, 86

N

narrow stance, 15, 30, 48, 136
Nautilus, 3-4
neuromuscular adaptation, 290
neuromuscular system, 87, 294

O

obliques, 104, 152
Olympic squat, 222, 225
Olympic weightlifting, 12, 136, 148, 150, 154, 168,
    181, 182, 191, 226, 231, 252, 289
overtraining, 285

P

partial squat, 9, 11, 13, 216, 217, 218, 262
patella, 8, 9, 11, 15, 29, 183, 209, 210
PCL, see posterior cruciate ligament
Pearl, Bill, 208
pectoralis major, 67, 82
pectoralis minor, 67
pelvis, 10, 34, 35, 36, 39, 40, 45, 46, 50, 94, 118, 123,
    125, 131, 238, 249, 265
Pendlay, Glenn, 293
periodization, 299
plate racks, 307-308
platform, 57, 142, 203, 216, 236, 303, 304, 305, 307
plywood, 142, 214, 304-305
posterior chain, 17, 24, 41, 45
posterior cruciate (ligament), 12, 272
power, definintion of, 169-172
    use as a modifier, 168
power bar, 20, 68, 136, 233
power jerk, 168
power rack, 57, 68, 70, 110, 199, 210, 214, 216, 217,
    220, 227, 253, 254, 257, 303-304, 306
power snatch., 168
powerlifting, 30, 49, 60, 66-68, 78, 104, 141, 143, 148,
    150, 170, 213, 312
proprioception, 29
proximal function, 34, 46, 213, 269, 270
pubis, 40, 165
pull-up, 253-258, 260, 304
push press, 149, 150, 165, 250-252

Q

quadriceps, 4, 9-12, 34, 45, 49, 85, 127, 131, 132, 187, 191, 211-213, 218, 238, 281
quarter squat, 11
quickness, 169, 178

R

rack position, 172-173, 176, 179, 184, 185, 188, 191, 192, 197-202, 231
rack pull, 208-214, 221
racking the bar, 97, 178, 215
radius, 78, 274
range of motion, 3, 8, 9, 11, 40, 78, 84-85, 112, 117, 122, 199, 209, 215, 216, 219, 220, 222, 223, 226, 232, 233, 236, 238, 243-244, 246, 249, 252, 253, 256, 262, 263, 265, 268, 270, 271, 285, 290, 294, 311
Ray, Ronnie, 66
RDL, 238-239, see also *romanian deadlift*
rebound, 10, 38, 40-41, 49, 58, 77, 85, 86, 87, 114, 161, 216, 218-220
rectus abdominis, 165
rectus femoris, 45, 46
Reinhoudt, Don, 66
reverse hyper, 273-274
rhomboids, 33, 67, 121, 161-162, 197, 253
rib cage, 8, 67, 79-80, 82, 85, 88, 98, 99, 121, 160, 165, 198, 255, 262, 263, 278
roman chair, 165-166, 267-270
romanian deadlift, 246, see also *RDL*
rotator cuff, 67, 68, 81, 153-154, 161, 197, 253
round back, 22, 36, 118, 127, 195-196, 247-248
running shoes, 61

S

sacrum, 17, 38, 225, 229
safety hooks, 101, 305, 306
sartorius, 45, 46
scapula, 18, 19, 29, 30, 87, 89, 121-125, 127, 131, 135, 139, 154, 156, 157, 159, 161, 162, 176, 187, 190-191, 196, 197, 208, 209, 211-212, 226, 240, 241-242, 244, 246-247, 249, 255, 263, 264, 276
seated press, 149
second pull, 171, 191, 213, 215
semimembranosus, 34
semitendinosus, 34
set position, 90, 122, 134
sets across, 27, 219, 229, 244, 246, 259, 291, 293, 297, 298

shear, 11, 31, 134, 272, 273, 274
shorts, 8, 41, 61, 62, 309
shoulder flexion, 276-278
shrug, 89-90, 140, 156, 157, 161, 170, 177, 189-191, 194, 198, 201-204, 211, 215, 216
Simmons, Louie, 170, 217
SLDL, see *stiff-legged deadlift*
Smith machine, 55
soccer, 93, 312
soreness, 32, 223, 244, 288, 310-311
split clean, 168
split jerk, 251
spotting, 22, 23, 54-57, 70, 72, 74, 76, 97, 100-102, 220, 228, 234, 236, 306
squat shoes, 60-61
squat suits, 30, 57, 95, 104
Starr, Bill, 9, 148, 168
starting position, 23, 59, 63, 73, 96, 98, 106-107, 111, 113, 119, 120-126, 131, 134-135, 157, 159, 184-187, 189, 202, 204, 211, 236, 244, 248, 278
sternum, 12, 19, 25, 80, 82, 85, 154, 173, 197-199, 227, 228, 234, 236
stiff-legged deadlift, 243-246, 265
stomp, 178, 198, 201-202
straps, 60, 104, 107-108, 142-144, 210, 215, 243, 263, 310
strength, definition of, 169
stretch reflex, 40, 85-86, 112, 142, 152, 161, 216, 220, 239, 243, 250, 277
sumo, 49, 59, 105, 134-135, 293
supine grip, 254-255, 266, 274, 276-277

T

t-shirt, 61, 62, 66, 309
tank top, 61, 62
tendinitis, 11, 45-46, 220
tennis, 74, 312
tennis ball, 27
tennis elbow, 266
tension, 10, 12, 38, 45-46, 118, 123, 131, 139, 240, 241, 268, 271, 272, 278
tensor facia latae, 45-46
third class lever, 83
thumbless grip, 76, 77
tibia, 10-12, 34, 42, 45-48, 49, 84, 123, 125, 213, 225, 227, 269
torque, 19, 20, 49, 79, 122, 131, 133, 134, 222, 225, 229, 281
touch-and-go, 85, 219, 220
training log, 100, 309
trapezius, 23, 67, 121, 156, 161, 162, 197, 215
triceps, 67, 77-79, 96, 157, 161, 162, 165, 197, 199,

triceps (*Continued*)
  208, 219, 231-232, 259, 262, 274-276, 281, 288,
  298
two-hands press, 148

U

ulna, 78, 183, 274
upholstery, 68, 306
upright row, 195
upright support bench, 70, 305, 306
USAPL, 49

V

Valsalva maneuver, 50-54, 98, 104, 138, 198
variable resistance, 3
vascular column, 52, 54
velocity, 9, 85, 101, 117, 169-172, 179, 190, 193, 198
  definition of, 169
vertical jump, 11, 112, 114, 169, 173
Viator, Casey, 3
viscoelastic, 40, 86, 112
Vlad, Nicu, 237-238

W

warm-up, 59, 100, 117, 135, 154,163, 215, 223, 272,
  290-292, 311
watts, 169
Webster, David, 9
Westside, 170, 217
wide stance, 30, 49
Williams, Jim, 66
Willoughby, David, 3
work, definition of, 120
work set, 100, 101, 209, 215, 264, 291-293, 297-298
wrist curl, 252
wrist wraps, 109

Y

Young, Doug, 66

The Authors

Mark Rippetoe is the owner of Wichita Falls Athletic Club and CrossFit Wichita Falls. He has 10 years experience as a competitive powerlifter. He has coached athletes in barbell and strength sports since 1980, and has worked in the fitness industry since 1978. He is the author of *Starting Strength: Basic Barbell Training, Strong Enough?*, and co-author of *Practical Programming for Strength Training*. He has coached numerous national level competitors and thousands of people interested in improving their health and strength.

Lon Kilgore is a professor of kinesiology at Midwestern State University where he teaches sport physiology and anatomy. He has also held faculty appointments at Kansas State University and Warnborough University (IE). He graduated from Lincoln University with a Bachelor of Science in biology and earned a Ph.D. in Anatomy and Physiology from Kansas State University. He has competed in weightlifting to the national level since 1972 and coached his first athletes to national championship event medals in 1974. He has worked in-the-trenches as a coach or sports science consultant, with athletes from rank novices to professionals and the Olympic elite, and as a collegiate strength coach. His interest in developing better weightlifting coaches, strength coaches, and fitness professionals have driven much of his academic and professional efforts. He has been a certifying instructor for USA Weightlifting for more than a decade and a frequent lecturer at events at the US Olympic Training Center in Colorado Springs. His authorship efforts include books, magazine columns, and research journal publications.

"We define thinking as integrating data and arriving at correct answers."

Robert Heinlein

"I know the term "deathly quiet" is a bit overdone, but there are few things more quiet than fourteen dead elephants."

Peter Hathaway Capstick
Death in the Long Grass